IDRC

The first meeting of the IDRC board, 26–28 October 1970. *Seated, left to right:* Sir John Crawford, Anthony Lancelot Dias, Lila Engberg, Rt. Hon. Lester Pearson, Lady Barbara Ward Jackson, Puey Ungphakorn, Dr. Charles Bentley. *Standing, left to right:* A.F.W. Plumptre, Rex Nettleford, Prof. Irving Brecher, Dr. H.A. Oluwasanmi, David Hopper, Pierre Bauchet, Roberto Campos, Ralph Medjuck, John Bene. (IDRC photo)

IDRC: 40 YEARS OF IDEAS, INNOVATION, AND IMPACT

Bruce Muirhead and Ronald N. Harpelle

Wilfrid Laurier University Press

Wilfrid Laurier University Press acknowledges the financial support of the Government of Canada through the Canada Book Fund for our publishing activities.

Library and Archives Canada Cataloguing in Publication

Muirhead, Bruce
    IDRC : 40 years of ideas, innovation, and impact / Bruce Muirhead and Ronald N. Harpelle.

Includes bibliographical references and index.
Also issued in electronic format.
ISBN 978-1-55458-301-0

    1. International Development Research Centre (Canada)—History. 2. Research—Developing countries. 3. Economic assistance, Canadian. I. Harpelle, Ronald N., 1957– II. International Development Research Centre (Canada) III. Title.

HC60.M83 2010   338.91'7101724   C2010-903897-5

ISBN 978-1-55458-316-4
Electronic format.

    1. International Development Research Centre (Canada)—History. 2. Research—Developing countries. 3. Economic assistance, Canadian. I. Harpelle, Ronald N., 1957– II. International Development Research Centre (Canada) III. Title.

HC60.M83 2010a   338.91'7101724   C2010-903898-3

Cover design by Martyn Schmoll. Cover photo—showing a researcher interviewing fishermen at La Boquilla (near Cartagena), Columbia—by Richard Lord. Text design by Catharine Bonas-Taylor.

© 2010 Wilfrid Laurier University Press
Waterloo, Ontario, Canada
www.wlupress.wlu.ca

This book is printed on FSC recycled paper and is certified Ecologo. It is made from 100% post-consumer fibre, processed chlorine free, and manufactured using biogas energy.

Printed in Canada

CONTENTS

ACRONYMS AND ABBREVIATIONS

ACAST	Advisory Committee on the Application of Science and Technology
ADRF	Asia Development Research Forum
AERC	African Economic Research Consortium
AFNS	Agriculture, Food, and Nutrition Sciences Division
AG[O]	Auditor General [Office]
AGRIS	International Information System for the Agricultural Sciences and Technology
AIB	Anti-Inflation Board
ANC	African National Congress
ASRO	Regional Office for Southeast and East Asia
ATPS	African Technology Policy Studies
ATPSN	African Technology Policy Studies Network
BAIF	Bharatiya Agro Industries Development Research Foundation
CAI	Corporate Affairs and Initiatives Division
CBO	Community-Based Organization
CCA	Centre for Connectivity in Africa
CGIAR	Consultative Group on International Agricultural Research
CIAT	Centro Internacional de Agricultura Tropical (International Centre for Tropical Agriculture)
CIDA	Canadian International Development Agency
CIEPLAN	Corporación Latinoamericana de Investigación Económica
CIHR	Canadian Institutes for Health Research

CIMMYT	Centro Internacional de Mejoramiento de Maíz y Trigo
CNRA	Centre national de recherches agronomiques
COMSEC	Commonwealth Secretariat
CPF	Corporate Program Framework
CPU	Canadian Partnerships Unit
CPU	Cooperative Programs Unit
CREDA	Centre for Research on Dryland Agriculture
CSPF	Corporate Strategy and Program Framework
CTA	Technical Centre for Agricultural and Rural Cooperation
CUSO	Canadian University Service Overseas
DAC	Development Assistance Committee (OECD)
DEA	Department of External Affairs
DFAIT	Department of Foreign Affairs and International Trade
DFID	Department for International Development
DPA	Director of Program Area
DTI	Department of Trade and Industry
EAO	External Aid Office
EARO	East Africa Regional Office
EASF	Expert and Advisory Services Fund
ECA	Economic Commission for Africa
EEPSEA	Economy and Environment Program for Southeast Asia
EES	Earth and Engineering Sciences Division
ELSA	Evaluation and Learning System for Acacia
ENR	Environment and Natural Resources Division
ENRM	Environment and Natural Resources Management
EtK	Empowerment through Knowledge
FAD	Fellowships and Awards Division
FAO	Food and Agriculture Organization
FITC	Foundation for International Technological Cooperation
FLASCO	Facultad Latinoamericana de Ciencias Sociales
GAD	Gender and Development
GKP	Global Knowledge Partnership
GMI	Global Micronutrient Initiative
GPI	Global Program Initiative
HS	Health Sciences Division
IADB	Inter-American Development Bank
IAEA	International Atomic Energy Agency
IBRD	International Bank for Reconstruction and Development
ICARDA	International Centre for Agricultural Research in Dry Areas
ICCR	International Committee on Contraceptive Research

ICRIER	Indian Council for Research on International Economic Relations
ICRISAT	International Crops Research Institute for the Semi-Arid Tropics
ICT	Information and Communication Technologies
ICT4D	Information and Communication Technologies for Development
IDA	International Development Association
IDC	International Development Centre
IFAD	International Fund for Agricultural Development
IFPRI	International Food Policy Research Institute
IITA	International Institute of Tropical Agriculture
IMF	International Monetary Fund
IMPACT	Instructional Management by Parents, Community, and Teachers
INBAR	International Network for Bamboo and Rattan
INNOTECH	Educational Innovation and Technology
IRRI	International Rice Research Institute
IS	Information Sciences Division
ISS	Institute of Social Studies
ISTC	Institute for Scientific and Technological Cooperation
ITU	International Telecommunications Union
LACRO	Latin America and Caribbean Regional Office
LDC	Less Developed Country
MERO	Middle East Regional Office
MIMAP	Micro Impacts of Macroeconomic and Adjustment Policies
MOSST	Ministry of State for Science and Technology
MOU	Memorandum of Understanding
NEPAD	New Economic Partnership for Africa's Development
NGO	Non-governmental Organization
NIEO	New International Economic Order
NRC	National Research Council
OAG	Office of the Auditor General
ODA	Official Development Assistance
OECD	Organisation for Economic Co-operation and Development
OPE	Office of Planning and Evaluation
OPE	Office of Program Evaluations
OPEC	Organization of the Petroleum Exporting Countries
OPT	Occupied Palestinian Territories
ORSTOM	Institut de Recherche pour le Développement (Senegal)

OVPP	Office of the Vice-President, Programs
PA	Program Area
PCO	Privy Council Office
PCR	Project Completion Report
PHAC	Public Health Agency of Canada
PHS	Population and Health Sciences Division
PI	Program Initiative
PO	Program Officer
PRISM	Program on Innovation Systems Management
RD	Regional Director
RIA!	Research ICT Africa
RO	Regional Office
RoKS	Research on Knowledge Systems
ROSA	Regional Office for Southern Africa
RPO	Regional Program Officer
RUP	Research Utilization Program
SARO	South Asia Regional Office
SCITEC	Association of Scientists and Engineers of Canada
SDC	Sustainable Development Commission (UK)
SED	Sustainable and Equitable Development
SEE	Social and Economic Equity
SEP	Social and Economic Policy
SIMA	System-Wide Initiative on Malaria and Agriculture
SSA	Sub-Saharan Africa
SSHR	Social Sciences and Human Resources Division
SSTC	State Scientific and Technological Commission
ST	Science and Technology
STI	Science, Technology, and Innovation
STPI	Science and Technology Policy Instruments
TBS	Treasury Board Secretariat
TC	Toxicology Centre
TEHIP	Tanzania Essential Health Interventions Project
TIPS	Trade and Industrial Policy Secretariat
UNCED	United Nations Conference on Environment and Development
UNCSTD	United Nations Conference on Science and Technology for Development
UNCTAD	United Nations Conference on Trade and Development
UNDP	United Nations Development Programme
UN-DPCSD	United Nations Department for Policy Coordination and Sustainable Development

UNEP   United Nations Environment Programme
UNESCO   United Nations Educational, Scientific, and Cultural
           Organization
UNF   United Nations Foundation
UNITAR   United Nations Institute for Training and Research
USAID   United States Agency for International Development
USC   Unitarian Service Committee
WAD   Women and Development
WARO   West Africa Regional Office
WB/G   West Bank and Gaza
WHO   World Health Organization
WID   Women in Development

FOREWORD: IN OUR PRIME

The International Development Research Centre was born in auspicious circumstances. When the act launching the Crown corporation was passed by Canada's Parliament in 1970, the roll call was unanimous—a rare event for any sort of bill. One can hardly imagine a more ringing endorsement.

During the decades since the passage of the *IDRC Act*, the Centre has fully lived up to this non-partisan vote of confidence. It has pursued its mandate to foster research for development with vigour and imagination. Regardless of the domestic political climate, IDRC has always enjoyed the support of senior Canadian officials. Worldwide, especially in the developing countries, IDRC has long been one of Canada's most highly regarded public institutions. In my view, this has been an excellent bargain, because IDRC's draw on the public purse has never been more than about 4 percent of Canada's official development assistance.

Paradoxically, however, IDRC remains less well known among the citizens of its home country. As the organization approached its fortieth anniversary, therefore, IDRC intensified its efforts to tell its story to Canadians. To better highlight the lasting impacts of the scientific and technical knowledge it has helped create, IDRC planned a series of events, including the publication of this important book.

Researched and written by distinguished Canadian historians, this volume was intended to provide an academic history of IDRC. As it has turned out, however, the book is more than a simple chronicle of events. For the benefit of Canadian taxpayers who have funded most of IDRC's operations, it provides an objective assessment of the Centre's long-term performance. Because the authors were guaranteed intellectual independence—this is not an IDRC publication—their work contributes substantially to the public accounting the organization is obliged and privileged to undertake.

Does this condemn the book to being dull and earnest? In fact, the IDRC story makes for compelling reading. These pages present a multi-generational narrative, the ups and downs of a modestly scaled global actor in shifting circumstance, and the clash of forceful protagonists. The authors are particularly convincing on the importance of strong leadership and sound governance. In detailing the influence of IDRC's presidents—remarkably, there have been just five in forty years—and the importance of an engaged board of governors, they remind us that imaginative, decisive individuals truly can meet the challenge of steering a large organization in new directions.

IDRC remains a work in progress, as does the process of international development itself. Its goal, like that of any development organization, should be to make itself redundant, but, of course, that task is far from achieved. The one constant in IDRC's history has been the belief that only enhanced capacity in the developing world for economic management, public administration, agricultural growth, public health, and environmentally sustainable practices can lead to lasting progress.

As it approaches its fifth decade, IDRC is in its prime, filled with energy and with the wisdom gained from experience. It has recently engaged dynamic new leadership, and it has prepared, on the basis of many lessons learned, a fresh strategic framework to guide its activities during the coming years.

As a former Canadian Cabinet minister and lifelong student of public policy-making, I appreciate learning about institutional effectiveness, achievement, and success. The inspiring story presented in this book illustrates that good government really can improve human lives. IDRC does get the job done, and the world is a better place because of it.

Hon. Barbara McDougall
Chairman of the Board of Governors
International Development Research Centre
January 2010

PREFACE

The International Development Research Centre (IDRC) was conceived in the context of the need to assist the global South in developing scientific and technological skills. It also represented an interesting and untested idea, at least for a public sector organization—to provide funding to southern research partners and let them undertake work on projects that they had developed and that reflected local needs. Research imperialism, where institutions from wealthy industrialized countries determined aid priorities, was foreign to the Centre's lexicon. IDRC's focus was resolutely on the South and it eschewed the funding of Canadian researchers, despite demands that it do so. Indeed, the Centre began life with these very particular objectives in mind, guiding principles from which it has never really strayed. In this, and in other ways that are discussed in this volume, IDRC is pioneering and unique—a stark departure from the more usual development institutions.

While the Centre has suffered setbacks and failures in its programming—to have had none would have made it a strange creature indeed—it has also been in the forefront of change and innovation more often than not. IDRC has received international recognition both from its peers and from foreign governments, reflecting the esteem in which it is held. As this book demonstrates, it has for the most part been nimble, flexible, and willing to contemplate approaches to problems that more staid organizations could not. Unfortunately, it remains an institution of which most Canadians are woefully unaware, as unknown in the country of its birth as it is known in those parts of the developing world where it has funded such good work. Canadians should be as proud of what IDRC has accomplished over the past forty years as they should be of how it has done so.

We owe a debt of gratitude to a number of people who have been instrumental in helping us. First and foremost, Lauchlan Munro, IDRC vice-president, Corporate Strategy and Regional Management, and also our program officer, has provided us with tremendous encouragement and insight as we undertook the research and writing of this book. His attention to detail and his willingness to comment critically on drafts of chapters has saved us from errors. Not once did he attempt to guide our writing. The Centre gave us the freedom and autonomy to write as we saw fit, and its commitment to that principle was personified in Lauchlan. The same can be said of other IDRC officials interested in this project, such as Policy and Planning's Bruce Currie-Alder, who listened patiently as we probed his understanding of events. These officials all provided advice when asked and helped us to navigate the intricacies of IDRC operation and organization. Their perceptive suggestions have proved invaluable. Similarly, IDRC interns Adriana Gouvea, Asha Jalan, and Sarah Mohan demonstrated great willingness to dig up documents for us when our travels took us far from Ottawa. Hélène St-Martin did a fantastic job in keeping our financial records straight; we owe her a debt we can never repay. Tim Dottridge, now retired but lately director of Special Initiatives at the Centre, never lost his equanimity despite that we often pestered him with questions. For that we are grateful, as we are to the Evaluation Unit's Sarah Earl, who lives and breathes evaluations and who brought her lively, intelligent, and engaged mind to bear on the project over many lunches.

The list of people to whom we owe thanks is large, numbering in the hundreds. To all of them we are grateful. However, limited in space as we are, we would like to thank in particular Christine Hains, Sachiko Okuda, Bessem Khouaja, Raymond Vaillancourt, and, following his retirement, Alain St. Hilaire, as well as those regional directors who took time from their busy schedules to meet with us several times and submit to our questions: Stephen McGurk, Rich Fuchs, Gilles Forget, Connie Freeman, Federico Burone, and Eglal Rached. Many others went out of their way to provide us with insights into the Centre. Chief among these must be Chris Smart, a recently retired but always committed IDRC man. Gordon Smith, chair of the Centre's board until 2008, was similarly forthcoming, as was James Pfeiffer, now head of the IDRC alumni association. Too numerous to mention are those many Centre funding recipients in many countries who took us out to view their projects and fill us in on how critical IDRC is to their country's welfare. We were overwhelmed by their kindness and thoughtfulness.

IDRC's former president, Maureen O'Neil, was the driving force behind the IDRC History Project and laid out the rules regarding intellectual freedom that guided its forward movement. Maureen is keenly interested in the Centre's history and wanted to capture that IDRC memory from its earliest years, even as some of it was disappearing. For example, Ivan Head, president from 1978 to 1991, had died in 2004, and many other employees from the 1970s had also passed away or were in poor health. While documents stored in the Centre's archives could tell some of the story, only interviews would flesh them out. We are grateful for Maureen's prescience and for her commitment to the project.

Last but certainly not least, we thank our editors at Wilfrid Laurier University Press—managing editor Rob Kohlmeier and acquisitions editor Ryan Chynces. The speed with which this book moved ahead was blinding. The deadlines were very tight and the work onerous, yet neither flinched when confronted with exigencies. For that we are grateful.

This book is based on hundreds of interviews and tens of thousands of pages of documents from the IDRC archives. We have selected and interpreted from both sources. Some readers will question why we dealt with "x" instead of "y," and that is their right. We only hope that we have provided some sense of the dynamism, the excitement, the commitment, and the pathbreaking nature of much that IDRC does. If we have succeeded, this book has met its objective. Of course, given the nature of our work, any mistakes are our own.

Bruce Muirhead
Elmira, Ontario

Ron Harpelle
Thunder Bay, Ontario

INTRODUCTION: CANADA AND THE "EVOLUTION" OF DEVELOPMENT ASSISTANCE, 1945–70

The International Development Research Centre (IDRC) is a product of a certain time, place, and philosophy, pushed by what one critic has called the North American liberal technocratic elite of the 1960s. It reflected a confidence in government and that "development" remained possible, both views of which were to come under increasing fire into the mid-1970s.[1] Intellectually, it also reflected the times and paralleled what was happening domestically with the very activist agenda pursued by the Pearson government. Along with publicly funded health care, a Canadian pension plan, and the Canada Assistance Plan came support for funding research for development in the South, where the researcher was not merely the vessel into which Northern projects would be poured, but who would actually determine the program of work. The Office of the Auditor General put it well when it noted, following a comprehensive audit undertaken in 1982, that "The Centre's approach to research aid is based on the premise that the best people to decide what the developing countries really need are the people of those countries and that research aimed at meeting those needs is best carried out by scientists of the developing world. IDRC acts as a catalyst, an adviser and a supporter. It monitors but does not manage the research projects it supports."[2]

It was truly innovative and unique—a stark departure from the more usual development practice where the South was a recipient of Western largesse and not a partner, a relationship that some characterized as neo-colonial. The

IDRC Act established it at arm's length from government, which provided it with a certain independence to plough its own furrow and which imbued the organization with certain features absent from most other official development agencies. "It is," the current vice-president, programs, has noted, "in some ways, like a university, like an NGO [non-governmental organization] and like a government department. Like a university, it is intellectually curious and committed to scientific excellence; like the NGO it strongly believes in its mission and in the autonomy needed to carry out that mission; and, like a government department, it uses public funds and is publicly accountable for its actions and enjoys the confidence and protection of that official status."[3] This hybridization has served IDRC well.

Beginning with four divisions—Agriculture, Food and Nutrition Sciences, Information Sciences, Health Sciences and Social Sciences—and a very small budget of CAN$1 million, it committed itself to funding applied research on problems Southern researchers identified as crucial to their communities. Division-based program officers would provide expert advice to putative recipients as well as encouraging researchers in innovative and interesting areas to apply. IDRC's focus was resolutely on the South and it eschewed funding Canadian researchers despite demands that it do so. While that was to change somewhat in the 1980s, it resulted in the Centre being much better known in developing countries than it is in Canada.[4]

Growing through the 1970s and into the late 1980s, it added divisions and personnel, at its peak employing more than six hundred staff. It also supported regional offices, eventually settling on six by 2010. IDRC was also bestowed with an innovative and unique governance system that was to prove remarkable. Established as a Crown corporation, it had the freedom to pursue its own lines of enquiry not fettered by government direction. Its board structure of twenty-one helped—eleven, including the chair, were Canadian, with ten foreign appointments. Nowhere else in the development world does this arrangement occur with respect to a public corporation. It remains true to its initial calling, even forty years on, while also very successfully navigating the hazards of a very difficult and demanding file.

The Origins of Development Assistance

International development is a contentious issue, a fact demonstrated by the millions of words devoted to plumbing its depths, and the titles of the various articles and books staking out authors' positions in support of or against current development practices.[5] In the twenty-five years following the end of the Second World War, growth theory was the dominant paradigm, reflected by the fact that the terms "development" and "economic growth" became virtually synonymous.[6] Even Dag Hammarskjöld's United Nations targeted economic development as the objective of Southern policy. As well, most development planners over the period believed Northern country experiences were transferable to the South, and if the latter followed the planners' prescriptions, they, too, would prosper. For example, Walt Rostow, who influenced a generation of development experts with his anti-communist modernization theory, offered that "It is possible to identify all societies, in their economic dimensions, as lying within one of five categories: the traditional society, the preconditions for take-off, the take-off, the drive to maturity, and the age of high mass-consumption."[7] While by 2010, high mass consumption is viewed more skeptically than it was in 1960, it was then seen as the end point of civilization.

Given this belief in the perfectibility of humanity and the linear and forever upward conception of what might be called progress, nascent development agencies directed their effort toward these ends. The first international agency constituted for the express purpose of providing help to those perceived as less fortunate, through the provision of loans, was the International Bank for Reconstruction and Development (IBRD).[8] One of the so-called Bretton Woods twins, the other being the International Monetary Fund (IMF), it had come out of the conference of the same name held in the New Hampshire town in July 1944. Seen from the perspective of those from what would be called the developing world, the IBRD was much more interested in reconstruction than development; Europe lay in ruins after May 1945 and the Bank would do its part to help revive it at the expense of its other mandate. It was not until 1950 that it provided its first loan to a developing country, Colombia. The IBRD was also from its inception a Western club, controlled by the United States through a quota system with an American-appointed president. While the IBRD is usually cited as an example of Western interest in "development," it was clearly not so in its early years.

The idea of official development assistance (ODA) in the form that we know of it today dates from the late 1940s.[9] President Harry Truman's point four program, announced in his Inaugural Address on 20 January 1949, is the precise date usually ascribed to the beginning of a program of modern official development assistance.[10] Its first three bullets reflected late 1940s American foreign policy: (1) support for the United Nations; (2) continued funding for the European Recovery Program, commonly known as the Marshall Plan; and (3) backing for the North Atlantic Treaty Organization in Western Europe, soon to be established by treaty as a bulwark against Soviet expansionism. Point four followed a different trajectory and was a radical departure from past practice when judged in the context of the times. The president exhorted his fellow Americans to:

> embark on a bold new program for making the benefits of our scientific advances and industrial progress available for the improvement and growth of underdeveloped areas. More than half the people of the world are living in conditions approaching misery. Their food is inadequate. They are the victims of disease. Their economic life is primitive and stagnant. Their poverty is a handicap and a threat both to them and to more prosperous areas. For the first time in history, humanity possesses the knowledge and skill to relieve the suffering of these people.

With that humble beginning lay the foundation stone for the whole modern development enterprise.

It also quickly became a casualty of the Cold War being waged between the world's superpowers, the United States and the Union of Soviet Socialist Republics. While many developing countries aligned themselves with one or the other, some, like India, chose non-alignment following its independence in 1947.[11] Adherence to the non-aligned movement remained, for the most part, the exception rather than the rule, although a meeting of Asian and African states, which took place from 18 to 24 April 1955 in Bandung, Indonesia, did profess a commitment to non-alignment. Attended by twenty-nine countries representing more than half the world's population, it was also true that not many of them could afford to remain neutral as between 1945 and 1989, the Cold War was the fact of global life that influenced aid appropriations and defence and foreign policy formulation.

Ottawa, while less enamoured with the idea of official development assistance than its continental partner might have been, was encouraged to become involved through the Commonwealth and the much-vaunted Colombo Plan for Co-operative Economic Development in South and Southeast Asia. Usually touted as an early flagship program for Canadian ODA, according to political scientist Peyton Lyon, the country's interest really began as a desire to "assist the United Kingdom" in meeting its post-war obligations to past and present members of the British Empire.[12] It was also intended as a means of helping countries in South Asia with their transition to independence and to check the spread of communism in the region. Indeed, Keith Spicer, the author of one of the earliest scholarly treatments of Canada's aid program, felt the whole thing was launched "with virtually no policy aim beyond a lively anti-Communist instinct and an exhilarating vision of a free, multiracial Commonwealth."[13]

Despite these early steps, development efforts remained largely ad hoc, reactive, small in scale, and unfocused. Indeed, ODA's global beginnings were lurching and slow, with the US contributing about 50 percent of the total by 1950. That would change over the next half decade, partly a function of the quickening pace of decolonization, especially in Africa, where in 1960 there were nineteen independent states as compared with three a decade earlier. Partly as a reflection of that, the decade culminated, at least in the ODA sense, in the establishment of the International Development Association (IDA), a subsidiary of the World Bank and the largest single channel of concessionary aid to very poor countries, a group to which most newly decolonized African countries belonged. The IDA had not been established without a fight, however, and in one sense it was ironic that it became a part of the World Bank, given its strenuous opposition to such an organization, and its ongoing fight with the United Nations, which wanted an institution focused on concessional aid and managed by itself.[14] The result was a defeat for Southern efforts.

It also represented what would only become more clear over the next two decades—the North's total rejection of a certain development paradigm. As has been pointed out by Jean-Phillipe Thérien, the history of international development has been dominated by the conflict between the Bretton Woods model (the IMF, the World Bank, and the General Agreement on Tariffs and Trade) and that of the UN (the Economic and Social Council, the UN Development Program, and the UN Conference on Trade and Development): "Tightly controlled by the developed countries, the Bretton Woods institutions champion economic growth and the free functioning of markets—values traditionally associated with the Right. The UN agencies, more attuned to developing countries' interests, tend to stress social justice and the need for political regulation—ideas associated with the Left. The (neo)liberalism of the Bretton Woods institutions has thus consistently opposed the more social democratic views of the UN agencies."[15] And by the early 1980s, the former had triumphed over the latter.

Still, broad Canadian experience with international development remained quite limited throughout the 1950s; instead, the action lay with unofficial groups. Protestant missionaries were keen to go abroad to proselytize as they had done in Canada. They were educators who had faith in progress and were intent upon applying "progressive" principles to the 1950s in locations as diverse as China and Latin America. Catholic missionaries were similarly active, particularly in Latin America.[16] Who better, or so it seemed, than these Canadian missionaries, representing a variety of denominations and with experience in remote regions of the world, to join in

Canada's international development efforts.[17] Given this impulse, it is not surprising that the Catholic Church in Canada founded Development and Peace, its official international development organization, at the Conférence des Eveques Catholiques du Canada in 1967, which followed closely upon the heels of the Second Vatican Council, held between 1962 and 1965, itself a gathering that promised fundamental change in the Church.[18] At one point, in proportion to its size and resources, Canada had "more missionaries at home and abroad than any other nation in Christendom" and in the absence of formal diplomatic relations with much of the world, the missionary movement represented the country's ties to many developing nations.[19]

Other Church-affiliated development organizations were established, like Operation Crossroads Africa, which moved into Canada in 1959 with the support of the United Church, in the process becoming Canadian Crossroads International.[20] It joined one of Canada's more famous non-governmental organizations, the Unitarian Service Committee (USC), which had been established by Lotta Hitschmanova, a refugee from Czechoslovakia who had fled the Nazi advance, arriving in Canada in 1942. By the 1950s, in parallel with Canada's efforts to assist the poor in other parts of the world, the USC emphasized international development assistance. Wearing a trademark army nurse's uniform with a military-style hat, and tirelessly working with missionary zeal to raise funds for the organization, Hitschmanova became a household name in Canada for a certain generation of baby boomers who, a half-century later, are able to recite her name and the USC's Ottawa address, 56 Sparks Street.

As well, organizations like the Canadian Save the Children Fund (1946), World University Services of Canada (1957), and the Canadian University Service Overseas (1961) worked in the South in various ways. In the spring of 1962, these groups came together in the Conference on Canadian Overseas Aid, sponsored jointly by the Canadian Institute of International Affairs and the University of Western Ontario (UWO) with officials from the UN secretariat, the World Bank, Canadian universities, the External Aid Office (EAO), and representatives of several federal government departments in attendance. It was one of the first such meetings to consider Canada's ODA policy in a multilateral setting; one part of the discussion focused on the role of NGOs in the aid process and it was decided that it was "useful because it increase[d] the total aid effort and because it involve[d] the Canadian community more directly in the process."[21] And that was seen as increasingly important for those concerned about Canada and its ODA effort as, according to the then-secretary of state for external affairs, Paul Martin, Canadians "generally are not convinced of the importance of foreign aid."[22]

Clearly, these NGOs were increasingly important in the context of the mid-
to later 1960s as Canada, if not Canadians, became increasingly aware of international responsibility. Part of this realization had to do with the celebra-
tion of Canada's 100th birthday in 1967, and the inauguration of the "Miles
for Millions" walks, which one of the authors of this volume remembers well,
ending a long day with very sore feet propped up in the old train station in
Ottawa. With the energetic Maurice Strong as director-general of the External Aid Office, NGO programs were established in November 1967, and the
idea of incorporating them more into the Canadian effort received a push.
A year later, CAN$5 million had been allocated to help fund non-govern-
mental organizations, with Canadian University Service Overseas (CUSO)
receiving the largest share. As well, Strong and others at EAO encouraged
volunteers from that organization and others to apply to work in the official
ODA effort, which they did; staff numbers increased from 350 to nearly 600
by 1970. Those organizations were to become important training grounds for
a revitalized aid component that was to emerge during the second half of the
1960s.

However, for the present, John Diefenbaker's government oversaw the
significant organizational change that resulted in the creation of the External Aid Office in place of the old shotgun approach to ODA disbursement as
it sought to rationalize and systematize Canada's slowly growing aid program. The prime minister, a committed Commonwealth man, was keen to promote policies that promised closer links with those partners, at least as long
as they did not create expectations among the developing Commonwealth
that Canada would find difficult to fulfill. For example, the results of a Commonwealth finance minister's conference held in Montreal in September
1958, when seen in the context of the time, were not insignificant. First,
Ottawa agreed to increase its annual contribution from CAN$35 million to
CAN$50 million to the Colombo Plan. As well, it would provide CAN$500,000
in technical assistance to Commonwealth territories in Africa, and would
provide help to the West Indies to the tune of CAN$10 million over five years.
Finally, along with the United Kingdom, the country launched a scheme of
Commonwealth scholarships and fellowships. With this kind of aid money
being discussed and glibly promised, and with a careful eye on the Canadian
penchant for frugality and rectitude, the government did give some thought
to how it should proceed.

Responsibility for Canada's economic assistance programs had been
divided between the Department of External Affairs and the Department
of Trade and Commerce, with the Department of Finance playing an important role, particularly with respect to questions of policy and financial

administration. That structure was now seen as less than ideal.[23] But more to the point, as the 1960s dawned, the Department of External Affairs was intent on bringing the provision of development assistance under its sole control—the under-secretary of state believed aid to be "an integral part of ... foreign policy."[24] To that end, the EAO was established as of 24 August 1960, which promised to consolidate all aid-related matters under one roof. Still, it was not to be much; along with its director-general, Herbert Moran, External allocated only three full-time officers to the EAO who were responsible for Canadian ODA, as well as a number of others whose remit lay with administration of the new department. Nor would others be hired; austerity measures following a late 1961 financial crisis/economic downturn had the civil service in its grip for several years, with the consequent freezing of EAO numbers.

However, that administrative shift did not change the fundamental disinterest most Canadians and their government expressed toward providing resources for Southern development despite the Commonwealth connection and the aid work done on that file to date. Canada devoted only .21 percent of its GNP to aid in 1960, a paltry amount that ranked far below the average of other industrial countries. Indeed, the chief of the US delegation to a meeting of the Development Assistance Committee (DAC) of the Organisation for Economic Co-operation and Development had commented on this: against the wishes of almost all other members, Canada did not want the 1962 DAC deliberations published because the country had "the lowest official assistance flow in relation to GNP [among all OECD members and] feared the domestic political effects of such implied criticism."[25] While Canadians might not be fervent supporters of ODA, neither did they want to know that their country ranked dead last with recovering states like Belgium, Italy, and Portugal well ahead of them.

Given the climate, Moran and the External Aid Office languished despite the United Nation's declaration of the 1960s as the First Development Decade. Reflecting this official unconcern were the miserly amounts of aid devoted to newly free francophone African countries as well as the government's admittedly cautious approach toward ODA and the Commonwealth. The former proved increasingly difficult following the election of the Jean Lesage government in Quebec in July 1960 and the beginning of the Quiet Revolution; it changed the nature of the relationship between the province and the rest of Canada, which began to ask with increasing urgency "What does Quebec want?" One of those demands was for greater equality both in Canada and abroad, which meant that some development assistance should be given to those African countries thus far ignored. Certainly, the deputy under-secretary of state for External Affairs (and soon to be under-secretary), Marcel Cadieux, a crusty and conservative Québécois, took that position as did the very influential André Laurendeau, editor of Quebec's *Le Devoir*, who thundered in its pages that "Le Commonwealth n'est pas toute l'humanité."[26]

However, that was easier said than done; as Moran was to point out, he did not have *any* French-speaking personnel on his staff who could handle such a program. Only following Cadieux's agreement to take it on was the tiny amount of CAN$300,000 allocated to that part of the initiative out of a total bilateral grant budget in 1963–64 of CAN$50 million. Clearly, francophone Africa was not a vital part of any Canadian aid program, remaining that way until Maurice Strong was named as EAO's director-general in 1966; until 1964, although the budget for that part remained a measly CAN$300,000 annually, over the three years from 1961 to 1964 only CAN$539,000 of the CAN$900,000 allocated had been spent. While in 1964–65, the first full year of the new Pearson government, which had been elected in April 1963, the figure for francophone Africa had been increased to CAN$4 million, an uncommitted balance of roughly CAN$2.8 million remained at year's end.[27] And while the ability to disburse funds to that region had improved with the opening of Canadian embassies in Senegal and Tunisia in 1966, it remained a poor aid cousin to the developing Commonwealth.

The so-called UN Development Decade, despite the fanfare with which it was launched following the proposal made by President Kennedy in a speech to the UN General Assembly in 1961, did not have significant impact on development discourse. This was the situation even though the new secretary-general appointed in 1961, U Thant, a Buddhist and socialist from Burma, saw the world through different glasses than had his predecessors and he set his sights on improving the condition of those billions who lived below the poverty line.[28] While raising the prestige of the organization, the reality fell short "of what were always optimistic targets and exaggerated expectations." Indeed, a case could be made that during the earlier 1960s, countries like Canada and international organizations like the United Nations were still feeling their way in terms of development strategies and plans despite more than ten years of devotion to that cause.

That also held true for the United States and the United Kingdom, both of which established new aid organizations, as had Canada, in the early 1960s. The US created the Agency for International Development in 1961, while in the UK, the Ministry of Overseas Development was set up with much fanfare in October 1964. Multilaterally, the Development Assistance Committee of the Organisation for Economic Co-operation and Development was created in September 1961 with a mandate to coordinate the aid efforts of member donors. However, support in Britain and the United States dissipated over the rest of the decade as public interest cooled and aid appropriations declined as a percentage of gross national product. The First Development Decade could not escape the ennui at best, or hostility at worst, that was now common with respect to the issues it promoted. As President Kennedy stated in a November 1963 press conference when asked about congressional reluctance to vote aid appropriations, "I don't know why we are suddenly so fatigued."[29] By the later 1960s, any development in that decade was construed largely as a failure even as planning for a Second Development Decade was under way.

Why was that so? Egon Glesinger, assistant director-general of the Food and Agriculture Organization, perhaps put it best in 1970: Among a number of serious errors of judgment, the most significant was the "excessive optimism" created by the Development Decade's announcement, creating expectations that could not be met. Further, the North "made the great mistake ... of thinking of their own pattern and their own problems and believing that these could be transposed. Today ... we are deeply convinced that development *can be planned and conceived only in the developing country itself*—that it is from its point of view that you determine the requirements, and then see where foreign assistance can fit in."[30] He was prescient; the International Development Research Centre, established by an Act of the Canadian Parliament in May 1970 to fund research for development, was designed to accomplish just that. Still, in a 1969 article, William Clark, then the director of information at the World Bank, suggested that "The Development Decade is dying of political inanition. Among the rich countries the will to assist development has faded and, partly as a result, in the poorer countries the will to develop is shriveling."[31]

But while the provision of aid to the South was increasingly a zero-sum game in the North, the countries of the former were more intent than ever on organizing themselves into some sort of coherent bloc to influence or badger their wealthier colleagues. For example, the non-aligned movement that emerged from Bandung had formally established itself at Belgrade in 1961. Further, the United Nations Conference on Trade and Development (UNCTAD) came into being in 1964 and was the favoured platform of the Group of 77, a loose coalition of developing countries whose mandate remains to promote their economic development. It was to represent the only major international institution created out of the experience of the First Development Decade.

Soon after its establishment, the UNCTAD "identified the need for special attention to 'the less developed among the developing countries'" and intended to create new policies of co-operation in the field of trade and development.[32] Those would be "firmly based on an acknowledgement of the economic and political inequality of nations."[33] Four years later a resolution was passed on the needs of those least developed countries, while in 1971, twenty-four countries were identified and placed on the original list of what became least developed countries. All of this activity made for a distrustful North and Colin Legum, the British editor of *The Observer*, suggested just that—the UNCTAD had set itself up to confront Western interests, leading the latter to regard it "with suspicion and resistance."[34]

So where did all this leave Canada's aid program by mid-decade? Certainly not in a good space as Canadians shared most of the sentiments expressed above and aid fatigue was already beginning to set in, partly caused by the perception that it was doing no good and might even be working against development. A German newspaper did nothing to dispel those doubts when it suggested to wide publicity in the West that "the poor in rich countries were helping the rich in poor countries."[35] Increasingly, the country was torn by domestic squabbles with Quebec, and political scandal had wounded the first Pearson minority government as it was to do to the second, elected in November 1965. Further, the prime minister was very busy with a national program that included the implementation of programs of publicly funded health care, enhanced social services, a national pension plan, a new flag, and a royal commission to study the issue of bilingualism and biculturalism. It was an activist and expensive agenda that left little time for other things that did not immediately further his domestic program. Perhaps that was why Pearson convinced Maurice Strong, the president of Power Corporation and one of the most powerful private sector operatives in Canada, to take over a floundering EAO as of September 1966, as well as to absorb an 85 percent cut in salary. Meanwhile, Herb Moran happily packed his bags and left for the peaceful confines of the Canadian embassy in Tokyo.

David Morrison notes that Strong was an excellent choice, injecting a new vigour and enthusiasm into EAO deliberations. Indeed, he "recruited some remarkably able people from the private and public sectors to take on senior responsibilities—and, as the establishment virtually doubled, returned CUSO volunteers and others injected youth, commitment and enthusiasm into the organization."[36] But his sense of place was similarly good; the 1960s was a decade of experimentation and change. External Aid, prompted by Strong but also pushed by those eager young officials, began to swim against the current including in its considerations, for example, the social dimension of development, a marked departure from past practice. Similarly, influential books were published in support of development by influential people with traction at the highest levels. Barbara Ward's celebrated *Spaceship Earth* in 1966 began to popularize the issue of underdevelopment and its effects in a way that had not happened before.[37] Similarly, R. Buckminster Fuller put out *Operating Manual for Spaceship Earth* in 1969, which imagined the human species as a crew, united by a shared fate, on a tiny spaceship travelling through infinity; clearly, or so Canadians were increasingly told, we were all in this together.[38]

Still, those considerations and the appointment of Strong did not mean that aid's path was suddenly clear of obstacles; Ottawa turf wars continued to infect the process. Should External Aid post its own officers overseas? Not if James Langley, an assistant undersecretary of state, had any say in the matter. Should EAO be permitted to offer independent policy advice to the minister? Not if J.R. Francis of the undersecretary's office had any sway with his boss; his take was that "more precise ground rules for cooperation with the External Aid Office" should be developed "in order to ensure that our thinking coincides with theirs" or the other way around. There was also "a certain degree of mistrust from both sides [that] must be resolved," noted Thomas Carter, the head of the African and Middle Eastern division at the department.[39] Strong was also very aware of the potential of departmental regulars to hold up his advance.[40] While international development might be a very slow process so, too, was forward movement in Ottawa.

And development was slow and largely dependent on the activities of the people so affected, or so Lester Pearson believed. He articulated that on a number of occasions; indeed, it became his mantra and would find expression in IDRC as the organization *funded* research *in* the South undertaken by Southerners designed to address important issues. For example, asked by the British Broadcasting Corporation to present the 1968 Reith Lecture, he did so calling it "Peace in the Family of Man." It focused on uneven development and the necessity of helping those who would help themselves. As he noted, "in external aid for development there should be maximum participation on the part of the receiving country. To the greatest possible extent we should place responsibility on the governments and the people of the country."[41] Similarly, when presenting the 1969 Russell C. Leffingwell Lectures sponsored by the influential US Council on Foreign Relations, he asserted that "Aid is no fairy godmother touching everything with her magic wand so that, presto, the little mice and pumpkins of local effort are turned into large luxury carriages. Development is a long, slogging, grinding effort by the people themselves of each country."[42] In his lecture to a crowd at Scarborough College of the University of Toronto in 1970, he raised the same theme: "No country will be able to go ahead except by its own effort and its own policies and the wise use of its own resources, human and material. All that external aid can do ... is to help the country help itself. The final responsibility rests at home. However, if a country is trying to go forward, to help itself, then we who are more fortunate have an obligation to assist in that process."[43]

Pearson, too, had become much more active on the aid front than he ever had been as prime minister. Following his resignation from office in April 1968 he was asked by Robert McNamara, then only recently appointed to head the World Bank, to lead an independent effort by a group of international development experts and assess past practice and determine why donor countries had scaled back on contributions; in 1968, for the first time, there had been a reduction in ODA. Known as the Commission on International Development, it was equally perceived as the Pearson Commission so closely was his style and personality reflected in its work, which was published as *Partners in Development: Report of the Commission on International Development*. While not influencing the debate in the way that it had hoped, especially with respect to its recommendation that Northern governments devote 0.7 percent of their GNP to ODA, it did raise the issue of Southern development.[44] Still, by 1970, aggregate official aid had *fallen* to 0.33 percent of gross national income, compared with more than 0.5 percent at the beginning of the 1960s and was to fall even further, to 0.22 percent of GNP on average among OECD countries in the late 1990s.

The Pragmatic IDRC

So, where does this bring us in our pending consideration of the history of IDRC? First, that this pragmatic Pearsonian conception of development permeated his ideas about what was to become the International Development Research Centre. Certainly he remained in close contact with Maurice Strong following his return to private life and was instrumental in the hiring of the very pragmatic David Hopper as IDRC's first president. Pearson was also able to influence the Centre's very early development as first chair of the board following the passage by Parliament of the *International Development Centre Act* on 13 May 1970. In a direct way, the pragmatism that animated his consideration of the international aid environment and found expression in *Partners in Development* did likewise in how he conceived of his baby. Strong, too, was a pragmatist. Both were interested in *how* to accomplish objectives by overcoming bureaucratic opposition. And the establishment of IDRC was first and foremost a *pragmatic* political act that demonstrated the success of their campaign; it did not reflect elements of intellectual ferment and debate or raise questions as, say, the establishment of the United Nations had, causing people to reflect on who they are or where they were going as a civilization.

As a result of that and its three midwives, Hopper, Pearson, and Strong, IDRC was and remains an intensely pragmatic organization, espousing a number of overriding principles as its organizational framework. These might include its emphasis on funding research for development and its idea of the role of knowledge "as the lynchpin and foundation stone of development."[45] That spoke to capacity building in the South, which was all about partnership, a philosophy that David Hopper embedded in the Centre and which had a particular IDRC bent: "You cannot build the capacity of others—they need to be partners of and in the process."[46] Further, there is one solid intellectual direction from which IDRC has never strayed and which sets it apart from most of its colleagues in the aid business—that Southern researchers are instrumental in establishing the agenda within the Centre's delineated programming, and that developing countries would have to help themselves, albeit with Canadian financial assistance. That is certainly clear from Pearson's various addresses noted above. From its very beginning, it embraced responsiveness and rejected notions of research imperialism or fitting itself into any sort of neo-colonial programming. In a sense, this pragmatism has been its greatest intellectual contribution to the world of development. Significantly, being a Crown corporation with its own board and Act also meant that it has not had to assiduously observe government strictures about working in certain countries for diplomatic, strategic, or official reasons. We will see this below in the cases of the southern cone of South America during the 1980s or South Africa in the early 1990s.

This does not mean that IDRC did not pull itself up by its own roots to see what was happening—it did that often and to great effect. Nor does it mean that the organization did not continually debate and question the appropriate way to move forward. It did that, too. Indeed, the stories of Hopper moving around the Centre in its early days, demanding of all he encountered, whether research scientist, program officer, or secretary, to explain themselves and why what they were doing was important and would contribute to Southern development, are legion. Ivan Head's establishment of an evaluations section, rudimentary though it may have been, was also indicative of the ferment that characterized IDRC's activities to improve itself, as did Keith Bezanson's move into program initiatives. Maureen O'Neil was to bring gender considerations into the Centre mainstream for the first time. As well, it evolved into a more participatory and inclusive "inter/trans/multi-disciplinary" sort of organization that valued linking research to the need for policy utilization and implementation. This, in turn, would lead to "a reduced emphasis on the natural sciences as the social sciences and community aspects of development has grown in stature and been favoured."[47]

As well, early on, it began funding Canadian area and development studies associations, their conferences, journals, and research-gathering and communication activities, "in doing so allowing Canadian-based scholars to network and constitute autonomous Canadian forums for the discussion of development issues. The Canadian Association of Latin American and Caribbean Studies, the Canadian Asian Studies Association, the Canadian Association of African Studies, and the Canadian Association of Studies in International Development have received substantial core funding from IDRC, intermittently in the 1970s and 1980s, and continuously since 1990. This has allowed Canadian-based scholars to create networks outside of US-dominated anglophone North American academic associations for discussion of development and area studies issues, and assists them in bringing scholars and agents from developing countries to Canada to participate in those discussions."[48] This meant better links with Canadian institutions and researchers, which became increasingly important over time. These examples only scratch the surface of the intense commitment of staff and management to ideas about development and process.

It is our judgment that IDRC began life with a very particular objective in mind, funding research for development in the South, from which it has never really strayed. While it has suffered setbacks and failures in its programming—not to have done so would have made it a very strange creature indeed—it has also been in the forefront of change and innovation more often than not. It has received international recognition from both its peers and governments, reflecting the esteem in which it is held. As this book will demonstrate, it has been, for the most part, nimble, flexible, and willing to contemplate approaches to problems that would not occur to more staid organizations. Unfortunately, it remains an institution of which most Canadians are woefully unaware, as unknown in the country of its birth as it is known in those parts of the developing world where it has funded such good work. Canadians should be as proud of what it has accomplished over the past forty years as they should be of how it has done so.

Notes

This book is largely based on documents retrieved from the IDRC archives. These span the period since 1970 and were subject to a variety of cataloguing processes and notations, which changed over time. This is reflected in our Notes. This said, we think that any researchers who follow us will be able to find our documents despite the sometimes idiosyncratic nature of some of our citations. This was necessary because IDRC's purpose in filing papers was not to make things easier for future researchers but to allow for easy retrieval of information by its own officials.

1 Anonymous reader, University of Toronto Press assessment.
2 "Comprehensive Audit Report to the Board of Governors of the International Development Research Centre," August 1982. Accessed at http://www.idrc.ca/uploads/user-S/11558266111Comprehensive_Audit_(1982).pdf.
3 Interview with Rohinton Medhora, Ottawa.
4 IDRC is rarely mentioned in general histories of Canada, or even of Canadian foreign policy development. And when it is, even the most highly regarded historians sometimes get it wrong. On this, see Norman Hillmer and J.L. Granatstein, *Empire to Umpire: Canada and the World to the 1990s* (Toronto: Nelson, 2007), 287. They state that "IDRC was instituted in 1978 by Trudeau to foster research ... (and to provide a job for his former aide, Ivan Head)." This is erroneous on both counts. A similar omission can be seen in Brian Tomlin, Norman Hillmer, and Fen Hampson, *Canada's International Policies: Agendas, Alternatives, and Politics* (Toronto: Oxford University Press, 2007).
5 See, for example, William Easterly (ed.), *Reinventing Foreign Aid* (Cambridge: MIT Press, 2008); William Easterly, *The White Man's Burden: Why the West's Effort to Aid the Rest Have Done So Much Ill and So Little Good* (New York: Penguin Press, 2005); William Easterly, *The Elusive Quest for Growth: Economists' Adventures and Misadventures in the Tropics* (Cambridge: MIT Press, 2001). In each of these, the author presents a sustained critique of Western practices vis-à-vis the provision of aid to the developing South. For example, in the introduction to *Reinventing Foreign Aid*, he notes that "I chose to reflect on the dissatisfaction that I and others feel with a dysfunctional business that is supposed to be benefiting the most desperate people in the world" (2). Richard Kozul-Wright and Paul Rayment, *The Resistible Rise of Market Fundamentalism: Rethinking Development Policy in an Unbalanced World* (London: Zed, 2007) suggest that "the developed world needs to show not only more humility in lecturing developing countries on how they should solve their problems but also more tolerance in accepting the possibility of different economic and social arrangements from those prevailing in the west" (xii). Ha-Joon Chang, *Kicking away the Ladder: Development Strategy in Historical Perspective* (London: Anthem, 2007) questions the policy prescriptions that developed countries imposed on the South. For example, he notes that the mantra most often espoused by established sources in the West in explanation for its economic success is that this was attained "through 'good' policies and institutions" like the protection of intellectual property rights, laissez-faire policies, and good governance. Rhetorically, he asks, "But is it really true that the policies and institutions currently recommended to the developing countries are those that were adopted by the developed countries when they themselves were developing?" (2). The answer is no. And so that list gets ever longer: Stephen Browne, *Aid and Influence: Do Donors Help or Hinder?* (London: Earthscan, 2007); Erik S. Reinert, *How Rich Countries Got Rich ... and Why Poor Countries Stay Poor* (London: Constable, 2007); Paul Mosely, Jane Harrigan, and John Toye, *Aid and Power: The World Bank and Policy Based Lending*, vol. 1 (London: Routledge, 1991), among many others. This tiny sample is merely representative of the approach taken by those thousands of critics who deplore the sort of Western meddling in the developing world that, to their minds, has perpetuated a system based on inequality, exploitation, and underdevelopment. A more recent, perhaps neo-liberal, contribution is Dambisa Moyo, *Dead Aid: Why Aid Is Not Working and How There Is a Better*

Way for Africa (New York: Farrar, Straus, and Giroux, 2009), who argues that aid has been counterproductive for Africa and that foreign direct investment in the continent would be better.

Those who favour the system as presently practised are far less numerous and come primarily from the approximately eighty multilateral and bilateral institutions that do the provisioning, although some, like Jeffrey Sachs, called by the *New York Time Magazine* "probably the most important economist in the world," also support the present system, or want more of it. See, for example, Jeffrey Sachs, *The End of Poverty: Economic Possibilities for Our Time* (New York: Penguin, 2006). He states that in order to achieve the goal of eliminating global poverty, clinical economics must be backed by greater funding; he argues that development aid must be raised from US$65 billion globally as of 2002 to between US$135 billion and US$195 billion a year by 2015. This would ensure the path out of extreme poverty for the world's poorest citizens. The book's foreword is written by the rock star Bono of U2, also a proponent of increasing development assistance. Sachs has called Moyo's interpretation "cruel." See also Daphne Eviatar, "Spend $150 Billion per Year to Cure World Poverty," *New York Times Magazine*, 7 November 2004, 7.

6 Browne, *Aid and Influence*, 24.

7 Walt W. Rostow, *The Stages of Economic Growth: A Non-Communist Manifesto* (Cambridge: Cambridge University Press, 1960), 1. See also John Toye and Richard Toye, *The UN and Global Political Economy: Trade, Finance, and Development* (Bloomington: Indiana University Press, 2004), 168–72, for critics of Rostow's approach.

8 The literature on the World Bank is voluminous. Important studies include Edward S. Mason and Robert E. Asher, *The World Bank since Bretton Woods* (Washington, DC: Brookings Institution, 1973). This book was initiated by the World Bank on the occasion of its twenty-fifth birthday and was called an "authorized but independent history." A similar effort was produced for the Bank's fiftieth— a commissioned but independent book, Devesh Kapur, John P. Lewis, and Richard Webb, *The World Bank: Its First Half-Century* (Washington, DC: Brookings Institution, 1997). There are also literally hundreds of other analyses, mostly critical of World Bank operations.

9 Gilbert Rist, *The History of Development: From Western Origins to Global Faith* (London: Zed Books, 2002), 8–46. He also traces such a concept back to the Europe of the 1700s.

10 However, some such as Gilbert Rist trace its origins much farther back. See Rist, *The History of Development*.

11 The literature dealing with the non-aligned movement is extensive. See, for example, Cecil V. Crabb, *The Elephants and the Grass: A Study of Nonalignment* (New York: Praeger, 1965); Hans Köchler (ed.), *The Principles of Non-alignment: The Non-aligned Countries in the Eighties—Results and Perspectives* (London: Third World Centre, 1982); Subrata Banerjee, *Non-alignment Today: Challenges and Prospects* (New Delhi: Allied Publishers, 1985); Roy Allison, *The Soviet Union and the Strategy of Non-alignment in the Third World* (Cambridge: Cambridge University Press, 1988); Steven R. David, *Choosing Sides: Alignment and Realignment in the Third World* (Baltimore: Johns Hopkins University Press, 1991).

12 Peyton Lyon and Tareq Ismael (eds.), *Canada and the Third World* (Toronto: Macmillan, 1976), xxi. Canada spent the first decade following the end of the Second World War attempting to help resurrect the British economy. For an account of this, see B.W. Muirhead, *The Development of Post-war Canadian Trade Policy: The Failure of the Anglo-European Option* (Montreal and Kingston: McGill-Queen's University Press, 1992).

13   Keith Spicer, *A Samaritan State? External Aid in Canada's Foreign Policy* (Toronto: University of Toronto Press, 1966), 3.

14   See Richard Jolly, "UN and Development Thinking and Practice," *Forum for Development Studies*, no. 1-2005, June 2005, 67. Accessed at www.unhistory.org/reviews/FDS_Jolly.pdf. As Jolly writes, beginning in the early 1950s, "The UN produced ... a succession of reports, arguing the case for concessional funding for developing countries. The World Bank, notably its then-president Eugene Black, dismissed the case, arguing that concessional funding would be anti-market, dependent on subsidies from the industrial countries and altogether against the interests of developing countries. Only in 1957, after nine years of highly contentious and often tortuous debate, was the matter brought to a resolution, with a historic compromise. The UN would be allowed to have an expanded program of technical assistance funded by a separate special fund in the UN.... The provision of concessional funding would become a program of the World Bank, notwithstanding their nine years of steady opposition. Thus the International Development Association was born, which of course continues to this day as the major international instrument for providing concessional assistance to the poorest countries." See also Robert E. Wood, *From Marshall Plan to Debt Crisis: Foreign Aid and Development Choices in the World Economy* (Berkeley: University of California Press, 1986), 73; Raymond F. Mikesell, *The Economics of Foreign Aid* (London: Weidenfeld and Nicolson, 1968), 2. Mikesell notes that "Foreign aid doctrine in the recipient countries ... is usually based on an entirely different philosophy of aid from that held by the donors. Recipient countries regard aid as a *obligation* of rich countries, a *right* of the recipients; they are frequently resentful or suspicious of the donor countries' national objectives that are served by aid. Thus, most recipient countries would prefer that aid be provided by United Nations' agencies or regional agencies largely controlled by developing countries, but by the developed, donor countries" (emphasis in original).

15   Jean-Phillipe Thérien, "The Brandt Commission: The End of an Era in North-South Politics," in Ramesh Thakur, Andrew Cooper, and John English (eds.), *International Commissions and the Power of Ideas* (Tokyo: United Nations University Press, 2005), 37.

16   See Catherine LeGrand for interesting perspectives on Quebec missionaries in Latin America. Catherine Legrand, "L'axe missionaire catholique entre le Québec et l'Amérique Latine: Une exploration préliminaire," *Globe*, vol. 12, no. 1, 2009: 43–66.

17   A good example of a missionary turned international development specialist is Jacques Amyot, who worked for IDRC in the 1970s. Born in northern Alberta to francophone parents who sent him to Valleyfield, Quebec, for an education, Amyot became a Jesuit priest and was working as a missionary in China at the time of the Revolution in 1949. He spent from 1947 to 1952 in the newly established People's Republic of China and was then sent to the University of Chicago to study social anthropology, receiving his Ph.D. in 1960. His graduate research took him to the Philippines, but when he graduated in 1961 he was sent to Thailand, where he joined other Jesuit priests teaching at Chulalonkorn University. Amyot was responsible for setting up the departments of anthropology and sociology, as well as the Institute of Social Studies (ISS) in 1969. He left the Jesuits in 1972 and two years later did likewise from ISS, allowing Thai researchers to assume control over the institute and its research agenda. In September 1974 he signed a contract with IDRC, almost by accident. Upon leaving ISS he hoped to obtain funding from the Canadian International Development Agency (CIDA) to conduct research on resettlement in the Mekong Delta. Upon

arrival in Ottawa, however, he discovered that "CIDA was a dead end," whereupon he investigated prospects at the International Development Research Centre, where he was offered a Pearson fellowship. However, Ruth Zagorin, the director of the Social Sciences division, offered him the position of IDRC representative in Southeast Asia. Thus, Jacques Amyot, the former Jesuit and Thai university professor, became a program officer living in Singapore working for the regional director, Nihal Kappagoda. He stayed with the Centre for five years and then returned to Thailand, where he settled, working at the university and occasionally for IDRC, the US·Agency for International Development, and other organizations. Interview with Jacques Amyot, Bangkok, Thailand, 29 November 2006.

18 Vatican II was held in response to a number of factors, chief among them that the world's bishops faced tremendous challenges driven by political, social, economic, and technological change. Some of these bishops sought new ways of addressing those challenges. See Jean-Guy Vaillancourt for a full discussion of the Catholic left in Quebec during the 1960s and 1970s. "Les groupes socio-politiques progressistes dans le Catholicisme québécois contemporain," in Jean-Paul Rouleau and Jacques Zylberberg (eds.), *Les mouvements religieux aujourd'hui: Theories et pratiques* (Quebec: Presses de l'Université Laval, 1984), 277.

19 Alvyn J. Austin and James S. Scott, "Introduction," in *Canadian Missionaries, Indigenous Peoples: Representing Religion at Home and Abroad* (Toronto: University of Toronto Press, 1986), 4.

20 Ian Smillie and Henny Helmich, *Non-governmental Organizations and Governments: Stakeholders for Development* (Paris: Development Centre of the Organisation for Economic Co-operation and Development, 1993), 103.

21 Arghyrios A. Fatouros and Robert Kelson, *Canada's Overseas Aid* (Toronto: CIIA, 1964), 93.

22 Paul Martin, "Address at Carleton University," *Overseas Institute of Canada Bulletin*, July 1963, 6. See also Paul Martin, "The Canadian Aid Programme," *Globe and Mail*, 15 November 1963, 9 for the first Liberal demarche into ODA.

23 Memorandum from Minister of Trade and Commerce, Minister of Finance, and Secretary of State for External Affairs to Cabinet, "Administration of Canada's Economic Assistance Programmes: Proposed Reorganization," 15 August 1960, *Documents on Canadian External Relations*, vol. 27, 1960 (Ottawa: Canada Communication Group, 2006), 647.

24 John Hilliker and Donald Barry, *Canada's Department of External Affairs:* vol. II, *Coming of Age, 1946–1968* (Montreal and Kingston: McGill-Queen's University Press, 1995), 179.

25 JFK Library, Papers as President, National Security Files, Carl Kaysen, Box 372, File: Economic Policy—Subjects—OECD Development Center, 6/62-12/62, "Personal Report and Evaluation of Meeting of the Development Assistance Committee of OECD, July 25, 26, 1962, by Frank M. Coffin, Deputy Administrator for Operations, AID, Chairman of the American Delegation," n.d.

26 André Laurendeau, "Le Commonwealth n'est pas toute l'humanité," *Le Devoir*, 16 January 1960, 4, as quoted in Spicer, *A Samaritan State?*, 56. However, Robin Gendron, *Towards a Francophone Community: Canada's Relations with France and French Africa, 1945–1968* (Montreal and Kingston: McGill-Queen's University Press, 2006) has a different interpretation. Canada was not so much loathe to move into aid programming in West Africa as it was in undermining it relations with France, especially given the Cold War context that characterized the period covered by the book.

27 Hilliker and Barry, *Canada's Department of External Affairs:* vol. II, 336.
28 John Toye and Richard Toye, *The UN and Global Political Economy: Trade, Finance, and Development* (Bloomington: Indiana University Press, 2004), 3. U Thant "had experienced colonialism at first hand and ... saw the major division of the world as that between rich and poor countries rather than between capitalism and communism," which gave the UN greater credibility among Southern governments.
29 See President John F. Kennedy, "News Conference #64," State Department Auditorium, Washington, DC, 14 November 1963. The part about ODA demonstrates critical congressional attitudes. See also JFK Library, Boston, MA, President's Office Files, Special Correspondents, Box 28, File: Bowles, Chester, Bowles to Kennedy, 11 October 1962. In the letter, Bowles, the undersecretary of state and a firm supporter of ODA, writes of "the Congressional fireworks in regard to foreign economic assistance [which] hit a new peak."
30 Egon Glesinger, "Discussion," in Colin Legum (ed.), *The First Development Decade and Its Lessons for the 1970s* (New York: Praeger, 1970), 39; emphasis added. The book, all 307 pages of it, focuses on the First Development Decade's failures. They are too numerous to go into here.
31 William D. Clark, "Creating Political Will," in Colin Legum (ed.), *The First Development Decade and Its Lessons for the 1970s* (New York: Praeger, 1970), 147. He went on to note that "If the world is not to drift apart into two hostile camps, the political will for development must be reinvigorated. The first responsibility lies with the richer, donor countries, which alone can give accelerated impetus to the development efforts of the poorer countries. What we need today is not more experts; it is not more economists; it is not more money—it is more determination on the part of the politically decisive to do something effective about the growing gap between rich and poor."
32 Jolly, "UN and Development Thinking and Practice," 65.
33 Toye and Toye, *The UN and Global Political Economy*, 12.
34 Colin Legum, "Discussion," in Colin Legum (ed.), *The First Development Decade and Its Lessons for the 1970s* (New York: Praeger, 1970), 161. See also Toye and Toye, *The UN and Global Political Economy*, 4.
35 David Morrison, *Aid and Ebb Tide: A History of CIDA and Canadian Development Assistance* (Waterloo: Wilfrid Laurier University Press, 1998), 59.
36 Morrison, *Aid and Ebb Tide*, 57.
37 Barbara Ward Jackson, *Spaceship Earth* (New York: Columbia University Press, 1966).
38 R. Buckminster Fuller, *Operating Manual for Spaceship Earth* (New York: Simon and Shuster, 1969).
39 Hilliker and Barry, *Canada's Department of External Affairs:* vol. II, 338–39.
40 Interview with Maurice Strong, Ottawa, 1 May 2006.
41 Lester Pearson, *Peace in the Family of Man* (Toronto: Oxford University Press, 1969), 65.
42 Lester Pearson, *The Crisis of Development* (New York: Praeger, 1970), 49.
43 L.B. Pearson, "Partners in Development," F.B. Watts Memorial Series Lecture, 1970, 5–6.
44 However, the verdict on the Pearson Commission is that it failed in its purpose "because shortly after its publication, the Bretton Woods system began to come apart, the industrial countries became preoccupied with their own troubles, and a little later, the oil crisis of 1973 changed the context of international discussion." Hans Wolfgang Singer and Javed A. Ansari, *Rich and Poor Countries: Consequences of International Disorder* (Baltimore: Johns Hopkins Press, 1977), 160.

45 Eva Rathgeber, "Turning Failure into Success: The Deconstruction of IDRC Develop-
    ment Discourse, 1970–2000" (Ottawa: IDRC, September 2001), 1.
46 Charles Lufthaus and Stephanie Nelson, "Capacity Building at IDRC: Some Prelimi-
    nary Thoughts," *Universalia*, April 2005, Appendix I, 5.
47 Rathgeber, *Turning Failure into Success*, 1.
48 Anonymous reviewer.

Canadian Learned Societies Supported

Canadian Council for Area Studies Learned Societies
> Date first funded: 21 August 1995   Date last funded: 7 October 2009

Canadian Association of African Studies
> Date first funded: 1 May 1974   Date last funded: ongoing
> • CAAS is an established professional association of Canadian scholars, representing
>   a variety of disciplines, interested in African studies.

Canadian Asian Studies Association
> Date first funded: 9 January 1975   Date last funded: ongoing
> • CSAS is an association of Canadian scholars interested in Asian studies.

Canadian Association for Latin American and Caribbean Studies
> Date first funded: 1 January 1974   Date last funded: 19 March 2009

Canadian Committee of the Middle East Studies Association of North America
> Date first funded: 12 July 2001   Date last funded: 7 October 2009
> • CANMES is the Canadian Committee of the Middle East Studies Association, estab-
>   lished in 1995 to encourage communication among scholars of Middle Eastern
>   studies resident in Canada, and to further the development of joint projects and
>   conference participation on the part of its membership.

Canadian Association for the Study of International Development
> Date first funded: 4 February 1999   Date last funded: ongoing
> • CASID is a national, bilingual, multidisciplinary and pluralistic association devoted
>   to the study of international development in all parts of the world.

Canadian Development Economics Study Group
> Date first funded: 1 July 2008   Date last funded: ongoing
> • CDESG aims to promote academic excellence and policy dialogue between Canada-
>   and developing country-based researchers in the field of development economics.

Canadian Society for Ecological Economics
> Date first funded: 17 April 2007   Date last funded: 11 June 2009
> • CSEE fosters interdisciplinary research, activities and dialogue among natural and
>   social scientists, to deepen understanding of the interactions between humans and
>   nature and to inform the sustainable stewardship of our common natural, human,
>   social and produced capital endowments.

Canadian Society for International Health
> Date first funded: 4 January 1984   Date last funded: 29 January 2010
> • CSIH is a national non-governmental organization that works domestically and
>   internationally to reduce global health inequities and strengthen health systems.

American Learned Societies Supported

International Studies Association
   Date first funded: 5 May 2003   Funding ongoing

International Association for Feminist Economics
   Date first funded: 21 May 2003   Date last funded: 31 October 2007

With thanks to Sarah Mohan, IDRC intern, for this information.

Chapter 1

THE IDEA BEARS FRUIT, 1967–70

> *You see things and say "why"? But I dream things
> that never were, and I say "why not"?*
> —George Bernard Shaw, Back to
> Methuselah, *Part 1, Act 1, 1921*

The dazzling fireworks display that lit up Parliament Hill on 1 July 1967, commemorating 100 years of Canada's nationhood, symbolized all that had gone right. The blues and yellows and purples that danced off the old limestone of the Centre Block with each explosion spoke of a country that was confident, dynamic, and capable. Its new flag, a red maple leaf between two red bars and first raised to the top of the Peace Tower on a very cold day in February 1965, suggested that anything was possible. For an entire year the country was consumed by celebrations, and joined in early summer for a week by Queen Elizabeth II, who lent a certain aura and lustre to the party. The world's fair, Expo 67 held in Montreal, was in full swing by the time she arrived, and the millions who visited symbolized the optimism and confidence of the decade. In 1967, the country had something to offer that made it exciting and different, or so it seemed; it was "cool."

That confidence was partly given shape by the introduction of social programs on an unheard of scale; medicare, the Canada Pension Plan, and an increase in social legislation generally, both federally and provincially, made Canadians much more secure. They could also feel smug about the problems of their neighbour, the United States, involved as it was in race riots and a very unpopular war in Vietnam. American difficulties, oddly, made Canadians feel superior; they were too intelligent and too humane to be afflicted by those issues. The songwriter Gordon Lightfoot put his finger on what increasingly separated the two North American countries with songs like his 1968 "Black Day in July." Canadians could only shake their heads, confirmed in the belief that theirs was the better part of the continent.

There were other reasons for optimism for those who knew about such things. The developing world seemed to be making advances toward economic independence, and decolonization was proceeding apace. For example, the so-called green revolution, a term coined in 1968 by William Gaud, then the director of the US Agency for International Development, was under way in several regions of the developing world, and India, it was thought, could look forward to a future free from hunger. Monkombu Sambasivan (M.S.) Swaminathan, the Indian geneticist and future IDRC funding recipient, was in the forefront of the movement.[1] While the revolution has turned out to be less than its billing and India has suffered as many agricultural setbacks as advances as a result, in the later 1960s the idea that the application of science and technology to the problems faced by a developing country *would* bestow huge benefits swept all before it. The problem of the clash of two civilizations that the French academic, Jean-Jacques Salomon, laid out—of the Northern one based "on the growth of science as the main knowledge-generating activity, the rapid evolution of science-related technologies, the incorporation of these technologies into productive processes, and the emergence of new forms of working and living deeply influenced by the *Weltanschauung* of modern science and science-related technologies" and the other, the Southern, "characterized by its inability to generate scientific knowledge on a large scale"—seemed amenable to resolution in those heady days of the late 1960s.[2]

Increasingly, scientists, economists, and political leaders around the world saw the need to extend technical and scientific knowledge to the developing world as the key to global prosperity and security. As one United Nations committee had noted, "Only a very small fraction of the world's scientific and technical resources are devoted to the problems of the developing countries; the overwhelming proportion of the world's intellectual capital, as well as its physical capital, is applied toward ... the highly developed countries."[3] That had partly been the rationale behind the convening of the United Nations conference on science and technology in 1963, which itself had come out of an idea raised in 1961 at the UN Scientific and Advisory Committee. Its report, with the rather unwieldy title of *Science and Technology for*

Development: Report on the United Nations Conference on the Application of Science and Technology for the Benefit of Less Developed Areas, did have an impact on world thinking. As P.M.S. Blackett of the United Kingdom described it, the conference was "a supermarket where delegates from the less developed countries can window-shop to help them decide on priorities."[4] Indeed, Southern delegates wanted a new agency set up by the UN specifically to deal with the application of science to development. The problem, of course, was that "window shoppers" did not normally have the money to purchase all of the things they saw, and many of the priorities the delegates identified were beyond their means. The idea of a new agency was rejected by Secretary General U Thant and senior management at the UN. As a partial response to the desires of Southern delegates, a subcommittee on science and technology was established, but, like many good ideas at the UN, it languished.

Imagine a New Organization

The International Development Research Centre was conceived in the context of the need to assist developing countries in developing scientific and technological priorities. In Canada, the idea of supporting science and technology for development was on the mind of Maurice Strong, the new director general of the External Aid Office[5] (EAO), the precursor to the Canadian International Development Agency, who used his influence in Ottawa to pursue this novel concept of development assistance. The country's scientific and technological base had developed to the point where a definite contribution in that area was a possibility. Lester Pearson, then prime minister of Canada and later head of the UN Commission on International Development and primary author of its report, *Partners in Development* (1969), was also an adherent. IDRC grew out of a late 1960s trend in development assistance: How did societies develop appropriate technology? It was also established to address a glaring gap in the provision of official development assistance— that of any organization dedicated to helping foster *research* in the South *done by Southern researchers* but funded by wealthy governments. It was true that some had done this, like the Rockefeller or Ford foundations, but they were not public corporations. Strong had an almost intuitive early understanding of an issue that would become much more prevalent by the 1990s: That "few Western aid programs ever seek feedback from their consumers, the world's poor. Aid bureaucrats seldom feel accountable to anyone other than their rich-country principals, who rate results not on how money is used but on how much of it is given out."[6] Strong had come from the private sector's Power Corporation and his appointment in 1966 to the EAO by Prime

Minister Pearson reflected the state of flux in the capital. It also mirrored what David Hopper, IDRC's first president, was to call Pearson's desire to put some muscle into Canadian development assistance; appointing Strong certainly did that.[7]

Arriving in Ottawa, Strong could not understand why government organizations like the External Aid Office did not have research and development (R and D) arms. As he mulled over this situation, it became more clear to him that such an entity should be created: his new charge should have an R and D department and, while he did not know exactly what should be built, he was interested in setting the wheels in motion.[8] Very soon after becoming director general, Strong embarked on a broad process of consulting with many of the leading thinkers and practitioners in the world of development assistance on the concept. As he well knew, approximately 98 percent of research and development expenditures continued to be made in the wealthy industrialized nations that already had the scientific and technological infrastructure that enabled them to maintain high growth rates; that huge disparity led to a technology gap. Strong believed that Canada could build "all the bridges and hospitals it wanted in the less developed countries without resolving basic problems of development unless we tackle the 'technology gap.'"[9] As it stood, less than one half of 1 percent of Canada's total aid flows was given to development research. Meanwhile, commercial enterprises often allocated up to 6 percent of their revenues for R and D, and nations in the 2–4 percent range. What was required, Strong thought, was a deliberate act of policy to correct the situation and give voice to his belief that there was more to development than rising allocation figures; he became convinced that an autonomous research-funding institution was the way forward. In those early days, as Strong conceived of it, the organization would identify, initiate, encourage, support, and undertake research into the problems involved in the development of economically deprived regions of the world. Through its research programs it would discover the most effective allocation of science and technology to the needs of the people of those regions for their social and economic growth. The idea was also that a centre would help Southern countries to acquire their own problem-solving capabilities so they would not become mere welfare recipients of the global village but, as one official put it, "creative contributors to the increased well-being of its members."[10]

Strong had done a lot of thinking about development following his arrival at the External Aid Office and realized that developing countries spent little on research and development. It seemed to him that, "given that knowledge is the principal source of wealth creation, if the education gap wasn't closed, then the development gap was just going to widen. If you wanted to get at this, you had to address it."[11] Closing the education gap was where his initial conception of what was to become IDRC came in. This reflected his larger vision of development assistance. He was increasingly appalled that the average income of Canadians in the late 1960s was multiplying annually by an amount almost equal to the total annual income of most people in less developed countries (LDC). "This imbalance," he noted, "is in large measure due to our mastery of science and technology and our lopsided application of it to LDCs. Most of the population growth is taking place in less developed countries.... By the end of the century, Canadians may have to justify before the world our right to continue to occupy a disproportionate share of the world's living space.... It would be folly to think that we could live securely in our sanctuaries of privilege and affluence with the tides of hungry and restless people rising all around us ... [This would be] morally devastating."[12]

Strong had also had some hands-on experience. Educating himself about the state of the South, his first overseas trip as director general of EAO in March 1967 was to India, then in the midst of the devastating Bihar famine, which had begun the year prior. Ironically, the famine occurred in the midst of *increased* food production generally in India as the high-yielding varieties of wheat that signalled the beginning of the green revolution became more widespread throughout the country. The affected population was approximately 34 million, of whom almost 14 million lived in the area directly hit by drought.[13] In the midst of this natural carnage, Strong met David Hopper at the Agricultural Research Institute in New Delhi, where Hopper was undertaking research with a Rockefeller Foundation grant.[14] The two men travelled to the field and admired the new dwarf wheat at the Institute, and Hopper had emphasized that agricultural research was a key to development. While others had also talked about this, Hopper's very forceful personality drove the point home and Strong came away convinced.[15] Following India, Strong moved on to the Philippines, where he visited the International Rice Research Institute, set up in 1960 with Ford and Rockefeller foundation funding in co-operation with the national government, at the University of the Philippines Los Baños. He came away greatly impressed with what he saw.

He also thought that it was extremely difficult, if not impossible, to provide through the mechanisms of his External Aid Office the kind of support for science and technology that was required in LDCs. First and foremost he had been impressed by Ford and Rockefeller's flexibility in terms of assembling an international staff of first-rate professionals. This was what really set his cat among Ottawa's pigeons as he considered the sort of organization he wanted. Strong thought about a foundation type of structure with an endowment that would have a board of governors with absolute autonomy. Later the discourse would shift to research meeting the needs of developing countries, and later still to the concept of research being done *in* the South by *Southern* researchers, which was quite radical for its time.

The Prime Minister Comes on Board

However, Ottawa in the mid-1960s was run as an old boys' club and Strong was a definite outsider. Even his personal appearance was seen as somehow deficient. As he noted years later, "It was once said of me that I dressed as though I had picked out my clothes from the Salvation Army store in the dark."[16] He was also not Oxford- or Harvard-educated, nor did he have a degree from Queen's, the favoured university of the mandarin set, or even the University of Toronto. Indeed, he had not finished high school, and many of his new colleagues, who had occupied their positions of power and influence for years, saw him as an outsider without the necessary grace or background to rub shoulders with them. Certainly that was the attitude of Marcel Cadieux, the undersecretary of state for external affairs; foreign affairs was his turf and an upstart like Maurice Strong would not dictate pace or policy to him.

But Strong had commissioned A.F.W. Plumptre the previous year to begin establishing what he had tentatively called the Canadian Foundation for International Development. How it would evolve and what it would do was anyone's guess in late 1966, but the director general was determined that something should result. Plumptre, a former assistant deputy minister of finance, had been appointed the principal at the University of Toronto's newly established Scarborough campus, and was widely respected throughout the Canadian public service. The selection of Plumptre for the job was pure Strong, who thought it important to enlist some outside credible help in making the case for the new Centre. As Strong remembered, "Even with the prime minister's approval, the bureaucracy can slow down or change things. That's when I decided that I had to get all the officials onside. Who was really respected by the others, a real traditional figure, to head up my little task force through which we could refine this proposal and have it accepted by the others, and I asked Wynn Plumptre.... He was not a person who I could have subverted; he was attracted to the idea and had flair and imagination."[17] Plumptre would need flair and imagination as he cast his net to its fullest extent during the next six months.

Strong's position was also shored up as the prime minister boarded the IDRC Express. On the evening of 8 June of Canada's centennial year,

Pearson laid out his vision of an international development organization to the Canadian Political Science Association. This came upon the heels of a lunch he had hosted, which included Jim Coutts, his personal adviser, and Strong, where the topic had been raised and thoroughly discussed. The EAO president had put it to the prime minister that the new organization he contemplated would be "the brains of [the External Aid Organization]."[18] In short, he stressed that the "big challenge facing the world is to use advances in technology to solve man's economic and social problems on a global basis and narrow the gap between rich and poor nations."[19] The organization would be dedicated to applying space-age technologies and modern systems of management to the development problem. This notion was, of course, entirely consistent with the ethos of the time where space *was* the final frontier, as had been exemplified by *Star Trek*, the television series that began in 1966. Anything scientific and extraterrestrial was seen as good; the preparations for *Apollo 11* were well under way, which would result in astronauts Armstrong and Aldrin walking on the moon. Anything was possible and if human resources could be mobilized to accomplish that, addressing the problems of earthly development should be easy if attacked with the right tools. In his speech at Carleton, the prime minister had noted:

> If free civilization is to survive and grow, we must very soon find vastly improved methods for extending the benefits of modern existence to the whole world community of man.... One idea for a new Canadian initiative in meeting this challenge that should be considered is for the establishment of a Centre for International Development.... Perhaps it will now prove possible for us to add a new dimension to our modest role in the world community by providing for a sharpened focus on the challenge of international development facing every country.[20]

Government policy often flows from prime ministerial interest, and this was no exception. As federal planners gave shape to Pearson's ruminations, ideas emerged over what any new organization of the kind envisaged would tackle. As the prime minister had pointed out at Carleton, the big challenge facing the world was to use advances in technology to solve economic and social problems: "A lot of the excitement in using new techniques for the purposes of peace and universal human progress, instead of war and universal human destruction, is simply not getting across, either to world statesmen or to the people of the developed countries."[21] To Pearson's mind, the idea of the Centre that he had in mind would examine the issue of famine, the production and distribution of food, and control of the global climate, among other things. Importantly, its work would also not conflict with that being done in government and university laboratories; it would be "mission-oriented research" in which specific objectives would be targeted and policy developed. Toronto's *Globe and Mail*, not usually a proponent of things Liberal during the 1960s, came out in unabashed support of the initiative. It was, an editorial proclaimed, "an imaginative idea, one which Canadians could seize with enthusiasm once they comprehended its possibilities.... It might even be made into a national goal, which would serve to rally the forces of industry, science, and technology the way President John Kennedy's goal of a US man on the moon by 1970 mobilized similar forces and sentiments in the United States."[22]

A small committee comprising Matthew Gaasenbeek, a former stockbroker and by 1967 a special consultant hired in early March by the president of EAO to do the groundwork, Lewis Perimbam, also a consultant working on the file who was part-time with the World Bank and who had been the founding director general of Canadian University Service Overseas, and J.D. Edmonds, a former executive assistant to Paul Martin, Sr., the secretary of state for external affairs, was struck to provide some flesh to cover the growing bones of the proposed centre. Gaasenbeek's job was to meet with influential people in North America and sound them out about their ideas of such a creature. The result of these preliminary deliberations led the committee to brainstorm about the shape the proposed organization would take. The only thing certain was that it would not "compete" with the normal operations of the External Aid Office. That sat well with the bureaucracy—any proposed new centre should not tread on others' toes.

Cabinet Gives Thumbs-Up and Plumptre Gets Busy

On an unusually cool August day, the Cabinet considered the arguments that had been raised.[23] Most importantly, it was agreed that a steering committee comprised of senior officials be established by Cabinet decision to study the desirability of creating some sort of centre and how to best go about accomplishing that objective. As well, the committee was to offer its recommendation as to the efficacy of using such a program to strengthen the resources of Canadian universities for research. Its instructions were to develop a proposal "to set up in Canada, but on an international basis, a centre for the promotion of research directed towards Developing Countries." In pursuit of that request, Plumptre had canvassed a range of opinion from aid organizations and informed people, including the World Bank and its president, Eugene Black; the International Monetary Fund and its managing director, Pierre Paul Schweitzer; US Agency for International Development, the Brookings Institution, and the three most important US foundations, Carnegie, Ford, and Rockefeller.[24] However, the proposed Canadian centre would differ from those foundations in two significant ways: it would be a *public* as opposed to a private corporation and would therefore be subject to the scrutiny of Parliament. US foundations, as has been pointed out, were "shielded from public oversight. They operated behind a veil of privacy long defended by founders, their families, and the fiduciaries appointed to oversee them. Foundation trustees regarded the endowments as their private domain for which they were accountable to no one."[25] At times, foundations were also instruments of American foreign policy; what would become IDRC would not adopt this role for Canada. Indeed, as will be discussed below, its Act explicitly stated that it was not an agency of Her Majesty. Where the Centre would copy foundation organization was in its ability to be active in areas where government was not for one reason or another. As has been pointed out with respect to US foundations, "Being free from political oversight ... [foundations can] address social issues that require immediate attention but may be too hot for government to handle."[26] As 1967 wound to an end, Plumptre had progressed enough to be able to offer preliminary conclusions. Most importantly, he believed that an international basis did exist for the proposed initiative; he had discerned "a genuine feeling ... that the world (not just Canada) was very short of research in some of the fields we are considering and that Canada has capabilities, perhaps rather special capabilities, in such research."[27]

Plumptre also thought that Canadians had various advantages with respect to the provision of official development assistance (ODA) that would benefit the new organization, and that had been brought out by many of those with whom he had spoken; Canada was bilingual and bicultural (a Royal Commission on Bilingualism and Biculturalism, struck by the Pearson government in 1963, now proclaimed that), it was a major Western economy with access to advanced technology and with a sizable research and development sector itself, but it had never "shared the taint of colonialism," a fact that counted in the developing South. Plumptre thought that against that background, it would be possible to turn the attention of young Canadians toward working in the field of international aid, a not unimportant consideration. Given this emphasis, he concluded that it might be possible to increase the flow of volunteers into Canadian University Service Overseas, as well as try to ensure that "graduates of CUSO make full and productive use in government, in business, in education, in research, of their remarkable [and] unique experience."

Further, and surprisingly, among those with whom Plumptre discussed ideas about a new centre, there was "*unanimous opposition*" that the research operations of the proposed centre should be gathered together into a single office.[28] Respondents emphasized that the research funded by the organization should take place in developing countries, "in the cultural, social, economic, industrial and agricultural surroundings where the results of the research will have to be applied." In other words, fieldwork was of the utmost importance, and that research should be carried out at existing universities and industrial research facilities. Montreal, Toronto, and Vancouver would house the sub-centres from which the flow of data for application in the South would come. Plumptre had given some preliminary thought to the practicality of creating sub-centres in those three cities.

The head office, the "holding company," would be in Ottawa, close to the seat of Canadian federal power. It was important that its first president be well known to the international research community so as to attract top-ranked international researchers. Finally, Plumptre was prescient when suggesting that the new Centre establish an agency equipped to appraise and post-audit aid programs with a view to developing criteria and principles to apply to the future. As he noted, "there has been all too little review and appraisal of the results of aid over the past 15 years." Canada's External Aid Office followed that up later, suggesting that "as soon as possible after its establishment, [the Centre] should set up evaluation procedures relating to specified current EAO programmes or projects."[29] That was very true then, and was to be in the future. And IDRC was to develop expertise in evaluations and its models set the standard for other organizations in the future.

Consideration of the shape of the Centre went on over the next several months under the loose heading of "Centre for International Development"; there were eventually about 100 name possibilities mooted. At each of these meetings, the committee, almost as if it were frightened of losing the core idea, reiterated that each project should be approached on an interdisciplinary basis, "in its totality, embracing all aspects from engineering and science to sociological considerations such as social attitudes, including perhaps religion."[30] Groups across the country would be "re-assured that our interests, while focusing on science and technology actually spread out broadly to embrace economic, social and political issues."[31] As well, "Canadian experience, Canadian inventiveness, whether in agriculture, forestry, fisheries, manufacture, communications or education, and in the social and natural sciences, would be developed for the benefit of other countries."[32]

The mechanics of the proposed Centre's operation were also discussed at various meetings. For example, who was to fund it? Strong was firmly of the opinion that as it was desirable—at least in the beginning—to have an organization clearly of Canadian parentage, it should be financed primarily from Canadian sources. While some support for specific projects might be invited from foreign governments or international institutions, this should not be allowed to jeopardize the Canadian content of the operation. This was the first institution of this sort that had been proposed by the federal government, "and political sensitivities to it might be particularly acute."[33] In accepting Plumptre's report on the establishment of a centre, it was decided that:

> The basic purpose of the Institution be to carry out research and develop-ment into the application of the latest techniques, technology and scientific knowledge (in both the natural and the social sciences) to the problems of economic and social development within the less developed countries with particular emphasis on those which have relevance to Canadian experience and Canadian problems.[34]

The Centre Takes Shape

By the end of February 1968, there was a consensus on the feasibility of the proposed Centre. The steering committee had concluded that there was a need for new research in Canada, and that it would be appropriate to make pri-ority provision in the aid budget for that purpose. As well, it had been decided that the research should be undertaken on a decentralized basis in existing Canadian institutions and in developing countries. As well, some work might be done by Canadian industry. Furthermore, Ottawa's contribution to the new Centre would have to be in the range of $20 million per year over a five- to ten-year period.[35] The committee had also agreed to further points on which action was required. First, priority should be given to determining the specific programs that the Centre would carry out and in what areas they might fall. Similarly, the government would want to know precisely what types of activity the proposed Centre would engage in and the effects that it would have on Canadian interests. It was also pointed out that some inter-agency coordination was required; for example, the Department of Agricul-ture was already undertaking work along the lines suggested for the Centre, and the Science Council had in mind the question of the application of sci-ence to the problems of developing countries as one of the factors in its delib-erations on national science priorities in Canada.[36]

That information raised certain questions, among them: Why add another development institute to those already in existence? Indeed, as Strong was to tell the subcommittee on international development in early

1970, he had initially been against creating another organization given that there were "a great many institutions in the development field in the world."[37] However, his decision to adopt the course of action was based on his analysis of the total amounts of funding for research and development in the developing South; there were few institutions doing R and D that had the necessary resources to maintain continuity and depth in their operations. There was a feeling that too much of the current work was short-term with no follow-up, and was thinly spread over too many projects. The models for this approach were the big foundations, Ford and Rockefeller and the Harvard development advisory service, founded in 1963 by Edward Mason and which provided advice on certain projects in the South. Similarly, the principal coordinating agency on the level of policy was the UN's advisory committee on the application of science and technology to development, with which Strong anticipated a very close relationship. By early 1970, Canada, through CIDA, had been invited to serve on that committee. As well, the feeling was that the new Centre should operate in advisory and training work at a high level; it should also be agile in terms of its ability to respond to opportunity.

There were other issues raised by interlocutors. Among them was E.C. Parsons, the director of the Organisation for Economic Co-operation and Development's Assistance Committee. In an amazingly lucid and prescient letter to Stuart Peters, he pointed to a number of critical areas that eventually informed (although not necessarily because of his interjection) the legislation creating IDRC. Some of it also flew in the face of Canadian government policy. Parsons suggested that it should not be an appendage of an academic institution and should attempt to bridge the "huge gap" between the economist/sociologist specialties and the applied sciences. It should also refrain from launching long-range research programs designed to discover the philosopher's stone of development and concentrate on policy issues requiring solutions over the next five to ten years—research must be seen to serve policy. Finally, he thought that there was a need to bring together the Western European "humanist" and the North American technically oriented approaches to development. This was reflected in a number of very practical ways—the need for a new and intensified approach to technical co-operation to building up new political relationships with developing countries increasingly influenced by the trade/aid/private investment aspects in the post-colonial world.[38]

Another meeting of the steering committee took place on 23 May 1968, about one month after Pearson's resignation as Liberal Party leader and prime minister in favour of Pierre Elliott Trudeau. In the ensuing election campaign as Trudeau asked Canadians for his own mandate, he told an election crowd that "We will give speedy and favourable consideration to the creation of an International Development Centre."[39] Following his smashing electoral victory, in which he took 154 seats to the Conservative's seventy-two, the issue about "the feasibility and desirability of establishing in Canada an International Development Centre for the purpose of tying the latest scientific and technological resources to the economic and social problems of developing countries" was revisited, with the new secretary of state for external affairs, Mitchell Sharp, pressing Trudeau for forward movement.[40] Given that the steering committee report was due in Cabinet by mid-August, it seemed appropriate that the government deal with the matter and prepare the necessary legislation for the forthcoming session of Parliament. Sharp thought it desirable, given the election promise, "to give this some priority."

Interestingly, in a margin note, the prime minister asked "Is this the time to raise the question of a Brookings Institute? Or should Sharp's centre proceed on its own?... While [he] was extremely interested in the concept of the International Development Centre, [he was] also strongly of the view that there [was] a great need for us to establish a research and consulting centre in Canada *for the use of governments at all levels,* somewhat along the lines of the Brookings Institute in the United States. We have given some thought to this idea in my office and Mr. Stoner has already had some informal conversations with Mr. Strong about how this kind of initiative could be coordinated with and associated with the intention to establish an International Development Centre."[41] Nor would there be any Centre legislation at that session of Parliament; the docket was already full and the Canadian Brookings idea had to be pursued further. Trudeau had "not reached a firm view on this subject and ... it was important to have a chance to jointly examine this matter with our colleagues."

Despite that, the steering committee, with Strong pushing it on, continued to meet. As spring turned into summer, certain decisions were taken: the headquarters would be in Ottawa, given the necessity of liaising with government, and especially the External Aid Office, and close relations would exist between the Centre, the EAO, and other government departments and agencies that had an interest in development research. Further, each research project would find what Plumptre had called its "natural home," whether in a university, an industry, or in some foreign country.[42] The idea of what became regional offices was also mooted at that meeting; they would help "to facilitate a two-way dialogue on development problems between Canadians and the people of the region."

Plumptre ended his May memorandum to the Cabinet committee outlining the objectives of the Centre as a basis for discussion. These included
raising production and consumption in the South, improving methods of
work and ways of life, the alleviation of sickness and suffering, and the betterment of humankind in the less developed regions of the world. For the
achievement of those objectives, he suggested that the duties of the Centre
should be to initiate and conduct research designed to apply and adapt to
Southern needs the benefits, experience, and experiments in Canada and
elsewhere in the fields of science, technology, and the social sciences. This
would help "to enlarge the horizons and enrich the experience of Canadians engaging in these studies to the benefit of Canada and the general benefit of the whole family of nations." That was quite a mouthful and to a
hard-bitten group of Ottawa mandarins, it was also a bit much. Given the
committee's horror with the language, Plumptre committed to having the
memorandum redrafted by the end of July.

The Steering Committee Reports

The last steering committee meeting was held on 15 August. Plumptre's
final draft weighed in at a hefty seventy-nine pages and ran the gamut from
organizational structure to program design. It focused on the science and
technology that he believed had allowed the West to prosper. However,
there was "no incentive for the application of this technology to the economic and social problems of the developing countries. This gap can be
filled [only] through assistance programs which are especially designed
to provide the impetus required to bring these resources to bear on fundamental development needs." The proposed Centre was designed to plug
that hole.

Its supporters anticipated that it would help to improve the nature, quality, and direction of Canada's external aid program but, more to the point,
it possessed much broader possibilities if it was established in a "wise" way
(whatever Plumptre meant by that) and managed well. As he noted,
"Throughout the entire field of international development it is now widely
recognized that far too little emphasis has been given to research and development and, in particular, to the application and adaptation of modern science and technology to the fundamental problems of underdevelopment." The
Centre would be unique in doing this as well as in bringing thinkers and
experts to Canada from around the world to investigate the issues of economic
and social development. The problems selected for study would be those to
whose solution Canadian expertise and experience could make some spe-

cial and distinctive contribution. Government was bound to like that phrase. It is also safe to say that that objective lasted only until David Hopper was appointed as the first president of the newly established IDRC in 1970. He would agree, however, that the studies would be action-oriented rather than purely theoretical.

What were the aims and objectives of the proposed Centre that would distinguish it as a unique institution in the world of international development? The steering committee suggested for Cabinet consideration that the Centre would initiate, conduct, and support projects designed to apply and adapt to the socio-economic needs of the developing South the knowledge and experience available in Canada in the fields of the social and physical sciences and technology. Further, it would assist the less developed regions of the world in developing and applying the scientific and technological capabilities required to meet their needs and aspirations. Moreover, the Centre would focus on those areas—agriculture, forestry, mining, water resources, transportation, environmental pollution, communications, and the problems of multicultural communities—that had special relevance to Canadian experience and expertise.

The steering committee also felt the proposed Centre would play a domestic role in Canada, perhaps as a sop to the prime minister's earlier intervention in the debate.[43] The new organization would fill an important gap in the institutional mechanisms available to meet domestic research needs. This would make it more saleable to politicians, or so it was believed, and would be a logical extension of its principal role; domestic and international activities would reinforce and support each other. Indeed, this insertion in the report could not be ignored. It had been the new prime minister's and would result in a domestic counterpart to the International Development Centre. It could assist other agencies in the application and adaptation of what Plumptre called "new insights in the dynamics of socio-economic growth and the techniques for encouraging the best direction of the emerging growth patterns of less developed areas across Canada." Maritime fishing villages or a Western Canada Aboriginal reserve might respond to practices and new ideas that originated in parts of Africa or Latin America. Similarly, environmental pollution, urban congestion, the effects of automation, crime, and juvenile delinquency were problems with solutions of broad applicability with which the Centre could be concerned. It would fill a gap in Canada that had been occupied in the United States by organizations like the Rand Corporation or the Hudson Institute. Even if—and Plumptre thought it a big "if"—the Centre was concerned only with the developing South, "there would [still] be a direct and necessary relationship to the similar problems within

Canada." This potential thrust did not, of course, survive the final cut. IDRC, when established, was truly "international."

The basic framework of what became the International Development Research Centre began to emerge from the report. The committee conceived of an organization that would be radical in its approach to development in a number of ways. Research, for example, would be remedy-oriented, akin to today's action research. Its impact in the South would be maximized by the implementation of policy that had been developed through this investigation. Indeed, the report came down firmly in favour of the Centre supporting "studies [that] would be 'action-oriented' rather than purely theoretical."[44] Science and technology would be applied to the fundamental challenges of the developing world, and it would be a research for development organization that would put the fruits of its funded research at the disposal of decision makers. As well, as has been noted above, it would be interdisciplinary since this was the most logical route to a more complete understanding of international development problems. And interdisciplinarity required more than uttering platitudes "that praise motherhood and condemn sin." If the real causes of underdevelopment were ever to be adequately understood, they would be so only through a combined operation by a variety of disciplines. Quite apart from the norm, the Centre's research projects were also conceived as being regional rather than national. As the report correctly pointed out, "for most poor countries, real progress may well be less firmly tied to national growth than to development of the region of which it forms a part."[45] Further, preference would be given by the Centre, when considering research programs, to those raising issues that extended far beyond the region under study to have the widest application within the South. And this IDRC has accomplished. Indeed, the resulting networks, which were dimly visible to steering committee members, have become the Centre's stock-in-trade, spanning continents and linking researchers undertaking similar projects together.

The Post-Steering Committee World

While no report had yet gone to Cabinet, in its Speech from the Throne the first Trudeau government made reference to process and intent; it intended "to press forward in its plans and programs for international cooperation and development which include the establishment in Canada of an International Development Centre."[46] The developing IDRC also seemed to encapsulate the spirit of the foreign policy review that Trudeau had initiated in 1968. The new prime minister had "made it plain that the changed circumstances of the world in the late sixties demanded a fresh look at the fundamentals of Canadian foreign policy to determine how the government might serve more effectively Canada's current interests, objectives and priorities."[47] The result of the foreign policy ferment comprising a general booklet and the five sector papers was tabled in the House of Commons as *Foreign Policy for Canadians* shortly after Parliament had passed the *IDRC Act* in May 1970. One of these papers, which focused on international development, committed the government to building a "more just world society" through an increase in the amount of foreign aid provided, greater emphasis on multilateral institutions in its distribution, and encouragement of private sector initiatives. The subjects of the other four theme booklets give a sense of the new prime minister's thinking: Europe, the United Nations, the Pacific region, and Latin America.[48] The newly established Canadian International Development Agency, which had emerged from the old External Aid Office in September 1968, was also swept up in the foreign policy review in January 1969, undertaking the first, but by no means the last, review of its policies.

Throughout the autumn of 1968, further consultations took place, this time with a view to determining the shape of the organization and not if one should be established. On 6 December 1968, the Cabinet Committee on External Policy and Defence met to consider the IDRC brief. Approval in principle was given to its establishment. The full Cabinet ratified the committee's decision on 17 December. Strong interpreted full Cabinet approval as the signal to push ahead with a document that would include "all the salient features required for the centre's operation and upon which legislative authority would be based."[49] Strong took the Justice department's James Pfeiffer on board to accomplish the latter, a propitious appointment as later developments would suggest. All the pieces were now in place.

First was the legislation that would give IDC its mandate. Peters had reviewed several pieces with, as he said, an eye to plagiarism. His idea was to incorporate both the research initiative and research-supporting capabilities with participation into one unique organization. The concept was not explicitly mentioned in the Cabinet submission, and when Peters brought it to the associate deputy minister of justice, D.S. Thorson, for interpretation, he was told that he did not have the authority to incorporate those ideas into the legislation without prior approval by Cabinet. Following confidential discussions with others in justice, it was decided to proceed on Peters' lines without further Cabinet authority. From the very beginning, IDRC would skate close to the edges of what might be deemed permissible by government. This iconoclastic flavour would quickly permeate the Centre's first employees, who saw themselves, not without reason, as free spirits out to "do good" in a world in need of their help.

And IDRC it would become. The first mention of an International Development Research Centre of Canada (although the "of Canada" was soon dropped) was made by the Cabinet committee on legislation and House planning and dated 23 January 1970. It would be a Canadian-sponsored, independent, non-profit organization with an international character. Its purpose would be "to initiate, encourage, support and undertake research into the problems involved in the development of economically underdeveloped regions ... [it would] focus its attention particularly on the adaptation and application of scientific and technological knowledge to the needs of the peoples of those regions for social and economic development ... [as well as] assist these peoples to develop their own capabilities to solve the problems of economic underdevelopment which confront them."[50] The Centre would enlist the talents of natural and social scientists not only from Canada but from around the world. Its personnel would identify development issues and use multidisciplinary approaches to solve them. It would also be action-oriented in that its areas of research would be designed to be of practical use to decision makers in the formulation and implementation of policy. Further, IDRC would emphasize programs and methods of work that would assist the developing South in building up its own capabilities and innovative skills, which would be required to resolve its own development problems. In doing so it would promote the establishment of global networks in forging close links with those engaged in similar research elsewhere. IDRC would enable Canada to make a major contribution to alleviating problems associated with poverty and the need for social innovation in many of the economically underdeveloped regions of the world.

Trudeau announced the pending establishment of IDRC in October 1969, soon after it had received Cabinet approval on 21 October. He prefaced his comments in the Speech from the Throne with a quote from the French novelist François-René Chateaubriand: "Try to convince the poor man, once he has learned to read and ceased to believe, once he has become as well informed as yourself, try to convince him that he must submit to every sort of privation, while his neighbour possesses a thousand times what he needs; in the last result you would have to kill him."[51] The prime minister had also noted the two-thirds of humanity who lived in poverty. The world, he had noted, "was too small to permit such disparities to continue." That was why his government, "at a time of austerity," was increasing the official development assistance budget, and to create "an International Development Research Centre which will be charged with the responsibility of improving the qualitative effect of Canadian and other aid projects." The Centre was, Trudeau went on, "an exciting concept; a recognition that accelerated economic growth is a complex task, and is deeply interrelated with the problems of social development." Its initial budget appropriation was set at CAN$30 million spread over its first half-decade of existence.

As committees hunkered down to discuss IDRC, one of the first orders of business was its name, the International Development Research Centre *of Canada*. The last part caused some tension among its midwives and there was some lobbying that it should be dropped completely or, if the government refused to accede, that it be changed to "in Canada." There should be nothing, or at least very little, that indicated from whence the new Centre came. Indeed, New Democratic Party MP David Lewis spent his question time as a member of the House of Commons Subcommittee on International Development posing that to Strong when the latter appeared as a witness on 14 January 1970. Why should the new Centre be identified in any way as based in Canada? Why should a majority of its board, or the president or chair, necessarily be Canadian? "Why not," he asked, "just call it the International Development Research Centre?"[52] While Strong might agree, he could not do that; it would be a political decision. In any event, when Bill C-12 was tabled for third reading in the House on 20 February, Sharp did point out an amendment: the "of Canada" had been removed, recognizing the international responsibilities of the Centre. As well, members of Parliament, perhaps reflecting the age in which they considering the document, also insisted that no military research be undertaken by Centre-funded projects. Strong was happy to say that none would happen directly, "but the relationship between military activities and development might be studied."[53] His objective was to ensure that the Centre be free to determine its own fields of study independent of any government directive. Later, during David Hopper's tenure as president of IDRC (1970–77), he was vigorously criticized by some groups in Canada for ruling military research off the agenda. However, a part of Strong's concern was to ensure the IDRC's freedom from government, which quickly became a cherished ideal by the organization, and to guarantee its independence to chart its own path subject only to the dictates of its Act.

Those concepts, however, could be realized only by a certain administrative structure that would allow the free flow of ideas and practices throughout the organization. It was thought that administrative arrangements would determine intellectual credibility. It was also terribly important as to who would be chosen as its first president, a fact not lost on Strong or his advisers. The Centre had to establish and maintain a set of characteristics consistent with its focus upon developing an environment that would foster creative problem-solving within a rapidly changing and technologically complex world. IDRC had to be decentralized, with self-motivated personnel. Staff should be grouped into rapidly changing and dynamic temporary systems organized around problems to be addressed, suggestive, almost, of program initiatives introduced at the Centre in 1995. As an individual could be a member of more than one group, the Centre's functional structure could be described as a series of overlapping circles. Groups of relative strangers with diverse personal skills would be brought together; they would complete their task and then the groups would dissolve. Personal and informal communication would become extremely important. There would be little routine: "Leadership in the organization must be an active method for producing conditions where people, ideas and resources can be seeded, cultivated and integrated for optimum effectiveness and creativity." And who might fit the demanding criteria for the new organization? David Hopper, an economics professor at the India Agricultural Research Institute but formerly a Rockefeller (and Ford) Foundation funding recipient investigating plant breeding, was the choice, appointed by order-in-council on 21 May 1970.

Why was Hopper chosen as the first president of IDRC? In large part it was because Maurice Strong was "quite taken by him, [and] he was Canadian, even though no one in Canada knew of him."[54] He was Strong's choice and his alone. Hopper had worked in India, in dusty villages, living in a hut with a dirt floor, doing research on strains of rice that would yield better results before moving to New Delhi, where he had taken up a position in the Indian Agricultural Research Institute, of which the Indian geneticist, M.S. Swaminathan, was head. Pearson and Strong, in India on a reconnaissance mission, had been invited to lunch by Swaminathan, who had asked Hopper, a colleague but also one of the very few Canadians on site, to join them; prior to this, Strong had only a passing professional acquaintance with Hopper, having met him while on his first trip through India in 1967. However, Hopper's family had known Pearson's socially in times past; his father had been a civil servant in Ottawa in the 1950s, and Geoffrey Pearson, Lester's son, had been a sometime playmate of Hopper's.[55] As well, his brother, Wilbert Hopper, was well known in Canada as an executive with Imperial Oil; he would later become the assistant deputy minister of energy, mines, and resources and, later still, the first chief executive officer of the newly established national oil company, Petrocan. Hopper's pedigree was known, but so were his unique talents. When combined, the two were an unbeatable combination. Pearson and Strong were very impressed with the latter's grasp of development details.

Mitchell Sharp, Canada's secretary of state for external affairs, moved that Bill C-12—to establish IDRC—be tabled for second reading on 12 January 1970. As he pointed out, the development gap was, to a large extent, a science and technology gap that conventional aid programs had done little to address in terms of supporting the kind of research, experimentation, and innovation that would assist developing countries to do something about it. Two days later Strong was explaining the Act's terms to the Subcommittee on International Development Assistance, a meeting that Hopper attended as a spectator: "There was one particular area in which there had not been sufficient work done—understanding the fundamental relationships between technological change on the one hand and social and economic and political change on the other."[56] It was obvious to him that this disparity between the developing South and the developed North was the degree to which the latter had produced a scientific and technological capability, and a set of attitudes and an infrastructure that was conducive to applying technology to the productive process:

It is now quite apparent that the science and technology which we develop for our own purposes, and which may be relevant to our kind of society and our value system, may not be relevant at all or may only be partially relevant to the needs of less developed countries. One of the important constraints on the application of science and technology is the very system of values which the less developed countries possess.

The new Centre's job would be to help the developing South discover what was relevant and then help it to develop institutions and techniques that would enable researchers to translate that knowledge into their own societies as reflective of *their* experiences, society, culture, and political systems, in the process improving the qualitative and quantitative aspects of their lives. That was where an IDRC radical innovation, the division of social sciences and human resources, would come into play, as will be discussed in Chapter 2. And while Canada did not have all the answers, it did have "a storehouse of knowledge" that could be shared with the South. To make the structure of the new Centre match its mandate, it would have an innovation that no other organization would—an international board comprised of eleven Canadians and ten foreigners with the chair, by law, being the former.

The *IDRC Act* moved inexorably forward as it leapt subcommittee hurdles, sprinted through committee discussions, and raced past various readings in the House and Senate. Forward momentum, however, threatened to come to a crashing halt in late April 1970. The Senate, in its second reading of the bill, proposed an amendment to the Act—that two members of Parliament may be appointed to the IDRC board. This did not meet with the approbation of the government, especially Mitchell Sharp, who told the House on 24 April that he would not appoint anyone of that description to the new board. David Lewis, the NDP member for York South, led the charge in Sharp's favour, telling assembled MPs that he thought "it would be an egregious error to make any appointments under this clause."[57] Lewis, the minister, and other interested members succeeded in convincing their colleagues that the amendment should be neutered and so it was, being revised from "shall" to "may." The *IDRC Act* passed Parliament unanimously, a remarkable occurrence. Strong put this down, at least in part, to his keeping the Opposition informed of his activities, both Robert Stanfield, the leader of the Progressive Conservatives, and the New Democratic Party's Tommy Douglas.

So what were the Centre's guiding principles to be as set forth in its bylaws, which were made possible by its relative freedom resulting from its act of establishment, what Australia's Sir John Crawford called "a unique piece of legislation"?[58] While remaining a part of the broader Canadian public sector, it has some latitude not normally accorded to Crown corporations to pursue its mandate. As Raymond Auger, IDRC's director general of finance and administration through much of its history, was to suggest to an incoming president much later, in terms of its operations, flexibility was the key word that could describe IDRC operations: "The operational mandate confided to the Centre is extremely broad and indeed easily encompasses any activity so long as it relates to research for or on development."[59]

More importantly, the *IDRC Act* stated, in section 18 (1), that the Centre was not an agency of Her Majesty, and IDRC employees were not members of the Canadian public service, a situation not unlike that of the Bank of Canada or the Canadian Broadcasting Corporation, where the objective was to prevent politicians from meddling with their operations. From that flowed its exemption from many of the rules internal to the government of Canada, although not from acts of Parliament, which applied more generally to the federally regulated sector. It also provided IDRC with much of its legendary freedom. A good relationship has also generally prevailed with the Department of External Affairs (DEA) and its minister, through whom the Centre reports to Parliament. As an important part of the covenant, IDRC did not operate in countries without DEA knowing about it, which went some distance toward easing the latter's concerns.

It was, however, a delicate relationship that did require some cultivation, but also distance. Early on in the Centre's existence, Hopper circulated a memorandum outlining his conception of appropriate interaction between

IDRC officers and Canadian diplomatic missions. As he noted, "I think it is important that we try to find the intermediate position which will give Centre staff freedom and independence of Canadian Government presence in their relations with professionals, individuals, institutions and governments in other countries but which, at the same time, will not occasion any embarrassment to members of any Canadian mission abroad because the mission lacks information about our plans and operations."[60] It was also imperative that officers bear in mind the clear parliamentary intent in establishing the Centre that was independent of the details of Canadian aid policy. Hopper did not want to become "too closely identified with the institutions of Canadian diplomacy." He pointed out that "In seeking to walk the tightrope between independence as a Canadian quasi-governmental organization and being a Canadian quasi-governmental organization that claims independence, we should not overlook our need to remain flexible and responsive to the way in which different recipient peoples will view the Centre." Hopper remained an outsider in Ottawa, which some saw as good; it kept IDRC's "distinctive character as not just another government entity." Strong, being an outsider himself, viewed this as an advantage and a necessity in doing the job.

This combination of characteristics made IDRC unlike any other international development organization. It was a problem-oriented, multidisciplinary (in theory), and international research centre. With respect to the first, the Centre chose to concern itself almost exclusively with research related to specific development problems and to apply the findings to concrete solutions. As has been pointed out, even the most apparently simple development problem becomes highly complex when viewed in its own cultural setting. And only a working combination of social and natural sciences could point to a possible solution. Further, IDRC would do its utmost to remain clear of explicit or implicit research "imperialism," a favourite theme of Hopper's. That could be extended to imperialism of any kind; as Rex Nettleford, a Jamaican member of IDRC's board, was to point out years later of the industrialized states, "there was confidence around the world in Canada as an ex-colonial country with no imperialistic designs on anyone else, itself in the shadow of a great nation and still suffering from the dependency syndrome. Many in the Third World feel that Canada understands their situation, is tuned into their sensibilities, and therefore can help. It has no axe to grind."[61] IDRC remained focused on putting the onus on the developing country researcher and institution to develop and articulate projects, as will be seen in Chapter 2. It was a part of the Centre's uniqueness, as was its structure: creation by one government, governance by an international board, independence from the usual aid strings and requirements, multinational staffing, and, perhaps most importantly, an exemption from the requirement that aid be tied to purchases in the home country.

And so IDRC was born, the progeny of many. As the old saying has it, success has many fathers, while failure is an orphan. The legion claiming parental status is indicative of the former. It was innovative, unusual, and special, as even members of Parliament seemed to realize when it passed through their hands. When, on 7 June 1970, David Hopper spoke at the first IDRC meeting following the passage of its act, he laid out his broad vision for its future, and the hopes on which it was launched:

> By the turn of the century, when the Centre will be a young 30 years old, the heavy, awkward footprints of astronauts will have marked many planets, and the shape and pace of our life on earth will have changed beyond belief. But by that time also, about 5½ billion people will live in what we now call the world's "developing" countries. Will their lives have changed too? We hope so. We hope that through a higher standard of living and economic integration with the "developed" world, they may have the freedom to enrich all of the earth's peoples by the quality of their lives and cultures. And we hope that the International Development Research Centre of Canada might contribute to that.[62]

While Hopper was wrong, at least on how many planets astronauts would have stepped on by 2000, he was correct when contemplating the effect of IDRC on the lives of many in the developing South. It would be a long-term process; as Rome was not built in a day, neither were the effects of development felt in the same period. Stamina would be a major requirement, both for the government of Canada and for the Centre. It is to that to which we now turn.

Notes

1   Known as the "Father of the Green Revolution in India," M.S. Swaminathan introduced high-yielding varieties of wheat to India and became the founder of the M.S. Swaminathan Research Foundation in Chennai, India. Swaminathan has been associated with IDRC since its inception.

2   Jean-Jacques Salomon, "The Uncertain Quest: Mobilising Science and Technology for Development," *Science and Public Policy*, vol. 22, February 1995, 57. See also JFK Library, Papers as President, National Security Files, Carl Kaysen, Box 372, File: Economic Policy—Subjects—OECD Development Center, 3/61-6/61, Isaiah Franks to Secretary, 26 June 1961. Interestingly, Franks notes that "The major obstacles to development are social and political, not scientific. They are not amenable to quick solutions. Scientific breakthroughs would not mean development breakthroughs and

could lead to disillusionment if great expectations were aroused that results could be accomplished in a short time."

3 Economic and Social Council *Official Records*, 39th Session, Supplement 14, UN Document E/4026, 7 as quoted in Sherman Katz, "The Application of Science and Technology to Development," *International Organization*, vol. 22, no. 1, 1968, 392.

4 Katz, "The Application of Science and Technology to Development," 395.

5 CIDA was created in September 1968 out of Canada's External Aid Office, which itself had been established in 1960 to better reflect the growing importance of ODA in Canadian calculations.

6 Review article, Joshua Kurlantzick, "Planners & Seekers: William Easterly, '*The White Man's Burden': Why the West's Efforts to Aid the Rest Have Done So Much Ill and So Little Good*," *Commentary Magazine*, June 2006, accessed at www.nyu.edu/fas/institute/dri/Easterly/File/commentary_plannersandseekers.pdf.

7 Interview, David Hopper by Robert Reford, Ottawa, n.d.

8 Interview, Maurice Strong, 15 August 2007, Ottawa.

9 Interview, Maurice Strong, 15 August 2007.

10 International Development Research Centre Archives (IDRC–A), Ottawa, Joe Hulse Papers (JHP), Stuart Peters, "The International Development Research Centre of Canada," 17 November 1969.

11 Interview with Maurice Strong, Ottawa, 10 May 2006. However, other countries had also considered these sorts of innovations. See JFK Library, Papers as President, Departments and Agencies, Box 86A, File: PSAC, Development Assistance Plan 3/7/61, Development Assistance Panel, President's Science Advisory Committee, "Research and Development in the New Development Assistance Program," 7 March 1961. While it was a different sort of animal the Americans considered birthing, it did contain significant elements of Strong's conception. For example, "It is not enough that these [development] limitations be seen and assessed from the outside. The development assistance program must stimulate the less developed countries themselves ... to identify and assess their own needs and wants and to create a development program that will meet them" (5). With respect to research and development more generally, Strong would certainly have agreed with the committee deliberation that "A private enterprise, faced with problems as novel and as broad as [those facing developing nations], would be considered derelict if it did not set aside 8% to 10% of its gross revenue to research and development.... This is the unadorned case for an R & D Unit within the development assistance program" (3). The US did not set up such a unit, despite the recommendations of the committee.

12 Peter Newman, "Think Tank for Foreign Aid," *Montreal Star*, 19 December 1968, 11.

13 For an account of the Bihar famine, see Paul Brass, "The Political Uses of Crisis: The Bihar Famine of 1966–67," *The Journal of Asian Studies*, vol. 45, no. 2, 1986, 245–67.

14 The Rockefeller Foundation had been active since its establishment in supporting research in crop science. While much of this was done in the United States, by 1923 it was funding work in China; in the early 1940s, in Mexico; and after 1945 in other parts of Latin America, including Brazil and Colombia, and India by 1956. The Foundation also provided scholarships to promising young developing world researchers to study in the US. As well, it encouraged locals it trained to oversee projects it funded. See Raymond F. Fosdick, *The Story of the Rockefeller Foundation* (New Brunswick: Transaction Publishers, 1989), 197–98.

15 Interview with Maurice Strong, 10 May 2006, Ottawa.

16 IDRC–A, Meeting of the Board of Governors, BG (33) 10/85, 112.

17 Interview with Maurice Strong, 10 May 2006, Ottawa.
18 Interview with Maurice Strong, Ottawa, 15 August 2007. Interview with David Hopper done by Robert Reford, n.d.
19 Gordon Pape, "After Expo: Research Centre for All the World," *Montreal Gazette*, 15 June 1967, 8.
20 *Globe and Mail*, 9 June 1967, 14.
21 Editorial, Toronto *Globe and Mail*, 17 June 1967, 12. See also *Time*, vol. 89, no. 25, 23 June 1967, 15. As the magazine pointed out, Pearson's idea was to turn Expo 67 into "a centre for international development," which would seek "vastly improved methods for extending the benefits of modern existence to the whole world community of man." Nowhere in the world "was there a think tank on the order of California's Rand Corporation designed to apply space age technology to the problem of world poverty."
22 Ibid.
23 IDRC–A, JHP, Section D, subsection (i), File #36, Record of Cabinet Decision, "Centre for International Development," 11 August 1967. The steering committee would consist of Strong (chair), J. Baldwin, R.B. Bryce, deputy minister of finance; Marcel Cadieux, the undersecretary of state for external affairs; G.F. Davidson; A.D.P. Heeney, the assistant deputy minister of finance; C.M. Isbister, the deputy minister of trade and commerce; T.M. Kent, former policy secretary to the prime minister and, in 1967, deputy minister of citizenship and immigration; Louis Rasminsky, the governor of the Bank of Canada; S.S. Reisman of the department of finance; Robertson, Ernie Steele, Jake Warren, S.B. Williams, J.W. Willard, and J.R. Weir.
24 A complete list of the foreign institutions Plumptre visited includes: *US:* World Bank, IMF, USAID, Brookings Institute, Ford Foundation, Carnegie Endowment, Rockefeller Foundation, UN Economic Division, UN Development Program, UNICEF, Harvard University Center for International Affairs, MIT Center for International Studies. *UK:* Commonwealth Secretariat, Ministry of Overseas Development, Overseas Development Institute, Institute for Development Studies. *France:* OECD, DAC, Quai d'Orsay interviews with a minister and four groups of officials, International Institute for Educational Planning, Institut de Developpement Economique et Social, Institut International de Recherches et de Formation en vue du Developpement Harmonise, Institut de la Vie.
25 Mark Dowie, *American Foundations: An Investigative History* (Cambridge: MIT Press, 2001), xix. This condition has, however, been changing in recent years.
26 Dowie, *American Foundations*, 251. He is quoting Peter Frumkin, a Harvard professor of public policy. However, Dowie also believes that this is not often the case. Still, as Plumptre made his rounds of willing interlocutors, this would have been one of the points made.
27 IDRC–A, JHP, A.F.W. Plumptre (AFWP) to Maurice Strong (MS), 22 December 1967.
28 IDRC–A, JHP, AFWP to MS, 22 December 1967; emphasis in original.
29 IDRC–A, JHP, AFWP to Gaasenbeek, 27 May 1968. As it turns out, External Affairs had an ulterior motive in requesting evaluations of programs. David Kirkwood, then a foreign service officer, suggested an initial program of appraising the role of paramilitary aid. External had been anxious for EAO to get into this field, but the latter had been reluctant for, as Plumptre noted, "quite understandable reasons."
30 IDRC–A, JHP, "Notes of a Meeting Held February 29, 1968 in Mr. Strong's Office."
31 IDRC–A, JHP, AFWP to MS, 8 March 1968.
32 IDRC–A, JHP, AFWP to MS, "An International Development Centre for Canada," 7 May 1968, Statement of Ministers.

33 Library and Archives Canada (LAC), Department of Finance Records (DFR) RG 19, vol. 246, file: 7810-03-4 pt. 2, "Proposed Centre for International Development," 28 February 1968.

34 Ibid.

35 DFR, vol. 246, file: 7810-03-4 pt. 2, V.J. Chapin to E.A. Oestreicher, "International Development Centre," 9 May 1968.

36 See DRF, vol. 246, file: 7810-03-4 pt. 2, Steering Committee, "International Development Centre," 23 May 1968. In the event, John Bene (EAO) was appointed to investigate forestry; Dean C.F. Bentley from the University of Alberta assumed responsibility for studies in the field of agriculture; Irving Brecher, from McGill's Centre for Developing Area Studies, had responsibility for general socio-economic and political studies; York University's Tillo Kuhn focused on transportation, while Prof. Edward Pleva from Western was the water expert.

37 IDRC–A, JHP, Canada, House of Commons, Sub-committee on International Development Assistance, 14 January 1970, 13:85.

38 IDRC–A, JHP, E.C. Parsons to Peters, 8 January 1968.

39 The speech occurred on 29 June 1968.

40 Library and Archives Canada, Department of External Affairs Records DEA-R (RG 25), vol. 11850, file: 38-4-IDRC p. 2, Sharp to the Prime Minister, 2 July 1968.

41 DEA-R, vol. 11850, file: 38-4-IDRC p. 2, Prime Minister to Sharp, 16 July 1968; emphasis not in original.

42 DFR, vol. 246, file: 7810-03-4 pt. 2, Memorandum to the Steering Committee, "Development Centre—Organization," 15 May 1968.

43 About 10 percent of the steering committee's report focused on the potential domestic role that the Centre would play.

44 Report of the Steering Committee, 5, as quoted in Tahira Gonsalves and Stephen Baranyi, "Research for Policy Influence: A History of IDRC Intent," January 2003, 6.

45 Report of the Steering Committee, 51.

46 Canada, House of Commons Debates, vol. 113, no. 1, 12 September 1968, 8.

47 Mary Halloran, John Hilliker, and Greg Donaghy, "The White Paper Impulse: Reviewing Foreign Policy under Trudeau and Clark," accessed at http://www.cpsa-acsp.ca/papers-2005/Halloran.pdf.

48 Secretary of State for External Affairs, Foreign Policy for Canadians (Ottawa: Information Canada, 1970).

49 IDRC–A, JHP, Strong to Thorson, n.d.

50 IDRC–A, JHP, Section D, ss(i), F#40, Record of Cabinet Documents, Meeting of 23 January 1969.

51 Canada House of Commons Debates, vol. 114, 24 October 1969, 37.

52 IDRC–A, JHP, Canada, House of Commons, Sub-committee on International Development Assistance, 14 January 1970, 13:77–13:83.

53 IDRC–A, JHP, "Process of Bill C-12," n.d.

54 Interview with Maurice Strong, Ottawa, 10 May 2006.

55 Interview with M.S. Swaminathan, Chennai, India, 10 December 2007.

56 Canada, House of Commons Sub-committee on International Development Assistance, 14 January 1970, Mr. Maurice Strong, 13:72–13:101.

57 Canada House of Commons Debates, vol. 114, 24 April 1970, 6267. Lewis went on to say that "I look to this centre to make a really valuable contribution to the problem of development in the less developed countries of the world. It will be able to do that only if it is a genuinely international body, if its entire orientation is towards

developing countries and not toward Canada or any other developed country. In my estimation it will do this only if the board of governors includes in high positions, as well as among the membership of the board, fair representation from the developing countries."

58 IDRC–A, JHP, IDRC, "News Conference—Oct. 28, 1970."

59 IDRC–A, Raymond Auger to the President, "Legal Matters," 7 May 1991.

60 IDRC–A, JHP, Hopper to All Officers, "Relations of Officers and IDRC Staff to Canadian Diplomatic Missions Abroad," 23 December 1970.

61 IDRC–A, JHP, Meeting of the Board, March 1978.

62 IDRC–A, JHP, "Comments," 7 July 1970.

Chapter 2

IDRC TAKES SHAPE: DAVID HOPPER
SETS THE PACE, 1970–77

The new name for Peace is Development.
—Pope John XXIII, 1963

The 1970s was a tumultuous decade, relatively prosperous in the West during its earlier years and disastrously not so during the latter half. Still, there were bumps early on. For example, the so-called Nixon Shock of August 1971 was still working its way through the global economic system. It had a number of effects on Canada and resulted in the collapse of the Bretton Woods system by 1973, which had been established in July 1944. As well, following a terrible campaign by the Trudeau Liberals in the 1972 election, a minority Liberal government was elected in October 1972. What government would do to make itself more palatable to voters was anyone's guess, although David Hopper, the newly appointed president of the International Development Research Centre, thought the politicking might not do the fledgling IDRC much good. Further, "stagflation" was a word coined during the period after the first oil shock in 1973 that severely disrupted Western societies, combining high inflation and high unemployment, a theoretical impossibility in Keynesian economics. That would result in the imposition of price and wage controls following Pierre Trudeau's return to majority government as a result of the 1974 election, and the establishment of the Anti-Inflation Board in 1975, along with unemployment, recession, and a lingering malaise in Canada that almost defied description, capped off with another "oil shock" in 1979 and an intense recession in 1980–81. Governments seemed powerless to address the drift.

In the international arena, the new international economic order (NIEO), a set of proposals referring to a wide range of trade, financial, commodity, and debt-related issues that affected developing countries, was articulated. These were first raised through the United Nations Conference on Trade and Development, a UN organization established in 1964 to promote less developed countries' interests, and especially those worst off. The NIEO was sanctified in 1974 through its adoption by the United Nations General Assembly, although ultimately to little effect.[1] As a result, Hopper could speak of at least one more "world" to go along with the three already in existence: "a fourth world composed of those nations 'most seriously affected' by the combination of world inflation and recession."[2] It was these countries that had become, or so he thought, "increasingly shrill in their demands for a new international economic order that will ensure progress." In short, this very incomplete list of possible sources of destabilization for the Centre could signal all sorts of difficulties in the years ahead.

The First Strategic Plan: Conceptualizing the Centre

IDRC owes its organizational and philosophical footprint to David Hopper. The Treasury Board Secretariat (TBS) pointed out that fact in its assessment of the Centre undertaken in October 1978 following his departure to the World Bank: "Its evolution [had been] *dominated* by … Hopper."[3] As well, the adoption of a unique style of operation was the result of Hopper's interpretation of the Centre's broad mandate. Nor were there any to protest that direction; the president's position "within the international scientific and academic community, together with his extensive experience in the development forum via previous associations with the World Bank and the Ford and Rockefeller Foundations" (he had been called "Foundation" Hopper) allowed him a relatively free hand. Maurice Strong was absolutely correct when he pushed for his selection; he wanted an iconoclast and also someone who would pull the new organization in the direction that Strong thought appropriate—against prevailing wisdom, but with a minimum of tilting needlessly at windmills.

With a willing board of governors and the wording of the *IDRC Act* permitting it, this is exactly what happened. As James Pfeifer remembered, "it was a wild time … because no one was sure what IDRC was going to be."[4] Intellectual and organizational ferment characterized its establishment as the new executive group began the process of separating IDRC "from the

CIDA womb." It would become, at least it was hoped, an organization that would fund research used by policy-makers in developing countries; as has been pointed out, staff were directed "not on whether they should ensure use of research results, but how they should do so."[5] As well, another early employee recalled that "there was no formal procedure for recruitment, nor an administrative manual. It was all *ad hoc*."[6] But that made it more exciting, as did the armed troops patrolling the streets of Ottawa as Hopper met with his board of governors for the first time on 26 October 1970; the so-called October Crisis was in full swing as the Québécois group, the Front de libération du Québec, demanded independence from Canada. Lester Pearson, a former prime minister, now IDRC chair and considered a high-value target for the FLQ, was protected by bodyguards supplied by the government. They also attended that first IDRC board meeting.

Still, that seemed not to have affected the gathering. The new president had long been absent from Canada and had little inkling of Quebec grievances. As well, he and his board tended to be "internationals," their focus not necessarily on this country.[7] Hopper's impassioned address to the board made no reference to events outside the Pebb Building. Instead, a self-described "field man," he emphasized that he did not want the Centre to become a think tank, but instead play a vital role in actively working with Southern researchers as they sought to make the lives of their citizens better. As Tony Price, one of the first regional directors, remembered about Hopper, "He was a good person to go on a field trip with; he never complained about the vehicle or the hotel or the conditions.... When Hopper was with IDRC, it was a field-oriented operation. The input from the field would be listened to, would get a sympathetic hearing."[8]

Hopper's statement to the October 1970 board meeting, which came to be unofficially known as IDRC's first strategic plan, did inform its activities and the general sentiment expressed persists to the present. What it did *not* become is interesting and had certainly shaped the impressions of the yet-to-be established organization among official Ottawa. It would not be research active but research supportive. His statement reflected that approach and, while lengthy (it runs to six double-columned pages), is worth exploring here. "In the next few months," he began, "our task is to nurture the Centre's internal organizational ethos and its capacity to address the issues of development."[9] An IDRC that was adaptive, flexible, extremely professional, and hard-working came out of the dedication and commitment of those first employees, supported and pushed by the president with his very firm view of what he wanted to accomplish:

We begin with many assets. The broad scope granted to us by Parliament is virtually unprecedented among world instruments of development assistance created by governments. The proposed resource base for our operations initially and in the longer term is sufficient to permit us to plan and execute an aggressive programme which will equal the efforts of all but the largest of the world's private foundations. Indeed, we are constrained only by the awesome knowledge that our individual and collective skills must be reckoned in direct proportion to the freedom and support given to us.

He went on to lay out his vision of what the Centre should begin to accomplish, and the challenges that it would have to overcome. It was his firm belief, for example, that all humanity would achieve "modernity" as it was lived in the later twentieth century, and to suggest that modern technology should be avoided because it might carry with it the seeds of the destruction of the culture that was being "helped" had no place in the discourse. For Hopper, "the alternative to scientifically derived technology is not a society free of the effects of technology, it is a stagnant society built upon older means of fashioning tools and organizing and practising the arts of production. Eschewing modernity can stay modernity only temporarily, the power of science and its technical spawn for altering the pattern of cultures and civilizations cannot be countered by wishful asceticism or vigorous proclamation of the virtues of peasant nobility." Applied science, with its way of making life better for those affected by its discoveries, would sweep all before it and the abundance that poured "from applied scientific technology promise[d] the elimination of human want." Visions of happy peasants sitting on dirt floors weaving textiles for sale to the next tourist had no place in his repertoire; he knew too well the reality. However, it was not up to IDRC or any other agency to implement the benefits of the bounty of the age into a culture: "This step must necessarily be the perogative of sovereign peoples, for it is a step that they alone can design and take."

In concert with that, Hopper's sure, deliberative way forward in October 1970 was to suggest that IDRC focus on farm and non-farm people living in rural areas as these were the global citizens who were most affected by the change from neolithic to modern. This in itself was contentious; not until 1974 was rural development recognized as a central issue at the World Bank and taken up by others following its lead. The Centre was very much ahead of the curve in setting its priorities. Such a focus would provide a "broad umbrella under which the Centre's staff would select and develop worthy projects for consideration." A total program of interlocking activities could be set up that would "form the ribs of the umbrella onto which could be sewn the fabric of world advance[!]"

While the board (and others) would eventually successfully lobby for the inclusion of urban priorities, for the present and under what he called his topical umbrella, Hopper's Centre would support research in agriculture, forestry, and fisheries; indeed, the whole space of rural life would become IDRC's beat—education, nutrition, local government and administration, social institutions, the rural environment, and the physical health of the rural family. Further, program leaders could address issues like population expansion and the attendant issues of providing gainful employment for rural people by "improving productivity and enhancing livelihood opportunities in farm and off-farm occupations, stressing particularly the creation of expanded labour absorption potentials within the frame of a dynamic rural village, small town, and larger growth centre in an effort to reduce the flow of people into the cities." While the latter proved impossible to accomplish over the next four decades, IDRC did develop, fund, and implement programs like small and medium-sized enterprises policy in the South, which did address many of the issues that Hopper had laid out. This would be one huge umbrella!

Importantly, Hopper also talked of the Centre's "philosophy of approach" to projects that would establish the welcome accorded to it among Southern peoples. Over the next forty years, a unique IDRC perspective was established that became one of its identifiable features—what advertisers might call its brand. IDRC's image would be very different from that of others; as he told the board, "The Pearson Commission identified an aid weariness in many donor nations. I am sure the Commission also encountered an aid weariness among recipients. It is a weariness born of being too long a supplicant suffering the donor's quiet arrogance and his implicit denial of sovereign equality." How would the Centre be different in operation? For its new president, the most important of its tasks was that outlined in the *IDRC Act*'s section 4.1 (b): "to assist the developing regions to build up the research capabilities, the innovation skills and the institutions required to solve their problems." The Centre's objective must be the creation of *local* capabilities to foster development through the application of science to *local* problems, through the activities of *local* researchers. In later years this would become known as participatory research, in which "the beneficiaries of research are encouraged to help identify problems to be solved, to identify and implement the research methods and activities to be undertaken, to evaluate the results, and to help determine the subsequent activities or programs which will enhance the beneficiaries' quality of life."[10] IDRC would become a global leader in the use of participatory research and, by the turn of the century, would be looked to by organizations like the World Bank for best practices.

Indigenous researchers, after all, were the best judges of what was relevant to their circumstances. As the president told a CBC International Service reporter following the conclusion of the board meeting, "It is fairly simple to take technology and transfer it. It's a little more complex, but it's not an insurmountable problem to take technology and adapt it to the conditions, circumstances, climatic requirements and so on, of a developing country.... Those men of good will within the metropolitan group who are interested and concerned about the developmental process have to recognize that they play a role as partners, and even junior partners, in the process of working with developing countries, in the game of building institutions."[11]

The Centre would begin with those Southern scientists and technologists who could contribute to the foundations of their own development process, and also recognize the right of developing countries to make their own mistakes in the pursuit of their research. It was only through mistakes that they would learn something of their trade. Hopper told the board at its meeting of March 1972 that "They can only make mistakes if they are doing something; they can only be doing something if they have resources to do it with. In my view, this is the purpose of our help and support. It is when they make mistakes, when they learn, and when they use resources successfully that the ground will be laid for the transformation of peoples and societies."[12] That fed into the president's belief that the second enabling provision of the *IDRC Act*—the apposition between the creation of technology outside a particular nation and its subsequent transfer to the users within that nation, and the creation within the nation of the skills and capacities to derive their own technologies—would also be an important one guiding the Centre's development. If that was to be achieved, some tears must necessarily be shed along the way.

Hopper expected that a researcher or a network would devise techniques for self-monitoring so that a minimum of supervision would be required from Centre personnel. If this was possible, he told the board, "then we will have pioneered a new style of international operation that can remove the stigma of charity and donor control from the support of research in development." Ultimately, the objective of the Centre was to secure the benefits of modern science and technology for the development of countries in the South. Hopper and his executive would shape the new organization as it emerged from the *IDRC Act*; he was not afraid "to use mallet and chisel to sculpture the shape that will be known as the International Development Research Centre." Further, because of the purpose in which they were involved, they, too, would make mistakes, but they, too, would "learn as much from our artlessness as from our art."

Hopper's final words were as inspirational and as directive as his first: "The early period of the Centre's history must inevitably be devoted to a search for its role in world development and for its methods of operation within that role. We need a clear delineation of the bounds within which the search will take place and the flexibility to bring to its accomplishment both artistry and craftsmanship." As well, he spoke openly about his commitment to capacity building over all else, because that was the source of "fundamental change."[13] Years later, as he looked back on his seven-year stint as president, he commented that he believed that IDRC's major contribution during his time in office had been in building people. If anyone could inspire a newly formed board comprised of cynical warriors of international development or former Canadian civil servants, university professors or administrators—what the president later called a "a collection of competencies"—Hopper could.[14] Clearly, the new president laid out a vision of the Centre that remains with it to this day—all the things on which the Centre prides itself.

In 2010, Hopper's words seem commonplace, even trite. However, throughout most of IDRC's existence, his view was not the one taken by development agencies or Northern governments. Indeed, a Decima poll of elite attitudes taken in Canada in September 1993 demonstrated that his words remained the exception twenty-three years after the establishment of IDRC.[15] Of the fifty-five whose attitudes were plumbed, the great majority referenced "mistakes of the past" that included "the old technical model in which Northern experts headed South to tell Southerners how to build their cities, manage their resources, train their people and grow their food." As the Decima document noted, "newer approaches [were] not strikingly different [in 1993] in terms of what is attempted." IDRC remained an exception.

Following Hopper's address, the board did as he had suggested; in the very dry language of the first *Annual Report*, the spotlight was shone on "the broad spectrum of dynamic development problems that hold substantial hope of solution through the application of scientific research methodologies and investigations into applied technology, and especially those problems which affect the welfare of peoples who are living in rural areas and are undergoing the transition from a traditional to a modern way of life."[16] But not just any people; IDRC would have at the centre of its calculations the "ordinary man," whom the benefit of "development" had largely bypassed. As Puey Ungphakorn, the governor of Thailand's central bank and the dean of economics at Thammasat University in Bangkok, as well as a member of IDRC's board, noted, "parity between the incomes of the various levels of people have widened; the division of income has become more unequal ... and the fact that the Centre is going to concentrate and emphasize this point will benefit the development process in our various countries."[17] That was a radical innovation, a phrase attached often to IDRC. As well, Ungphakorn would have wholeheartedly agreed with the characterization of what IDRC was doing as expressed by his board colleague, Rex Nettleford from Jamaica. Its remit, or so Nettleford believed, was "the humanization of development assistance."[18]

In other words, IDRC was not an institution devoted to basic research—there was a lot of that being done in universities and special research organizations around the world. It would deal with what was commonly perceived as *the* problem in the late 1960s and into the next decade—of the transfer of technology and new ideas that research scientists had brought forth. As Hopper had told the Society of Industrial Accountants of Canada in June 1970, support for the type of research funded by IDRC was critical: "Direct aid is necessary as a temporary palliative, but in the long run it will be no more effective or adequate as a basis for relationships between the rich and the poor nations than the dole and the soup kitchens were to the basis of relationships between the rich and the poor within our own societies."[19] Hopper also made clear that the new Centre's choices were constrained by reality; most of its funding would go to nations "midway up the development scale, nations that have a middle-grade set of institutions and a middle-sized pool of trained scientists who can benefit from the limited research assistance the Centre can provide. Centre support for the least developed nations is necessarily slight because of their lack of research institutions and small number of trained people."[20] That was reflected in the percentages of IDRC funding that flowed to Asia and Africa by the time of Hopper's departure in late 1977—about 40 percent to the former and only 19 percent to the latter, even though Africa, as a whole, was much worse off in development terms than Asia.

The Development of the CGIAR

Hopper's experience with the green revolution certainly informed his later work and his unremitting support for an umbrella organization that would become so important in global agricultural research—the Consultative Group on International Agricultural Research (CGIAR). He certainly would have agreed with the assertion that "There is something absurd about a technology which can hope to put a man on the moon in 1970, but seems likely to fail to feed adequately many millions of men left behind on earth. How can science, always active at the promotions of knowledge, be turned in on itself so as to help solve the age-old problems of hunger, ignorance and disease?"[21]

The green revolution, while often associated with India, was really a global phenomenon. Work was undertaken in Mexico as early as 1943 on wheat hybridization with the benefits then passing to Indian researchers. As some board members saw it, this could be an IDRC role, too; it would help developing countries get the results of work done in major centres around the world with the transfer of research technologies and methods. In 1971, this emphasis on agricultural research was given focus through the establishment, with Centre help, of CGIAR, described by a former IDRC director as "the best and most significant international collaborative activity in international development."[22] It eventually encompassed under its broad mandate research on commodities as diverse as rice, yams, and trees.

The Consultative Group experiment had begun in April 1969 with Bellagio I, where the World Bank, under the urging of its president, Robert McNamara, had been one of the prime sponsors of the meeting. The Rockefeller Foundation hosted the gathering at its villa in Bellagio, Italy, keen to incorporate those with deeper pockets than itself into helping to fund developing country agricultural research. Clearly, it was far beyond Foundation means to do an adequate job of financially supporting even the four agricultural research organizations extant at that time.[23] Strong, while head of CIDA, had been approached to attend the April 1969 meeting and those held subsequently to provide support largely, he thought, because he was "the new boy and had been floating around on this question a lot. Ford and Rockefeller were the drivers on this [agricultural centre funding] and they made the case that they could not continue to do it on the scale necessary."[24]

While everyone attending Bellagio agreed on the nature of the problem, the question remained how to administer any new organization that emerged, especially as public money would be involved. Sitting beside McNamara at lunch one day on the patio of the Foundation's Villa Serbelloni under a strengthening Italian sun, Strong suggested a consultative group. They existed for country financial issues and could take the shape of, say, the World Bank-sponsored Aid India consortium. Agriculture was arguably the most important area to address in developing countries, so why not have a consultative group for rice research, with donors meeting recipients to work out a program? Strong had travelled extensively while still with CIDA (he left the organization in 1970), trying to drum up support for the sort of thing he had proposed. When the president of the World Bank, Robert McNamara, took up Strong's suggestion and used his considerable powers of influence and persuasion to convince others, the consultative group system was the result.

A further organizational meeting to which IDRC was invited was held in Washington, DC, in January 1971, a scant two months after the Centre's initial board meeting. The CGIAR was officially inaugurated in May 1971 in the US capital and by that time, IDRC had come in as one of the charter supporting agencies. CIDA was also a member, but IDRC's attachment was different; when the Treasury Board Secretariat raised the question with Hopper as to why the Canadian taxpayer had a double representation with the group, he responded that CIDA was there as a government agency while the Centre "[sat] with the foundation section, [its] board having successfully washed the governmental taint off our money."[25] Sir John Crawford, the Australian but also a contributing member of the Centre's board, was named as chair of CGIAR's technical advisory committee, made up of agricultural experts from the North and South, whose job it was to advise the parent organization on agricultural research priorities, which ultimately bore some resemblance to the Centre's. Later, Hopper was identified as one of the leading policy-makers who collaborated in the effort to establish the group.

Developing Southern Research Capability

As was the case with the CGIAR, IDRC was to play a significant role in developing Southern research, as well as leadership, capabilities in developing country institutions. Barry Nestel, an early program officer in agriculture, food, and nutrition sciences, recalled that unlike more mainstream development organizations "where a foreign expert came in and the locals picked up the crumbs ... IDRC definitely broke a great deal of new ground in trying to place most of the money into indigenous institutions rather than into foreign experts."[26] While other agencies would eventually pick up on this way of operating, the Centre certainly blazed that trail.

That work of funding Southern researchers would be facilitated through the four divisions that had been established: (1) Agriculture, Food, and Nutrition Sciences (AFNS), (2) Information Sciences (IS), (3) Population and Health Sciences (PHS), and (4) Social Sciences and Human Resources (SSHR). They became known among IDRC staff as the four fiefdoms, each jealously guarded by its director. Multi-disciplinarity, or even interdisciplinarity, was foreign to their lexicon, and joint projects almost never happened during the Hopper era as the divisions maintained what they would have said was their integrity. It would only be during the tumultuous years of the 1990s that the walls dividing divisions were smashed apart under the force of external circumstances and program initiatives took the place of divisional projects. The divisions were headed by a director—Joseph Hulse, John Woolston, George Brown, and Ruth Zagorin, respectively. Zagorin was one of the few women in the organization in a professional position. Hulse's division, intensely focused on the scientific, was, by general agreement, the strongest in the Centre as was to be expected given Hopper's professional pedigree, rooted as it was in India's green revolution. Some board members also believed that Hopper's experience was the impetus for IDRC's initial emphasis on rural people when, as some objected, urban problems were equally as taxing. As has been pointed out elsewhere, Hopper had a tremendous belief—indeed, faith—in science and technology working for the betterment of civilization.[27] He was convinced that he had personally witnessed that result while in India in the 1960s as the green revolution had unfolded, ensuring Indian food security forever, or so it had seemed at the time. The new president's commitment to the benefits of technology in all its applications was total. The untested Social Sciences and Information Sciences divisions were relative unknowns to governors, but would come into their own over the next few years.

But why include social sciences at all? Because it was a reflection of the mindset of those who had conceived of the Centre and had written its act. One of those architects felt very strongly "that you had to have ... social science research. One of the first needs of a country as it proceeds in its development is to be able to make sensible decisions about what sort of science and technology it needs. That means a capability to analyze the issues and to do social science research related to the policy for science and technology."[28] Lester Pearson had also spoken about different approaches at the post-board press conference in October 1970. Social science was an integral part of the exercise; the research was technical, to be sure, but also had a presence in the social realm, the domain of Zagorin's division. An example of that were the social consequences of new agricultural production techniques in Tanzania: "While the technical achievements ... have been fantastic," Pearson noted, "they have also brought with them certain social and economic consequences ... [S]ome of them have been quite, if not disturbing, deserving of consideration and action.... Technical progress is not going to be held up because of possible social consequences in the future. But I think we ought to be more aware of the problem of social consequences when we begin the technical development" than the world was fifteen years ago.[29]

The irony was that most of the early governors would have styled themselves as social scientists of one description or another. That was part of Zagorin's problem when pushing the social science context; they all thought they knew the way forward, although their personal experience in the use of social science for development was limited. In terms of the early 1970s context, it was, as Zagorin has pointed out, "a tie between [SSHR and IS] in terms of the board not understanding what each was about [despite their knowledge of the 'social sciences'] and why each was important in its own right." Both were innovative and suggested that IDRC was indeed serious about a holistic approach to development problems, although that would really only begin to happen in earnest in the later 1980s.

Information Sciences, then in its infancy, was indeed a departure from the norm and very little known by governors. As Ruth Zagorin pointed out, "It was a generation ahead of its time. It was just astonishing! To start this in the 1970s was just remarkable." And Hopper went one further in his conception of the Centre. As Paul McConnell remembered, the president had a specific conception of IS in mind. While program directors often questioned the advisability of having a separate division for Information Sciences, he was certain that information would be crucial for everything that went on at IDRC: "There was something bigger at play here and we needed to be building networks between disciplines, and between researchers and the capacity of human beings who can deal with any subject matter if they have the skills and technology that can be communicated through IS."[30]

Here, management had to overcome board skepticism about the merits of information technologies as they then were. It was a mandated area for the Centre, one that was close to Hopper's heart. In India he had been concerned with the lack of information availability and exchange, concluding that developing countries were not capable of disseminating information appropriately. The division's primary objective was "to support cooperative initiatives ... to develop information systems to which international, national and voluntary agencies can supply, and from which they can obtain, development information."[31] How could that be done but by attending at a library or some other facility that contained information? And if this was the case, why was such a division needed? By and large, the board did not see its purpose, viewing it as a diversion of scarce resources.

To convince the board at its September 1973 meeting, Hopper encouraged members to troop down to the National Research Council (NRC) on Sussex Drive in Ottawa to view the results of a computer search that would be undertaken by John Woolston. He was familiar with NRC; he had come to IDRC from a position at Chalk River Nuclear Laboratories and Atomic Energy of Canada via Vienna and the International Atomic Energy Agency (IAEA), where he had been in charge of the production of scientific publications, and where early computing had been his stock in trade. He was in Europe when the International Nuclear Information System, a super-library, had been established, which worked on the formula of each country, reporting what had been published on the subject within its own national boundaries. The total file was then made available to all members.

When it was suggested that the Food and Agriculture Organization (FAO) do something similar, Woolston, now at IDRC, was brought on board in 1973 as chair of the panel that advised FAO on the development of the new system, International Information System for the Agricultural Sciences and Technology (AGRIS). Woolston had told the board that "the first priority in the information sciences is the need for a system that contains within it a great deal of information on the development process. If this information is stored by each producer of information, through a network there will be a merging of development information and each participating institution and agency will have a mechanism to draw on the stored information as needed."[32] That was his objective for AGRIS. However, given the lack of time in which to develop their own computing system, he convinced IAEA to let FAO use its system rather than putting scarce resources into the development of one of its own, not an easy task. Indeed, the initial co-operation soon turned sour and the co-operating agencies—FAO, the Commonwealth Agricultural Bureaus, and the US National Agricultural Library—were at each other's throats.

These problems contributed to those IDRC experienced with this initiative, and Woolston eventually spent much of his time working within UN agencies in trying to sort out difficulties and pushing the information science agenda forward rather than in developing projects. That was in part because of the nature of the beast as well as competing ideologies, and partly because much of the information work was completely new. However, despite the problematic nature of the project, it was a very important one and developing countries were also brought on board during the design discussion, which, to that point, had been dominated by experts from the North. IDRC sponsored a meeting held in Rome, inviting fourteen people from the South who were responsible for agricultural information in their countries, to review the design and comment on it. They did and the result included one of the first IDRC publications, *AGRIS and the Developing Countries*.[33]

Given his baptism by fire in the AGRIS negotiations, his extensive international experience in bibliographic reference systems and familiarity with them, it was child's play for Woolston to demonstrate to the board (through the NRC computer system, which searched the developing AGRIS site) the incredible power of this emerging technology. In this, he was helped by the University of Chicago's Theodore Schultz, who would win the 1979 Nobel Prize in economics, and who was a board member as of the September 1973 meeting. Schultz served up what some on the board considered to be a soft pitch, and Woolston hit a home run. As the board stood around looking at the blank screen, could, Schultz asked, a search of the system for references to education and agricultural productivity be attempted? It was and Woolston found fifteen different articles on the subject, eight of which had been written by Schultz, four others of which the American knew, and three that were unknown to him. Hopper remembered that "the penny then dropped for board members."

With their approval, the president ordered an early Hewlitt-Packard computer for the Centre, travelling to California to meet in person with William Hewlitt to enquire as to what would be necessary for IDRC to be able to support developing countries through its Information Services division. He purchased an HP 3000 series II with 200 kilobytes of core storage and 200 megabytes of disc storage, then one of the most powerful computers in the world. Its capacity was demonstrated to the board in December 1977 for the first time. Hopper told governors that he would like to expand the community of participants in the exercise to LDCs and to representatives from the Soviet Union, which also had an HP 3000 on order, "provided they will commit themselves to some input in an experimental phase."[34] Later, Ivan Head, Hopper's successor as president, could report to governors the intense interest of the Soviet Academy of Sciences in IDRC-developed software. At the time, IDRC was the only development organization in the world using computers in its relations with the South. It also recognized at a very early date the information/knowledge gap between North and South, doing what it could to help close it.

The short stroll to the National Research Council that the board took represented a preliminary recognition that this was missing. It really was very unique and unusual. When Hopper moved to the World Bank in late 1977 as vice-president for South Asia, he brought ideas about the installation of computer technology with him and encouraged the implementation of policies designed to wire that institution. However, as things then stood, the president was to tell the board in early 1976 that the Centre *was* the international agency for development information sciences, and that it gave leadership at both the country and global levels in developing systems of information dissemination, storage, and retrieval.[35] That also resulted in the establishment of MINISIS, a retrieval system that proved to be very popular among users around the world, boasting 125 installations on six continents by 1984. Many institutions were making enquiries about its use, while a number actually employed it, including the United Nations, the French Senate, the World Bank, the International Monetary Fund, the United States Agency for International Development (USAID), the Pentagon, as well as a number of Canadian federal departments and, perhaps most importantly,

Paramount Pictures. As Head was glad to tell the standing Senate Committee on External Affairs, all of those influential bodies for whom cost was no object chose "to organize [their] files on IDRC software."[36] The International Labour Organization in Geneva was keen to buy the HP hardware and enter into a licensing agreement with IDRC for its software, while the Soviet involvement had resulted in an invitation to Moscow, where the Soviet Academy of Sciences wanted to make a deal. Similarly, it was functioning in a number of languages, including Arabic, Chinese, Russian, Thai, and five European tongues.[37] As well, it was being offered to LDCs and a project funded in 1979 devoted CAN$137,500 to extend MINISIS storage and retrieval systems to Tunisia, Zaire, and other countries in francophone Africa that were to be selected.

It remained more difficult to convince the board of the relevance of Social Sciences as a contributing part of IDRC, given that epiphenomenal moments where social science pennies dropped were harder to come by even given the preponderance of social scientists on the board. Hopper put it down to the fact that they all had their own quite firmly held opinions about where social science, and what sort of social science, fitted into the mix.[38] Zagorin did have difficulty because of the *nature* of her division—social science in a natural science world and in an organization resolutely devoted to the application of *hard scientific* principle. SSHR would, or so some thought, take scarce resources away from more deserving divisions. And, as Zagorin clearly remembered, the board was difficult, "making no contribution to the social sciences until Ted Schultz, an economist and very supportive Nobel Prize winner, came on [in September 1973].... The most difficult projects to get through the board, to get them to understand what we were trying to do, were those from social science."

It helped that Zagorin was "very assertive and smart—aggressive."[39] Still, as time passed, more governors evinced concern over the necessity of social science research, although it remained "a poor cousin" over much of Hopper's tenure.[40] Only as the Centre reached early adolescence was it was more common to hear governors declaim on its virtues. As was pointed out in what became a more typical comment, "after 30 or 40 years of experience in development, [the lesson must be drawn] of how dangerous it is to de-link development as an economic process from political, social and institutional development. The lack of progress in some developing countries often has to do with non-economic factors that lie embedded in culture, in institutions, [and] in the educational system. Development can no longer be divorced from considerations on culture, social factors. In fact ... we ignore the centrality of culture at our peril."[41]

There were a few examples of perceived SSHR relevance demonstrated by certain IDRC projects, although program officers chose not to imagine them as such. While scientific objectives were attained and new lines of cultivars or varieties with the desired characteristics like improved yield or disease and drought resistance were developed, at times they were not taken up by farmers. Indeed, this point had been raised by the Canadian deputy minister of fisheries and oceans during the autumn of 1969 at a meeting of the deputy minister's Committee on Science and Technology that had on its agenda the developing IDRC. He had pointed out that many fisheries innovations had come from research done in Canada, but relatively few of them had been adopted by fishermen. "How," he had asked, "can we expect people in developing countries to take up innovations as a result of research carried out when it is so difficult for Canadian fishermen to do so?" Maurice Strong, appearing as a witness, had explained that the Centre would have social science research carried out in conjunction with research to develop "hardware," and that the social science focus would be concerned with how to introduce the innovations with the minimum of social disruption.[42] The fact that new methods were often not taken up by farmers was attributed to their "conservatism," but also to the fact that researchers had not paid sufficient attention to the social and cultural impediments to the acceptance of change, which was the purview of SSHR. The underlying lesson, which IDRC learned, was that it could not be assumed that a piece of successful research would be used simply because it was a national priority and was deemed as such by the appropriate authorities. Social and cultural factors had to be considered, as well as other elements like marketing infrastructure, distribution, and credit and pricing systems. Finally, the Centre absorbed the fact that the utilization and dissemination of new methods of cropping, or new varieties of sorghum, was not automatically a national responsibility. Just as often it would fall to the Centre to ensure that the fruits of research escaped the walls of the research station.

These points—the conservatism of farmers, the at times lackadaisical attitudes demonstrated by governments in implementing policy that resulted from research, and the social and cultural factors involved in the dissemination of new types of seeds—are illustrated by two projects. The first was concerned with intercropping and situated in the southern highlands of Tanzania, in Morogoro Region, and suffered from this intense focus on the science; on-farm research did produce sorghum cultivars that were superior in size, nutritional value, and value to those grown by farmers, but the new, high-yielding varieties were not readily accepted. The traditional specimens remained favoured because of their long stalks, which were used for various purposes, including fences for animals and shelters for people and their live-stock. Another example dealt with the development of bird-resistant varieties of sorghum, which had been developed by the Arid Lands Agricultural Development program in the Middle East in the early 1970s. The research objectives were attained and new varieties bred that were successful in discouraging birds. However, the cultivars were not widely used, despite their advantageous characteristics; the colour of the seed coat, which was no longer white, and the taste of the sorghum (because of a high tannin content) precluded the new cultivars from being widely used even though their net yield potential was much higher than the traditional varieties. Clearly, this was a social science problem that emerged from a natural science innovation. It was also not a problem unique to IDRC. Indeed, to their credit, most Centre program officers promoted what M.S. Swaminathan called the "learning by doing and not by lecture" approach.[43] AFNS scientists recognized that a top-down paradigm would usually not yield the results that were expected. It was quickly discovered by those in the field that it was impossible to work out improved agricultural methods and systems without any input from the locals, nor could they be expected to adopt the products of that research.

The division was certainly sensitive to the translocation of what has been described as inappropriate or inapplicable technologies from developed into less developed economies. One of its strategy documents noted this: "The need for research to create technologies better suited to the conditions that exist among rural communities and households of Africa, Asia and Latin America has long been neglected. It will be [our] objective to address this need."[44] However, while they might try their hand at attempting this, it more clearly lay within the expertise of SSHR, which was largely kept out of AFNS business. While some program officers, like Hubert Zandstra or Gordon Banta, might be able to demonstrate the benefits of adopting a new seed, many others were not, nor were they necessarily interested. Those two, as program officer Hugh Doggett recalled, "learnt how to get alongside the local farmer, they knew what information they wanted from him, how to use it, and how to persuade local farmers to try out some different seeds and methodologies.... [They] played key roles in the development of [an] essential holistic approach."[45] Later, what came to be known as adaptive research methodology owed much to this thinking.

Still, that situation remained the exception and a June 1988 IDRC assessment, *Crop and Animal Production Systems Programme Report*, commented on why many of the research-generated technological packages in the tropics and subtropics of Africa had not been adopted by the majority of farmers:[46]

a) most of the farmers are small-scale who are economically rational and generally only willing to adopt innovations they consider to be advantageous;
b) most of these small-scale farmers live in highly unpredictable environments, where input and marketing infrastructures are often unreliable;
c) most of them cannot simply take risks; d) all too often, research objectives
are based on the preconceptions of scientists who have little appreciation of
the real problems of small-scale farmers; and e) in some cases the technological packages are in a language not easily understood by the farmers.

Again, social science inputs, combined with the work undertaken by AFNS,
could have resulted in more utilized project outcomes, but in the structure,
values, and personalities then prevailing, that was not always realized. IDRC
would absorb these lessons as it matured.

Still, much of that discussion was in the future while during the mid-
1970s, SSHR fought a rearguard action against those who would do it harm,
primarily by questioning its budget appropriation or its strength. For example, during Hopper's term as president, several governors remained dissat-
isfied with the relative budget split between SSHR and Health Sciences—
25 percent to the former and about 10 percent to the latter. There was some
pressure to better equalize those percentages. A few of those battles were also
conducted at board meetings in developing countries as Hopper introduced
another innovation, one that has since been copied by other development
organizations—holding one meeting per year in the South. The motivation
for doing this was to "educate" the Canadian board members about the developing world, many of whom were political appointments and woefully uninformed about development. The first such meeting was held in 1972 in New
Delhi. While there, the board travelled to Kathmandu and the then King of
Nepal, Birendra Bir Bikram Shah Dev, gave his first-ever audience to foreigners, attended by Lester Pearson, Hopper, and the Nepali vice-president
of IDRC (and soon to be finance minister and later foreign affairs minister
in Nepal), Bekh Thapa.

Regional Offices and Networks

The Centre was also sensitive to its president's desire to establish a presence
in the field. For Hopper, this meant setting up regional offices (and a few others), which he authorized almost as soon as he moved into the Pebb Building.[47] During the first several years, three were formed: Southeast Asia, based
in Singapore and dealing with Southeast and East Asia in 1971, while two
years later the Latin America and the Caribbean regional office (Latin America and Caribbean Regional Office—LACRO) situated in Bogota, Colombia

(which was closed in 1989 and reopened in Montevideo, Uruguay, because of violence), and the West Africa Regional Office (WARO), established in Dakar, Senegal, were opened. Others were soon to follow: in Beirut, Lebanon, in 1974 (at least until civil war ended that experiment in 1976), Nairobi (East Africa Regional Office) and Cairo (Middle East Regional Office) in 1975, New Delhi (South Asia Regional Office) in 1983, and Johannesburg (Regional Office for Southern Africa) opened in 1992 and closed nine years later. Intellectually, as well as in practice, Hopper preferred to hire directors in the offices from the regions. For example, Nihal Kappagoda, a Sri Lankan, was appointed as the first regional director (RD) in Singapore, followed by Jingjai Hanchanlash, a Thai, while Henrique Tono, a Colombian, was the first for LACRO, succeeded by Fernando Chaparro in May 1981. Others were to follow—Adzei Bekoe at the East Africa Regional Office (EARO); Vijay Pande in New Delhi; and Saleh Dessouki, then Fawzy Kishk, at the Middle East Regional Office (MERO). Stanislav Adotvie of Dahomey (now Benin) was appointed as first RD of the West Africa office, although he was quickly followed by Tony Price, a Canadian. Further, the president took steps to open liaison offices in London, New York, Paris, and Washington, DC, to ensure that he would have antennae in place to receive information from, and share it with, other donor institutions, especially the Ford and Rockefeller Foundations, the United Nations, and the World Bank.

Staff in the regional offices (ROs) was generally from the region as well, although ultimately nationality was not an issue, a tradition that has survived to the present. Hiring was program-driven and if a particular sort of person was required, "and if that person came from Denmark or the Philippines, that was the person you took."[48] Dogmatism was foreign to the lexicon of the Centre, and having foreign nationals working shoulder to shoulder with Canadians in pursuit of excellence was seen by virtually all program officers and senior management as a strength. When Price went to open the Nairobi office in 1975, EARO was very international—virtually all support positions were from Kenya, while the professionals were from the Philippines, the United Kingdom, Jamaica, and Venezuela. Thirty years later, EARO had no Canadians, at least by birth, on staff, and the regional director was American.

During Hopper's term, these regional offices strove to fit themselves into the developing IDRC matrix, although sometimes uneasily. Their role was as administrative agent for the Centre in the regions, and not necessarily as project generator. Furthermore, program officers stationed in an RO reported in a direct line to their divisional leadership in Ottawa for scientific project development, monitoring, and all other professional responsibilities. They were to be guided by the regional director in matters relative to behaviour and appropriate relations with the people of the region. This created some tension and, at times, misunderstanding. Indeed, the president felt that during IDRC's formative period, the concept that he was striving for with respect to regional offices "never quite came off."[49] For example, there was much interest in certain regional offices, like LACRO, in assessing the primary needs and requirements of the region on the basis of country priorities, development plans, and programs. While this was done by regional staff, there was virtually no follow-up by Ottawa. As was pointed out, "interesting data had been collected but a problem existed in the integration of the regional office initiatives with the program-related activities of the Centre. If the first activity of data collection and analysis [did not] feed into what program divisions [were] doing, then whatever area you carry out tends to be 'in the air.'"[50] Further, certain RDs were keen to take a more proactive hand in determining program formation in their regions, as was the case with the Ford Foundation. However, in its first incarnation, program emphasis and components were decided in Ottawa. It quickly became clear that the degree of decentralization that the Canada-based directors were prepared to give was not nearly as great as was required under the Hopper scheme. This tension would resurface periodically over IDRC's history.

During the 1970s, RDs served primarily as liaison between headquarters and governments in their regions, as well as diplomatic and managerial hubs. Further, they would have kept Ottawa in touch with regional issues, apprised of the execution of local projects, and ensured that the program was reasonable given conditions. As one early RD recalled, the system, despite the confrontations that occurred at times, "did not work too badly."[51] That was because of IDRC structure and intellectual tradition, nebulous though it may have been. It was also because IDRC's professional staff *were* of high quality, enjoying considerable field experience, to the extent that the Treasury Board Secretariat, in its 1978 assessment of the Centre, thought it necessary to comment on that phenomenon.[52] And that, Tony Price said, "made the relationship between the field and the head office much easier because the people from the programs in Ottawa who you were dealing with were in almost every case professionally competent, had a lot of field experience, and consequently had a lot of credibility in the countries where they were working and with the people in the regional office."

Senior management thinking on regional offices had also evolved since very early days; Hopper told the board, for example, that IDRC's search for viable projects would continue to centre on activities that had implications stretching beyond the borders of one country, which the ROs could help to identify and support.[53] In other words, networks, some of which were housed in regional offices and all of which would help to define Centre operations, were already being touted as best reflecting developing practice. By the time of Hopper's departure, IDRC had funded about 150 of them; from its beginning until 31 December 1979, "over 35 percent of its projects and 43 percent of its program budget related to activities associated with networks."[54] Ivan Head, the new president as of March 1978, continued that practice; he "had no ideology" about them: "the point was the cross-fertilization you got out of the network ... [and] they were very productive of indigenous research."

Some networks were very specifically focused, such as the one between Newfoundland's Memorial University and Upper Volta (now Burkina Faso), which dealt with the blackfly. The networks in social science were more global and amorphous, a group of people, Hopper pointed out, who got together and decided that an area was important: "The city researchers, for example, were brought together to identify common problems that could be engaged in research. The science and technology group were focused on science and technology, and out of that came the science and technology policy instruments (STPI) project. The network formed for public enterprises was specifically drawn together for that purpose." The Centre was stimulated by networks and their possibilities and, as Hopper was to say, "he wasn't a bit concerned about how they got there."[55]

This was another reason the president was keen to establish regional offices to expedite this network policy initiative. The issue, as he defined it, was attempting to divine a sensitivity to the developing country rather than sitting around in Ottawa, "trying to dream up what they ought to do."[56] That was key: Hopper was trying to construct some sort of system that allowed relatively equal interaction between Ottawa and regional offices. That was based on his firm view that offices in the regions were key to building research capability in the developing world. This would, he thought, come to dominate IDRC's project and program activities. Presence was, to some extent, what counted and the Centre had laid a foundation upon which it would build a philosophical superstructure of assistance to Southern researchers that would be unusual among aid agencies in the world.

In short, the president wanted to ensure IDRC played a catalytic role in Southern development, and that it not be regarded merely as another funding organization. Part of that would come down to the *way* it did business—IDRC's flexibility and speed in terms of its turnaround time for grant approval played a major role in a catalytic sense. Some saw the *way* in which IDRC could operate networks, based in ROs, as a major contribution to development, one that would eventually be copied by other agencies. In the late 1970s and into the next decade, "networks" became a buzz word and in many of them, *participants* were the *recipients* of assistance rather than *part-ners* in development, as was the philosophy with IDRC. The Centre saw net-works as a tool for developing indigenous institutional capacities, as opposed to the way in which many agencies saw them as subsidiary activities.

The power and influence of networks were also cumulative and, to that end, "figures on projects located in countries and their financial dimensions [were] not altogether a faithful illustration of the Centre's support."[57] What was important to IDRC was not so much the country from which a particu-lar proposal came or the status of the putative researcher as whether a pro-ject's findings were to have wide applicability. Networks allowed researchers to work not in isolation but in collaboration with their fellows in other coun-tries and regions, to compare methodologies, exchange ideas, and share results. They were to prove extraordinarily successful for organizing, mobi-lizing, and giving experience to Southern researchers.

Still, they were not easy to supervise, operate, or fund, and some later complained that IDRC had too many network projects and too little synthe-sis. Under the pressure of increasing budgets in the early 1970s and of the requirement to give the bulk of the funding directly to developing country institutions that required an enormous amount of very difficult fieldwork, it was easy to lose sight of the bigger picture, of what the program officer or the division might be hoping to accomplish. And to encourage the creation of networks in addition to that was, at times, very difficult as well as time-consuming for an organization in which time was at a premium. Even then, IDRC officials felt the pressures associated with being away from home and family for long periods of time. These absences would cut careers short and eventually become a topic discussed at board meetings. A common senti-ment during the decade was that the Centre had achieved a certain level of accomplishment through what the wags called a two-for-one special; the husband would be hired and travel the world, while his spouse was left behind to maintain the house, raise the children, and see to his needs when he returned.[58]

In the early 1970s, various regional organizations were established, often with IDRC assistance, to share information, overcome isolation, and con-tribute to the professional development of participants. A good example, and one of many that IDRC funded, was Technonet Asia, an Asian network for industrial technology information and extension that began operations in September 1972. John Woolston dreamed up this project that brought people together. It is useful in terms of demonstrating what the Centre hoped to accomplish through these networks, as well as some of the pitfalls asso-ciated with them. Its role was to provide technical information and industrial extension services, particularly to small-scale industries in those countries that participated. This orientation fitted in with early IDRC thinking; particular subject concentrations would coincide with what were perceived to be regional strengths. For example, Africa was marked for library development, Southeast Asia for industrial information, and Latin America for communication science. This suggested regional focus was due to the perception of area needs and resources, a perception that was, admittedly, not always accurate. The Technonet report discussed the importance of local training in industrial extension and the development of a self-supporting network of participating organizations.[59] The concern here was small industry extension and how one obtained information; that grew in part out of the National Research Council's experience in trying to provide technical information to small industrialists in developing countries.

However, the board and some program directors thought IDRC had reached too far; the general feeling was that the Centre should not be involved in actual network *operations,* as opposed to funding the start-up process. The fact that headquarters in Ottawa was administering this network in its entirety was confusing: "IDRC was in reality operating an information service," one observer noted; "there was more emphasis on training industrial extension workers than on actually moving documents and providing information," which lay outside of the Centre's mandate, at least according to some.[60] But Technonet did fulfill a real purpose and provided a valuable service, and it was hived off from IDRC funding in 1983. It also demonstrated the flexibility, in a good sense, of IDRC policies.

It remains very active in 2010, is self-financed, and has been used by other bilateral and multilateral donors as a template, the model of an excellent network. As its website now proclaims, it "is a non-stock, non-profit and non-political international development organization comprising nine small, micro and medium enterprises promotion and development organizations from eight Asian countries, with its secretariat based in Singapore."[61] The early lesson learned at IDRC, raised at sundry board meetings following the Technonet experience, was that it was necessary to have a project where a parent institution would eventually take over the network—when new institutions were being set up in the South, unexpected pitfalls were the norm.[62]

Ruth Zagorin, the director of the Social Sciences and Human Resources Division, recalled years later the centrality of networks. These were a Centre innovation that largely sprang from SSHR, dealing as it did "with so many very touchy areas."[63] They quickly spread to other divisions. Fascinating results came from networks, she believed, as researchers were introduced to each other, links that were maintained over years in many cases. As Zagorin

remembered, "you [had] a group of researchers interested in the same problem, agreeing to a set of questions that had to be addressed in the research,
to a common research design, and to a timetable." The result was always
greater than the parts. They were also one way to spread the word. Hopper
told the *Globe and Mail* that "for most developing country governments, support for research comes very far down on the list of priorities. For most politicians the pay off that comes from scientific research is very uncertain. We try
to build international networks to bring researchers in an area together so
they can share their talents and experience."[64]

There were also quality of research issues that networks helped to address
because of the defined purpose of the work. What was most important was
its purpose. Publication in a peer-reviewed Western journal was not necessarily—indeed, almost never—the objective. Most often, IDRC-funded
research in the South was to bring knowledge, information, and experience
for policy purposes. The researcher was looking for a definition of the issues,
an explanation, and a set of options a policy-maker could handle—in short,
to support action. For that reason Zagorin often encouraged program officers
to include policy-makers in research design, an unheard of innovation for the
time, despite the almost constant tension between officials and the academics who undertook the projects. The former, according to a number of program officers, simply dismissed social scientists with the claim that they
never gave government officials what they wanted. Social scientists retorted
that government never listened to them. IDRC was very keen that the two
groups learn to speak the same language; that social scientists become adept
at answering policy-makers' questions and to translate their research findings into a form usable by the latter. Policy-makers, for their part, should
articulate their objectives with greater precision.

"Initially," Zagorin recounted, "this [new] approach drove the social scientists up the wall."[65] Still, early on its effectiveness was demonstrated. As
it evolved, it was not unusual to find officials sitting in on sessions going
over the research results prepared by social scientists. They would also provide feedback. It was a rewarding experience as both came to understand each
other better, and Zagorin was gratified over the number of researchers who
subsequently moved into positions of responsibility in government or in public services. Indeed, the names of those who have held IDRC grants and gone
into their country's service in a senior capacity would fill many pages, among
them René Cortazar (Chile), Danilo Astori (Uruguay), Rashad Cassim (South
Africa), and M.V. Rajasekharan (India).[66]

One other issue plagued IDRC in its early years, especially as it sought
to operate in certain parts of Africa where French was the *lingua franca* and

France the dominant power. The region, it seemed, was regarded by the French as a *chasse gardée*, a preserve for their aid and influence.[67] Bilingual Canada could prove to be competition. When the Centre came to establish a regional office for West Africa, the focus was on Côte d'Ivoire (the favourite), Nigeria, and Ghana.[68] Senegal was eventually included in the list as Côte d'Ivoire was removed, presumably counselled by their omnipresent French advisers not to allow it. Paris seemed not very enthusiastic over the possibility of a Canadian presence in Abidjan or anywhere else in the country, for that matter. Indeed, at one point in late November 1972, negotiations with Côte d'Ivoire had reached a critical point (they ultimately collapsed), and Hopper banned all travel to the country "until a government decision [was] reached on [IDRC's] request to open a regional office."[69] Senegal, which nominally fell into the same category as its neighbour to the south, did not feel so constrained. The office was established in Dakar.

Taking Care of Business

IDRC's first years were extremely busy as administrative operations were established, the conceptualization of the Centre proceeded apace, and staff were hired. All of these components affected its evolution. As Gerry Bourrier, a former official at IDRC, has pointed out, employees, and particularly the earlier ones, seemed to be possessed of "a missionary zeal" that motivated their desire to participate in the work of the Centre, especially if they had had experience with a much more bureaucratic organization like the United Nations, the World Bank, or even CIDA.[70] The same could be said, he recalled, for the ex–Canadian University Service Overseas (CUSO) cohort who came on board, which IDRC was especially keen to hire; "[their] attributes were always sought when we recruited new staff." The foundation, and what Bourrier called ideology, laid by those early hires has persisted in IDRC, affecting its evolution in a positive manner.

Part of that included the very close identification of the Centre with professionalism. As many remembered, during the Hopper era (and later) it wanted the best trained and equipped international scientists. That excellent cadre of personnel helped IDRC to establish a reputation that was the envy of many other development organizations. Program officers had much autonomy and discretionary authority, which fitted in well with the developing Centre ethos and was a reflection of Hopper's personality. Here, it was helped by its relatively small size and meagre budget. That, combined with the Centre's early legendary flexibility, proved to be a huge advantage. IDRC suppleness was demonstrated by activity in Uganda, Ethiopia, the southern cone of

South America, South Africa, and Palestine—anywhere in which social strife, political trouble, or *coups d'état* made life untenable. The Centre was often the only Canadian agency that stuck it out when conditions deteriorated.

For example, Hopper authorized IDRC personnel through the Nairobi office to remain active in Uganda once Idi Amin had taken over government in January 1971, and Prod Laquian at EARO, following its establishment, ran, as he called it, a Ugandan underground railway for refugee intellectuals. IDRC would support them either through grants or by finding displaced academics a position at a university in the region. Tony Price, working out of the Nairobi office, helped Ethiopian intellectuals in distress leave the country following the beginning of that country's civil war in September 1974. Similarly, Tony Tillett, with Elizabeth Fox in tow, often swept through the southern cone of Latin America, dispensing research funding designed to preserve recipients from the military's wrath during the years of dictatorship in the 1980s. Marc Van Ameringen worked with the African National Congress (ANC) in the late 1980s and into the 1990s, quietly fighting against apartheid in South Africa until the ANC could take over. As Laquian pointed out, but which also holds for other hot spots, if Uganda had invested years of education in a person "who was only going to be killed by Idi Amin, you were saving the world a great deal of investment" if they were supported elsewhere until it was safe to return.[71]

IDRC flexibility was appreciated by other donor agencies as well. Laquian noted that in Nairobi he "played footsie with Ford Foundation, with UNDP [United Nations Development Programme], with UNEP [United Nations Environment Programme] because they were also identifying problem cases and they did not have the flexibility of IDRC, so they naturally came to us and said 'we need your help on this.'" He also never felt that he was part of the Canadian foreign aid bureaucracy. As he recalled, he served in Nairobi for two years, and went to the Canadian High Commission only once—to record his address in case he needed to be evacuated. IDRC personnel saw themselves "as a completely autonomous operation.... We took pride in the fact that [the Centre] had an international staff. It was easy for me to work in Africa because they didn't see me as any kind of a White colonialist. That was also what made IDRC so successful in Asia—that kind of recruiting."

This flexibility, however conceived, did not mean that IDRC had lax accounting practices; Bourrier noted that the Centre practised "honest conservatism" and husbanded its financial resources as carefully as possible to maximize output while ensuring proper accountability. As was pointed out, "The fact that [IDRC] was one of three agencies, out of 43, which received a 'clean bill of health' during the Comprehensive Audit conducted by the

Auditor General in 1980, is a tribute to the scientific, fiscal and administrative integrity of the management and staff of [the Centre]."[72]

When the first board worried about how the Centre would get projects, Hopper assured them that as their product was money, project numbers would not be an issue.[73] That was true; about fifteen were approved during 1970–71, totalling approximately CAN$1.3 million. Taken together, these demonstrated little cohesion, each emerging from an activity generated in one of the four program areas. As one of the first program officers hired at the Centre, Andrew Barnett related that in late 1970 and into the next year, he was travelling almost continuously in order to sign up researchers. His orders were, as he recalled, to find someone who was capable and convince them to take up an IDRC-funded project.[74] This was mostly to do with the fact that procedural and administrative mechanisms remained undeveloped early on. The Centre was keen to add to its resumé in that first year.

However, by the end of the second year, the president was already growing concerned about spreading resources too thinly. He was increasingly focused on what seemed to him to be the rather amorphous nature of IDRC practice on the ground and "being all over the map." From the perspective of the 1970s, the Centre was beginning to address what it thought to be the critical issues in which Canada had a capability and which IDRC could handle within the framework of its resources. Given his budgetary concerns, Hopper was also not at all keen on moving into in-house research either with IDRC laboratories or with research libraries and scholars in Canada, thereby spreading resources even more thinly. As he noted, the Centre "came out of the foreign assistance budget and I did not see tapping this to help Canadian university students and professors. I did see the point of tapping Canadian know-how and did so at several universities, to do something in which the developing countries needed assistance and partnerships."[75] Tap Canadian know-how he did, although not to the extent demanded by universities and research centres.

As a result of his anxieties about the Centre's direction, he told the board that management wanted "to bring a greater unity to the projects spawned within each of the program areas and to insuring a closer interaction among the activities of all four areas."[76] He expected to see in the coming year a shift in focus from building the activities of the four separate programs to a greater concentration on unifying the work of the divisions to bring each into an emerging matrix. As well, Hopper reiterated his philosophical approach to development that had guided, and would continue to guide, IDRC's progress— the Centre would remain focused on the micro because forward movement in development came through small steps. It would continue its concentration on the country-by-country research problems that involved the creation, development, and expansion of new ideas, and on the smaller problems of development within those countries. Indeed, IDRC was an intellectual enterprise, financing and distributing certain types of knowledge with certain attributes. Knowledge, as the Centre and its creators knew, was the most powerful engine of production over time. Advances resulted in the creation of new global skills and capital, and Hopper had early on laid out his perspective, which was to support projects "of merit and importance even if that support must be given through some of the screwiest arrangements imaginable."[77]

Eleven-Point Wisdom

But how to refine IDRC programming, which was becoming a bit scattered, and at least begin to position the Centre for the future while continuing to provide autonomy to program staff and minimize the number of policy constraints that could inhibit their degree of responsiveness in any particular case? How to balance, for example, competing goals, of maintaining Centre support for problem-oriented or applied research, *and* assistance for phenomenon-oriented or basic research, as well as keeping the right weight "between Centre assistance for analytical research, *and* support for direct, comprehensive action development projects"?[78] Hopper prepared a brief analysis of eleven research policy issues for the board's consideration at the 19 March 1973 meeting held in Bogota, Colombia.[79] He believed that 1973 marked the end of the first phase of the Centre's existence; six new governors would be appointed and a new chair would convene the September meeting following the untimely death of Lester Pearson on 27 December 1972. While his eleven-points paper was largely based on his October 1970 statement, which remained the major guideline for Centre endeavours and would remain the basic policy document, at least in the near future, policy and its implications should be periodically tested against a standard. As well, it came out of the guidelines for the handling of projects that were received at the Centre and that had been passed by the board's executive committee in January 1971. These threads were brought together with the eleven research principles and reaffirmed by the full board meeting in March of that year. Each issue was reviewed against two extreme positions on a continuum, with the intent of selecting a middling one that, judging by the comments recorded at the meeting, the board accepted in its entirety. As an official policy document that spelled out Centre policy precisely did not exist, the 1973 statement served as the sole indication of IDRC policy until much later.[80]

But why produce this paper when the Centre had prospered without such a document for the previous three years? In short, Hopper felt that greater formality was necessary, especially as the Centre grew.[81] Furthermore, as this is the only policy document that was to receive board approval during Hopper's tenure as president and for some years after, it is as important, intellectually, in codifying Centre practice as had been Hopper's October 1970 statement. It was a tangible expression of IDRC's philosophy and why it supported projects where it did. What were the policies as articulated by the document? First and foremost, it emphasized the Centre's commitment to the funding of science and technology research, as well as maintaining "a strong orientation to assisting research that has a practical, or an applied significance for the economic and social advancement of developing nations." Everything else flowed from those simple premises.

Hopper viewed the first four policies as forming a unity of purpose. The first spoke to the Centre's willingness to fund Southern researchers who "after some suspicion and much doubt as to the true willingness of the Centre to provide virtually untied assistance," welcomed its support and the vote of confidence in their abilities that it implied. Policy issue II was the balance between Centre acceptance of Southern research agendas, and its judgment about what those should be, combined with IDRC support for its enunciated development research objectives. The Centre had been overwhelmingly responsive to Southern research enquiries and had "encouraged innovative departures from the usual run of research activities." That said, it was also true that the Centre was not always completely responsive to researcher demands in the sense that it would fund any project. That was partly a reflection of its very limited budget, but also because the evolving organization wanted a certain coherence to its work, as has been seen above. Then, as now, IDRC had a set of thematic approaches that its officers believed to be important, and to which it more or less stuck. That sometimes occasioned caustic comment in the 1970s by those whose work did not easily fit into the prescribed direction. One thing was sure, as Ruth Zagorin was to note, the Centre "could not do everything."[82]

The next policy issue articulated a balance between improving the innovative research skills of LDC research scientists and technologists by providing on-the-job training and Centre assistance to ensuring quality outcomes for the research. As IDRC had discovered over its short life, the former was variable and dependent on the experience of the researcher. As a result, it had quickly come to the determination that developing potential human talent was part of its remit. Training of LDC researchers and the development of human skill, as laid out in 4.1 (b) of the *IDRC Act*, was the justification.

Theirs was a longer-term strategy of investment in scientists who, in many cases, were just starting out. As could be expected, this policy had generated huge excitement in the Southern research community. The final policy issue of the first four spoke to the balance in IDRC support between applied and basic research, and the Centre's fixation on the first.

The remaining seven items dealt largely with administrative issues like the balance between institution building, research training, and research support; IDRC's reluctance to provide core support for institutions (although that would change); and the proper weight accorded to Centre support for research projects and direct support for post-secondary training. It did the former and not the latter, but that would also change. For example, Africa confounded Hopper and over his time in office, the president came to believe there were good reasons for adopting a different position, especially as the continent was in dire need of research funding, but did not have the capability to absorb it.

Implementing the Hopper Vision

This list informed IDRC practice, which, in turn, animated its program priorities. Coming out of the 1960s and early 1970s, these generally concentrated on the application of science and technology, or social sciences, or a combination of the two, to the problem at hand: How did countries feed growing populations in Asia? What crops were most suitable? What could be grown most easily? How was population growth to be contained? How should children be educated? About 75 percent of Centre funding during the Hopper era could be roughly construed as falling under section 4.1(b): "to assist the developing regions to build up the research capabilities, the innovation skills and the institutions required to solve their problems." Further, 70 percent of projects, by number, were focused on finding new technologies or growth potential, and about 10 percent on miscellaneous activities that included training. Very little went to institution-building. In the context of those first years, the food issue was one that science and technology could effectively address, or so it was believed, along with health and education.

Early on, Joe Hulse set about ploughing the agricultural field. His philosophy, and that of the division, could be summed up by quoting Jonathan Swift's *Gulliver's Travels*, which Hulse did in the Centre's *Annual Report, 1971–1972*: "And he gave it for his opinion that whoever could make two ears of corn or two blades of grass grow upon a spot of ground where only one grew before, would deserve better of mankind, and do more essential service to his country, than the whole race of politicians put together." At the

March 1972 board meeting, Hulse offered his division's vision, and it remained its guiding wisdom for the better part of two decades. These included identifying and supporting programs in agriculture designed to ameliorate the condition of life of rural communities in the South, in large part by promoting research by food and agricultural scientists.

It also included the innovative approach of supporting research that looked at farming in its totality. Most often, donors were commodity-centred—they would provide funding to improve, say, rice or livestock. Further, some projects would support storage investigations, while some looked at drying and others at milling. That, Hulse believed, distorted results, which led his division to promote a systems approach for a whole farming system "from the time a crop was harvested until somebody ate it." The condition in which it was eaten was dependent on all the intermediate stages.[83] Swaminathan appreciated that, especially in the case of India; from every part of the biomass—the straw, the husk, the bran, of whatever crop it might be—there was an attempt made to yield a living. Swaminathan called it "paddy to prosperity," what he hoped would be a reversal of the more common "paddy and poverty."

A significant part of that was encouraging work on less "glamorous" and perhaps more "neglected" crops like chickpea, pigeon pea, and cowpea, collectively known as the poor man's meat. As well, the division cultivated researcher capability for millet, oil seeds like safflower and niger, and sorghum. With respect to the last noted, Hopper later remarked that "we know a lot more about the enzymic structures of sorghum and how the plant really works in a drought than we would have known without IDRC," which was critical for its improvement.[84] Cassava was also supported given its centrality as a food staple for more than 300 million people; CIDA devoted CAN$6.5 million over five years to it, with the Centre as the executing agency. IDRC funding would allow them improved opportunities to meet, to communicate, and to co-operate with each other in support of the common good. And if Hulse's division could pique the interest of Canadian crop scientists to undertake work on their own, so much the better.

The cassava program had an interesting provenance and demonstrated a number of IDRC philosophical strands that had been woven together. A proposal for research had come from the Centro Internacional de Agricultura Tropical (CIAT) in Colombia, which saw the root as a useful source of pig feed. What began as the cassava swine project never developed in that way; instead, it became the cassava improvement project, which focused on providing it to people. IDRC funded that research, while CIDA supported CIAT to the tune of CAN$3.25 million, a fund that the Centre managed. That contract, according to Maurice Strong, was the value of the Centre to CIDA—the latter would not have to build up its own expertise in the area.[85] During the 1976–77 fiscal year, the Centre took over sole responsibility for the program.

IDRC program officers suggested locating all the people who had ever worked on cassava in Indonesia, Malaysia, and parts of Africa and Latin America, a daunting task made more so by the many who had never published their findings. The next step was to examine what bibliographies existed; some were discovered, but not one was complete. A consultant was found with the help of John Woolston's information science division to weave all these into one coherent piece, and eventually the Cassava Information Centre was established at CIAT, with the most complete expertise on this important crop.

On the more purely science side, problems also had to be overcome. For example, cassava was "vegetatively propagated," meaning that the "seed" was taken from a cutting off the main stem with two nodes about 22 centimetres apart, one for the root and one for the stem. Given that there were certain cassava diseases on some continents, researchers did not want to transmit them through this method of propagation. As a result, a contract was let to the Prairie Regional Laboratories in Saskatoon to develop tissue culture propagation from the new shoot before it became infected. This made the growing of disease-free plants possible, even from diseased roots. The plantlets could also be distributed in test tubes, which was a huge advantage. It also began a link with Canadian universities, where more basic research was required. McGill University in Montreal received a contract to classify cassava in taxonomical tables, while its counterpart in Guelph determined how much of the dry matter went into the leaves. As Hulse pointed out, "Whenever you do applied research, sooner or later you will bang your head up against an obstacle that cannot be solved in the field. More fundamental research is needed. The scientist needs to examine the biochemistry and physiology of the plant to learn what it is that is causing the difficulty [and that happened at Canadian universities]."[86]

As was the case with cassava, the development of triticale, a drought-resistant, high-protein grain, encapsulated many of the developing thrusts of IDRC policy as it moved forward in the 1970s, including networks and association through research with CGIAR. IDRC did not fund work on wheat, but it did have a project on the development of a new grain, triticale, a wheat-rye cross, which it underwrote to the tune of about CAN$3.25 million during the early 1970s. It was one of the first projects that the Centre funded, and its potential was clearly huge; triticale was often dubbed "the miracle grain" or "the super plant." Gerry Bourrier, then an AFNS program officer, recalled that he had a sheaf on his desk for about a dozen years to remind him of its centrality to the division's work.[87]

Triticale was, as Hopper explained at a news conference, "a wide-out cross … like a mule, a cross between a donkey and a horse, and the problem with it has been the problem with the mule.… It was an infertile grain … and produced a very shriveled grain. It was a biological curiosity." It had been around for many years and had been extensively researched at the University of Manitoba (UM). By the late 1960s, Mexican researchers had taken up the cause, both domestically and in partnership with UM, which had resulted in a significant breakthrough in its development. If triticale was successful, it could have significant implications for dry farming areas around the world as the rye part of its parentage was drought resistant without the grain possessing rye's relatively unacceptable eating quality. And that would materially help countries like Kenya, which had 57 million hectares of land area, of which 70 percent was semi-arid.[88]

It was also important that IDRC fund research on market structures, on the handling and processing of the grain, and the credit facilities that farmers needed to buy inputs for triticale cultivation. Hopper noted early on that "this is one of the kind of projects that the Centre would … [launch]; to sustain and follow over a period of time," and did help to establish a working relationship between UM and the International Centre for Maize and Wheat Research in Mexico, as well as research centres in India, Kenya, and Tanzania in order to test the grain in global conditions.[89] AFNS's report to the board during the September 1976 meeting referred to three networks of note—cassava, triticale, and crops of the semi-arid tropics. However, for reasons beyond our purpose here, triticale was not successful in the way Hopper had hoped. In 2010, the major triticale producers are Australia, Belarus, China, France, Germany, and Poland; they and twenty-two other countries harvested about 14 million tons in 2008.

Hulse planned to link up cassava, triticale, and a host of other crops with national centres that were being established as the CGIAR system was gearing up. His intent was to transfer knowledge from international to national to rural communities. This focus, in the case of India, led to the first large India–Canada project, which investigated dryland agriculture and which eventually resulted in the birth of a specifically Indian organization, the Centre for Research on Dryland Agriculture (CREDA), established with the help of the Canadian government. Later, the International Crops Research Institute for the Semi-Arid Tropics (ICRISAT), affiliated with the CGIAR system and with the Indian office based in Patancheru, Andhra Pradesh, was set up on a basis similar to CREDA. The Centre had also played a critical role in the establishment of the International Centre for Agricultural Research in Dry Areas (ICARDA) in Aleppo, Syria, in 1975. This concern for the semi-arid tropics reflected dire need; those regions, like the Sahel in North Africa, were generally thought to be among the poorest of the poor. That Canadians "would not have known whether the Sahel was in Africa or on the other side of Mars" meant little;[90] in totality, semi-arid agriculture supported millions, and the land on which it was pursued totalled about one-third of the world's usable arable area. In short, it remained critical if those populations were to experience any quality of life.

Further, IDRC was key to the establishment of the International Food Policy Research Institute (IFPRI) in early 1975, along with the Ford and Rockefeller foundations. It followed on the World Food Conference of November 1974, convened by the FAO and attended by representatives from 135 governments. It had produced the Universal Declaration for the Eradication of Hunger and Malnutrition, which had noted in its first sentence that "Every man, woman and child has the inalienable right to be free from hunger and malnutrition in order to develop their physical and mental faculties."[91] Headquartered in Washington, DC, IFPRI was chartered as a non-profit corporation, and its objectives reflected prevailing wisdom: to identify through research important constraints that were likely to be impediments to the improved production, consumption, and availability of foodstuffs throughout the world, with particular emphasis on the needs of low-income countries. As well, it was tasked with determining those actions that could be taken or influenced by governments and international organizations to alleviate these constraints by changes in policies and programs relating to the production, trade, and distribution of food.[92] Reminiscent of IDRC, IFPRI would be governed by a board of trustees drawn equally from developed and developing countries, with Sir John Crawford serving as chair in its first incarnation. The Centre, along with the Ford and Rockefeller foundations, would each appoint one member, while the World Bank and FAO had agreed to co-operate with the recommendations made as a result of research undertaken.

IDRC was also interested in health and population through its Population and Health Science division (PHS), which changed its name in 1975 to health sciences. Both incarnations were suggestive of approach; the division was focused on preventive, basic issues, not sophisticated, clinical responses to exotic diseases, although, admittedly, it did a bit of that, too. The development context into which the division was born was one in which concern over population was beginning to surface. It was perceived in terms of contraception, fertility regulation, and the problems of abortion, particularly the terrible effects of induced abortion. As the World Health Organization

(WHO) has pointed out, "Ending the silent pandemic of unsafe abortion is an urgent public-health and human-rights imperative ... this scourge threatens women throughout the developing world. Every year, about 20 million abortions are done by individuals without the requisite skills, or in environments below minimum medical standards, or both. Nearly all unsafe abortions (97 percent) are in developing countries. An estimated 68,000 women die as a result, and millions more have complications, many permanent."[93] Nor were the statistics any better for maternal mortality. In 2010, they remain appalling. As Geoffrey York has recently pointed out, "Close to 550,000 women die in pregnancy and childbirth every year—a rate of about one woman every minute—along with nearly 4 million infants who die within a month of birth.... For women in Africa and Asia, the act of ... having a child is one of the most dangerous risks they can take. Their chances of dying in childbirth can be more than 100 times greater than a Canadian ... woman would face."[94] Despite the risks presented, however, large families were the norm in the developing world because of the risk of loss of children due to high infant mortality rates.

George Brown, who became the division's first director, had propounded from the beginning a primary health care approach to the family, and that health and family planning must go together; only when the health of mothers was included, when the health of babies could be improved, would family planning programs have an impact. As one of his colleagues later noted, "Brown really rode the bandwagon on primary health care" after helping to build the vehicle.[95] This IDRC focus predated international concern as articulated by the Alma-Ata Declaration of 12 September 1978, made under World Health Organization/UNICEF auspices, which "express[ed] the need for urgent action by all governments, all health and development workers, and the world community to protect and promote the health of all the people of the world."[96] IDRC was certainly among the first in terms of seeing primary health care as good. It included not only personal medical and health protection services, but also such basic environmental concerns as clean water and sanitary disposal of human waste. As it had done in helping with the AGRIS project undertaken by FAO, IDRC also built a computer-based bibliographical reference tool, SALUS, which by the end of the decade provided about seven hundred references to articles, papers, and monographs relating to the area. It also represented a good example of the conjunction that IDRC worked to achieve, of social science with its natural science counterpart.

Significantly, when IDRC had been a glint in Maurice Strong's eye, Brown had given some thought to the shape of any emerging unit. He had been a special population adviser at CIDA, tasked with developing a population strategy. The initial idea had been for a division of population studies. Brown's memorandum had defined the areas that became division sectors: contraceptive technology, the prospects emerging from research, and population policy. These had flowed from concerns about population and family planning, and developing countries' need to undertake their own research to understand policy issues. Only later was health added. There were many major health issues that could properly be linked to population, for example, the provision of basic health services to rural areas, which related as well to other activities such as agriculture. This was connected to family planning operations research, which, it was felt, should be combined with primary health care. Hopper had seen Brown's memorandum, talked to others, then asked him if he would accept a position at the Centre.

The population technology field was also an area in which research was funded. At the global level, PHS was at the forefront of discussions of what emerged as the WHO program in human reproduction. An IDRC grant had put a consultant into the mix, and the tiny Centre was helping the WHO to act. This was the definition of punching above one's weight. It was also busy in many associated areas, for example, developing a network in Mexico on collaborative research and human reproduction, which was enormously successful, in the process making Mexico one of the outstanding leaders in the field of reproduction and reproduction technology. Another project—thromboembolism—in Hong Kong focused on the effect of oral contraceptives on women and was linked to a whole series of projects in Southeast Asia. Finally, a major global project in contraceptives, the International Committee on Contraceptive Research (ICCR), run by the New York City–based Population Council, was funded by IDRC and the Ford and Rockefeller foundations. In the estimation of experts in the field, this turned out to be the most successful contraceptive research development program undertaken to that time in the public sector. The ICCR developed a series of usable contraceptives, working with IDRC funding for the better part of fifteen years.

It also began funding a program of research in 1975 on fertility regulation, focused on an anti-pregnancy vaccine, which continued to receive Centre support into the mid-1980s. Funding went to the Population Council, although the project itself was based at the All-India Institute of Medical Sciences and headed by the physician G.P. Talwar, a world-renowned immunologist. Its attraction was in its simplicity; it offered the promise of a simple, very effective method of preventing conception and would surely be welcomed by those women keen to prevent pregnancy. The test population comprised women in India, as well as some in Finland, Sweden, and the United States.

Given the subject and the vulnerable position of the women participants, some Centre governors demonstrated a level of discomfort. Liliane Filion-Laporte, herself a physician, claimed it to be "science fiction" and was very concerned about the ethics of testing the product.[97] John Gill, now director of Health Sciences, thought it would be a major breakthrough: "If you look at the amount of female sterilization that is going on in the world today with women who have reached thirty and have four or five children and don't want any more, I think the possibility of a vaccine is far more acceptable than sterilization." Further, he emphasized that the project's ombudsman, a condition of IDRC support, made sure that all protocols were observed. Whatever misgivings some governors might have voiced, they voted CAN$550,000 for phase II at its meeting in March 1980 and more than CAN$711,000 for phase III in early 1983. However, with the board increasingly nervous about possible outcomes, phase III of the project was accepted subject to three conditions. The first was that the results of the toxicological studies on animals be reviewed by a qualified group within Canada or a qualified group acceptable to Canadians; the second was the government of India's acceptance of both the short- and the long-term medical risks of what was being done; and, third, that IDRC participation would be reassessed before the project entered the clinical phase. It did indeed prove to be a problematic project—Centre support ended with phase III.[98]

Education was much less contentious than pregnancy vaccines, and it became an area of focus as the 1970s wore on, especially the education of children. Early on, the governor, Puey Ungphakorn, had stated that "education should be the first and foremost consideration."[99] With the support of the board and management, it had begun a substantial program of support for education within its social sciences program by the mid-1970s. When IDRC began to fund research focused on primary schools, few other agencies were doing so. Moreover, it did not dismiss the existing school system as irrelevant and antiquated, a common practice among those agencies that were active in the field.[100] David Hopper felt that "the rejection of the school system is bolstered by a widespread belief—only weakly supported by actual observation—that established schooling have left large numbers of educated unfitted for employment." Still, that could not diminish the fact that in most areas of the developing world, education systems had been created to serve colonial requirements and even into the 1970s (and later) they largely retained their elite-oriented characteristics. An important function of those systems was to identify the "bright" children and provide them with higher, more specialized training so that they could fit into managerial, administrative, technical, and professional roles. The underprivileged became dropouts;

in Indonesia and Thailand, for example, while over 90 percent of all children enrolled in primary schools, only 30 percent continued on in secondary schools. In Malaysia, it was 92 and 53 percent respectively, but only 3 percent went on to university. Far from being vehicles for upward mobility, those education systems perpetuated inequality.[101]

The Centre very quickly came to believe that social returns from education were greatest at the lower levels, while the private returns were similarly so from universities; if a country had limited resources, they should not go to the latter, which was where most money from international donors was placed. Usually, buildings that were either inappropriate or very difficult to maintain were built and were better suited to a campus in North America or Europe. Further, as Joseph Hulse pointed out years later, albeit in a slightly different context, he had "turned [his] face against 'bricks and mortar' or building institutions without a sharply defined focus. The United Nations Development Program had put very substantial amounts of money into creating large institutions that were later left to be maintained by the developing country. In erecting bricks and mortar, you not only put physical walls around people, you also put intellectual and philosophical walls around them so that they don't ever see outside those walls."[102]

Indeed, research did demonstrate the groundbreaking point that the influence of primary education was extraordinary; in order to achieve sustained literacy, children had to be kept in school for at least four years, which might then propel them on to higher grades and out of the poverty trap. Conversely, as was pointed out at IDRC, there was no country where it could be demonstrated that despite vast investment, adult education had worked. Institutions like the United Nations Educational, Scientific, and Cultural Organization (UNESCO) had done research on that, as IDRC was funding work focusing on the primary level; a country did not—indeed, could not— sustain literacy with adult education. It could, however, if it got a critical mass through grade 4. Similarly, females and primary education should be investigated as preliminary research found that a mother with a minimum of education could have a very significant effect on the whole development process in terms of providing suitable nutrition for her own children, as well as an enhanced ability to control her own fertility.

Though annual budgets for education sector work rarely exceeded CAN$5 million, by the early 1980s, from its very tentative beginnings the previous decade, IDRC had become a central player in international educational assistance, prominent for its support of Southern-based solutions to educational problems.[103] IDRC's education sector projects were typically small research projects. Yet "because of the support of education staff in six regional offices and the Centre's commitment to disseminating the findings of the educational research it supported, IDRC's work in education gained large regional and international audiences. The unique nature of its mission also allowed IDRC to support small-scale educational innovations, an unusual undertaking among Northern donor agencies. Included among these was support for the development of regional educational research networks."

Centre educational policy was reflected in a CAN$360,000 grant to a project based in Manila, Philippines, with work also being done in Indonesia. The Regional Centre for Educational Innovation and, IDRC's first venture into support for research in mass education, was very successful and set the Centre on a path that would reap major rewards. The project was designed to investigate the possibility of providing teaching material to large numbers of children with minimal teacher supervision that would allow them to move forward and acquire the kind of basic education that was necessary. It was an attempt to cut by 50 percent the cost of education per child in order to educate all primary school children with no increase in the overall education budget. Over forty-five months, beginning in 1973, it focused on improving the effectiveness and economy of the delivery system for primary education, the role of teachers in non-formal education, and alternative educational systems.[104] The project established a primary education system known as Instructional Management by Parents, Community, and Teachers (IMPACT) and was implemented in five villages in Naga, Cebu Island, Philippines, and four villages in Solo, Central Java, Indonesia. Instead of conventional teachers, instructional supervisors directed and organized a variety of modules or learning activities for as many as two hundred students. Skilled community members, volunteers, and older students helped with the modules, and parents monitored their child's progress. During early 1974, researchers in the Philippines conducted a survey and acceptance campaign for IMPACT and developed the modules. Over the year following July 1974, the modules were then tested at the grade 4 level only. Evaluations showed such promising results that Indonesia implemented the system in 1976, with other countries following quickly.

Still, the Educational Innovation and Technology (INNOTECH) project was not all clear sailing and accolades, and an early incident tested IDRC's mettle about what sort of development agency it was. One of the fundamental philosophies of the Centre was to place confidence and faith in the integrity and purpose of the recipient. At the board meeting in September 1974, Zagorin noted that IDRC had experienced some difficulties with the Indonesian component of the project; the Centre's practice was not to make a second payment to the team until a project report and financial statement had been filed that accounted for the previous instalment. Although the request had been made repeatedly, the documentation was not produced until September 1974. This was worrying because, even though there was a considerable balance showing for the project, there were cost overruns on certain items and some discussion of the abuse of Centre funds. After much discussion among senior management at IDRC, Zagorin wrote a letter to the organizations concerned, which brought the project and its financial irregularities to the attention of higher authorities in Jakarta.

Project partners felt that the severity of the letter could result in IDRC being asked to leave Indonesia, to which Hopper had replied "that if this was to happen, there are still many other countries looking for funds and this will be the attitude taken with other countries who abuse Centre funds."[105] It was important early on to set the precedent. IDRC was not asked to leave the country and indeed, researchers rallied round the beleaguered project and helped it live up to its commitments. Furthermore, "some of the government officials who had acted as [paid] consultants actually returned the funds." Hopper ended his intervention to the board, noting that "The Centre cannot deal and work in good faith with recipients of resources if the recipients are not prepared to insist that they also demonstrate similar good faith in how they handle our funds and meet the commitments." While the result in this case was good, it just as easily might not have been. Clearly, the Centre was etching its line in granite across which it would not go. As a result, it enhanced its reputation among LDC researchers and among a certain cadre of officialdom as an organization of the utmost integrity devoted to the advancement of capacity building in the South.

Science and Technology Policy Instruments Project

Hopper was also keen to use Centre resources to expand program activity to include a fifth category that focused on something like science and technology (ST) as it related to the problems of small and medium-sized industries. As well, he was interested in the growth of applied sciences in low-income regions. This was the genesis of one of the first truly big IDRC undertakings, the science and technology policy instruments project (STPI), which was coordinated by the Peruvian, Francisco Sagasti, and overseen by Geoff Oldham, a British citizen who held a joint appointment at IDRC and the Science Policy Research Unit at the University of Sussex in England. Labelled by Jorge Sabato, then research professor and member of the board of directors of Argentina's Bariloche Foundation, as "one of the most interesting [projects] ever carried out," it was also, in a sense, quintessential IDRC; as

Maurice Strong had earlier noted with respect to the establishment of the Centre, "In the beginning, we started with an issue. Is the science and technology gap an important one? (and the answer was fairly quickly yes); if so, by what means can we best address that gap? ... We started out with the feeling that this gap in science and technology was a fundamental one, that not enough was being done in this area."[106] STPI attempted to address that problem through analysis, as well as exerting influence on ST policies in the South. Lasting more than three years, the project involved ten different countries in all regions of the world,[107] and was based on two principles: whenever possible, work should have relevance to more than one country, and programs should be interdisciplinary. Three assumptions were drawn out of the early exercise: (1) that LDCs were becoming increasingly determined to make their own decisions on all matters pertaining to technology and development; (2) that the ability to make good decisions depended on having both the prior capability to define the problems about which the decisions are to be taken and having access to a body of knowledge that will make it possible to predict the likely outcome of the those decisions; and (3) that social science research carried out in the South would not only help to generate that knowledge, but would also help to develop capabilities to analyze and define complex problems. STPI encapsulates many of the ideas that animated IDRC during the Hopper years and is therefore worthy of brief examination.

The idea for the project originated in February 1971 at a meeting of representatives of Latin American science policy organizations. The participants believed "a situation had been reached where many policy recommendations had been made by national experts, international organizations, and academic institutions for the development of science and technology but there was practically no information about how to put them into practice and make them work."[108] It represented a novel form of collaboration among Southern countries in the field of science and technology policy research. It was also one of the few that sought primarily to provide information and advice to policy-makers and decision makers in the participating countries. At the end, it was hoped that STPI would result in the transfer of technology among nations, the diffusion of industrial technologies within nations, and the development of a world bibliography on science policy. As Hopper put it, IDRC had come into existence at a time when support for science and technology as an ingredient of development "was an exotic item in most aid budgets."[109] It was because of Centre efforts and projects like STPI that that was less true when he left office. "The paths," he opined, "carefully opened by IDRC in its early months [were] now being slowly turned into roads."

During the summer of 1970, Hopper had asked Oldham to prepare a paper to convince him that science and technology policy should be a part of the research portfolio of the Centre. The president had said that there were the four "princesses" of IDRC, which then constituted the divisions. He also had "several toads around which were areas where there were problems but he didn't see how to get hold of them. He was waiting for a prince to come along and convert these toads into princesses."[110] He offered Oldham a month-long assignment to act the role of science and technology prince. As the toad changed shape, it was agreed that an ST policy program would be initiated, which Oldham would lead. It would not become another division but remain a program, which would feed into IDRC through SSHR.

It was an ambitious undertaking. As was pointed out, its general purpose was to gather, analyze, evaluate, and generate information that would help policy-makers, planners, and decision makers in LDCs "to specify the ways and means for orienting science and technology toward the achievement of development objectives."[111] It was believed that the project would help to: "develop indigenous capabilities in science and technology appropriate to the countries' needs; better utilize these capabilities in the productive sector and other areas of socioeconomic activity; improve the process of importing technology in such a way as to maximize its beneficial effects; and, absorb and adapt the imported technology linking it to indigenous scientific and technical activities." The project document listed a number of variables that it would focus on, which would make it possible for policy-makers concerned with applying ST to the achievement of development objectives to identify the mechanisms and instruments that were most likely to have the desired effect.

Was it successful, or merely one of the more costly of IDRC's projects? That depended in part on the perspective of the respondent. Some at the Centre believed that it was not their job to fund downstream activities—like the implementation of STPI's findings—and that investing too much in this kind of activity could jeopardize IDRC's ability to respond to proposals for other projects. That would only come years later with ideas like "closing the loop," where emphasis was placed on influencing policy-makers and turning project results into policy. However, the organizers thought it to be a tremendous success. As Sagasti wrote, "There is no adequate way of summarizing the research results obtained in the STPI project. Furthermore, some results are especially difficult to capture and convey through written reports because they are intangible, coming from the close interaction between researchers and policymakers." There were other factors at work—the increasing reluctance during a period of high unemployment and inflation among developed countries to transfer technology to the South and the increasing differentiation among LDCs, with a few, like South Korea, beginning to emerge as intermediate industrial powers. STPI, its fathers firmly maintained, was an action-oriented research project that aimed at reducing uncertainties in ST policy-making through improved information.

The project report was absolutely correct in pointing out that the next few years would see the rise of science and technology as the key determinants of relations between industrialized countries and LDCs. Because of that, it was important to learn more about the social conditions that led to their development. STPI was an attempt in that direction, linking policy-makers and researchers, and paying attention to the dictum expressed by Francis Bacon four hundred years earlier: *Nam et ipsa scientia potestas est*— knowledge in itself is the source of power. STPI's value lay in pointing a way to further research efforts, and perhaps also to the United Nations Conference on Science and Technology Development (UNCSTD), held in August 1979 in Vienna. While this event falls outside of Hopper's tenure, it presents a continuity with the Hopper-encouraged project and so will be briefly addressed here.

The Centre, together with the Canadian Ministry of State for Science and Technology, financed an elaborate study, carried out by the Association of Scientists and Engineers of Canada (SCITEC) jointly with the Royal Society of Canada, to identify the potential contribution of the Canadian community to ST for development. David Steedman, the new director of SSHR following Zagorin's 1978 departure, had suggested that the question should not be simply "what technology" for Southern countries, but the more fundamental issue of "technology for what?"[112] It was also important that the questions be asked in the appropriate order so that governments might not only enquire about "know-how," but "know-why" as well. IDRC had urged the Association Canadien-Français pour l'avancement des Sciences to host a day-long symposium on the transfer of technology in relation to international development, which was held in May 1978. Attended by 250 Canadian scientists, technologists, development economists, administrators, and policy-makers, and more than thirty representatives from LDCs, it resulted in what might be termed the first IDRC history, edited by David Spurgeon, the director of communications—*Give Us the Tools: Science and Technology for Development*.[113] The proceedings were edited by King Gordon in *Science and Technology for Development: Proceedings of a Symposium Held at the Ontario Science Centre* and featured the likes of Geoff Oldham, Rex Nettleford, the National Research Council's Omond Solandt, and Tuzo Wilson. As Gordon noted in his introduction, "It was natural that IDRC should display a keen interest in the plans for the UNCSTD meeting, the goals of which appeared to correspond so closely to its own. Here was an initiative that might harness more effectively the world's scientific and technological resources to meet the needs of the majority of the world's people."[114]

In a very real sense, the key IDRC role in the organizational mechanics of the UN conference was the payoff for STPI. Indeed, at the special request of the UN Secretariat, the Centre seconded Sagasti and Emile Sahana to help synthesize the national and regional papers for the plan of action presented at UNCSTD even though, as Louis Berlinguet, the IDRC's senior vice-president, told the board at its October meeting, the conference was expected to fail "like many of the other confrontations between North and South."[115] That it did not surprised most, providing "some proof that there could be a few bridges established between North and South." The negotiations would continue throughout 1980.

Conclusion

The Hopper years were very successful ones at IDRC as the organization got off on a sound footing. Researchers were supported and projects were funded that in many cases were groundbreaking and innovative. Hopper's implementation strategy for IDRC was designed to satisfy two goals: the establishment of the Centre in a manner that would preserve its unique character relative to its Act, and the buildup of credibility among LDCs and within the international development community.[116] The president put it best when describing the phenomenon to the board in 1975:

> The Centre began with what I am going to call a smorgasbord approach. What we did essentially was to put out some dishes and said those were the ones that we working on and asked the developing country researchers to indicate to us what their choices would be from the smorgasbord.... And we have tailored the dishes very much to the priorities expressed to us by the developing countries. It is not merely because some researcher in a developing country would like to undertake certain work that we would support it. It would have to be quite clear that the additional knowledge to come from this research would have to add substantially to what is already a large body of investigations and to our understanding of how to conduct better research. We have no model of development that we seek to impose; we have no model that we insist the research pattern adapt itself to; but we do hold the right to lay out certain dishes on smorgasbord and not others.[117]

This was a unique approach, to say nothing of the language in the quote above, in approaching international development in the 1970s. Even the

Treasury Board Secretariat, much to its own surprise it seemed, had to agree: "From a client point of view the concept of promoting indigenous self-reliance and cooperation have proven to be viable. Several developed countries have studied the IDRC concept and structure as the 'ideal' research support model and US Congress representatives are currently considering the IDRC experience for possible application to the USAID program." Its "great stroke of genius," as one governor was to remark almost a quarter-century later, "was to be a problem-focused organization, to work where the problems are, and to listen and help Southerners to identify and research their own problems."[118] By 1977 IDRC punched, as the old adage has it, above its weight in the international arena, exerting an influence on, for example, the Ford Foundation, which added non-Americans to its board, while the Australian Agricultural Centre was structurally affected by its operations, and the Swedish Department for Research Cooperation (SAREC) was constructed on the IDRC model.

Indeed, from the beginning, IDRC philosophy had focused on the support of direct funding for LDC scientists. In 1970, that approach had broken new ground. Other agencies funding ST for development had provided support coupled with external technical assistance, and often only for research problems that met donor agency priorities. By the end of Hopper's tenure, the Centre's philosophy was shared by some other donors. It was perceived as an organization with integrity, as well as one that was extraordinarily sympathetic and empathetic with the South. IDRC consciously rejected the notion of research imperialism, putting the onus on LDC researchers and institutions to develop and articulate projects. That was a fundamental part of the Centre's uniqueness. But perhaps most importantly from a government perspective, the Centre seemed to be good value for the money. One reason for that, the Treasury Board Secretariat suggested, was "the quality of [its] staff [which] unquestionably contributed to its high state of efficiency."

The early days were also "'passionate and hot' and hardly bureaucratic at all," as John Woolston remembered. Program officers (POs) had an immense amount of freedom to go out and investigate what could be done in co-operation with Southern researchers. While there was accountability to both the board and senior management, they were also very much on their own. POs were not unlike early pilots—they flew "by the seat of their pants."[119] Roving program officers also contributed to the betterment of IDRC—if they saw something innovative and interesting in one place, they would tell of it in another. They were sometimes compared with "wandering minstrels from the Middle Ages," travelling from country to country, singing about what they had seen elsewhere. Woolston thought that "the IDRC wandering minstrels were quite effective in bringing people up to date and alerting them as to possibilities." That did not mean, however, that the Centre could rest on its laurels. As wandering minstrels eventually saw their employment wither by new methods of communication and entertainment, so IDRC would have to work hard to stay ahead. Moreover, there were a number of unsettling issues appearing on the horizon. One, pointed out by the Treasury Board Secretariat, cautioned new management to protect the Centre against "the normal tendencies towards stagnation and insularity as the organization reaches maturity."

Moreover, there were very serious macro issues in the international arena, which will be raised in Chapter 3. Suffice it to say here that some on the board, and especially Pierre Bauchet, scientific director of the French National Centre for Scientific Research, thought IDRC had to evolve in order to stay current. He had asked the board to consider a more global view of development problems, especially those problems vital to the economic future of LDCs—trade, commodity prices, global inflation, transfers of technology, private and public capital movements, and forms and amounts of assistance— all areas that were terra incognita to the Centre. As his intervention during the September 1975 board meeting was welcomed, it was also rejected. Hopper maintained that "the plight of low-income nations may be eased somewhat by the workings of international negotiation, but lasting development for today's poor countries depends fundamentally not on an easing of circumstances, however welcome, but on the transforming of traditional economies and societies from a technological base of lore and folk practice to one of applied science, social and physical and natural. [The task] demands a micro focus."[120]

Ivan Head, the incoming president of IDRC, was a relative unknown in development circles, being better known as an international lawyer and Trudeau's foreign policy adviser. His new job was a consolation prize of sorts, or so it was interpreted by some; Robert Bothwell has written that international development was not Head's strong suit. He was awarded the job because of his relationship with Prime Minister Pierre Trudeau, but also, perhaps more importantly, because he was perceived as a foreign policy competitor by the new minister of external affairs, Allan MacEachen. In short, MacEachen, as he assumed his new office, "was not prepared to tolerate the continuation of Ivan Head as Trudeau's foreign policy adviser. Head must go, and he did, leaving for the position of president of … the International Development Research Centre."[121] Treasury Board Secretariat also put into words what many at the Centre feared: Head was a "pragmatist" who would, in all likelihood, support the need for a domestic IDRC role based on mutual benefit, whatever that meant. For Centre officials, that was not part of their swashbuckling, devil-may-care self-image, but the Treasury Board offered a different reality to the one most employees liked to think about: "IDRC appropriations are an integral component of ODA; IDRC is internationally recognized as a Canadian organization; IDRC has become totally dependent on the Canadian government for unrestricted funding, and; the interests of the Canadian government are taken into consideration by the Centre in some cases." Further, linkages with CIDA were required, or so the Treasury Board thought, as well as with Canadian universities. And in the final analysis, another micromanager of Centre affairs, as Hopper had been, would have been the worst thing possible.

The Treasury Board Secretariat had also zeroed in on the fact that an official directive policy did not exist, and that the Centre instead relied on the eleven principles that Hopper had articulated at the Bogota board meeting. Accordingly, "one of the most important tasks of the new Board and Chief Executive Officer will be to establish a comprehensive set of policy directives."[122] That would perhaps not be good for an organization that prided itself on its ability to go anywhere and do anything within its remit. Concrete policies would not necessarily serve its purposes well. The list of Treasury Board recommendations was long and would, if implemented, significantly change the method of IDRC operations, so many employees thought.

However, Hopper had come around to a slightly different point of view about interagency co-operation, between IDRC and the more official elements of Canadian foreign policy. In mid-1975 he had told Centre staff that they "must bear in mind that [it] is a Canadian institution, established by the Parliament of Canada and derives its financial support from the Canadian government, which also appoints the individual members of our board of governors."[123] His position was a retreat from the one articulated in 1970 as he set about building IDRC without a template to consult. By mid-decade, in what had turned out to be a terrible global economic situation, Centre officers should now make an effort to inform the heads of Canadian missions in the countries that they visited of their trip as much in advance as possible. Furthermore, Canadian offices in those cities where UN agencies maintained representatives focused on aid issues, as well as those operating where the Organisation for Economic Co-operation and Development maintained a presence, should be kept informed of IDRC business. The memorandum was full of phrases like "courtesy calls," "notification," "copies of correspondence sent to," "notify the Aid and Development division of the department of external affairs," and so it went. There was a new reality in Ottawa by 1975, one that was not necessarily conducive to the kind of work the Centre did. Hopper ended the memorandum, noting that "With good will, tactful discretion and a flexible approach, we should be able to develop a fruitful pattern of relationship with all concerned."

There was some nervousness as the Centre's founding father and guiding light departed the scene. Certainly, a large part of that was caused by Hopper's departure, but some was also undoubtedly provoked by the plunge in IDRC's budget allocation—from the CAN$35 million anticipated for 1976 to the CAN$29.7 million that was actually allocated, given the government's austerity program, to be discussed in Chapter 3. And while the budget for 1977 had been provided (at CAN$35.5 million), the Centre, as most other agencies in Ottawa dependent on Canadian government coin, was picking its way carefully through the minefield. Staffing levels would not necessarily reflect the increased amount. Those two items—the budget cut and the president's departure—were almost inconceivable for that early staff. Ivan Head was an unknown quantity with very close ties to the political establishment. The Treasury Board Secretariat, while acknowledging that IDRC was a well-run and effective organization, had a long list of suggested changes, some of which went to the heart of its being. Eight new governors would be appointed as Head assumed office, also reducing the continuity from times past. How all this would figure into continuing operations was a mystery. Crossing one's fingers and hoping for the best did not seem a particularly appropriate response, but what else was left?

Notes

1   Rene Wadlow review of Ramesh Thakur, Andrew Cooper, John English (eds.), *International Commissions and the Power of Ideas* (Tokyo: United Nations University Press, 2005). The non-aligned movement in the United Nations, encouraged by the impact of the Organization of Petroleum Exporting Countries, had tried to create a new international economic order. The effort failed, beaten back by the US and the UK, which slowed down and then destroyed all possibilities of discussion within the UN, but proposed no alternatives. The failure of the NIEO negotiations left a legacy of bitterness among the non-aligned, which came to believe that the rich states were interested in neither development nor social justice. Accessed at www.transnational-perspectives.org/transnational/articles/article301.pdf. See also John Toye and Richard Toye, *The UN and Global Political Economy: Trade, Finance, and Development* (Bloomington: Indiana University Press, 2004), 4. As they note, "the North–South dialogue was effectively dead by 1981.... The global political and ideological climate, partly in reaction to the South's demands for a NIEO but partly as a result of the Latin American debt crisis, underwent a major transformation thereafter."
2   DRC–A, "Statement Made by the President, IDRC, to the Board of Governors of the IDRC, March 14–15, 1976," Mexico City.

3   Library and Archives Canada, Treasury Board Records (RG 55), Accession 90-91/164, Box 31, file 8068-03, "Evaluation of the International Development Research Centre—Documentation of Phase I—General Review," Program Branch, Treasury Board Secretariat, 30 October 1978; emphasis not in original. See also Gerry Helleiner, unpublished memoir, "IDRC Again and Again." Indicative of this sort of attitude, Helleiner has written "During the period of IDRC's creation I was invited to a lively international meeting (at Château Montebello) at which ideas were exchanged as to what exactly it should do and I had an opportunity to meet him. As one of my international friends there put it: 'You Canadians are very funny people. You set up a wonderful and innovative new Canadian institution. Then you appoint such an *American* sort of person to run it.'"

4   Interview with James Pfeiffer by Joe Hulse, 14 June 1988.

5   IDRC–A, Interview with Geoffrey Oldham, 23 July 2002, as quoted in Tahira Gonsalves and Stephen Baranyi, "Research for Policy Influence: A History of IDRC," January 2003, 7.

6   IDRC–A, Interview with Michael Brandreth by Joe Hulse, 18 March 1988.

7   Of course, this was not the case with all board members. For example, Louis Berlinguet would surely have had an intense interest in the affairs of his province.

8   Interview with Tony Price by Joe Hulse, 8 February 1988.

9   See "Statement to the Inaugural Meeting of the Board of Governors of the International Development Research Centre, 26 October 1970, accessed at https://idlbnc.idrc.ca/dspace/bitstream/123456789/2215/1/Hopper18.pdf. Much of the ensuing discussion comes from this document.

10   IDRC–A, William Found, "Participatory Research and Development: An Assessment of IDRC's Experience and Prospects," Evaluation no. 295, 30 June 1995, 1. In his evaluation, Found points out that the World Bank came around to the merits of participatory research by the mid-1990s. CIDA produced a study of the advantages of PR in 1994. It is not, however, suitable in all cases of development.

11   IDRC–A, "Canadian Broadcasting Corporation, International Service, Round Table Discussion with members of the IDRC following the conclusion of the first board of governors meeting, held in Ottawa, October 26–28, 1970."

12   IDRC–A, Minutes of Board Meetings, Fourth Meeting, March 1972.

13   Interview with David Hopper, Washington, DC, by Joe Hulse, 5 January 1988.

14   Hopper interview. Hopper also claimed that the first board was "pretty savvy about what was relevant and what was not."

15   IDRC–A, Karen Spierkel to SMC, 7 October 1993. See Decima Research Report to the International Development Research Centre, "Elite Interview Study on Development Assistance," October 1993. Fifty-five elite interviews were conducted by Decima Research with selected members of Canada's wider development community. The sample contained fifteen representatives of NGOs, six from national associations, ten academics, eight from the print and electronic media, nine from government, and seven from the private sector. Each interview took about forty-five minutes.

16   *Annual Report, 1970–1971* (Ottawa: IDRC, 1971), 7.

17   IDRC–A, IDRC, "News Conference—Oct. 28, 1970."

18   IDRC–A, Rex Nettleford to Joseph Hulse, 29 December 1987. Hopper interview.

19   IDRC–A, file: 4402-1, Hopper, W.D., Addresses/Writings, vol. 2, Speech delivered to Society of Industrial Accountants of Canada by David Hopper, "Canada and International Development," June 1970.

20 IDRC–A, "Statement Made by the President, IDRC, to the Board of Governors of the International Development Research Centre, 14–15 March 1976," Mexico City.

21 William Clark, "Preface," in Sir John Cockcroft, *Technology for Developing Countries* (London: Overseas Development Institute, 1966).

22 IDRC–A, Interview with Andrew Brown by Joe Hulse, 4 January 1988.

23 The four were: (1) the International Rice Research Institute (IRRI) at Los Baños, Philippines, which dated from 1960; (2) the Centro Internacional de Mejoramiento de Maíz y Trigo (CIMMYT), set up in Mexico in 1966 but emerging out of an initiative that had been under way between Mexico City and Rockefeller since 1943; (3) the Centro Internacional de Agricultura Tropical (CIAT), established in 1967 in Palmira, Colombia; and (4) the International Institute of Tropical Agriculture (IITA), also formed in 1967 in Ibadan, Oyo State, Nigeria.

24 Interview with Maurice Strong, 10 May 2006.

25 DRC–A, Board of Governors (B of G) Notes, (14) 3/77, p. 63.

26 IDRC–A, Barry Nestel to Hulse, 24 March 1988.

27 Peter Stockdale, "Pearsonian Internationalism in Practice: The International Development Research Centre," unpublished Ph.D. thesis, McGill University, 1995, 174.

28 Interview with Geoffrey Oldham, Seaforth, England, May 2006.

29 IDRC–A, IDRC, "News Conference—Oct. 28, 1970."

30 Interview with Paul McConnell, Ottawa, 22 December 2008.

31 IDRC, *Annual Report, 1970–1971* (Ottawa: IDRC, 1971), 9.

32 IDRC–A, Meeting of the Board, March 1973.

33 AGRIS is the international information system for the agricultural sciences and technology. It was created by the Food and Agriculture Organization of the United Nations (FAO) in 1974 to facilitate information exchange and to bring together world literature dealing with all aspects of agriculture. AGRIS is a co-operative system in which participating countries input references to the literature produced within their boundaries and, in return, draw on the information provided by the other participants. For further information, see http://www.fao.org/AGRIS/. See also "FAO in Action, 30/09/80," *Ceres*, vol. 13, no. 5, September–October 1980, 12. The publication notes that AGRIS "is increasingly reflecting its nature as a decentralized partnership between developed and developing countries. All told, 40 languages are now represented in the AGRIS input, and although last year nearly half the documents processed were in English, that represented a very sharp drop from the previous year when nearly two-thirds of all documents were in English."

34 IDRC–A, B of G Notes (15) 9/77, 36.

35 IDRC–A, "Statement Made by the President, IDRC, to the Board of Governors of the International Development Research Centre, March 14–15, 1976," Mexico City.

36 Canada, Standing Senate Committee on External Affairs, First Session, 33rd Parliament, Issue no. 10, 29 April 1986.

37 Canada, *Minutes of Proceedings and Evidence of the Standing Committee on External Affairs and National Defence*, Issue no. 25, 28 May 1985, 25:6.

38 Oldham interview. As he recalls, Hulse intensely disapproved of Zagorin's marriage to Hopper while she remained a director. Further, during senior management meetings, "Ruth would come in and critique Joe's projects quite strenuously. But on one occasion, Joe came in and critiqued one of her projects very strongly, and the president jumped down his throat. For Hulse, this demonstrated the inappropriateness of having Ruth there as a director and he vowed that he would have nothing more to do with that division." Only after Zagorin departed IDRC in early 1978 did co-operation between the two divisions become more of a possibility.

39   Interview with Maurice Strong, 10 May 2006.
40   IDRC–A, Interview with Vijay Pande by Joe Hulse, 18 May 1988.
41   IDRC–A, Soedjatmoko to Hulse, 18 December 1987. See also IDRC–A, Sixth Board Meeting, March 1973. Irving Brecher, a Canadian board member and director of McGill University's Centre for Developing Area Studies, noted at the March 1973 meeting that he had "the impression the Centre may be underestimating the importance of the social sciences in developing countries."
42   IDRC–A, "The Origins of the IDRC: A Personal View by C.H.G. Oldham," n.d.
43   Swaminathan interview, 10 December 2006, Chennai, India.
44   IDRC–A, Tenth Board Meeting.
45   IDRC–A, Interview with Hugh Doggett by Joe Hulse, 30 August 1988.
46   For the full account of the meeting, see http://www.ilri.org/InfoServ/Webpub/ Fulldocs/X5536e/x5536e02.htm.
47   It is interesting to note that Ruth Zagorin, who in 1975 became Hopper's wife, did not subscribe to the notion that ROs were an advantage. As she later noted, "Decentralization was not the answer. The issues are not regional, they are global. If an agency like IDRC did not take advantage of the learning across regions, it wasn't maximizing its resources."
48   Interview with Prod Laquian, Vancouver, 17 May 2006.
49   Hopper interview.
50   IDRC–A, Interview with Fernando Chaparro, 18 May 1988.
51   Price interview.
52   IDRC–A, Treasury Board Secretariat, Program Branch, "Evaluation of the International Development Research Centre, Phase One," 30 October 1978.
53   IDRC–A, Meeting of the Board, "President's Statement to the Board," 20–21 September 1971.
54   Barry Nestel, Jingjai Hanchanlash, and Henrique Toño, A, Conclusions, (A), 1.1, IDRC Project Networks, Office of the Vice-President, Planning, August 1980, IDRC Library.
55   Interview with David Hopper, Washington, DC, by Joe Hulse, 5 January 1988.
56   Hopper interview.
57   IDRC–A, Jingjai to Irene McCullough, 25 March 1988.
58   The number of days on the road per year for IDRC program officers often reached staggering counts. At times, two hundred days per year were spent away from home! The subject of overwork because of days on the road came up periodically at board meetings during the 1970s, especially as IDRC lost good people as they burned out. In one instance, Brian Davy, an early hire by IDRC, recalled during one year he spent 228 days on the road. Interview with Brian Davy, Ottawa, 13 August 2008.
59   For further information on Technonet, see http://idlbnc.idrc.ca/dspace/handle/ 123456789/741.
60   IDRC–A, Interview with Michael Brandreth by Joe Hulse, 18 March 1988.
61   For more information on Technonet, see http://www.technonet.org.sg/taprof.htm.
62   A similar situation occurred with the African Economic Research Consortium (AERC), modelled on IDRC.
63   Zagorin interview.
64   IDRC–A, Minutes of Board Meeting, March 1972, Hopper as quoted in Toronto *Globe and Mail*, 12 January 1972, 10.
65   Zagorin interview.
66   René Cortazar is minister of transportation and communication in the Chilean government. Between 1990 and 1994 he was minister of labour and later executive

director of Televisión National de Chile. Danilo Astori was minister of finance in Uruguay and is now vice-president. Rashad Cassim is deputy director general, economic statistics in statistics, South Africa. M.V. Rajasekharan is minister of state for planning in the Indian federal government. IDRC has recently (2008) completed a study of former research award holders or scholarship recipients who have made a significant contribution to politics or academe. The list does indeed extend to hundreds of names.

67 See Robin Gendron, *Towards a Francophone Community: Canada's Relations with France and French Africa, 1945–1968* (Montreal and Kingston: McGill-Queen's University Press, 2006). See also J.F. Bosher, *The Gaullist Attack on Canada, 1967–1997* (Montreal and Kingston: McGill-Queen's University Press, 1999).

68 IDRC–A, Minutes of Board Meeting, March 1972.

69 IDRC–A, Hopper to Vice Presidents/Program Directors, "Cancellation of Visits to Côte d'Ivoire," 30 November 1975.

70 IDRC–A, Interview with Gerry Bourrier by Joe Hulse, 4 January 1988. Bourrier occupied a number of positions at IDRC over his twenty-five years of service, including regional director, West and Central Africa; director, fellowships and awards division; director, human resources division; and deputy director, agriculture, food, and nutrition sciences division.

71 Interview with Prodocio Laquian, Vancouver, 25 April 2006.

72 Interview with Gerry Bourrier, 15 August 2008, Ottawa.

73 Hopper interview.

74 Interview with Andrew Barnett, Sussex, England, 12 May 2006.

75 There was an interesting exchange between IDRC personnel and George Beaton, professor and chair of the Department of Nutrition at the University of Toronto, which went on for some months with respect to this topic. For the exchange, see Library and Archives Canada, Department of External Affairs Records (RG25), Series N5, vol. 18, file: IDRC Jan. 1972–Mar. 1973, Beaton to Ferguson, 5 May 1972 up until Hopper to Beaton, 29 September 1972.

76 IDRC–A, Meeting of the Board of Governors, "President's Statement to the Board," Third Meeting, 20–21 September 1971.

77 IDRC–A, "Statement of the President," Fourth Board Meeting, March 1972.

78 IDRC–A, David Hopper, "Research Policy: Eleven Issues," IDRC-014e.

79 This section comes from IDRC–A, David Hopper, "Research Policy: Eleven Issues," IDRC-014e.

80 Library and Archives Canada, Treasury Board Records (RG55), Accession 90-91/164, Box 31, file: 8068-03, Program Branch, Treasury Board Secretariat, "Evaluation of the International Development Research Centre: Documentation of Phase One— General Review," 20 October 1978.

81 IDRC–A, Sixth Board Meeting, March 1973. The following paragraphs are based on the minutes of this board meeting, where the paper proposing the policies was considered. In terms of budget growth, IDRC had indicated to the government that it would request grants at the level of:

	Current CAN$	
1972–73	$8 million	
1973–74	$14 million	+75 percent growth
1974–75	$20 million	+43 percent growth
1975–76	$27 million	+35 percent growth
1976–77	$34 million	+26 percent growth
1977–78	$41 million	+21 percent growth

82 Interview with Ruth Zagorin, Washington, DC, by Joe Hulse, 5 January 1988.
83 IDRC–A, Interview with Joe Hulse, 17 May 1988.
84 IDRC–A, Interview with David Hopper.
85 IDRC–A, "AFNS," n.d.
86 IDRC–A, Interview with Joe Hulse, 17 May 1988.
87 Interview with Gerry Bourrier, 16 August 2008.
88 "Man-Made Cereal Finally Gaining Recognition," *Ceres*, vol. 13, no. 5, September–October 1980, 4.
89 IDRC–A, IDRC, "News Conference—Oct. 28, 1970."
90 Interview with Joe Hulse, 17 May 1988.
91 United Nations, *Report of the World Food Conference Rome 5–16 November 1974*, New York, 1975, accessed at FAORLC-41001 World Food Conference.
92 IDRC–A, David Hopper, "Message to Governors," 27 January 1975.
93 David A. Grimes, Janie Benson, Susheela Singh, Mariana Romero, Bela Ganatra, Friday E. Okonofua, Iqbal H. Shah, "Unsafe Abortion: The Preventable Pandemic," *Sexual and Reproductive Health* 4, World Health Organization, 1, accessed at http://www.who.int/reproductivehealth/topics/unsafe_abortion/article_unsafe_abortion.pdf.
94 Geoffrey York, "Maternal Mortality: Why It's a Crisis," *Globe and Mail*, 29 January 2010, accessed at http://www.theglobeandmail.com/news/world/maternal-mortality-why-its-a-crisis/article1449826/. Similarly, unsafe abortions for women who did not want to carry a baby to term are also debilitating. They remain one of the leading causes of maternal mortality in developing nations. According to the WHO, nearly 70,000 women worldwide die from unsafe abortions annually, and millions more are injured, many permanently.
95 Interview with William Jeannes.
96 International Conference on Primary Health Care, Alma-Ata, USSR, 6–12 September 1978, "Declaration of Alma-Ata," accessed at http://www.who.int/hpr/NPH/docs/declaration_almaata.pdf. The article dealing with primary health care read: "Primary health care is essential health care based on practical, scientifically sound and socially acceptable methods and technology made universally accessible to individuals and families in the community through their full participation and at a cost that the community and country can afford to maintain at every stage of their development in the spirit of self-reliance and self-determination. It forms an integral part both of the country's health system, of which it is the central function and main focus, and of the overall social and economic development of the community. It is the first level of contact of individuals, the family and community with the national health system bringing health care as close as possible to where people live and work, and constitutes the first element of a continuing health care process."
97 IDRC–A, Meeting of the Board of Governors, B of G Notes (22) 3/80, 16.
98 Nor did the questioning end in 1983. Christine Stewart, the Liberal member of Parliament for Northumberland, appointed secretary of state for African and Latin American Affairs in 1993, officially enquired as to the IDRC's involvement in 1993.
99 IDRC–A, IDRC, First Meeting of the Board, 26–28 October 1970. His colleague, René Dubos, objected, saying that "before education becomes the primary development emphasis, the problems of protein and calorie malnutrition must be solved."
100 Patricia Bell, "Education: A Policy for Serving the Most Children," *IDRC Reports*,
101 IDRC–A, "Development Research: Issues and Possible Future Directions for IDRC," Evaluation no. 65, December 1983, 13–14.
102 IDRC–A, Interview with Joe Hulse, 17 May 1988.

103 This paragraph largely comes from Karen Mundy, "Canada's Response to the 'Education for All' Initiative," *NORAAG News*, NN19.

104 See IDRC, *Projects in Indonesia*, "Delivery System for Mass Primary Education," 1977, accessed at http://www.crdi.ca/en/ev-83016-201_720122-1-IDRC_ADM_INFO.html.

105 IDRC–A, Board Meeting Minutes, September 1974.

106 David Spurgeon (ed.), *Give Us the Tools: Science and Technology for Development* (Ottawa: IDRC, 1979), 11.

107 The ten were Argentina, Brazil, Colombia, Egypt, India, Mexico, Peru, South Korea, Venezuela, and the Yugoslavian province of Macedonia.

108 Francisco Sagasti, *Science and Technology for Development: Main Comparative Report of the Science and Technology Policy Instruments Project* (Ottawa: IDRC, 1978), 25.

109 Interview with David Hopper, Washington, DC, by Joe Hulse, 5 January 1988.

110 IDRC–A, "The Origins of the IDRC."

111 IDRC, *The Science and Technology Policy Instruments Project*, IDRC–050e, 1975, 7. Interestingly, there is a 2008 paper produced by a researcher for the Indian Council for Research on International Economic Relations (ICRIER) that deals with similar material by Saradindu Bhaduri and Janashruti Chandra, "Informal Values and Formal Policies: A Study of Japanese Technology Policy and Significance for India," ICRIER Working Paper no. 219.

112 IDRC–A, file: B of G Notes (20) 3/79, Meeting of the Board, 1 March 1979, 12.

113 *Give Us the Tools: Science and Technology for Development* (Ottawa: IDRC, 1979).

114 See J. King Gordon, *Science and Technology for Development: Proceedings of a Symposium Held at the Ontario Science Centre* (Ottawa: IDRC, 1979).

115 IDRC–A, Meeting of the Board, October 1979.

116 IDRC–A, Treasury Board Secretariat, Program Branch, "Evaluation of the International Development Research Centre, Phase One," 30 October 1978.

117 IDRC–A, President's Statement to the Board, March 1975.

118 IDRC–A, BOG 2006 (06) 07, Lauchlan Munro to Board, 24 May 2006, 17. Here Munro is quoting a governor from an October 2003 meeting of the board.

119 Woolston interview.

120 IDRC–A, "Statement Made by the President, IDRC …"

121 Robert Bothwell, *Alliance and Illusion: Canada and the World, 1945–1984* (Vancouver: UBC Press, 2007), 376.

122 IDRC–A, Treasury Board Secretariat, Program Branch, "Evaluation of the International Development Research Centre, Phase One," 30 October 1978.

123 IDRC–A, David Hopper, "Relations of Officers and Professional Staff of IDRC with Canadian Government Representatives and Diplomatic Missions abroad," 11 April 1975.

Chapter 3

IVAN HEAD AT THE HELM, PART I, 1978–83: IDRC IN HIGH GEAR: PROJECTS, PLANS, AND OPERATIONS

We in the developing world need more IDRCs.
—Vinyu Vichit-Vadakan, UN Asian
Development Institute

Despite the IDRC staff's anxieties about the departure of the only president the Centre had known and the arrival of a new one, Ivan Head, as of 13 March 1978, it remained, by and large, unchanged during his tenure. Indeed, apart from certain administrative changes, David Hopper would have recognized the essential structure and IDRC's intellectual underpinnings when Head retired in 1991. Allan Gotleib, then sitting on IDRC's board but also the undersecretary of state for external affairs, highlighted this at a board meeting in late 1980 following the president's statement to the board, summarizing his conception of events: after considering the Centre's trajectory over the eighteen months since Head's appointment, it appeared to him "that the basic areas of concentration of research efforts [over the next years] will probably be in areas that were similar to these past ten years."[1]

Most fundamentally, for example, as has been seen in Chapter 2, Hopper's Centre had consciously turned its focus to the welfare of peoples living in the rural areas of developing countries. In Head's Centre, that emphasis would remain; the 1980 Brandt Commission report, *North-South: A Program for Survival*, had observed that "mass poverty remains overwhelmingly a rural affliction, and it is rural poverty that seems so harshly intractable. The mass urban poverty of Kinshasa, Mexico City or Cairo is a relatively modern phenomenon. For all its squalor, it is one step up from rural deprivation. To some extent, that is why these cities have grown. But the poor in India, Bangladesh, Indonesia and nearly all of Africa are still, to the extent of 70 percent or more of the total population, in rural villages."[2] That reflected the IDRC rationale well and argued for the continuing investment in increasing food production, research that would lead to the provision of adequate health care, water supply and sanitation facilities, education, and renewable resources.

As well, IDRC would continue to cultivate research networks. By the mid-1980s, the Centre was supporting more than three hundred, which took an enormous amount of time, energy, and resources. It also emphasized practical, action research, and remained reluctant to support research activities unless there was some sort of payoff in terms of application; indeed, this became a greater priority for both board members and senior management over the 1980s, and its consideration would take much more time. As will be discussed below, John Hardie, then in the Office of Program Evaluations (OPE), submitted a paper for board consideration in early 1982 that called for what he and his team had labelled affirmative action. Its fundamental point was that policy-makers should be included in project development rather than after the fact in order to make the results more palatable and perhaps useful to that community. However, that was difficult and required constant work; in *With Our Own Hands*, a compendium of articles on IDRC funding successes, published in 1979, some of the contributors examined the difficulties of achieving policy influence through the sort of research that the Centre usually supported.

IDRC philosophy remained largely unaltered—a commitment to fund research in the South, undertaken by Southern researchers, that was designed to ameliorate the condition of life in developing countries. The intent of that support was to allow less developed countries (LDCs) to be better able to walk in partnership with the more economically and technologically advanced North through the enhancement of their capabilities. Head was keen to carry on where his predecessor had left off, albeit with a nod to Canada's political realities through the incorporation of some Canadian content into a few Centre projects. This was impressed on him by the context in which his institution operated; greater sensitivity was now demanded. That imperative found expression in the establishment of the Cooperative Programs Unit (CPU) in 1981, an innovation that encouraged and supported projects linking Canadian researchers with those from developing countries.

Head was an inspired choice as president—thoughtful, diplomatic, and possessed of a skill set appropriate to IDRC's stage of development. He had also worked, albeit very briefly, in Canada's Department of External Affairs, being posted to Kuala Lumpur, Malaysia, for a few years in the early 1960s. As well, he was a lawyer, having graduated from the University of Alberta's law school in 1952; he had received a master's of law from Harvard eight years later. He had returned to the U of A and was made full professor in the law school by 1967, the same year that he became associate counsel to then-Minister of Justice Pierre Trudeau for constitutional matters. When Trudeau became prime minister the following year, Head had gone along, becoming his legal assistant; in 1970, he had been appointed as special assistant, with responsibility for foreign policy. Neither technocrat nor scientist as Hopper had been, he was also not a politician, although closely associated with politics, and the Liberal Party in particular. While the Liberals remained in power, that was a good linkage. However, even when the Progressive Conservatives under Brian Mulroney took over in 1984, IDRC did not suffer unduly largely because of the activities and sensibilities of Joe Clark, as well as the prime minister; both were Red Tories with social consciences.[3] Further, John Hardie has speculated that Head and Clark were both Albertans and lawyers, and the president made sure that the minister knew what he was about.[4] Head also worked both sides of the street assiduously, and it paid off for the organization, and that was his strength. Unlike Hopper, who was a micromanager in the sense that he was consumed with project detail and would spend much time critiquing them if given the chance, the new president was not.

Head's thirteen years at IDRC were successful, although there was some turbulence along the way; of most importance, its parliamentary appropriation increased from CAN$36.9 million to CAN$114.1 million, a significant hike even given the ravages of inflation during the period and the much less propitious climate in which to pursue a development agenda. Stagflation, inflation, interest rates that hit 22 percent, budget deficits, rocketing unemployment, and federal-provincial discord all sapped Canadians' will. Still, it appeared that he was the perfect choice for IDRC in 1978. An argument can be made that, had Hopper remained, the Centre would have evolved very differently and, in all likelihood, not to its benefit. He had prided himself on his "maverick" status and had rejected the necessity of cultivating relationships among Ottawa's political and bureaucratic elite, which, by the later 1970s, was a necessity. Why was that?

The Parti Québécois, dedicated to Quebec's independence, was elected to office in November 1976 and the reverberations were felt throughout the country, exacerbated by the first referendum on separation, held in 1980. Prime Minister Pierre Trudeau was now focused on defeating the separatist threat, almost to the exclusion of former priorities. Nor were Canadians optimistic on the economic front; they had taken a beating over the previous half-decade and their governments were in a state of shock. This was a new situation and innovative ideas were significant by their absence. In a sense, the best Canadians could come up with was to kick Trudeau from office as of 4 June 1979 and replace him with a minority government headed by the Progressive Conservative, Joe Clark, at least until another election removed him from office and re-elected Trudeau on 3 March 1980. Price and wage controls, overseen by Beryl Plumptre, head of the Anti-Inflation Board (AIB), had been introduced in 1975 by the *Anti-Inflation Act*, a sure sign of economic desperation, only to be removed in 1979, an indication of economic uncertainty. Inflation had soared to almost 11 percent by mid-decade, which had undermined the country's economy and its ability to compete internationally. Unemployment also rose steadily over the later 1970s and into the next decade, approaching 13 percent in December 1982, the highest rate experienced since the Great Depression of the 1930s. This phenomenon—high inflation and high unemployment—thought to be impossible in Keynesian economic theory, led to the coining of the word "stagflation." Government retrenched with tighter fiscal and monetary policies, and ran ever higher deficits as optimistic revenue collection projections failed to materialize; by 1993, the country's debt would reach a staggering CAN$550 billion, roughly 75 percent of Canada's gross national product, a clearly unsustainable level.

The deteriorating economic situation was made worse by another oil shock that hit in 1979. The entire Western world slipped into recession. It also provoked enormous tension between the federal government and Alberta as Ottawa passed the National Energy Program, which was designed, among other things, to subsidize Eastern consumers at the expense of Alberta producers, leading to Western outrage and bumper stickers with the slogan "Let Eastern bastards freeze in the dark." In short, Canada seemed to be coming apart at the seams—economic difficulty with Alberta, political trouble with Quebec, and the rest of the country mired in the molasses of an economic recession.

Nor were things much better internationally. As noted in the previous chapter, by early 1976 Hopper could talk of the "MSAs," those Southern countries "most seriously affected" by the downturn experienced around the world. This concern would parallel that expressed for the "HIPCs," the heavily indebted poor countries of the early 2000s, which tended to the same ones. It was estimated that the current account trade deficit of non-oil Third World countries had gone from about US$11 billion in 1973 to more than US$40 billion by 1975 and higher yet by the early 1980s. Nor were the big multilateral agencies co-operating, or at least not their donors. For example, the United States, suffering its own economic downturn, refused to increase its International Monetary Fund quota. Further, it would not break through the US$750 million per year plateau of contributions to the World Bank subsidiary, the International Development Association, which had been established in 1960 to provide low-interest loans to the poorest countries to help alleviate poverty. Latin American countries were also in crisis as the Big Three—Argentina, Brazil, and Mexico—spoke openly about a moratorium on debt payments. At the same time, concessional aid transfers to Southern countries from the Organization of Oil Exporting Countries and the industrial country members of the Development Assistance Committee (DAC) of the Organisation for Economic Co-operation and Development amounted to US$13.5 billion. In addition, DAC members provided US$15.4 billion and OPEC US$2.4 billion in net capital transfers. As a result, non-oil LDCs balanced their trading account deficit by adding significantly to their indebtedness, a very bleak situation.

The early 1980s also spawned a raft of literature decrying the decline of countries like Argentina, Brazil, Mexico, and Zaire, all topped off with the imposition of World Bank structural adjustment programs that arguably did far more damage than good. For the South, the existing world economic order seemed to be collapsing, a paradigm that had been constructed and sustained following the Second World War by and for the industrialized nations of the world. A US Agency for International Development (USAID) official perhaps put it best when he noted in late 1983 that "developing countries are being put through an economic wringer that is undoing the achievement of several decades. Countries that achieved independence in the early 1960s and began the process of modernization in the early 1970s are now being demodernized. Investment projects are lying idle, children are not being taught, disease is spreading, beggars are filling the streets from which they have been absent for decades, people are looting food shops, and the middle class is being destroyed by bankruptcy and high interest rates." It almost sounded like Armageddon or, even worse, *Mad Max*. The UN's Economic Commission for Africa also highlighted the point that the impact of those events was most pronounced in those countries least able to absorb them. Its authors wrote that global trends in development could lead to "poverty of unimaginable dimensions in rural areas and to increased crime rates and misery in urban areas."[5] The World Bank spoke of a "crisis" in Sub-Saharan Africa (SSA), while in the Sahel, a ferocious drought was scouring the land and desiccating people's hopes. LDCs had had virtually no voice in shaping the development model, and because they had seemed to gain only marginal benefit from its operation, there was, by the later 1970s, a determination that any new world economic system must be built and managed with the concurrence and participation of the poorer nations and must include in its operation a clear recognition of their special needs and interests.

It was that sentiment that had resulted in the establishment of the United Nations Conference on Trade and Development in 1964, and the UN's adoption of the new international economic order (NIEO) in 1974. However, it remained that power and resources were concentrated on one side—that of the industrialized countries—and discussion did not necessarily yield much fruit for the less advantaged. A conference on international economic co-operation, held in Paris, which began in June 1976 with high hopes, ended with a whimper a year later, having resulted in little of substance. In the words of Jahangir Amuzegar, an executive director of the International Monetary Fund and Iran's ambassador-at-large and principal resident representative to the International Monetary Fund and World Bank, it was hopeless: "The conference came to a battered and confused end—more than a hectic day behind its scheduled final ministerial meeting. An 18-month 'dialogue' between the rich North and the poor South, which had begun with much enthusiasm and great hope in Paris, finished on a faint and joyless note."6

Still, what seemed to be a hopeless external environment did not hinder the Centre's ability to do its work. Seen in that light, Head's appointment was inspired—critically, he was able to use his political connections in Ottawa to protect his new charge from adverse attention. That job was made easier by what Maurice Strong, the chair of IDRC's board following the resignation of Louis Rasminsky in the autumn of 1977, called "the ablest group of professionals that I believe exist in any institution.... [Head] has come into command of a solid ship which is the pride of the fleet, and we believe too that as its new captain he is fully up to the challenge and to the new expectations that we have for this institution in the [difficult] period ahead."7 In that, he would be helped by the quality of his staff, who blended a distinctive mix of sectoral and geographic qualifications and experience, possessed among themselves hundreds of university degrees and technical certificates, spoke more than sixty languages fluently, and came from more than fifty countries. From Ivan Head, mostly bereft of international development experience, that must surely have elicited a huge "Amen."

The New Regime Settles in

Head's first board meeting occurred three days after his appointment. It was a time for stock-taking, peering into a murky future to determine what might be a suitable path to follow. To 1978, IDRC had reflected the sentiment expressed in the Robert Frost poem "The Road Not Taken," in which the poet speaks of two roads diverging in a wood where he "took the one less traveled by, / And that has made all the difference." It remained for Head and the Centre to determine if the road less travelled remained the most appropriate course for the 1980s, given the reality of a different political, economic, and social context. Early on, the new president was told that the Centre's parliamentary appropriation was to be frozen during the 1979–80 fiscal year at the same CAN$37 million figure that it had received for 1978–79 as the new minority government evaluated its priorities. However, even before the election of the Conservatives, the Trudeau government was making noises about balancing the national budget, and that could only harm IDRC.

For example, during the in-camera board session of March 1978, Strong had laid out in fairly stark terms a new reality for the Centre; the secretary of state for external affairs, Donald Jamieson, had directed "that we are going to have to put in front of [Jamieson] a new rationale for IDRC. We have to start from the premise that he and his colleagues really don't know much about IDRC [which was true]. He said that as a matter of fact, even some of the people in cabinet really didn't know what it was until their attention was attracted to IDRC by the fact that Ivan Head was going to become its president, and that was when they thought it must be pretty important."[8] While it was all well and good to be known, and maybe even revered, beyond Canada's borders, it was also increasingly politically important that the IDRC brand be better appreciated within the country; in those parlous times a domestic constituency might come in handy in terms of protecting the work (and budget) of the organization.

Strong told the board that he wanted to reserve some time during the second day of deliberations for another in-camera session to discuss "in total frankness, the present policy of the IDRC."[9] While he was not, he emphasized, implying any criticism of the past (all board members at that meeting had served with Hopper and had been responsible for Centre policy), in a transition period "we should take a new and fresh look at where we are, how we got there, and where we should like to go." That was caused in part by the fact that, while the board then had the funds necessary to cover all projects to be considered at the meeting, for the first time in its history its program appropriations budget, as opposed to it parliamentary appropriation, would be CAN$5 million *less* in the coming year than it was in 1978. And that, Jon Church, the vice-president of administration, told the board, represented the case for "financial restraint."

Finally, aside from budgetary issues, Head had some thoughts about IDRC's supposed commitment to a multidisciplinary approach. Strong noted that "some of us who realize that this was one of the main rationales for the Centre when it was created have questioned the degree to which, in practice, our program now reflects a genuine multidisciplinarity." Of course, as Strong had implied, programming generally reflected no such thing. Terry Smutylo, shortly following his employment at the Centre in 1982, was under no illusions about multi-disciplinarity; while there was a real need to work across divisions if IDRC was to maximize its potential, it did not. He remembered: "I would enter the elevator in the morning and realize that no one in the elevator knew each other because they had never worked together. It [would take] a lot to overcome this lack of cooperation."[10] John Hardie had a similar recollection; when he arrived at IDRC in 1980, he had very quickly heard about the four fiefdoms and that "they didn't really talk to one another."

Clearly, as seen in Chapter 2, interdivisional co-operation had not been a priority. Further, Head was increasingly convinced that project criteria would have to be tightened and some sort of strategic plan would need to be developed given that the Hopper Centre had not, in the strict sense of the phrase, had one. That would come in 1981. However, Strong would not be around long to oversee the projects his comments brought into being. He resigned as chair of the board in the fall of 1978 after less than one year, and was replaced in the fall of 1980 by a former Trudeau Cabinet minister, Donald Macdonald, who served only until early 1984. Macdonald had been appointed to head of the Royal Commission on the Economic Union and Development Prospects for Canada, which left little time for other things. Janet Wardlaw, a professor from the University of Guelph and protegé of William Winegard, former president of that institution and now member of Parliament, succeeded him.

Head also laid out his ideas: first and foremost, he would work to continue to assure the relative independence, albeit in a new context, of the Centre within the Canadian matrix. However, it was also clear that it depended on a constituency that now needed more massaging than in the past that began and ended with a government that was "looking for ways of dealing with developmental issues and foreign policy issues, as well as budgetary controls and the rest."[11] His strength was not in the minutia of project work but in the broad strokes that guided Centre labours. He told the board during his first meeting that he would "jealously protect the worldwide reputation of this Centre ... pursue with dedication [the board's] policy directives, and encourage program directors to develop for your consideration projects of a demonstrable validity, dynamism and imagination."[12] Staff could go about their work sure in the knowledge that he would be on the front line, safeguarding their interests.

The new president would be hard pressed in following through on those commitments. To make matters more difficult, Canada's budgetary crisis was made worse by "a degree of national introspection ... that gives some of us grave pause, because there is an immense need for Canadians to be aware of the world about them and to forget that our own stature, our own image and our continuing existence as a political society depends in some large degree upon the attitudes of others." Head hoped that his background and his knowledge of governmental processes (and perhaps his connections with the senior elements of power) would permit him to anticipate roadblocks and to work his way around any that materialized so that the Centre would not find itself faced with any surprises. Finally, it was imperative that Canadians be told about IDRC, to take joy in celebrating its achievements, as well as to make "perhaps slightly more clear the Canadian parentage of the Centre around the world."

While IDRC purists of the Hopper mode would have experienced a sharp intake of breath at that audacious comment, it also reflected the new reality in which the Centre now operated. It was also why, to the disgust of many in the organization, Head replaced the "of Canada" in IDRC's name, which had been removed in 1970 in the *IDRC Act*. At the October 1978 board meeting, so serious was Head about the necessity of alerting Canadians of the existence of the Centre that members of the press were invited to join the board at lunch. Also, CTV's Bruce Page was permitted to bring his cameras to record governors for posterity (and its public affairs program), downing food and drink. With a straight face, the new president told the board that it was "in keeping with the Centre's need for some exposure within Canada."[13]

Head did move quickly on this issue of publicity. In early 1981, he appointed Ernest Corea, a Sri Lankan national, to head a new division, the Cooperative Programs Unit (CPU), which came into existence on April Fool's Day, surely seen as appropriate by some holdovers from the Hopper era.[14] However, just as quickly, Corea was made his country's ambassador to the United States and Mexico, which led to James Mullin, formerly with the Ministry of State for Science and Technology, taking over in August. Efforts at increasing IDRC exposure to Canadians and enhancing co-operation also involved a new emphasis on post-secondary institutions in Canada. With the same vigour that Hopper and his IDRC had largely steered clear of entanglements with Canada's universities, Head's operation consciously articulated a policy of promoting collaboration between research groups in Canada and in LDCs. He was embarrassed, he later said to the House of Commons Standing Committee on External Affairs and National Defence, that between 1975 and 1979, the Centre had spent a miniscule 1.61 percent of its funding at Canadian universities.[15]

The provenance of the Cooperative Programs Unit could be traced back to the United Nations Conference on Science and Technology for Development (UNCSTD). The view of developing countries coming from that meeting was that they wanted more access to the research systems of the North. As a result, Ottawa offered another 1 percent of official development assistance (ODA) toward collaborative research. The new division at IDRC spread some of the new money through existing divisions and kept another bit for itself. Over the next several years, the unit worked out in which areas it should concentrate and one of these, Earth and Engineering Sciences, became a new division in 1987. Still, not all agreed. Gerry Helleiner, while on the board during the mid-1980s, thought it to be "an infringement by the Government of Canada on the independence of IDRC."[16] The Centre was not a national granting institution but an international development organization. However, there was little IDRC could do to turn the clock back given the forces buffeting Canada and also the Centre.

It also led to some interesting possibilities that might have been passed up but for new arrangements. For example, the Canadian government tasked the Centre to be the lead agency in implementing the recommendations of the United Nations Conference on New and Renewable Sources of Energy, which had been held in Nairobi between 10 and 21 August 1981. Along with that responsibility came CAN$10 million, spread over four years, to be used in a multidisciplinary way in the pursuit of energy research in the South. That was where CPU proved its worth; if the anticipated requests for funding, which would come for energy-related activities, did not fall within the historic activities of existing divisions, the Cooperative Programs Unit would be called upon to provide the necessary home. Quite rightly, Head celebrated the establishment of the Unit, noting that "we are now blessed with this extraordinarily flexible vehicle."[17] Co-operation in this instance was a method of strengthening the research capabilities of LDC research groups by providing them with a link to at least one part of the international scientific community, often difficult to obtain if the Southern researcher was in a small institution.

CPU also conducted what Mullin had earlier called his subversive campaign. He was convinced that the best way to change the direction of Canadian scientific research was to put it directly in touch with LDC problems and issues. Through the process of having Canadian scientists collaborate with their colleagues in the South, he hoped that the former would be made more aware and more likely to choose more things to work on that were directly applicable to the Third World. It was partly as a result of that aspiration that the Centre inaugurated what Head called "a novel exercise" in May

1980, sponsoring a day-long seminar at the University of Guelph to which interested members of faculties of universities in the region—Brock University, University of Toronto, University of Western Ontario, University of Waterloo, Wilfrid Laurier University, and York University—would attend. IDRC would send its four division directors and other officers. The University of British Columbia and the University of Alberta had enquired if a similar meeting could be held later on their campuses. The emphasis remained on LDCs throughout, and the day-long show-and-tell was to encourage Canadian researchers to immerse themselves in LDC issues that could be shared.

By the early 1980s, the CPU was necessary, underwriting the public relations dimension that was essential "for our own survival."[18] Rex Nettleford, a board member until 1982, remained "very aware that we need to convince the Canadian constituency that we really are serious." At the October 1981 board meeting Head also emphasized that the new division would not be "vertical" in the sense that IDRC would not hand down judgment from on high, but more horizontal. This response was welcomed by many governors, but in particular by the Philippines governor, Geila Castillo. "You may," she had offered, "have something to learn from us, too." Head certainly had no quarrel with that.

The Empire Strikes Back

But that was in the future, and for the present, Head seemed intent on soothing the concerns of his new employees as he assumed office. That was not easy; Treasury Board Secretariat (TBS) had thrown a bit of a wrench into IDRC machinery with a report that the Cabinet had demanded with respect to the allocation of Canadian bilateral development assistance funds for 1977–78. The result was extensive and suggested that the Centre should be reined in vis-à-vis its independence from the normal mechanisms of official Ottawa, and should now be regarded as a product of *Canada's* foreign aid policy. When it was established in 1970 as a creation of the Parliament of Canada, IDRC was in theory bound by the general rules as set out in Canada's *Financial Administration Act*. However, it was made exempt from the Act's specific rules governing Crown corporations, as were eight of its fellows, including the Bank of Canada and the Canadian Broadcasting Corporation. It was (and is) audited once per year and the results made available to Parliament. By the later 1970s, Treasury Board Secretariat was doing what it did best— attempting to treat all Crown corporations in similar fashion, even if it meant trying to force square pegs into round holes. Indeed, several years later a new chair of the board, Donald Macdonald, put the situation succinctly. Citing the government's ongoing legislative project to draw within one structure all of those public institutions that loosely fell under the rubric of Crown Corporation, he noted that the Treasury Board lawyer would say "IDRC is a corporation incorporated by the Government of Canada. We are engaged in looking at the corporations incorporated by the Government of Canada, therefore, IDRC should be fitted into this framework."[19]

As well, committed as it was to the methodology articulated by the generally accepted accounting principles, TBS did not appreciate a freelancing Centre, jetting about the globe without much input into, or control by, its officials. As one IDRC official noted, the process whereby TBS had turned its baleful eye Sauron-like on the Centre suggested something not unlike "the empire striking back."[20] Treasury Board Secretariat noted that "no other developed country has been prepared to accept the same degree of political autonomy and international representation" as had been given IDRC—the implicit assumption was why should Canada? And since IDRC had become "much more "Canadianized" than was ever anticipated (that description drove Centre management to distraction—what did it mean?), the question of a domestic role should now be considered.[21] Head called that one of many unsophisticated and uninformed comments made in the report. All of this government attention was rather disconcerting and had some at the Centre reminiscing about the good old days when it had been possible for them to fly below the radar, invisible to all but the most determined observer.

In David Hopper's interpretation of the *IDRC Act*, objective 4(1) b, "building developing country research capability," was singled out as being the most crucial. The emphasis was to be on promoting indigenous self-reliance and the ideal of "responsiveness" was chosen to promote that end. His second priority stemmed from 4(1) a, "enlisting scientists and technologists and that considerable attention would be given to high standards of professional competence. Finally, 4(1) c, involving "coordination of international development research," was to have special significance; research networks were established among developing countries with common interests. This approach was reinforced through the use of regional offices (ROs), information-sharing, and seminars as additional means of furthering coordination.

As a result, the elements of internationalism, political independence from the mechanisms of the Canadian government, financial flexibility, and the focus on research done by Southern researchers in developing countries had come to characterize IDRC. As TBS noted in a memorandum speaking to the operation of the Centre, "Clearly, Dr. Hopper's implementation strategy was designed to satisfy two intermediate and survival-related goals; the establishment of the Centre in a manner that would preserve its unique character relative to its *Act*, and the build-up of credibility and respect among developing countries and within the international development community."[22] Treasury Board Secretariat believed that Hopper had accomplished his objectives effectively even if it might have disagreed on direction. Certainly, the International Development Research Centre had established credibility among LDCs and had stimulated the development and training of Southern researchers. Its model had been studied by other developed countries, and even as TBS was penning its report, the US Congress was considering whether or not to establish its own version of IDRC, the Institute for Scientific and Technological Cooperation (ISTC), whose enabling legislation had been submitted by US President Jimmy Carter.[23] It was not to be, a squabbling Senate and House of Representatives decided, and it remained stillborn. It *was* a fact that only one other Northern country, Sweden, with its Swedish Agency for Research Cooperation with Developing Countries, was prepared to accept the degree of political autonomy and international representation that had shaped the Centre.[24]

IDRC needed to strategize for the future, especially with respect to evaluation machinery as no formal mechanism existed for evaluating programs, and assessing new opportunities and improvement in project performance and resource allocation was not based on what had been done in the past. TBS had some areas where IDRC could improve, most of which related to a more made-in-Canada approach. For example, it pointed to "an absence of any form of overview in terms of budgetary or program impact; a lack of priorities and criteria to guide project selection; and, program objectives and priorities resulting from a corporate planning exercise should guide program divisions in their efforts."

There were a number of other recommendations: more internal coordination and integration; a greater sense of the organizational needs of IDRC; the rationalization of ROs, which could only be done once the broader issues regarding regional involvement and decentralization of authority were resolved, with regional offices more involved in project implementation and evaluation. Interestingly, TBS focused in on the "four fiefdoms" of IDRC; it suggested the breakup of the Social Sciences and Human Resources division and the relocation of many of its social scientists within other divisions as that could lead to more multi-disciplinarity. As well, Treasury Board Secretariat suggested the establishment of an evaluations mechanism to objectively measure the success, or not, of IDRC programming.

Surprisingly, given this litany of criticism, Treasury Board Secretariat, as well as the Privy Council Office (PCO), were unanimous in their praise of Centre activity; indeed an official at PCO had taken the unusual step of telephoning the senior vice-president, Louis Berlinguet, to say that IDRC "had been given a clean bill of health" by both and that there would be no follow-up.[25] Head speculated that the reason they had backed off was "the indication we have given ... that we intend to stand up for ourselves, to demand the opportunity to return arguments, and to insist on some degree of clarity and scientific analysis of these activities." That might have been, but that was not the only reason IDRC sailed through; the investigations had revealed an extremely well-run organization that had more than lived up to the promise encapsulated in its Act.

The Centre Moves On

As Head got his feet under him, division directors rehearsed their situations and, for the most part, it was "steady as she goes." Joseph Hulse, of Agriculture, Food, and Nutrition Sciences (AFNS), led off as perhaps reflected the order of importance of IDRC at that time. Continued areas of emphasis included marginal lands, multiple cropping systems, use of wastes and by-products, aquaculture, post-production systems, and small forestry projects. With respect to the last, IDRC-funded projects focused on micro forests, which it had been alone in pioneering. This was a relatively new direction and was showing some benefit in terms of wood for fuel and the protection of crops in small villages, as distinct from the large plantation type of forestry more commonly supported by other development agencies.

There was quite a diversity of content in view of the fact that AFNS was supporting projects in so many different socio-economic and agro-climatic environments; the crop science program, for example, was taking place in forty-six different countries, fisheries in nineteen, animal sciences in nineteen, and forestry in eighteen. Hulse and his division continued to concentrate their priorities on the well-being of the rural poor, which had been Hopper's primary focus, and within that general concentration, had been particularly concerned with the semi-arid tropics, in particular, the Sahel, then ravaged by a horrible drought. Further, and of some note for IDRC's reputation in Sub-Saharan Africa, following the overthrow of Uganda's Idi Amin in 1979, the new government asked the Centre for advice on agricultural research priorities. This was uncharted territory and, while leery about taking it on, IDRC's Hugh Doggett did so, leading a team to Kampala and spending some time in the country.

As well, the Centre became similarly involved in Zimbabwe following its independence on 18 April 1980, signing a general project agreement with Harare on 8 July 1981. However, Hulse had visited the country earlier in order to acquaint the government of Robert Mugabe with what IDRC did and how his government should go about applying for assistance. He had also led a team that examined the needs of Zimbabwe and a number of other southern African countries in the post-production and post-harvest sector of agricultural activities. Similarly, in the autumn of 1980, Nihal Kappagoda was asked to be a member of a Commonwealth Secretariat team in Zimbabwe to examine the whole area of economic development and prepare for a major donors' meeting. Indeed, IDRC personnel in one guise or another visited the country regularly following independence; the RD from Nairobi, for example, went six times in the two years to early 1982. Clearly, the Centre was fulfilling, "with some dispatch, its earlier offers of assistance to Zimbabwe."[26]

Agriculture, Food, and Nutrition Sciences, almost alone among the divisions, had veered off the road less travelled during the Hopper years, lightly cultivating the Canadian academic community. The division had stationed an officer at five universities across the country, and had also funded some work in those.[27] Hulse told the board that "We have an immense talent in Canada in the field of agriculture, food and nutrition, which is comparatively untapped. When one looks at the program [the UK's Ministry of Overseas Development] has with various universities, we have nothing comparable to this in Canada, and I think it unfortunate that we don't have a single Canadian director-general of an international agricultural research centre."[28] Further, AFNS had begun discussions with CIDA on greater co-operation in areas like those ripe for the Agency's "pre-investment," the strengthening of national agricultural research and training institutions, the introduction of research components into some of CIDA's development projects, and the coordination of Canadian talent and competence from the academic, industrial, and private sectors. That initiative would intensify in the years ahead and represented quite a change from the Hopper era; it was also more in tune with the evolving mandate of the Centre under Head. As well, it received kudos from at least one board member during the meeting held in early 1980. William Winegard, the president of the University of Guelph, had checked with academic colleagues across the country with respect to IDRC activity housed in Canadian universities and Hulse had received "full marks."[29]

The division had managed about 380 projects to 1978, 344 funded by IDRC along with thirty-six special projects, primarily supported by CIDA. As well, it had handled more than US$7 million as executing agency for five different international activities involving a number of donors. Hulse was also careful to repeat what had been a mantra of sorts through the 1970s—agricultural research was not a revolutionary process but rather one of slow evolution, "assisted by man's ingenuity and industry."[30] And that would take time; he did not "believe in Green Revolution, [a concept] not of scientists, but of journalists."[31] He also thought that research being done in farmers' fields was most important because "research in farmers' fields or in rural processing or industrial units is invariably more revealing and meaningful than research undertaken on experimental stations or in bio-chemistry research laboratories."[32] That position, even then, was quite rare among development agencies.

Finally, AFNS was also embarking on a new approach to development— farming systems research, which marked a breakthrough in the conceptualization of agricultural research. This was a necessity, or so many of the division's program officers believed, because there had been very serious shortcomings in earlier attempts to introduce new technologies to farmers in developing countries. Farming systems was an attempt to incorporate a multidisciplinary focus into agricultural research. By the 1980s, most Centre-supported agronomy projects were using a farming systems research methodology even though "it was considered to take 'a great deal of time to organize.'"[33] As Eva Rathgeber has noted, "For the first time, researchers were looking at the farm as a small, family-owned business with inter-related systems of production and resource utilization." IDRC began support for this approach early; the first project was funded in 1979 through the International Rice Research Institute. It moved beyond the traditional commodities approach and began to reflect the reality of small farmers in Africa, Asia, and Latin America.

John Gill, who had taken over what was now called Health Sciences (HS) from the departed George Brown, told Head that late in that year the division had changed its direction with the elimination of demography and the de-emphasis on family planning research. The focus of its activities was reduced from six to four, including fertility regulation methods, tropical diseases, rural health care, and rural water and sanitation. It was also significant, or so Gill thought, that all of the work funded had been undertaken without using any expatriates, which had meant better value for money— he had not needed to "top off projects with $50,000 or $60,000 a year" with a First World salary. IDRC continued to subsidize research in Southern countries in this area where more immediate results might be obtained from developed country laboratories, but where LDC training would have been negligible.[34] As a result, the average project cost had been very modest, in the range of CAN$100,000 as opposed to CAN$150,000–$160,000, which had permitted more projects to be funded. Since 1970, the division had been involved in fertility regulation, investigating new methods in technology,

clinical trials, safety measures against contraceptives in use, and some training as part of the grants program. As well, what Gill called social obstetrics
had been a focus during the last decade—this examined maternal problems
during pregnancy, issues with mother and child immediately following birth,
and any that occurred during the child's first year.

The division's primary emphasis, however, remained centred on the
question of health care delivery, a very difficult problem given that health ministry budgets in the South were lamentably small; this was simply not a priority for most LDC governments with very limited resources. IDRC had
invested much in funding research in the area of auxiliary health personnel—those not officially trained but capable of improving health outcomes.
Indeed, the director then felt that enough had been done in this area and the
emphasis should now be on implementation. Most ministries of health in
LDCs did not have the personnel to carry orders from the top to the bottom,
or communication in the other direction, nor any adequate supervision for
auxiliary and paramedical personnel, who might sit around for five months
out of every six with nothing to do because they did not have the necessary
tools, like drugs, to do anything with. The issue was how to get health care
to the people.

One aspect of primary health care research was the rural health development program in Colombia. To some extent, it presaged IDRC's very successful ecohealth program of some years later; health, the Colombian
researchers suggested, was not merely the absence of disease, and they
adopted a more holistic approach to primary health care. To that end they
investigated drinking water services and waste disposal; they actively involved
the family and the community in the project; and incorporated environmental considerations into program design more generally. Its goals were a 60
percent reduction over five years in the rate of maternal mortality; a 50 percent decrease in infant mortality; a decline in complications during pregnancy, delivery, and parasite-related illness among school-age children, and,
finally, a reduction in adult morbidity. While all the objectives were not met,
the project did have a major impact on primary health care programs in rural
areas in Colombia. Further, the Ministry of Health, in conjunction with
UNICEF, replicated many of the model components in several regions of the
country, developing a national primary health care policy. It also had an
impact in other Latin American countries, in particular Bolivia and Ecuador.[35]

Health Sciences was also assiduously funding workshops in Africa in
which potential trainers had been selected from various countries and taught
the new technologies and methods of health preservation. They then returned
to their regions to close the circle. Into the 1980s, this practice of hosting

training workshops in African countries was to become a more common strain in Centre funding. Given the very rudimentary level at which knowledge about health inputs and outcomes rested, this was seen as a necessary beginning point. The *idea* of workshops did not always inspire confidence in the uninitiated, however; at Donald Macdonald's first executive committee meeting following his appointment as chair of the board and perhaps thinking back on what meetings had meant in Ottawa, he asked, "Is the holding of workshops really significant towards achieving the objectives or is it merely an opportunity for people to get together to chat?"[36] Head quickly set the record straight.

The fact remained, however, that IDRC's pockets were not deep, and hosting meaningful training sessions in Africa, where internal flights were very expensive and very circuitous, cost a significant amount of money. That they were very necessary did not obviate that fact. The Centre did what it could, but it was often only scratching one part of a very large surface. This issue did become more prominent at the Centre; by the mid-1980s, the board was concerned that "training in research planning, administration and management has been neglected and is actually non-existent in some regions. This results in inefficient use of IDRC contributions, excessive vehicle wear, unacceptable financial reporting, excessive red tape, and the absence of long-term research goals."[37] So, workshops designed to address these problems *were* important. Gill often lamented the fact that millions of dollars were wasted by better-heeled donors because of the top-down approach favoured by most of them, unfamiliar as they might be with local conditions.

Information Sciences' John Woolston told the new president and the board that he was especially motivated by the idea of building a framework to permit work done in one place to be available to all others. That was, for instance, the case of AGRIS, the system that he had helped develop; it "now contained more information from developing countries than any other file on agricultural information being produced either commercially or in the public sector."[38] The example of AGRIS had been one of the priorities that an ad hoc committee of governors, chaired by Winegard, had provided to IS in 1978—the development of bibliographic information systems in those subject areas where IDRC was active in research. During Head's first term in office, the division would also become involved with the development of another system called CARIS, concerned with information about research in progress, as opposed to AGRIS, which provided information about research already completed.

The governor's committee had also suggested that IS devote a greater proportion of its budget to communications research—how to convey the results that scientists produced to the larger audience of extension workers and farmers. That was a good idea, but the division had had only one specialist in communication science, who had since been transferred to the Latin American office. As a result, the whole initiative had migrated to Social Sciences, where "the methodologies and techniques of the social sciences [were] paramount, and [to which] it was appropriate to make that transfer." That was also a reflection of limited resources in IS. Among divisions, it was the most likely to lose experienced personnel to other organizations, like the United Nations, because of the skill set they possessed. As well, it had supported a number of projects, like Technonet, discussed briefly in Chapter 2, which had proved to be heavy in terms of time commitment.[39] Each expenditure had had to be decided at headquarters in Ottawa. All of that had taken a full-time person from the division whose time might have been better spent on other priorities. Woolston told the board that his division would not—indeed could not—undertake those heavy staffing responsibilities in the future without substantial investment in personnel.

The obverse of that situation were areas where IS should be expanding, but found it difficult to do so given its responsibilities. By the late 1970s the Centre's professional reputation in the field of information sciences had been steadily increasing, in large part because of the impact that MINISIS, its software package, had had upon users around the world.[40] Information scientists had for years wanted compatibility among systems in different institutions to avoid the situation that prevailed in the late 1970s, during which the same documents were catalogued and indexed many times in different institutions because of incompatible software and different cataloguing systems. That was where MINISIS made a difference.

The system was the standard by 1980 because hardware requirements for a powerful mini-computer like the HP 3000 Series II, which could support MINISIS, were 10 percent the cost of a large one. Woolston told the board that governors could "congratulate themselves on what turned out to be a very wise decision made in 1975, to take the risk and design this system."[41] A number of countries and institutions were fitting themselves out with the software—Tunisia, Morocco, and others represented by the Arab League, Malaysia, Zaire, the University of Singapore, and, perhaps more importantly, the People's Republic of China. CIDA followed suit, but much later. Perhaps indicative of the sorry state of the relationship, the Agency's president, Maggie Catley-Carlson, remarked that the organization had "finally adopted the MINISIS system, 847th in the world to do so. I guess something that's developed at home is something like being a prophet in your own land; it always takes a long time for it to go as far as across the [Ottawa] river."[42]

The downside to its popularity were the constraints it physically imposed on Information Sciences; Woolston commented that it was his division's responsibility to install MINISIS on the various computers and he had lost one of his senior computer staff. As a result, the division was behind in honouring its commitments; if it lost another computer specialist, "it would be a wipe-out." IS had also contracted out some of its rights to MINISIS with commercial organizations for distribution in specific territories—the Dutch software company RAET and SERIC in France. As well, Systemhouse, based in Toronto, had the Canadian and American rights. The Centre's proprietary rights were protected in the agreements with the private sector, and any revenues generated contributed profits to IDRC coffers.[43] However, the Centre also provided the software free of charge to agencies like USAID and UNDP.

This process was unusual for IDRC, to say the least. It was now involved in licensing arrangements with the private sector. James Pfeifer filled the board in on how that had come about. Given the development of MINISIS, there had been several options facing IDRC: "cut it loose and turn over the source codes to anyone who wanted them ... turn it over to a Canadian software company ... [or] try and make it work for us."[44] Clearly, the last was most compelling, especially given the resources the Centre had invested in the instrument, and accordingly, IDRC had formed the MINISIS Users Group. The corporation was the hub in the middle and MINISIS went out on spokes to anyone interested in using it. Because it was a desirable package, it was hoped that enough profit could be generated by commercial licensing to sustain both the core group at headquarters, as well as to allow IDRC to make the system available to LDCs at no cost to them. Its philosophy throughout the whole exercise had been that "if bright people in a public sector corporation generated a system which could return some money to the Canadian taxpayer ... [it was not] exceeding [its] mandate by doing so." The source codes were also kept in Ottawa to protect the Centre's investment and to prevent its licensing partners from making it incompatible with Southern needs in the name of profit. MINISIS remained housed in its building for years and was a great example of the Centre's support for information technology development and application, long before other agencies were doing so, that had provided practical results for developing country partners as well as being a commercially viable product. Indeed, by fiscal year 1998–99, the MINISIS Users Group was able to recoup 100 percent of the costs of its operation from fees collected from wealthy Northern clients. In December 2000, it was successfully spun off from the Centre, creating MINISIS Inc., an independent commercial enterprise.

Social Sciences remained a very active division where the broad outlines of the past seven years remained in place. David Steedman took over
as director on 27 November 1978, following Ruth Zagorin's departure to
join her husband in Washington, where he had become a vice-president at
the World Bank. This represented another shock to IDRC sensibilities almost
as profound as that given by David Hopper's retirement from the Centre.
That was reflected in staffing levels; the division experienced a transitional
phase of perhaps eighteen months during which there was a large staff
turnover and a significant dip in project development. With education, the
concentration remained on the elementary level and in a vindication of the
IDRC approach, other donor institutions were now turning their attention to
funding primary school projects. On the population front, the Centre would
have to learn something about suitable and productive intervention points,
and it needed a continuing assessment of ongoing work. With science and
technology, science and technology policy instruments now needed a period
of consolidation and dissemination. As Zagorin left, the new director would
impart his own character to the division.

And what might that be? First and foremost, Social Sciences was interested in *training* Southern researchers in various areas; he told governors at
the April 1979 meeting that "the most valuable work we do is not around this
table. It is not in Ottawa. It is not in the writing of projects for approval. It
is rather the process that takes place between program officers and potential recipients."[45] In pursuit of that objective, the division also wanted to
work more closely with junior researchers in areas where the research environment was weak. That would help, it was hoped, with respect to policy relevance. If the product could be improved in such cases, perhaps government
would be more prepared to implement the results. Steedman told the board
that that was why "you may have noticed in the research policy workshop
evaluation a great deal of emphasis upon the use of training policy-makers
to use the results of research, as well as training research workers to do the
research."[46] It was also important that the Centre not limit funding in the social
sciences. The Ford Foundation, with which IDRC had worked in the past,
was going through an evaluation process that might result in a greatly reduced
presence in that field. As a result, the Centre had become "the primary source
to which [researchers] will turn for funding. This is a relatively new situation in which we have a moral obligation to our constituency."[47]

Steedman would return to this idea of obligation throughout his term
at IDRC. He viewed it as a tragedy in the making if the big bilateral and multilateral donors reduced their funding in certain areas like institution-building, into which IDRC was moving by the early 1980s, and which will be

discussed below. The Centre would have to shift its priorities carefully (although it was imperative to keep up with the demands of researchers), and avoid what he called "fickleness," which could only damage its credibility and work in the South. It was important not to be put in a position of narrowly defining IDRC objectives and implementing them in such a rigid fashion that it became more prescriptive than responsive; that would surely lead to research imperialism.[48]

Training had come to be perceived as vitally important for the developing Centre, especially since the publication of Hopper's eleven-point program. That had noted that IDRC "had no programs of scholarships or other formal training assistance at any educational level," which was regarded as a deficiency even then. By the early 1980s, about 10 percent of all program support was directed toward training, and indicators suggested that that would increase. As all divisions began to consider putting more resources into Africa, the training aspect became more important given that the institutional base in large swathes of the continent was embryonic. While all countries in the region had established universities (if sometimes not very good), the emphasis at all of them was in teaching, not research, to train students to the graduate level. Few universities had developed postgraduate programs, and funds for research were very scarce. Given this situation, a bright student had to travel to Europe, North America, or the Eastern bloc for training and, once there, often chose not to return to the sponsoring country. The worsening economic condition during the late 1970s and early 1980s only made this more difficult both for the return of students and because it resulted in the reduction of research funding that was provided by national governments to universities.

The board was onside. It had endorsed the notion that the Centre should concentrate on developing research skills by enabling scientists to do research. And as David Steedman pointed out, that did cost money, but it also set the Centre apart from other donors: "In my view, the uniqueness of IDRC ... lies in that percentage of our budget which goes to technical support.... It is not just monitoring: project development, working with researchers to look at the variables that we have stated, is an enormously complex and difficult operation in those parts of the world where social science is weak." But more than this, the situation in LDCs often raised the question as to whether or not it was possible to cultivate a general appreciation of the role of science, technology, and research in the lives of ordinary people. The answer was distressingly no, unless the program began in the elementary grades, which generally remained weak, especially in Africa. That was a part of the training exercise that the Centre would undertake.

Program divisions were redirecting support to countries with weak research infrastructures, again, unlike the situation during the Hopper years, which had favoured those countries that could successfully absorb research funding. In a paper prepared by the office of the director of planning, guidelines were laid down, for example, that training was a necessary condition for effective research and for building research capacity.[49] Furthermore, the same principles of responding to LDC needs and of maximizing the involvement of developing country researchers in designing, managing, and implementing their research programs should also apply to training. In pursuit of that, IDRC recognized that it could play a useful role in building research capability in new areas and in testing innovative methods by financing specific training activities. To do that, it was also agreed that priority should be given to training in the trainee's own country, a policy designed in part to address the brain drain. And that would, at least in some circumstances, require funding to build up selected training institutions in the developing world. This marked a shift in the philosophy and practice of the Centre.

This increased importance accorded to training in Africa in particular was the result of a shortage of skilled personnel who could undertake the sort of research IDRC funded. While there were a number of significant international institutions operating in Africa by the later 1970s—like the Institute of Agriculture for Rwanda, Burundi, and Zaire, or the International Livestock Centre for Africa—most of these lacked sufficiently trained local human resources, especially in the more recently independent countries of southern Africa. As well, a similar situation pertained with respect to those IDRC had been instrumental in creating and supporting, like the International Centre for Research in Agroforestry, based in Nairobi, and the Pan African Development Information System, located in Addis Ababa, Ethiopia. The Centre had provided core grants and, in some cases, paid overhead charges and encouraged other donors to become involved. While it had not yet done the same at the national level, it would do so in the future as the health of regional organizations depended, in part, on that to be found in the various countries.

That, then, begged the question: Who, or what, determined a country's research priorities?[50] Head had earlier spoken of "research imperialism" and "colonial attitudes" adopted by Southern researchers to "cater" to what they perceived to be Northern priorities. Was IDRC implicated, "consciously or unconsciously affect[ing] this decision by its own activities and support" even though the sectors in which countries chose to develop research capacity were determined primarily by them? And if this were true, had researchers, as Yelavarthy Nayudamma, an Indian governor who was killed in the 1985

Air India bombing while returning home following a board meeting, asked, adopted those colonial attitudes, becoming intellectually dependent on granting agencies from the North? Many were, he thought, "alienated from the people [they] belong to." Further, Nayudamma raised the perennial issue for the Centre: Was it building only research capacity, or was it also building, almost more importantly, problem-solving capabilities that implied policymakers' use of the research? That conundrum was expressed in colloquial language some years later by Ivan Head: What came first? The chicken or the egg? That, as has been demonstrated above, concerned the Centre throughout its existence. The governor thought that a country like India had a large research capacity, yet not a similarly proportioned problem-solving capability. In short, decision makers had to be involved in the process or it was not as useful as it could be.

Not surprisingly, most staff agreed, although not all, which provoked some discussion within the Centre. Was utilization a linear process or was it a more iterative one of "generating, receiving and absorbing new knowledge?... [As well] it was not easy to distinguish between research that promoted new knowledge and that which promoted its use."[51] Still, when developing projects, it was wise to adopt a policy of affirmative action, at least according to a survey of attitudes prepared in July 1982 by the Office of Planning and Evaluation's (OPE) John Hardie. The idea held that utilization should really begin before a project was implemented. Involvement of potential users of the research, private or public sector, was crucial at the project development stage and sharpened the focus of the research and resulted in a demand-pull for the knowledge that had yet to be created. Donald Mills, in work he undertook for the Centre, was worried that "research is taking the place of wisdom."[52] What he meant was precisely what animated Hardie's concerns—"the business of insufficient consultation of the user or the farmer by researchers, which is a major problem in research." In the IDRC model, as reflected by Hardie, the probability of usefulness was significantly greater than if potential users were considered after the fact when it became more a question of supply-push. Head had earlier noted that "knowledge is a resource too precious to be stored; its value is enhanced, not diminished, through utilization," a belief that guided his Centre's activities.[53] While the questions of research imperialism or the utilization of research were not "solved" then, and indeed could probably never be dealt with to the satisfaction of all, the exercise was suggestive of the free-ranging discussions that characterized board deliberations.

Regional Offices (Again)

The issue of regional offices was raised once more, especially given resource pressures in other areas. Were they an unnecessary add-on or an integral part of the Centre? Each incoming president professed uncertainty as to how to integrate/use/reform them to some sort of standard. They are certainly important to the intellectual, as well as the administrative, history of IDRC as has been described in Chapter 2. In the early Hopper years, there had sometimes been a difference of opinion expressed as to the appropriate role of regional offices. Indeed, an ongoing debate about their cost-effectiveness had been typical. Following his appointment, Head wanted to "know" the truth, so he had commissioned Nihal Kappagoda, the Centre vice-president of planning, in 1981 to visit the issue, and his committee had made a number of recommendations. It was decided that ROs would be granted more responsibility; Head's objective was to create largely self-supporting structures, certainly accountable to Ottawa, yet less on a day-to-day basis than had been the case in the past.

In particular, regional offices were now tasked with apprising head office of the processes and priorities that were being assigned to development in their regions. In co-operation with the Office of Planning and Evaluation, ROs did become more involved in developing capacities to gather and analyze information on the research environment in their respective regions. The president felt that this enhanced ability was critical to future programs and would be increasingly reflected as new projects were developed. Further, as personnel changed, different perspectives were raised. For example, Steedman quickly became a supporter; his division, he thought, could not "fulfill the kinds of objectives [he had mentioned earlier] unless we are extremely close to our constituency. You [could not] fly to Manila for two or three days and say you know the research scene in the Philippines. You have to have two people in Singapore, as we do, who go to Manila once every six weeks to talk to the people. It is just not possible to do this from Ottawa."[54] Additionally, the program officer environment in regional offices was very rich, given that program officers were allowed a great deal of freedom to pursue projects, and also to think, which was a benefit to the Centre and which could be more easily appreciated as regional offices were brought in from the cold. As Jim Mullin later pointed out, among officers in ROs "there was a lot of 'toing and froing' of ideas."[55]

An even more ambitious effort with respect to ROs was undertaken in mid-1984, when Joe Hulse agreed to examine regional offices again. This exercise was important as it represented the first time, the earlier Kappagoda effort notwithstanding, that the experience and existing functions and responsibilities of the ROs had been documented and recorded. In short, while examining the administrative apparatus of the regional offices, the Hulse report also posed certain issues and questions about their intellectual roles and input in the IDRC process. The fundamental point in the Hulse report was that a larger presence in developing regions was consistent with the Centre's purpose and style. ROs were more consistently aware of their changing needs and opportunities, a conclusion similar to the one reached by Kappagoda's investigation. Program officers based in regional offices were unanimous when asked by Hulse; they did function more effectively in an RO than from Ottawa: "They claimed better contacts with recipients and governments; greater awareness of research requirements and activities of other agencies; and, better opportunities for interdivisional cooperation."[56]

How did regional directors receive the report? There was a consensus that ROs had five primary functions: (1) representation of the Centre, (2) management of the regional office, (3) project development and administration, (4) planning and evaluation, and (5) support for non-project activities of the Centre. Regional offices were in the best position, or so some thought, to have access to information relating to socio-economic development trends and research environments in their respective regions. Accordingly, regional offices had the responsibility to reflect the needs of the region to IDRC management. Furthermore, they believed that to ensure Centre projects reflected the development realities and specific research priorities of the regions, more attention should be given to gathering and analyzing information and ensuring its appropriate dissemination throughout IDRC.[57]

The development and use of this sort of information would enable those offices to help develop the framework of a strategy, or range of ideas, within which IDRC would work in the region. ROs would review Centre program activities in their region, analyze major policy options, and identify alternatives as well as new research areas that the Centre should consider. Finally, they would provide an analysis of the regional research environment, including the research needs of the region's countries. In order to accomplish these goals, regional offices would, in a new configuration, respond to the information needs of the Centre and they would be an integral part of its planning and evaluation activities. The change of direction suggested by a revision of RO roles would, of course, have an immense influence on the concepts and values that animated IDRC decision making. This will be further discussed in Chapter 4.

Changing Processes at the Centre

In Head's Centre, other changes were made that had a significant impact on its intellectual trajectory. For example, Treasury Board Secretariat had zeroed in on the gaping hole where forward planning capabilities should have been. To address that, Nihal Kappagoda was appointed vice-president of planning (VPP), soon after to become the less unwieldy Office of Planning and Evaluation (OPE). His group assumed two functions: (1) to create a mechanism that would permit the Centre to prepare a strategic plan, and (2) design an evaluation process for projects and a methodology for evaluation, two critically important variables. Prior to Kappagoda's elevation, most IDRC planning had had a divisional focus. Head hoped that the new committee chaired by the vice-president would take "a fresh look at the policies and directions of the [whole] Centre."[58]

This change of focus was necessitated by fact that the Centre's world had been transformed dramatically over the previous few years. One factor in particular lent that some weight; the number of projects begun had more than doubled for each five-year period: 272 to 1975, 675 from 1976 to 1980, and 1,473 up to 1985. Doug Daniels, the director of the Office of Planning and Evaluation, later told the president's committee that "IDRC has now moved out of its early experimental laissez-faire phase into corporate maturity. The accumulation of experience should now enable the Centre to create innovative programs with higher probabilities of greater effectiveness."[59] As a result, for the first time since it was established, it was obliged to employ its budget as a management and policy tool. During IDRC's first years, given the pressures placed upon it by a very activist board and senior management, it was a situation of dollars chasing projects. By 1978, that condition had reversed—projects were now chasing dollars. That increased the burden on the board in determining the Centre's policy priorities, but it also increased the load on staff to satisfy themselves that they were putting forward projects that effectively employed available funds. For that reason, budgeting was now an essential ingredient in IDRC's management process. The aim of evaluation was to feed information back into planning and management to facilitate and improve decision making. Its purposes were accountability, corporate memory, and future decision making. Evaluations, planning, and coordination figured prominently in this revised equation.

The evaluations committee was innovative—IDRC was among the first development organizations to engage in self-assessment. As it grew larger, there was agreement among senior management and program officers that the evaluation of programs and projects supported by the Centre, and of its internal operations, was critical to its accountability and essential to its management process.[60] As well, project completion reports (PCRs) at the end of each activity were added to the duties of project officers, as were written judgments of the utility of the projects they had supervised. While completion rates for PCRs remained disappointing (staff resisted filling them out), evaluations had a happier history. For the latter, it was expected that about 10 percent of completed projects would be assessed each year and, to that end, it was anticipated that a workshop on evaluation methodology would be conducted in early 1980. Of tremendous significance also, IDRC used, as often as possible, Southern evaluators.[61] That piqued the interest of other agencies, which began to follow the Centre's path.

By 1980, three major evaluations had been completed, two of which, Kappagoda thought, "have already been of assistance to the divisions in formulating future project activities in their respective areas."[62] These included the Latin America grants program on human reproduction and the science and technology workshop program evaluation. Similarly, the Centre completed the evaluation of five remote sensing projects that would, it was hoped, provide some guidance to information sciences. Finally, in that first iteration, a few studies had been undertaken on appropriate IDRC policies and practices in least developed countries, primarily in Africa, on network strategies and training policy. Further, IDRC was consulting with other research agencies to learn from their experiences. As Allan Gotlieb had correctly commented when the new program had been under discussion in late 1979, "the heart of the success of our efforts lies in the capacity to evaluate and thus to grow with experience, and to learn from our errors."[63] It was anticipated that about 1 percent of the Centre's budget would be allocated to evaluations.[64]

This emphasis was suggestive of a new route to decision making and planning. A Head objective was to make it easier for the board to assist the Centre in the formulation of policy, as distinct from a project-by-project approach. The board would be encouraged during one of its semi-annual meetings (as it transpired, the April meeting) to consider the Centre's overall policy. Senior management had chosen a three-year window rather arbitrarily, for little reason other than three years seemed far enough into the future to make some sense. It was also the time frame that Treasury Board had indicated suited its processes and that, CIDA's Michel Dupuy told the board, was "the very least IDRC needs to steer its way through Treasury Board." As well, the Privy Council Office had asked about the Centre's planning horizons, and the auditor general had emphasized that it was one of the key areas that it wished to examine in a comprehensive audit that was pending early in the decade.

Planning did impose some order on a Centre where little had existed before, but it came with a cost in that responsiveness to Southern requests was potentially reduced. Head cited this belief during his testimony to the House of Commons Standing Committee on External Affairs and National Defence: "My own board of governors is somewhat dubious about forward planning and vision. A remark made by one of the governors ... at [our] recent meeting was 'It is not so much a question of where we are going to take the Centre over the next three years ... the question is where are the researchers in the developing countries going to take us? If we continue to be responsive to their needs to their assessment of their priorities, we follow them.'"[65] Strictly following, however, was untenable in the political context then prevailing. As Kappagoda noted, it was necessary "for the Centre to monitor the changes in development trends in the Third World, and unless a strong independent capacity exists to assess alternative choices for the allocation of Centre resources, the IDRC runs the risk of not responding adequately to the emerging needs and interests of developing countries."[66] The 1970s were over.

The new process would begin as of the April 1980 board meeting, when Geila Castillo enthusiastically supported the news while also expressing some amazement that it had been accepted: "I must confess that when Nihal Kappagoda made his presentation last October, I didn't expect much to come out of it, not because I did not believe in the capability of his staff, but because, from personal experience, I know that this matter of evaluation is a terribly sensitive one. I am very pleased to note that he has been able to pull it off, and, judging from the looks of it, without much bloodshed."[67] Still, evaluations were indeed a contact sport and John Hardie, hired into the Office of the Vice-President, Programs (OVPP) in the summer of 1980, remembers directors like Hulse and Woolston making sarcastic remarks like "'Here are the evaluation police coming around.' So the office of planning and evaluation was viewed with some suspicion. What's this little group here sucking up resources and not doing anything that they viewed as useful.... But it was Ivan's creation, so they couldn't ignore it."[68]

A Troubled World and UNCSTD

The world of the later 1970s was not nearly as pleasant for Canadians and some others as had been the case in the roughly three decades following the Second World War. In office less than a year, Head was forced to address what he called the provision of "basic or essential needs ... which had been coming forward in increasing volume" as well as the "employment of science and technology, and particularly technology" in LDCs.[69] The second theme had been stimulated largely by the UN Conference on Science and Technology for Development (UNCSTD), and it was giving rise to new, but also very welcome, questions among Southern governments that went to the heart of IDRC activity in the field. These included not merely "What technology?" but, more importantly, "Technology for what?" These weighty questions would have to be contemplated with a static IDRC budget, however; it was frozen by Cabinet edict in early 1979 as Canada's fiscal and economic situation continued to experience difficulties.

Head was able to use these themes to segue in his address to the board in early March 1979 to the Iranian situation and the example and lesson that it held for IDRC in particular and development more generally. The Shah of Iran had fled the country in January of that year as demonstrations and strikes paralyzed it. While there were perhaps a half-dozen factors that contributed to the development of an Islamist state by the following December, the president concentrated on two basic issues that could be applicable to a number of other countries: unbalanced development and an inability to comprehend adequately the social impact of rapid industrialization and the other changes that were changing the face of Iranian society. This had resulted in what some had called the collapse of culture.

Further, Teheran's emphasis on industrialization as an integral part of its modernization program, an almost "total disregard for the needs of the rural areas," and the overemphasis on technological development without paying adequate heed to social ingredients had made a bad situation worse, or so Head believed. It was exacerbated by "the overwhelming presence, throughout this process, of outsiders, giving the impression to many in Iran that foreigners were in control of those processes." Each one of these elements was contrary to how IDRC perceived its mission in the South: "In each instance, the kind of work in which we are engaged and the attitudes we embrace and project attempt to ensure that that kind of situation does not happen in the countries or in the areas or provinces in which we have an opportunity to work." The president had just returned from a trip to the Middle East, and he was firm in his view that a greater sophistication and sensitivity in development matters was necessary.

In his statement he also cited the work of the Independent Commission on International Development Issues, also called the Brandt Commission, after its lead commissioner, former West German Chancellor Willy Brandt.[70] The reason for its 1977 creation was a concern over the misallocation of the globe's resources—the North, with about 25 percent of the world's population, consumed 80 percent of its resources, while the South, the remaining

75 percent, used what was left. Brandt had insisted that neither the World Bank nor the UN provide funding for his commission, which allowed IDRC to play a role in helping it to get on its wobbly feet. Hopper's Centre had made the commitment to provide the original source of funds, up to CAN$500,000, which permitted it to organize and begin functioning. Without that initial grant it is unlikely that Brandt Commission would have gone forward. Hopper had then extracted a *quid pro quo*, insisting on three criteria that would ensure continued Centre support: (1) commission members had to be dedicated to undertaking a solid and objective analysis of outstanding issues between North and South, including addressing commodity questions, and problems of trade, debt, and aid transfers; (2) they had to examine the present operational arrangements, establishments, and terms of reference of existing institutions "to see if these ... could not be made more effective in easing the problems between rich and poor nations; and (3) members must be "solidly devoted to the issues of raising productivity, the output of goods and services, and the distribution of this output within the Third World."[71] The purpose of the final criterion was to bore into the core of the problem of underdevelopment in the South. Hopper had also pointed out that the Commission was not a popular idea at the World Bank or among governments despite Robert McNamara's musings that had led to its establishment. Indeed, the British World Bank director had suggested that a private commission such as this would not have a great chance of success. He was to prove prescient.

While the Brandt Commission did go ahead and did address the issues Hopper had laid out, its effect was not unlike that of a meteor—a bright light in the sky, then nothing but a slowly disappearing tail. Its main report was published in February 1980 under the title *North-South: A Program for Survival*. The difference in title between this and the one prepared a decade earlier by Lester Pearson told the story about what had happened during those ten years; *Partners in Development* (1969) contrasted sharply with *A Program for Survival* (1980). Pearson's message had been one of hope that the South would prosper in coming years because of the transfer of resources from developed to less developed countries, which would surely occur in the near future. With Brandt, catastrophe was not far off; indeed, the Commission was an admission by McNamara that North–South dialogue needed to be re-energized. In a commentary, the Food and Agriculture Organization magazine, *Ceres*, contended that the real needs of LDCs "are subordinated to ideological preferences, commercial chicanery, historic and linguistic links, patronage, the desire to counterbalance one nation against another, and the whole arsenal of good intentions, not-so-good-after-thoughts, and, still worse, second thoughts."[72] Head believed it to be one of the great ironies that, at a time when the developed and less developed were more dependent than ever on each other, "the indifference of the industrialized countries is perhaps at a greater level than it has been for some time."[73] While the Brandt Commission was rather sober in its analysis of the issues affecting development, its report also remained compelling for IDRC, especially given its early support. The Centre funded a conference during the summer of 1980 designed to give some impetus to the Commission's recommendations. Brandt, the Commonwealth Secretary-General Shridath Rammphal, and Barbara Ward, the great development activist, among others, agreed to attend.

Amid continuing global gloom, the Commission's primary recommendation—that action should be taken following a meeting to be convened on North–South issues—fell apart. The anticipated conference was held in Cancun, Mexico, sponsored by President Lopez Portillo and Austrian Chancellor Bruno Kreisky, with strong support from Pierre Trudeau. As Brandt later observed, "Addressing itself to the issues which we had identified in our Emergency Program, this summit, the largest ever devoted exclusively to North–South issues, seemed to reflect a consensus of world leaders on the necessity for new initiatives in the fields of food and energy—and for launching global negotiations."[74] Brandt wrote of a "setback" following Cancun; it certainly was as if all forward movement stopped. Part of that came from strong American and British resistance. Prime Minister Margaret Thatcher later wrote that "The whole concept of 'North–South' dialogue, which the Brandt Commission had made the fashionable talk of the international community, was in my view wrong-headed."[75]

Cancun's failure necessitated another Commission meeting in Kuwait in January 1982, while during the summer, members came together in Brussels. As interest rates in Canada hit 19 percent, Brandt enquired as to the possibility of travelling to the country for the follow-up. When the Liberal government found it not to be a useful expenditure of resources, IDRC stepped into the breach, subject to certain conditions; commissioners would have to find their own way to Ottawa, the meeting would take place at IDRC headquarters, and they would stay at mid-level (read cheaper) hotels, for which IDRC would pay. They accepted and came, from former UK Prime Minister Edward Heath, to Sonny Ramphal, to Colombia's Rodrigo Botero Montoya. Sweden's Prime Minister Olaf Palme was also confirmed, although he was ultimately prevented from attending because of an emergency debate in his Parliament. This was quite a sight—former chancellors and prime ministers resting in hotels that were not used to their sort.

As events transpired, IDRC was the perfect location for the gathering; its word-processing units allowed the Commission to complete within four days camera-ready copy of its report, which was published on 6 February 1983. Entitled *Common Crisis: North–South Cooperation for World Recovery*, Brandt wrote "Deteriorating economic conditions already threaten the political stability of developing countries. Further decline will likely cause the disintegration of societies and create conditions of anarchy in many parts of the world.... Our situation is unique. Never before was the survival of mankind itself at stake."[76] While concrete action remained far removed from present-day reality, Head told IDRC's executive committee that "it was a moment of some considerable pride and, obviously, of assistance to the Brandt Commission that it met in these premises."[77] This marked the end of the Commission as an entity and, in a sense, it had come full circle. The Centre had given it a necessary funding boost in 1977 when other finances were scarce, and it had done the same in late 1982 for the same reason, which had allowed the Commission to write its final report.

The Brandt Commission accomplished very little. With no patron among governments and the election of Margaret Thatcher in 1979 in the United Kingdom and Ronald Reagan in 1980 in the US, there was now active opposition to its recommendations. As has been noted, "it would be hard to imagine a more hostile ideological/political environment for the 1980 Brandt report to navigate for its notions of a grand social pact between North and South, with the end of detente and ascendancy of the new vigorous wave of neo-conservatism."[78] Following 1983, "the ideas of the Brandt Commission were placed unequivocally at the bottom of the international agenda."[79]

IDRC viewed the UN Conference on Science and Technology for Development in largely the same way that it saw the Brandt Commission—as a part of the evolving situation in a world increasingly unfriendly to international development. That was partly because the conference, as Francisco Sagasti has pointed out, "marked the international legitimization of a number of concerns of developing countries in the area of science and technology policy."[80] As it had supported Brandt in the late 1970s, so it did the former, hoping that the UN conference would emerge a success. It considered not only science and technology policy instruments, which IDRC had pioneered in the early 1970s with Geoff Oldham and Sagasti, but more particularly technology; never before had there been such an attempt to come to grips with its application in development. As well, there was an increasing emphasis on ends as well as means, and on the requirement for equitable and sustainable development policy.

IDRC personnel were excited by UNCSTD, both before and during the actual conference. This occupied much Centre attention and many of its resources during mid-1979; its subject was very closely related to what IDRC stood for—linking science and technology with development. It was reasonable under those circumstances that IDRC had devoted almost CAN$290,000 for the conference. First, in conjunction with the Ministry of State for Science and Technology (MOSST), a study was done by the Association of Scientists and Engineers of Canada on the problems the Canadian scientific community was facing in extending its expertise to the problems of developing countries. This paper was given to the minister for science and technology and formed a part of the national document for UNCSTD. IDRC also participated in a one-day seminar hosted by the Quebec Association of Civil and Scientific Organizations on problems related to the transfer of technology. Furthermore, the Centre assisted the United Nations in the synthesis of some of the papers that had been received for the conference, and its funds were used to help bring Southern researchers to several meetings organized by IDRC and which it considered crucial to the success of UNCSTD. The first of these, held in Jamaica and co-chaired by Ivan Head and Barbara Ward, had resulted in a paper, "Mobilizing Technology for World Development." Louis Berlinguet was also present at an organizational meeting funded by the Soviet Union in Cali, Colombia. There were others attended by Centre staff in Singapore, Mexico, and Vienna. Berlinguet was also the vice-chair of the Advisory Committee on the Application of Science and Technology (ACAST), a UN agency that convened a colloquium one week before the Vienna meeting and which brought together scientists and policy-makers.

At the conference itself, the usual confrontation between North and South was evident. The group of seventy-seven developing countries was united in their request for a major undertaking to assist them in building up their indigenous scientific and technological capabilities, a fact made clear by the conference communiqué, what Sagasti called "sensible recommendations for developing indigenous science and technology capabilities, for restructuring international scientific relations, and for reorganizing the UN machinery in order to make it more responsive to the needs of developing countries in the field of S&T for development."[81] LDCs wanted the creation of a US$2 billion to US$4 billion fund at the UN to finance these activities, as well as the creation of a new international body within the United Nations to administer the new funds and to purchase technology on their behalf. Eventually, a "voluntary" and disappointing fund of about US$250 million was established, a far cry from the demands made.[82]

Finally, they wanted the industrialized countries to apply a substantial amount of their domestic research and development capacity to the solution of developing countries' problems. These demands were described as firm.[83] The word did not mean the same thing to Northern representatives, so very little of what was demanded was obtained; they remained more paper requests. Still, despite the rather tentative response to LDC issues, it was "one of the very few major UN conferences that did not fail [at least outright]. In fact, it achieved some proof that there could be a few bridges established between the North and the South, and the negotiations will continue during the coming years."[84] It was also the last "big jamboree" of the Second Development Decade. Mahindra Naraine, in the Department of Politics at the University of Lancaster, also thought that it contained "very little science and technology but was a political event envisaged as part of the New International Economic Order package."[85] In short, the conference was a success because "it was not a failure." Under the circumstances, that was a ringing endorsement.

So what did IDRC get from its investment of money and people power? Given that science and technology for development was a major part of its work, perhaps quite a bit. The General Assembly gave ACAST more responsibility, yet could not arrogate to itself more executive power; it remained an *advisory* body to a legislature that had very little power. Still, it continued to work on issues referred to it by the General Assembly and certain member governments, which helped to sharpen its expertise. Furthermore, the United Nations in particular perceived UNCSTD as an educational opportunity in partial justification of the cost and effort—Northern politicians now knew more about the scientific problems of developing countries than was the case before the high-profile gathering, and that was a step forward. Similarly, more scientists had learned about the political and economic implications of their discoveries, and it was hoped that dialogue between scientist and politician had been encouraged.

That would be a welcome development for the Centre, too, whose image had also been enhanced by exposure at the meeting. IDRC had set up a large booth filled with its materials, and its publications had flown off the shelves. While that had been a boost for the Centre, the announcement made by the Austrian minister of science and culture, Herta Firnberg, who had presided over UNCSTD, was in some ways more significant; she had told the conference that Austria would soon be establishing an institution modelled on IDRC. While that did not happen in part because of the economic downturn, it did demonstrate the esteem in which the Centre was held by some other countries. Importantly, many countries had also attended the speech of Martial Asselin, the minister of state for the Canadian International Development Agency in Joe Clark's short-lived government, in which the Centre had been singled out as a significant contributing organization. He had also announced that it was to become the focal point of Ottawa's new initiative of providing additional funds to allow *Canadian* scientists to become more involved in researching the problems of the South. A target figure of about 1 percent of ODA, roughly CAN$12 million, was to be set aside.[86] "We would expect IDRC," he intoned, "to build up its capacity to use such resources effectively fairly quickly, over the next few years."

How was that announcement received at the Centre? In two ways—cautiously and with some incredulity that additional funds would be allocated to ODA. Head would also make certain that this "cannot and must not be, or be seen to be, as any derogation of the independence of the Centre from the government of Canada, and as well the intention of the Centre to continue, even when this new activity begins, to be responsive to the stated needs of developing countries."[87] As well, such an effort, if and when it came to fruition, would be seen as quite separate from the kind of activity in which IDRC was normally engaged. It remained that it was not an institution whose traditional practice had included funding Canadian researchers. When the minority Clark government was defeated on a confidence vote in March 1980 and lost the ensuing election, the additional funds died on the order paper.

The early 1980s was shaping up to be a very tough time in terms of Canadian economic vitality. Nor could IDRC necessarily assume that its parliamentary appropriation would not be reduced. As it was, it was frozen in 1979–80 at the same level as the previous year, which actually meant a decrease in real terms.[88] Donald Macdonald told the board in October 1982 that further adverse pressure on the Centre's budget could result "because of domestic unemployment [the result of which might be] an attempt to shift funds without … creating a larger deficit."[89] The fact that that scenario did not play out stood as testament to IDRC's reputation with government. Instead, it received a 15 percent increase in its parliamentary appropriation for the 1980–81 fiscal year, and continued to experience additional revenues through to 1988–89. Head correctly called the government's refusal to reduce the Centre's parliamentary appropriation during the early 1980s "an extraordinary vote of confidence in a period of economic recession in Canada."[90]

Travelling to China

However, IDRC continued to search for new areas in which to invest the funds it did have, very sensitive to the criticism that it had stagnated around the four fiefdoms. While they remained essentially intact, the Centre was reaching out. The People's Republic of China (PRC) was an objective. Having opened up to more involvement with the West following the death of Mao in 1976, the PRC was keen to initiate discussions with IDRC, an intent based on the Centre's reputation for non-interference in the domestic affairs of the country in which it funded research, as well as IDRC's explicit rejection of research imperialism. To that end, the country's ambassador visited the Centre to determine more precisely its suitability for funding work in China. Head also met with the ambassador at the embassy and proposed that an IDRC delegation visit his country. The president had long been interested in the PRC and, in the early 1960s, had thought it a travesty that Canada had not recognized the Asian giant.[91]

The president was keen to proceed with China on a Centre-wide basis rather than through a number of individual approaches; indeed, he had instructed all program officers to cease their operations in the People's Republic until a coherent strategy could be worked out. This proposed approach was unusual and had reflected two concerns. The first was that Chinese needs were so great "that the resources of the Centre had to be of a significant amount in order to adequately do the task," while the second was "the obverse of that coin; that our other clients and research partners elsewhere in the world might become distressed if they felt that an enormity of funds from the Centre were likely to be channeled towards the PRC."[92] As a result, a target figure for research investment, CAN$2 million, was derived, spread over two years. (During the two-year period ending 31 December 1982, the Chinese spent CAN$1,946,975 of that.) Head was very eager to forge that link, telling the board that "we all accept the fact that we have much to gain from a relationship with China. There is much technological and scientific activity that we can benefit from, and we have much to offer ourselves."[93]

In September 1980, he signed a memorandum of understanding (MOU) with the State Scientific and Technological Commission (SSTC) of the PRC. A critical part of the MOU was IDRC's insistence on and China's agreement to marry its technologies and technicians with IDRC funding and research management experience for the benefit of *other* LDCs; that is, Chinese researchers would travel to other developing countries to spread the benefits of their work funded by the Centre. The arrangement was a first—the PRC had never done this before. It was also useful as Chinese scientists and technologists, often with IDRC backing, informed Asian colleagues of the results of their findings in bamboo cultivation, forestry practices, and aquaculture, among other areas. Given early success, Joe Hulse told an incredulous board that the Centre "was hoping to create the first scientific linkage between Taiwan and the People's Republic of China through a device in Thailand ... the Asian Vegetable Research Development Centre."[94] However, it would be best for all concerned, he dryly noted, if that was not brought to the attention of the Canadian press.

Because of the ravages of the Cultural Revolution, the Chinese were very keen that IDRC officers "train people, to bring them up to the point where they themselves could do things, to put them into universities, institutes and to create courses, workshops and conferences."[95] Some of this involved the Social Sciences Division, and its program officers had been all over China by late 1982. Indeed, that was a part of the bargain; the IDRC team had made it very clear to the Chinese that it wished to have an across-the-board program operating in the People's Republic, to which Beijing had agreed, which meant that as agricultural scientists would be funded, so, too, would those from social sciences. The problem for the Chinese government was that often research in the latter area led to criticism of the state, implied or overt, stemming from the results of projects. The Centre had also hired some officers fluent in Mandarin, which helped its efforts in the countryside, but which also meant they could do so independent of government interpreters. Similarly, in a few years, IDRC was making instructional films using Chinese characters and the use of simultaneous translation in PRC operations had fallen to a minimum. That simple measure, so quintessentially IDRC, led to an exceptional degree of collaboration and confidence developing between SSTC and the Centre, and contributed immeasurably to the effectiveness of the relationship.[96]

However, in its early funding of Chinese researchers, the primary Centre concern was to contribute to the strengthening of basic Chinese agricultural and forestry science with a view to increasing production; the focus was on building Chinese capacity, which was accomplished with help from Canadian scientists also funded by IDRC. Much of the work done on canola and pawlonia, for example, was undertaken at research stations; the Centre was active in encouraging the Chinese to move out into the field for real testing, which they did. As one IDRC regional director has written, "As field training, dissemination and institutionalization began in earnest, practical obstacles posed by the interconnectedness of farmland and forest systems became more obvious. Recognizing partner priorities, the focus of Centre support expanded towards production systems and their utilization and integration; new projects focused on bamboo or fuelwood utilization, on cropping systems and on integrated cropping and aquatic systems."[97] Into the 1990s, the emphasis was to shift away from production systems to involve more socio-economic considerations and to locate research efforts closer to the communities facing problems in ecosystems or at basin levels rather than in test plots or research stations. That was seen most clearly with the work of community-based natural resource management projects "in the marginal ecosystems of the arid Tarim Basin and the karst landscapes of rural Guizhou and with Centre support for work on biodiversity mapping and indigenous knowledge in the tropical Xishuangbanna Reserve." With these, Centre support helped provincially based, multidisciplinary Chinese research teams build capacity to work in a participatory fashion with poor communities and staff from local government.

Further, IDRC funded a program of research focusing on the cultivation of bamboo, which began in early 1982 and which would remain on its books for another two decades. This eventually led to the establishment of the International Network for Bamboo and Rattan (INBAR) in 1998, the first international organization to be based in the Chinese capital. Of the thirty-four participating countries, Canada is the only temperate country member, a reflection of INBAR's origins. As one Chinese researcher was to later note, "Canada has helped China improve its bamboo and rattan when it does not itself grow any of these trees. This shows the sincere intention of IDRC to help developing countries."[98] It did indeed seem to be the case that the various bamboo workshops the Centre had sponsored helped to take "the Chinese out from behind the bamboo curtain."[99] By 1990, the bamboo-funded research program grew to be the largest in size, measured in value in annual terms, administered by IDRC's South East and East Asia Regional Office, and one of the most significant in the world. By that time, the MOU had been amended twice, in 1983 and 1988, to reflect changes in Chinese organizational practices and in IDRC program support. Overall, the Chinese venture worked out very well, and IDRC has remained involved and vital, even as China has experienced tremendous growth rates over the past twenty years and is well on track to becoming a middle-income country.

The Centre Examines Itself

John Hardie's paper, "Using Knowledge for Development," was the result of what had become a greater issue for IDRC—the utilization of research results, which had launched a period of introspection and self-assessment.[100]The purpose of the paper was to stimulate discussion as the Centre set about considering its way forward during the second half of the decade. What animated all of its decisions was IDRC's status as a research for development organization, and that the research supported should be aimed at problem solving and not merely funding researchers to undertake research for its own sake. By the earlier 1980s, some senior management realized that IDRC was hazy, in some instances, about outcomes: What *was* the impact of the research it had funded in developing countries? Jim Mullin remembered the day that that simple question had sunk in at the Centre: "'Look [at what] we have spent'—at that time the aggregate spending of IDRC had reached a billion Canadian dollars and it didn't take too smart a program officer to understand that if we were going to continue to get large amounts of money in the temper of the times of government spending, we had to be able to show that that made a difference."[101] In the longer run the Centre would be assessed by its association with research work that contributed in some way to social and economic advancement, and it was incumbent upon staff to begin to document how and where this had occurred.

This also highlighted the second part of the Centre's philosophical orientation—that meaningful development came from within societies and not from Northern dictates. IDRC could not supply the answers or the questions, and it should respond and not impose. But what should it do if the affected country could not, for one reason or another, establish its own priorities? It would be very tempting for IDRC to make suggestions about what seemed to be obvious, but that would smack of paternalism, a dangerous development and a position that was alien to the Centre's culture.[102] It also followed that the research was not the Centre's, but belonged to the researcher. And if that meant the Centre helped to "re-invent the wheel" occasionally, that was a part of its philosophy and practice. As officers, who were well aware, knew, most projects did not deal "with great science in the sense of highly innovative, new things which result in spectacular publications and frontiers of knowledge."[103] Instead, IDRC focused its assistance more on existing knowledge, a degree of innovation, with excellent management capabilities behind the research, application of existing knowledge, and what one governor called "downstream rather than upstream frontiers."

IDRC was keen to determine the effectiveness of the utilization of research results accruing from projects it funded, hiring a consultant, Donald Mills, to prepare a report. Mills was certainly qualified, having had a distinguished career with the Jamaican public and foreign services, where one of his responsibilities had been to represent his country as its permanent representative to the UN. His mission was designed to help the Centre plan strategically in determining and measuring impact. This would be done through an investigation of research management and an evaluation of the process of research result implementation. He would also investigate researcher attitudes, as well as those of certain government officials in targeted countries about research utilization. As Head had said, "Research results are of no value to anybody if they bring nothing more than honour to the researcher or dust to the shelves where they sit."[104] A few years later, a similar program was undertaken for IDRC in francophone countries by Jacques Diouf, formerly the minister of scientific research in the government of Senegal and later head of the Food and Agricultural Organization.

When Mills toted up his interviews and assessments, the sum pointed to a reputation that was almost unequalled: "its flexibility, the fact that it does not seek to establish a high profile, the fact that its grants are not tied, and a number of things about IDRC have been recognized."[105] There remained some niggling questions: How would IDRC maintain the quality of its efforts as it programs expanded, which would surely happen with its increased parliamentary appropriation? As it grew, how could IDRC prevent itself from "becoming too large, too smug, and too stagnant"? How would (or could) the organization remain on the collegial path it had followed for the past thirteen years? Mills was excited by his findings; IDRC should run with what it said about itself and take it *literally*. Out of this analysis had come what Ivan Head called "new initiatives." He had canvassed board members during the spring of 1982 for their thoughts, and a hefty paper of the same name was later put together by staff to explore certain possibilities.

One contribution that met with universal approbation was earth sciences, an area ripe for examination with help from Canadian scientists; Mullin's group, the Canadian Partnerships Unit (CPU), would spend a significant proportion of its resources here. This area was chosen because it could help to improve Southern access to the strengths of the Canadian research system.[106] In a sense, earth sciences was a natural; Canada's oldest scientific institution was the Geological Survey, dating from the 1840s.[107] The Canadian experience in their own development had been very closely tied to the exploitation of natural resources and, as a result, there was a wide array of private, public, and academic institutions across the country that had experience in the subject. Conversely, there were a great many countries in the South that needed to develop expertise in the area. Mullin had consulted with the International Union of Geological Sciences, the Association of Geoscientists for International Development, and with the UNESCO Program on Geology for Development in Africa for insight into how to proceed. It was so typically IDRC.

Nor would the Centre replicate research or work being done by other development agencies; it would remain focused on the poorest parts of the population, particularly the rural poor, whom larger agencies tended to ignore. It would also concentrate on areas like soil analysis, beginning with a workshop to bring together soil scientists and geochemists from a more traditional geological background to work out ways to replace soil nutrients that had been leached out in tropical locations. The Amazon was one area in which to locate such a project. As well, water issues could be explored in, for example, the Andes with help from hydrologists at the University of British Columbia. The identification of suitable construction materials was also a promising area of research in the South, which would be a contribution toward improving the lifestyle of people in certain developing countries. The program would not fund projects like high-energy physics, the compilation of an anthology of creative English language writing in the islands of the South Pacific, or a project to determine which birds migrated annually between Quebec and Venezuela, all proposals received by IDRC. Other than that, however, the field was wide open. Indeed, Mullin's new responsibility could be called "the office of miscellaneous other areas of research. If it does not fit the four program divisions, it ha[d] to fit [his]."[108]

The first project to be funded was the Cyprus Crystal Study in conjunction with Dalhousie University and was "a classic project of what we will have in Cooperative Programs."[109] The project's objectives were threefold: (1) to investigate the formation of certain classes of mineral ores; (2) to examine its potential as a source of geothermal energy; and (3) to consider it as a source of groundwater. It had been developed via discussions with Canadian scientists who were contemplating a training element for developing countries to be attached to projects they were then undertaking. They had first approached CIDA, but without success, whereupon they had encouraged IDRC to be a putative partner, now a possibility because of CPU. The Centre had then funded an external review, undertaken discussions with the Canadians, and had examined the results of two previous projects on similar themes that the group had completed. Mullin told the executive committee that "Cyprus is one of the more advanced of the societies and is certainly a far step away from many of the activities that the Centre has had. The real attraction came from the proposal to add to the drilling project in the analysis of the cores, a training program where eligibility is determined first on geological grounds." The proposal was to invite about twenty mid-career LDC scientists to take part in the research activities, and then suggest that roughly ten of them come to various labs across Canada to participate in a more detailed laboratory analysis, thereby exposing them to the latest techniques for analyzing such structures. Mullin hoped that geological surveys and departments of mines from a wide range of LDCs would be helped through this effort. While project costs were heavy, Head noted that he looked forward to the involvement of Information Science's cartography program, and other relevant programs in Agriculture, Food, and Nutrition Sciences and Social Sciences. The template was set.

In the Southern Cone

One of the more controversial areas in which IDRC worked during the 1980s, and which demonstrates its commitment to research and preserving researchers in sometimes-hostile environments, was the Southern cone of South America. In the early 1970s, that region was subject to military dictatorship; Uruguay in June 1973, Chile the following September, and Argentina on 24 March 1976. The situation remained perilous for all those who opposed the various governments; for example, it was estimated that in 1976 Uruguay had more political prisoners per capita than any other country on earth, and that about 10 percent of its population had emigrated to escape the military. Further, the torture and killing of those identified as opponents of the regime numbered in the tens of thousands. It was a similar story in Argentina and Chile, where the murdered and the *desaparecidos* became the stuff of legend. In both countries, juntas led by generals Jorge Videla and Augusto Pinochet proved to be vicious and without mercy. Again, thousands were "disappeared" and many thousands more put in prisons— three thousand killed in Chile and about twenty-seven thousand tortured and in jail, while about thirty thousand were killed in Argentina. Further, Operation Condor pledged the three governments to work together against so-called insurgents, assassinating, disappearing, or incarcerating and torturing perceived opponents. By and large, those governments targeted social democratic opponents and those in the universities who did not subscribe to their notions of social organization and governance. Society was being remade as a result of economic policy; all three countries were experiencing an enormous concentration of wealth accompanied by a decreasing role of the state in providing health and education services, resulting in higher levels of malnutrition, illiteracy, infant mortality, and reductions in university enrolments.

IDRC, along with a few foundations, supported the research of displaced academics. It began in late 1976, when Hopper, on his own initiative, had provided Argentina's Bariloche Foundation, established in 1963 and dedicated to research and graduate training, with a CAN$50,000 grant to keep it alive following the military takeover. Its underlying credo was respect for democratic republicanism, which had, of course, alienated it from the military junta. Arguably, one of the best examples of IDRC support for the victims of authoritarianism in the region was the funding provided to the Corporación Latinoamericana de Investigación Económica (CIEPLAN), which was also partly funded by the Ford Foundation.[110] It is a rough model for what happened with other organizations located in Argentina, Brazil, and Uruguay, as well as Chile, like the Facultad Latinoamericana de Ciencias Sociales (FLASCO), which had been established in 1957 by UNESCO as a regional master's level training centre for Latin American sociologists.[111] In its researchers' own words, CIEPLAN "was motivated by the willingness of a group of social scientists to maintain a tradition of independent academic research on fundamental economic and social problems related to Chilean and Latin American societies under a context in which for a number of reasons, this activity has been seriously curtailed in the universities."[112] About 30 percent of all CIEPLAN's annual funding came from IDRC, while between 90 and 100 percent of its income derived from foreign sources through the support of five foreign donor agencies.

As former executive director Patricio Meller remembered, a very important thing for the Chileans was that IDRC "understood the priorities as to research had to be defined by us, not by them. In this way, it was different from most other foundations. [Moreover], in spite of the fact that some issues we thought important were not in their program, they listened and were able to stretch and accept our position."[113] René Cortazar, Meller's successor as executive director and later the minister of labour in the first Aylwin government and minister of transportation and communication in the last Bachelet administration, went further; he did not have any experience "with any other foundation where you felt that they were really interested in what *our* agenda was. IDRC tried to make it work through not forcing us to adapt to their agenda for Latin America."[114] And that was much appreciated and helped to distinguish the Centre from other institutions that had been actively funding dissident centres for a longer period of time and with greater resources.[115] Further, all of the very important macro-economic work being undertaken by the Corporation was funded by IDRC, including workshops, research dissemination, as well as research. Cortazar suggested that the funding provided by the Centre allowed them, as "leftists," to be fiscally responsible, a very unusual condition, or so he claimed. It was, he said, not unlike "nuns talking about sex." CIEPLAN initially consisted of about twenty-five people huddled together in a house, writing papers for a journal with a circulation of about a thousand. In the mid-1970s, the military harassed its staffers, but in Chile, oddly enough, given what had occurred with government, police were very careful about rules, and the Corporación had legal status from the pre-junta days. The military also undertook a cost-benefit analysis: Was it worth it to close down a small operation like CIEPLAN and risk it becoming an issue in countries like the United States and Canada, especially given the funding provided by foreign agencies? As well, program officers had pointed out to the board that as the decade ground on, those military regimes felt more comfortable and secure, which made them less fearful of popular (or academic) unrest. Furthermore, the sword, at least in the government's view, was mightier than the pen. For an authoritarian government, that was enough.

Finance was a pressing need for Southern cone research centres as inflation was a constant problem eroding the value of the currency, reaching the level of 150 percent per year in the case of Argentina in 1979. CIEPLAN was grateful for IDRC funding and also that it came with few strings attached.[116] If there was a caveat, it remained that the Centre was keen the Corporación develop policy, and not write only academic papers. Meller observed that IDRC trusted them to produce relevant research that would have an impact on Chilean society, whether or not the left was in quiet opposition or in power. And impact it they did. During the early 1980s, their macro-economic studies suggested that the government had downplayed the incidence of inflation afflicting the Chilean economy and undermined the military regime's claims of economic brilliance. Its economic policy had largely been constructed by the so-called Chicago boys, trained in the Chicago school of economics, led by Milton Friedman, which would be discredited throughout much of the world by the 1990s.

As the situation in the country began to stabilize, it became clear that organizations like CIEPLAN were the alternative to continued military rule; if IDRC had not continued funding the organization, it would not have been a point of reference "where people could say 'What is the alternative to the military?'"[117] When Chileans began mobilizing against the government, the Corporación had a growing impact. Part of this came as a result of a book published by CIEPLAN economists and funded by the Centre, *Political Macroeconomic Policy: A Latin American Perspective*. Would it have been possible to accomplish this in Chile, basically providing an alternative to military rule, without the foreign assistance of which IDRC constituted a significant part? René Cortazar thinks not: he could "not imagine there was a way to build a team of intellectuals—sociologists, economists, and others—under the military regime and through the transition without the aid of international organizations like IDRC." Without them, the evolving situation would have been completely different as the private sector in the country was very much marching in step with the dictatorship.

How did the Centre get to the point where it did this sort of thing in the Southern cone even though the Trudeau Liberals had recognized the Pinochet government the day after the coup? That had largely to do with the persistence of two IDRC program officers—Elizabeth Fox de Cardona, who worked out of the Centre's regional office in Bogota, and headquarter's Tony Tillett—as well as Nihal Kappagoda, Doug Daniels, and Chris Smart, and the Centre's Act and freedom from the "normal" constraints of behaviour for Canadian government institutions; IDRC was not, of course, an agency of Her Majesty, which did give it latitude. Fox wrote the first paper for board consumption in September 1980, "Support for Social Sciences Research in the Southern Cone," while Tillett contributed "Social Science Research in the Southern Cone of Latin America: An Evaluation of Centre Supported Institutions."[118] Chris Smart was also integrally involved in project design, as well as being the buffer between David Steedman and Tillett; the two despised each other and Smart's job "was to keep them from getting at each other's throats."[119] IDRC had begun supporting five social science research centres in Argentina, Chile, and Uruguay in 1977. "This was done," Fox concluded, "with the understanding that the grants were necessary given the political repression of the social sciences as part of the rapid and undemocratic changes of government." With military officers in each country approving curriculum and faculty, expertise in the social sciences was actively discouraged.

In hindsight, of course, IDRC support is seen as the "right thing" as those military governments have gone on to international opprobrium with one former president, Augusto Pinochet, suffering the ignominy of imprisonment in the United Kingdom in the 1990s for activities conducted by his regime during the seventeen years from 1973 to 1990. Similarly, in recent years Argentina and Uruguay have seen civilian governments charge and convict senior military officers for their involvement in some of the murders and disappearances that took place during the dictatorships. However, the crystal ball was not so clear when the subject came up for discussion at an in-camera session of the board in 1982. And one important board member, the chair Donald Macdonald, was resolutely opposed to offering assistance to dissident researchers. His position, and the response of Fox, Tillett, and Head, speaks to IDRC's commitment to what it would have seen as the cause of research pluralism. As well, it reflects a fundamental decency that animated most of the Centre's activities. Macdonald's statement and the various reactions are worth quoting here for those reasons. It also says a lot about IDRC's philosophy, one that would also be brought to bear in South Africa in the later 1980s, and which will be discussed in Chapter 4.

"There seems to be," Macdonald began when the project "Macroeconomics and Balance of Payments Research: Phase II" was brought up for consideration at the June 1982 executive committee meeting,

> a polemical quality running through this document. Do we want to be in the position of funding this sort of project? ... We have decided to hold our noses and deal with a lot of governments we may not like such as Chile, Zaire, Argentina, Ethiopia ... but are we serving our cause well and the people we are trying to assist by, in effect, running the research department of

the leader of the opposition? In other words, should we be getting into politics? I don't know what the initial framework of this Centre's mandate was, but if the answer to that question is yes, then I would be very surprised. I may not know a lot of things but I do know something about politics.... I think we should stay out of politics; this is getting us into politics.... I am not in support of it. If you don't get into trouble on this one, then I'll be a monkey's uncle.[120]

Even given the dry words recorded in the executive committee minutes, one can imagine the reaction. Head, among others present, emphatically rejected the chair's advice. That side of the president's personality was what Maggie Catley-Carlson called the "Ivan the good side.... He had a perversity of mind in some cases that was very good."[121] CIEPLAN was in the forefront as a producer of quality material. Moreover, Corporación researchers, and their dedication to their craft and their country, was what allowed IDRC to offer some help. Jeffrey Fine, a program officer working out of South America and who helped prepare the document under consideration, echoed the president's position: Phase II was "certainly not polemics ... due to the general situation in Chile, any type of independent economic criticism of government policies is going to be exaggerated simply because of the situation in Chile. There is no other group doing this type of research and, as a result, it may create a reaction. The focus of this is to provide alternatives for discussion, not simply to criticize." And when Head had visited Argentina in early 1982, the country's military-appointed deputy minister of foreign affairs had requested a meeting with him to discuss IDRC support of those research institutions that opposed the government's agenda; the Centre had not been "discouraged" from doing what it was, or "inhibited by the governments of Chile or Argentina.... I think it fair to say that the international reputation and quality of the institutions which we have selected—CIEPLAN among the foremost—is the best defence over any worry." Following an hour's heated debate and after letting it sit with members overnight, phase II was approved over Macdonald's objections. In Argentina, Dante Caputo, the country's foreign minister following the restoration of democracy, could tell Joe Clark in October 1985 that the greater part of the extensive monetary and fiscal reform policy introduced in the post-dictatorship period was a direct result of research funded by the Centre over the years.[122] IDRC involvement with CIEPLAN and others of its type in different countries would continue into the 1990s.

In the long run, far from getting into trouble, IDRC's support for researchers in the Southern cone during the dictatorships paid major dividends when democratic governments returned to power. It helped those countries to deal with the "lost decade" of the 1980s, plagued by "the worst economic and financial crisis ... in the last 50 years."[123] The result of the relatively small investment made by the International Development Research Centre was, first and foremost, the establishment of a Canadian reputation that was second to none among many Chilean academics and intellectuals. Alejandro Foxley, chair of CIEPLAN in the 1980s and, until 2009, Chile's foreign minister, has sung the praises of the IDRC, while Fernando Chaparro, then the regional director at the Latin America and Caribbean office, claimed that "the [successful] Chilean experience was based partly on IDRC."[124] He went on to note that "in [the Centre] they found not just a source of funding, it was people they could relate to in terms of the ideas, in terms of the workshops that were organized, and getting significant discussion of some of the major research, development and human rights issues that we were facing. And I think it's the quality that was the attraction with IDRC—besides the financial dimension." René Cortazar has said that without the involvement of IDRC, the vibrant democratic path that Chile has followed over the past sixteen years "could have been a very different story.... Canada was a big part of it."[125] How big? As Ivan Head was told when he visited Chile in late 1990, "no less than four ministers in the Aylwin government, and some twelve individuals in senior positions, [were] all long-time recipients of IDRC assistance.... The Centre's sustained support for independent research throughout much of the dark period of the military dictatorship was one of the major turning points in the victory of the democratic forces and now a significant element in the policies of the new government."[126] Indeed, in the years since the restoration of democracy, every Chilean budget director and every minister of finance first proved their mettle in CIEPLAN, marking a direct, although now increasingly distant, relationship with the Centre.

As they entered government, Canada was not forgotten, and a tangible result was the Canada–Chile free trade agreement, negotiated in the mid-1990s and which took effect on 7 July 1997. Then, Canada was the only industrialized country with which Chile had such a treaty. Trade flows increased, as did investment. Moreover, as Cortazar has said, the agreement was welcomed by his countrymen because "the legitimacy of working with Canada is very different from working with the United States because of the history of the US and Chile." Similarly, in recent years many high-level positions in the governments of the region were held by individuals who once benefited directly or indirectly from IDRC support for research, and they continue to associate Canada with their individual success and with a very different approach to development.

Conclusion

While this chapter began with the statement that the fundamental outlines of IDRC remained unchanged during Ivan Head's first term in office, clearly much happened *inside* the Centre as procedures were shaken up, evaluations were undertaken, and administrative processes altered. Perhaps of singular importance for its long-term survival, IDRC became much more conscious of its Canadian roots. Head's intent to "massage" his fellow Canadians, and especially their elected representatives, was key, or so it was becoming more clear, to the Centre's continuing operation. The Cooperative Programs Unit was an essential and flexible add-on to that effect, which would support its overall objectives. As well, IDRC opened up vistas to include the People's Republic of China, just emerging from the Cultural Revolution. That was very significant and was testimony to the Centre's global reputation—the Chinese sought it out and signed an MOU while most other development organizations were still scrambling, attempting to determine what the death of Mao meant for them.

But IDRC remained focused on its four divisions, and board considerations of projects as listed in the minutes, look more or less in 1982 as they did in 1972. For example, in June 1982, Agriculture, Food, and Nutrition Sciences put forward a project dealing with *Erythrina*, a bacteria that fixed nitrogen in the soil. It had done similarly in 1972. And that list went on—farming systems in Mali, groundnut improvements in Thailand, intercropping in Swaziland, and pasture development in Chile. Social Sciences was funding projects like the social aspects of rural technology in Latin America and a literacy campaign in Ethiopia, Information Sciences was providing money for the Barbados library, archive, and information centre network and for national agricultural information systems output services, while Health was supporting a project on acute respiratory infections in the Caribbean and another on advanced intrauterine devices with global application. Similarly, networks remained important for IDRC and were cultivated whenever and wherever possible. This general pattern remained in place at the Centre for the remainder of Head's time in office, but as its parliamentary appropriation increased from the roughly CAN$67 million when he was reappointed to office by Pierre Trudeau to CAN$114 million when Keith Bezanson took over, IDRC was obviously much more activist and its projects more widespread. What did this explosion of its parliamentary appropriation mean to the Centre? We will turn our attention to that in Chapter 4.

Notes

1 IDRC–A, Meeting of the Board of Governors, B of G Notes (23), 10/80, 12.
2 Willy Brandt, *North–South: A Program of Survival: Report of the Independent Commission on International Development Issues* (Cambridge: MIT Press, 1980), 50.
3 Joe Clark thought that the best thing he could do for IDRC while he was foreign minister was to leave it entirely alone. He knew its Act very well and was concerned not to meddle in its business. Interview with Joe Clark, Waterloo, 26 October 2008.
4 Interview with John Hardie, 17 August 2008, Ottawa. As well, Hardie noted that Head always said he saw his role as a fundraiser for IDRC and keeping on the good side of Clark made this easier.
5 United Nations Economic Commission for Africa as quoted in IDRC–A, Meeting of the Board of Governors, B of G Notes (23), 10/80, 10.
6 Jahangir Amuzegar, "A Requiem for the North–South Conference," *Foreign Affairs*, vol. 56, no. 1, October 1977, 136.
7 IDRC–A, Meeting of the Board, March 1978, *in camera* session, Maurice Strong.
8 IDRC–A, Meeting of the Board, March 1978, *in camera* session, Maurice Strong.
9 IDRC–A, Meeting of the Board, 16, 17, and 18 March 1978, B of G Notes in-camera session, 2.
10 Interview with Terry Smytylo by Martin Kreuzer, 15 June 2004, Ottawa.
11 IDRC–A, Meeting of the Board, March 1978, in-camera session, Ivan Head.
12 IDRC–A, Meeting of the Board, March 1978, in-camera session, Ivan Head.
13 IDRC–A, Meeting of the Board, October 1978.
14 The April Fool's date is, of course, fortuitous. The CPU came into existence as the new fiscal year, 1 April 1981, began. Still, the point remains.
15 Canada, House of Commons Standing Committee on External Affairs and National Defence, *Minutes of Proceedings and Evidence*, no. 3, 15 November 1979, 3:8–3:12. See also, Ivan Head, "IDRC: A New Focal Point," *IDRC Reports* 1979, 10.
16 IDRC–A, Meeting of the Executive Committee, EC (64) 6/86, 14. Helleiner believed that Canadian universities would use IDRC as a cash cow: "I do not like the program of grants in aid or excessive overheads to bail out what I hope are temporarily financially strapped Canadian universities in an international development institution. I regard this as a matter of principle."
17 IDRC–A, Meeting of the Board of Governors, B of G Notes (25) 10/81, 45.
18 IDRC–A, Meeting of the Board, October 1981, Rex Nettleford.
19 IDRC–A, Meeting of the Board of Governors, B of G Notes (25) 10/81, in-camera session, 21 October 1981, 1.
20 Interview with Lauchlan Munro, 7 August 2009.
21 Interview with Maggie Catley-Carlson, Chelsea, August 2006. Catley-Carlson related an interesting story that had to do with her tenure as president of CIDA. TBS officials, and those from the Auditor-General's Office, were always on her organization to account for every penny of public funds expended. Later, when she became deputy minister of health and was called into a meeting with TBS officials, she worried about the same thing: Had Health officials done something incorrect? As it turned out, TBS wanted to do all in its power to help her as she learned those ropes. It then struck her that TBS did not care one whit about helping *international* development as expressed through CIDA, but did very much about the those federal departments focusing on *domestic* issues.
22 IDRC–A, Program Branch, Treasury Board Secretariat, "Evaluation of the International Development Research Centre: Documentation of Phase One—General Review," 30 October 1978, 19.

23   Jimmy Carter Presidential Library, Atlanta, White House Central Files (WHCF), Box
     FO-28, file: FO 3-2 9/5/79-10/21/79, Carter to Senator Ernest Hollings, 1 October
     1979. Carter asked for US$19 million in support of the ISTC and later, US$126 mil-
     lion for the Foundation for International Technological Cooperation (FITC), as it
     became known in legislation. It was a way of "using aid more effectively. It will do
     good out of all proportion to its size, in helping developing countries carry out
     research on such problems as energy, health and agriculture. Dollar for dollar, noth-
     ing in the aid program will produce greater results." Congress was not so enthusias-
     tic. While the FITC would be stillborn, as it was being considered, Senator Charles
     Percy, the ranking minority member on the Senate Governmental Affairs Committee,
     told Carter that one way to make it more palatable was to involve "the technologi-
     cal know-how and ingenuity of the private sector ... into the development proposal."
     See Carter Library, Box FO-27, WHCF, file: FO 3-2 11/18/78-1/15/78, Percy to Carter,
     14 December 1978.
24   IDRC–A, Meeting of the Executive Committee, EC Notes (50) 1/83, 4. Later, during
     the Reagan presidency, the US government launched an ongoing effort to generate
     support for a new foundation, an international foundation for science and technol-
     ogy for development, which would not be part of the UN system and which was
     intended to combine all of the activities of organizations such as IDRC and to be
     given "the enlightened direction of the United States administration from day to day
     as to how these activities should be carried out." The American proposal did not
     elicit much support from any quarter, and especially not from the Group of 77. Head
     told the executive committee that with its approval, he would continue to oppose the
     creation of any such instrument as IDRC felt that "in its modest way, it can perform
     better following the judgment of its Board rather than that of the White House."
25   IDRC–A, Meeting of the Board of Governors, B of G Notes (20) 3/79, 46.
26   IDRC–A, Meeting of the Executive Committee, EC Notes (46) 1/82, 22.
27   The universities supported by IDRC personnel were: the University of British Colum-
     bia, the University of Saskatchewan, the University of Manitoba, the University of
     Laval, and Dalhousie University.
28   IDRC–A, Meeting of the Board, March 1978, Joe Hulse.
29   IDRC–A, Meeting of the Board of Governors, B of G Notes (22), 3/80, 79.
30   IDRC–A, Meeting of the Board of Governors, B of G Notes (22), 3/80, 75.
31   IDRC–A, Meeting of the Board of Governors, B of G Notes (23), 10/80, 23.
32   IDRC–A, Meeting of the Board of Governors, B of G Notes (23), 10/80, 24.
33   Eva Rathgeber, "Turning Failure into Success: The Deconstruction of IDRC Develop-
     ment Discourse, 1970–2000," Evaluation no. 479, September 2001, 37.
34   IDRC–A, Meeting of the Board of Governors, B of G Notes (22), 3/80, 82.
35   IDRC–A, Dr. Silvio Gomez Arango, "Rural Health Development Program (Colombia)
     and Multi-disciplinary Research Centre for Rural Development," Evaluation no. 46,
     May 1983, 47.
36   IDRC–A, Meeting of the Executive Committee, EC Notes (46) 1/82, 20.
37   IDRC–A, Meeting of the Board, B of G Notes (33), 10/85, 96.
38   IDRC–A, Meeting of the Board, March 1978, John Woolston.
39   L.J. Jarmai and S.S.B. Elwela, "Technonet Asia: An Evaluation," 17 December 1982,
     accessed at https://idl-bnc.idrc.ca/dspace/bitstream/123456789/7372/1/54318.pdf
40   MINISIS was developed as an affordable database management tool for organizations
     in the South. It is used by universities, governments, libraries, and other organiza-
     tions in more than sixty countries.
41   IDRC–A, Meeting of the Board of Governors, B of G Notes (22), 3/80, 87.

42   IDRC–A, Meeting of the Board of Governors, B of G Notes (33) 10/85, 119.

43   However, arrangements with the private sector did, on occasion, cause some angst. For example, a private organization in Brazil had applied to IDRC to become a distributor of MINISIS, which would have generated revenue for the Centre. However, as Woolston told the board, he agonized about the propriety of doing so: "We don't want to be competing with an indigenous software industry." Meeting of the Board of Governors, B of G Notes (23), 10/80, 34.

44   IDRC–A, Meeting of the Board of Governors, B of G Notes (22), 3/80, 91.

45   IDRC–A, Meeting of the Board of Governors, B of G Notes (23), 10/80, 34.

46   IDRC–A, Meeting of the Board of Governors, B of G Notes (22) 3/80, 100.

47   IDRC–A, Meeting of the Board of Governors, B of G Notes (24) 3/81, 13.

48   IDRC–A, Meeting of the Board of Governors, B of G Notes (24) 3/81, 13.

49   IDRC–A, President to All Program Staff, "Training Policy Study," 18 August 1981. See also B of G Notes (24) 3/81, 23. The Nigerian governor, A.A. Ayida, commented on certain types of social science research being undertaken in rural areas and was worried about its impact on researchers. He told the board that "It is not easy in the Third World to separate research activities from subversive activities in the social field."

50   IDRC–A, New Initiatives, 1982, 35. However, this issue of research imperialism was not as cut and dried as it seemed, a position drawn out by Geila Castillo, a long-serving governor from the Philippines: "I have heard more than once around the table the expression 'we do not want to impose; this is what they want.' I think we might be confusing the issues of responsiveness with something else. To me, the greatest imposition that a funding agency can make is not to allow a certain idea to prosper and develop, and say that we cannot support that. So that is an imposition by not giving it enough consideration.... When we decide we are going to support something, I don't know what it means when you say 'we don't want to impose.' ... And simply because researchers in the developing countries say 'this is what we want to do,' period, I think there should be a healthy debate between IDRC staff and the people from the developing countries ... it seems to me it is an insult to people from the developing countries when you do not debate with them. That means you are not treating us as equals because, if you were, let us get into a serious professional debate about proposals because these are issues of substance, issues of analysis, issues of information." See IDRC–A, Meeting of the Executive Committee, EC (64) 6/86, 72.

51   Tahira Gonsalves and Stephen Baranyi, "Research for Policy Influence: A History of IDRC Intent," January 2003, 10.

52   IDRC–A, Meeting of the Board of Governors, B of G Notes (28) 3/83, 110.

53   IDRC–A, Meeting of the Board of Governors, B of G Notes (26) 3/82, 5.

54   IDRC–A, Meeting of the Board of Governors, B of G Notes (24) 3/81, 18.

55   Interview with Jim Mullin by Martin Kreuzer, 10 August 2004, Ottawa.

56   Much of the following discussion comes from IDRC–A, Joseph Hulse, "IDRC Regional Offices—Their History and Responsibilities," MC 84/24, 13 June 1984.

57   IDRC–A, Joseph Hulse, "IDRC Regional Offices—Their History and Responsibilities," MC 84/24, 13 June 1984.

58   IDRC–A, Meeting of the Board of Governors, 19, 20, and 21 October 1978, B of G Notes (19) 10/78, 9.

59   IDRC–A, Memorandum: Doug Daniels to the President's Committee, "The IDRC Evaluation System," 12 September 1986.

60   IDRC–A, *Program and Policy Review VIII*, 1986, 13.

61 Memorandum: Doug Daniels to the President's Committee.
62 IDRC–A, Meeting of the Board of Governors, B of G Notes (22), 3/80, 60.
63 IDRC–A, Meeting of the Board of Governors, B of G Notes (20) 3/79, 50. Interest-ingly, Donald Macdonald, following his elevation to the chair, spoke against the appointment of senior government officials on IDRC's board, especially that of the undersecretary of state for external affairs. He asked the in-camera session held in October 1981 "What should the role of the Department of External Affairs be in rela-tion to this institution?... I do not think that the Under-Secretary of State for Exter-nal Affairs [USSEA], no matter how estimable a person, should be on the board of this particular institution.... I think we should be in the position where Governors not be embarrassed, knowing that the senior permanent public servant responsible for external affairs is going to be sitting at the table. They need not try to read the bumps on his or her head to decide what exactly it is that Government's policy wants." Gottlieb left to become Canada's ambassador to the US in early 1981. The presence of the CIDA president was also raised; Macdonald suggested that that was not a problem—they were "less central a figure in the power structure in this city than the Under-Secretary of State for External Affairs. Indeed, he has to fight for his own life to a certain degree. This, however, raises another question. As he sits at the table, is he thinking of his own life or is he thinking of the life of his institution?" See Meet-ing of the Board of Governors, B of G Notes (25) 10/81, in-camera session, 21 Octo-ber 1981, 2.
64 IDRC–A, Meeting of the Board of Governors, B of G Notes, (21) 10/79 56. The divi-sion directors received the revised structure relatively well. David Steedman of Social Sciences, and director only since November 1978, was most supportive. As he noted, "I think this is a very valuable exercise. In fact, I was one of the first to suggest a cou-ple of programs that should be evaluated. I believe it would be especially interest-ing for the evaluation unit to adopt mechanisms or approaches that are broad enough in scope to cut across divisional lines, and which can thereby throw light in an inter-disciplinary way on our own evaluations."
65 Canada, House of Commons, Standing Committee on External Affairs and National Defence *Minutes of Proceeding and Evidence*, 15 November 1979, Issue no. 3, 3–20.
66 IDRC–A, Meeting of the Board of Governors, B of G Notes (22), 3/80, 61.
67 IDRC–A, Meeting of the Board of Governors, B of G Notes (22), 3/80, 67.
68 Interview with John Hardie, 12 August 2008, Ottawa.
69 IDRC–A, Meeting of the Board of Governors, B of G Notes (20) 3/79, 12.
70 In January 14, 1977, Robert McNamara, the president of the World Bank, announced the idea of establishing a commission of experienced, respected politicians and econ-omists. He proposed that the members of this new international panel should not be official representatives of governments, but would work independently to formulate "basic proposals on which global agreement is both essential and possible." The com-mission was to make recommendations on ways of breaking through the existing international political impasse in North–South negotiations for global development.
     Willy Brandt was asked to preside over the commission, which was to be equally represented by the developed North and the developing South. On 28 September 1977, Brandt announced that he was prepared to form and chair an "Independent Commis-sion on International Development Issues." Among its members were three other former heads of state—Eduardo Frei, the Christian Democrat ex-president of Chile, Olaf Palme, the Social Democrat ex-prime minister of Sweden, and Edward Heath, the ex-Conservative prime minister of the United Kingdom. See Centre for Global

Negotiations, "The Brandt Equation: 21st Century Blueprint for the New Global Economy," accessed at www.brandt21forum.info/About_BrandtCommission.htm.

71 IDRC–A, Meeting of the Board of Governors, B of G Notes (14) 3/77, 40.

72 IDRC–A, Meeting of the Board of Governors, B of G Notes (20) 3/79, 12.

73 IDRC–A, Meeting of the Board of Governors, B of G Notes (20) 3/79, 13.

74 The Brandt Commission, *Common Crisis: North–South Cooperation for World Recovery* (Cambridge: MIT Press, 1983), 4.

75 Margaret Thatcher, *The Downing Street Years* (New York: Harper Collins, 1993), 168–69.

76 Brandt Commission, *Common Crisis*, 1.

77 IDRC–A, Meeting of the Executive Committee, EC Notes (50) 1/83, 3.

78 Andrew F. Cooper and John English, "International Commissions and the Mind of Global Governance," in Ramesh Thakur, Andrew Cooper, and John English (eds.), *International Commissions and the Power of Ideas* (Tokyo: United Nations University Press, 2005), 13.

79 Jean-Phillipe Thérien, "The Brandt Commission: The End of an Era in North–South Politics," in Ramesh Thakur, Andrew Cooper, and John English (eds.), *International Commissions and the Power of Ideas* (Tokyo: United Nations University Press, 2005), 39.

80 Francisco Sagasti, "The Changed Context of Science and Technology for Development," 18, accessed at https://idl-bnc.idrc.ca/dspace/bitstream/123456789/25473/1/111008.pdf.

81 Sagasti, "The Changed Context of Science and Technology for Development."

82 Mahindra Naraine, "Little Science and Technology, Much Politics: United Nations Conference on Science and Technology for Development," *Resources Policy*, no. 4, 1979, 309.

83 See, for example, Don Hinrichsen, "NGOs at Vienna: Next Stop Stockholm? *Ambio*, vol. 8, no. 5 (1979), 231–32.

84 IDRC–A, Meeting of the Board of Governors, B of G Notes (21), 10/79, 50.

85 Naraine, "Little Science and Technology," 309.

86 IDRC–A, UNCSTD, "Statement by the Hon. Martial Asselin, Minister of State for the Canadian International Development Agency," 21 August 1979.

87 IDRC–A, Meeting of the Board of Governors, B of G Notes (21), 10/79, 53.

88 The Centre received CAN$36.9 million during 1978–79 and 1979–80 in *actual* dollars. However, in *real terms using 1992–93 as the base year*, the parliamentary appropriation decreased to CAN$77.52 million from CAN$84.63 million. IDRC, "Relationship of IDRC Parliamentary Appropriation to ODA," n.d.

89 IDRC–A, Meeting of the Board of Governors, B of G Notes (27) 10/82, 34.

90 IDRC–A, Meeting of the Board of Governors, B of G Notes (26) 3/82, 5.

91 Brian L. Evans, "Pursuing China: Memoirs of a Sometime Peasant, Worker, Student, Scholar, and Diplomat," unpublished manuscript, 85 (under review by University of Alberta Press). In 1964, as a young assistant professor at the University of Alberta, Evans remembered that Ivan Head, then a professor of international law at the university, was part of a group that "bombarded" the visiting secretary of state for external affairs, Paul Martin, Sr., with questions ("the most pointed ones from Ivan Head") as to why Canada had not recognized the People's Republic: "Was it due to American pressure?" On 1 February 1971, Canada did so while Pierre Trudeau was prime minister and Head his chief foreign affairs adviser.

92 IDRC–A, Meeting of the Executive Committee, EC Notes (50) 1/83, 52.

93   IDRC–A, Meeting of the Executive Committee, EC Notes (38) 1/80, 3.

94   IDRC–A, Meeting of the Executive Committee, EC Notes (38) 1/80, 23.

95   IDRC–A, Meeting of the Board of Governors, B of G Notes (23) 10/80, 12.

96   The relationship went from strength to strength, as seen by the trip report filed upon Ivan Head's return from China in 1988. In 1986, a personal link had been established when Ivan Head had appointed Dr. Xi Huida, an agricultural scientist, to the board. Prime Minister Brian Mulroney put the request to Premier Zhao Zi Yang. See "China Trip Report," August 1988, accessed at https://idl-bnc.idrc.ca/dspace/handle/123456789/16309.

97   IDRC–A, Stephen McGurk to Terry Smutylo, "Review of 20 Years of S & T Cooperation with China," 17 September 2000, 3.

98   IDRC–A, Zhan Hongqi, Zheng Yongqi, Geoffrey Oldham, and Tan Say Yin, "An Assessment of Twenty Years of Research Collaboration between China and the International Development Research Centre," Evaluation no. 436, January 2000, 7.

99   IDRC–A, Meeting of the Executive Committee, EC Notes (46) 1/82, 24.

100 IDRC–A, John Hardie, "Utilization of Research Results: Discussion Paper," July 1982.

101 Interview with Jim Mullin by Martin Kreuzer.

102 This was not a black-and-white situation, however, and over the past decade the Centre's position had become more nuanced than when IDRC was a fledgling organization. Clearly, it had its priorities, into which Southern researchers had to fit themselves, although staff always retained the ability to respond to interesting ideas that lay outside of regular programming.

103 IDRC–A, Meeting of the Board of Governors, B of G Notes (37) 10/87, 115.

104 IDRC–A, Meeting of the Board of Governors, B of G Notes (30) 3/84, 16.

105 IDRC–A, Meeting of the Board of Governors, B of G Notes (28) 3/83, 103.

106 IDRC–A, Meeting of the Board of Governors, B of G Notes (27) 10/82, 40.

107 IDRC–A, Meeting of the Board of Governors, B of G Notes (27) 10/82, 54.

108 IDRC–A, Meeting of the Executive Committee, EC Notes (46) 1/82, 11.

109 IDRC–A, Meeting of the Executive Committee, EC Notes (46) 1/82, 9.

110 Ford had done the heavy lifting during the years following 1973, providing institutional support grants to a number of Southern cone institutions that had been established following the various coups. For example, it had provided "a hefty grant" to the first post-Pinochet government of Particio Alywin, which contained an abundance of former CIEPLAN members, a measure of its importance both during the junta era and after. These included:
    Alejandro Foxley, minister of housing
    René Cortazar, minister of labour
    José Pablo Arellano, budget director
    Pablo Pinera, undersecretary of finance
    Ricardo French-Davis, director of research, Central Bank of Chile
    Nicolás Flano, Chilean executive director to the World Bank
    Manuel Marfán, adviser, minister of housing and director of policy
    Mario Tercel, director of research, Department of Finance
    Ignado Walker, adviser in the Office of the President
    Claudia Serrano, director of social services, Santiago
    Esteban Jadresic, Research Department, Central Bank of Chile

111 In the aftermaths of the various coups, FLACSO's multinational staff and student body were severely affected. Staff were detained and several students were murdered by the authorities. Following the Chilean coup, its directive council closed the

teaching program in Chile, transferred their headquarters to Buenos Aires, and began to decentralize the FLACSO operation, eventually creating new centres in Ecuador and Mexico. Left behind in Santiago was a small number of Chilean researchers, who were gradually joined by a group of internal academic refugees, many of whom had been dislodged from the country's Catholic University. Having wreaked havoc on the organization, the government recalled that it was a regional organization protected by international treaty whose signatories comprised Chile, Costa Rica, Cuba, Ecuador, Mexico, and Panama. Recognizing that it would not be in its interests to unilaterally violate its treaty obligations, the regime adopted a relatively benign posture toward the Santiago group. Further, the military government *funded* FLACSO to meet its international obligations, at least until 1979, when it withdrew. This very brief account obscures the ups and downs FLACSO experienced, although it did survive through the military period.

112 A.D. Tillett, "Social Sciences Research in the Southern Cone of Latin America: An Evaluation of Centre Supported Institutions," vol. II, 11 September 1980, 17.

113 Interview with Patricio Meller, Santiago de Chile, 22 June 2006.

114 Interview with René Cortazar, Santiago de Chile, 22 June 2006.

115 For example, the Ford Foundation, partly because of its identification with the United States, did not receive the same accolades as IDRC, despite its much greater role in supporting dissident researchers. Ford provided US$50,000 as early as 1975 to CEDES, followed by a series of larger grants to other institutions over the next five years.

116 According to Diego Piñiero, dean of the Faculty of Social Sciences at the Universidad de la República in Uruguay, lengthy discussions took place among researchers about the agendas of international organizations, especially those from the United States, and the implications of accepting funding from them. IDRC was discussed in this context and was judged to be trustworthy. Interview with Diego Piñiero, 6 June 2008.

117 Interview with Patricio Meller, Santiago de Chile, 22 June 2006.

118 Elizabeth Fox de Cardona with the co-operation of Nita Manitzas, "Support for Social Sciences Research in the Southern Cone," vol. I, September 1980, and Tillett, "Social Sciences Research in the Southern Cone of Latin America."

119 Interview with Chris Smart, 12 July 2007, Ottawa.

120 IDRC–A, Meeting of the Executive Committee, EC Notes (48) 6/82, 17.

121 Interview with Maggie Catley-Carlson, Chelsea, August 2006.

122 IDRC–A, Meeting of the Board of Governors, B of G Notes (33) 10/85, 4.

123 IDRC–A, Meeting of the Board of Governors, B of G Notes 44/3, "1990 LARO Regional Report," March 1990.

124 IDRC–A, Nancy Smythe and Maggie Gorman, "Conversation with Fernando Chaparro," 5 November 2004. See also IDRC–A, "IDRC Institutional Support to the Southern Cone," B of G Notes 34/11, March 1986.

125 Interview with René Cortazar, Santiago de Chile, 22 June 2006.

126 IDRC–A, Meeting of the Executive Committee, 17–18 January 1991, 8–9.

Chapter 4

IVAN HEAD REDUX, 1983–91: A DARKENING HORIZON

> *The best way to keep a country dependent is to tell it
> everything and never let it find out anything by itself.*
> —Donald Mills, chair, Jamaica's permanent
> representative to the UN (1973–81)

Introduction

Ivan Head was appointed to his second five-year term on 13 March 1983 and a subsequent three years on that day in 1988. While the worst of the various crises seemed to have passed in Canada—the economy was improving, unemployment was moving downward, the fiscal situation was improving, and the threat of Quebec separation seemed to have diminished—new issues had arisen to take their place. For example, with the collapse of the old Soviet empire in 1989–90, Western Europeans began to look more favourably upon their economically disadvantaged eastern cousins, which meant the investment of social and political capital and also dollars, with a concomitant decrease in the number available for development financing in the South. Ivan Head made that point late in the decade when he quoted Joshua Ihora, the Nigerian ambassador to Belgium: "Our very real concern is not that the European Community will look to help the East. We understand that bonding. We are worried that in the process, they will turn their back on us."[1] There were statistics to support that concern; in 1990, the EC package of assistance for the sixty-six Africa/Caribbean/Pacific countries amounted to US$10 per capita over a five-year period, while EC offers to Hungary and Poland were six times as great over three years. IDRC itself, under contract to the Canadian International Development Agency, was to get involved in Ukraine in the late 1990s in support of development.

Other issues intruded as well. A fall in oil prices was both good and bad—good for those who bought the stuff, and bad for those, like Canada and Nigeria, who sold it. Commodity and agricultural prices remained depressed, which sapped demand for manufactured imports in less developed countries (LDCs). In Africa, Asia, and Latin America, social turmoil and political instability continued to adversely affect peoples and governments. Head, in his statement to the board shortly after his reappointment, told them that in addition to the items listed above, the age was characterized by "increasing protectionism, decreasing international trade, liquidity crises and intense human suffering."[2] As if that were not enough, "only three living species war[red] on their own kind—rats, ants and humans." And the first two did not make money off the activity. War was an intense preoccupation; forty-five of the world's 164 nations were engaged in it with 4 million soldiers, who had killed uncounted other millions.

Given the magnitude of horrific events afflicting humanity, what could IDRC do to help to make things a bit less ominous? First and foremost, the Centre remained committed to its support of various networks—hundreds of them by mid-decade in all areas of research for development. Indeed, over the two decades from 1971, IDRC was to spend more than CAN$240 million in network-related projects.[3] As well, in typical Centre fashion, it "could not assume that its own processes [were] so satisfactory that they need not be continuously evaluated." Head thought that its parliamentary appropriation could reach CAN$100 million by 1986–87 (it did), and CAN$200 million by 1988–89 (it did not).[4] With that kind of serious money it might be necessary to significantly shift the Centre's method of operation in ways he could not yet divine. The latter figure was massive for a development research organization like IDRC, but even CAN$100 million was huge. Head worried that the Centre's ability to function effectively was a product of the capability of developing countries' research communities to absorb those funds, which, to some extent, put IDRC's future in others' hands. But what if it could not appropriately disburse an increased parliamentary allocation to the satisfaction of senior management and Treasury Board Secretariat because of a dearth of personnel? What did the Centre then say to Parliament? "Thank you very much, we don't feel that we can really use those funds in those increments in an effective fashion."[5] That might be construed in the upper echelons of Cabinet as the crazed murmurings of disaffected people with a concomitant effect on future allocations.

Further, handling more than CAN$100 million of taxpayer money would require more staff, but Head was very concerned that the Centre's numbers, both the administrative apparatus and the program officer cohort, not grow at the same rate as did the parliamentary appropriation. IDRC prided itself on being a labour-intensive yet agile institution, and if its grant did rise to CAN$200 million, necessitating the hiring of more staff, it might become too unwieldy. As a result, Centre restructuring was a pressing need to prepare for growth in such a way that it did not distort its essential nature and character. Certainly, its definition of development would remain the same—that people in developing countries should be adequately fed, healthy, and literate. The list of basic development needs was correspondingly simple: food, water, sanitation, housing, education, health services, and disease control. Its qualities should also remain as they had developed. This reflected the notion that "development is a complex matrix of ingredients and problems, none of which are unrelated to others … development is investment—of people and resources—and development decisions are investment decisions. Those most capable of identifying the problems, assessing the risks, and fixing the priorities are the peoples of the developing countries themselves. They are the engines of development; they are the instruments of change."[6] Those qualities were also what had prompted the important Development Assistance Committee of the Organisation for Economic Co-operation and Development to note in the summer of 1985 that "Able to respond fast and flexibly to project opportunities, and with the bulk of its projects in and managed by the Third World, IDRC undoubtedly represents one of the most direct and innovative responses to the scientific needs of developing countries made by any industrialized nation."[7] But what after this?

Head put the idea to the board that IDRC should adjust its processes "in order to reduce the percentage of [its] expenditures which are now so overwhelmingly committed to staff-intensive project support." If it did not do so, it could not count on functioning at the high level it had achieved during the previous thirteen years. That meant longer term program funding was quickly becoming appropriate. In other words, IDRC could not simply continue to grow by doing what it had been doing in the past, but with a significant increase to its budget. That would become a basic policy question that the Centre would have to face over the next number of years: How would it change and what would it do? That suited Head as well: "Orthodoxy is often the opponent of discovery and advancement; habits of attitude and process become obstacles to achievement; an effective organization is one that retains its motivations for change."[8] Those questions (and that attitude) prompted IDRC to assess its mission statement in 1985 and strategize more clearly for the future. Furthermore, four issues were raised at various times in IDRC deliberations that had an impact on operations: (1) decentralization, (2) institutional development, (3) the balance between producing research results and building research capacity, and (4) concentration or dispersion of research funding. How did networks fit in? As this chapter will demonstrate, much time, effort, and paper was spent as the Centre grappled with ideas about its future.

Tinkering with Administration

This sort of introspection was accompanied by an administrative shakeup that altered the shape of IDRC through the adoption of a flatter management structure as of 1 October 1983, which was also made necessary by changes within the organization. Centre objectives were being broadened as its parliamentary appropriation increased. Staff levels were also up by 25 percent from 1980–81 to 1983–84, which translated into about six hundred employees worldwide. That prompted board member Sir Geoffrey Wilson to ask if the 25 percent increase in staff costs had resulted in a 25 percent decline in programming. It had not—indeed, the opposite had happened, and not only because of the infusion of extra parliamentary appropriation. Economies had been achieved in other areas. The amount the Centre devoted to administration, regional offices, and divisional management had remained at about 20 percent of its appropriation—a very good number. Those extra hands were now needed and Norman Currie, the chair of the Budget and Audit Committee, suggested a reason: "Several years ago, large amounts of our budget were going to core support of international institutions. We are now working with a much larger number of projects and much smaller amounts requiring better management and better supervision by our group. We therefore require more people to carry that out. The reason we have more people is because of the size of the projects." For example, in 1983, when a mini-census of projects had been undertaken, the Centre was supporting fifteen hundred projects in nine hundred institutions based in one hundred countries! The sheer scale was difficult to conceive, made more complicated by the way in which IDRC operated. The president, for one, was adamant that it was important not to lose "that essential element which was to work closely with scientists in LDCs in a way that was different from simple cheque-writing foundations that send something through the mail to them."[9]

    This intensity imposed its own imperatives on program staff—it was not unusual for them to spend 115 days per year on travel status, an incredible burden on the (mostly) men and their families. Furthermore, this travel tended to be difficult. Head noted that he often had to point out to officials at External Affairs that "it did not mean sitting in a Geneva hotel for two months at a time, engaging in boring but not necessarily environmentally deteriorating negotiations. These men and women are popping about a day here, two days there, all over the developing world, and this is tough on them." Nasir Islam put it thusly: "As the dictum in the academic world goes: 'Publish or Perish,' the popular dictum in the IDRC is 'Travel or Perish'. Frequent travel is ... regarded as a necessary evil."[10] While over the remainder of Head's time in office longer-term projects would slowly become the norm, it remained a very difficult problem made more complex as IDRC broadened its reach into new areas such as nutrition and women in development. Qualified program staff remained at a premium, a situation exacerbated by a freeze in civil service hiring imposed by the Mulroney government in 1985. Although IDRC was not a part of that group, it followed suit as was politically necessary. As Head told the board, if the Centre was seen to be "flying absolutely in the face of that government policy ... we would undoubtedly create difficulties for ourselves."[11]

What principles guided the Centre in revising its strategic planning system and much of its administrative apparatus? The key had been, as Doug Daniels pointed out, "that the process is as important as the product. For a responsive organization like IDRC with so many different markets and programs, we are skeptical about the benefits of global corporate strategic plans which impose a certain rigidity on all actors."[12] Still, as it matured and as its parliamentary appropriation climbed toward CAN$100 million, it could not be all things to all people. A planning document declaimed on the Centre's evolution: "The aim of the new phase of strategic planning is to create a less ambiguous atmosphere in which to exercise staff discretion, to provide broad indications of policy intentions and to initiate processes of information-sharing and consultation to improve operational effectiveness."[13] In other words, more rules. Still, IDRC would also emphasize "a strategic process [which] left to the program officer [some] discretion and judgment."[14] After all, that had characterized the Centre since its establishment and reflected its core values. "Flexibility," Head suggested, "begins to diminish if there is not a bit of fudging around the edges ... a little fuzziness, not on a case-by-case, but on a problem-by-problem and issue-by-issue, need-by-need analysis to allow us ... to look at needs and see how best we can respond to them."[15]

But growing complexity also prompted certain questions that arose from the planning document: Was the organization primarily *responsive* to Southern research demands as its self-perception suggested, or was it now *catalyzing* research? It was doing both, which was not much different from years past; each division had always been responsive within certain parameters. Even in the devil-may-care Hopper days, characterized by "a generous mandate allowing considerable freedom to explore, innovate and create,"[16] AFNS, for example, could not fund work in areas outside its expertise, making it non-responsive to certain researchers. However, it could, and did, catalyze research in, say, cassava or triticale, which the division could do well. As a result, it was very responsive to Southern researchers undertaking work on those two crops.

This situation had become more pronounced by the mid-1980s as the Centre grew and as government became more interested in periodically examining its operations through the Office of the Auditor General or the Treasury Board Secretariat. In a sense, IDRC became more "professional" with its *Programs of Work and Budget (PWB)* and *Program and Policy Reviews (PPR)*, which did indeed impose more order on its operations. It might have been the case, as a governor pointed out, that by mid-decade IDRC had "a fairly fundamental problem in trying to reconcile a responsive philosophy with five-year plans," but that did not necessarily make it non-responsive. Head was also correct in maintaining that "the Centre is responding to project requests that come to us.... There are no absolute priorities. The way in which the funds are distributed among the divisions represents the priorities attached to those research sectors by the developing countries themselves." While *PWBs* and *PPRs* might direct programming, they were not prescriptive; those documents were constructed, in part, through extensive conversations with Southern researchers. These were determined by input from regional offices and were also the result of intelligence gleaned by program officers on their travels, possessed as they were with a "set of antennae for day-to-day perception of the priorities of the developing countries."[17] An example is again provided by Agriculture, Food, and Nutrition Sciences; it was typically responsive in that it expected requests from scientists of developing countries where the submission of a project was taken as an expression of a need as defined by those scientists. While priorities could be set as far as program or regional support were concerned, the actual support of projects depended on program officers' consideration of them and might, or might not, coincide with those priorities.

The Centre also remained keen to continue the practice it had begun in Head's first term of ensuring the incorporation of policy-maker demands in project design, where possible, and evaluating results following project completion. As Yelavarthy Nayudamma noted, "If you could indicate the impact of any project which is helping a developing country, we will have done our job."[18] John Hardie's paper had commented approvingly on this a half-decade previously, while IDRC's fifteen-year history, *With Our Own Hands: Research for Third World Development: Canada's Contribution through the International Development Research Centre, 1970–1985*, had reinforced that perspective:

> International development is about change. It necessarily involves innovation, which is the process of delivering to people the knowledge generated by research in a form that has useful and enduring benefits in practical economic or social terms. Anyone who has spent time ... wrestling with this delivery process knows fully how intricate and difficult it is. Success cannot be claimed until a long sequence of careful steps is complete. With IDRC's focus on development for the benefit of people in need, the critical importance of establishing early cooperation and understanding between the transmitter of information and its eventual user becomes starkly clear.[19]

Head agreed with that although he also counted *enhancement* as a viable Centre product. By that, he meant enhancing the competence of the scientific community within a country. Indeed, the president often viewed projects as much as vehicles for that as for presenting a solution to specific problems.

Into the (Relative) Unknown

As the Centre considered its structure and the intellectual basis on which it made decisions, so too did it think about destinations for its research funding, like a concentration on Sub-Saharan Africa (SSA). This contrasted with the situation during Head's first term, and very sharply with that prevailing during the Hopper era whose Centre had not really put much into Africa, however pressing the need. In 1975, for example, IDRC had had about sixty projects under supervision in Thailand alone while other countries of the region had also seen a considerable injection of Centre support, which had totalled more than CAN$10 million. At the other extreme, twenty-four countries had had only one project from 1980 to 1985, and another twelve had had two projects each. All of these "under-serviced" countries were in Africa. The continent was, to a large extent, *terra incognita* to IDRC. Head quoted the late British prime minister Lord Salisbury, on the eve of the Fashoda Crisis of 1897, to demonstrate the difficulty: "It is as difficult to judge what is going on [in Africa] as it is as difficult to judge what is happening on the other side of the moon." By the mid-1980s, that hemisphere of the moon had been mapped; one could not say the same thing about SSA.[20] Such a shift had major implications for Centre program officers as those countries were less capable of generating results with concomitant additional pressure being placed on frontline officers, who would trek through the continent looking for business. IDRC would also have to put more resources into the "strengthening of institutions [and training] ... and projects [would] need to be less ambitious and last longer."[21] Moreover, impact might have to play second fiddle to enhancement, at least for a while; the research base in the region was at a relatively rudimentary level. The director of Social Sciences, David Steedman, was correct in his analysis that African countries were most in need of "building an indigenous research and planning capacity."[22]

This new determination changed the focus of some of the divisions at least. The issue of entering more forcefully into underrepresented areas was raised in the context of determining broad strategic direction. Should the Centre work primarily with mid-level research systems and leave out the very weak and the very strong? To what extent should IDRC attempt to shore up a sometimes crumbling and often inadequate supporting infrastructure of that system? Should the Centre support non-nationals of the country in which the institution or project being supported was located? Should it persevere with such institutions and countries if they proved unable to use Centre funds effectively, which was an increasingly common complaint by the mid-1980s as IDRC sought out more remote researchers and institutions? For example, at the October 1985 board meeting, it was pointed out that many new research partners needed a degree of coaching: "training in research planning, administration, and management has been neglected and is actually non-existent in some regions. This results in inefficient use of IDRC contributions, excessive vehicle wear, unacceptable financial reporting, excessive red tape, and the absence of long-term research goals."[23] Despite those hurdles to appropriate project development and supervision, however, IDRC put its money where its mouth was; by 1988, it was directing 30 percent of its appropriation to African institutions, up from 24 percent in 1986.[24] It could live with excessive vehicle wear.

This sort of discussion had led, as of 1 October 1983, to the establishment of the newest IDRC division, Fellowships and Awards (FAD), which was provided with roughly 8 percent of the Centre's budget and which took over the administration of about 55 percent of the Centre's training programs and awards. The two broad program areas were maintained—that is, programs for developing countries and those for Canadians. From its inception the Centre had reflected the close relationship between research and training, and although David Hopper had written in 1973 that "The Centre has no programs of scholarships or other formal training assistance at any educational level," several divisions had taken steps to deal with the dearth of trained researchers in the developing world.[25] Thus AFNS and Information Sciences had built training opportunities into many of their projects, while the Social Sciences division had made its concern for training explicit in its original designation as the Social Sciences and *Human Resources* division. That practice continued even after the establishment of FAD.

It was used as the principal vehicle for supporting training and was the mechanism IDRC used to experiment with forms of education. In its early years, it had supported almost exclusively individual training and individual awards for people to take formal training courses. During the mid-1980s, some novel ideas about group training had been introduced where the Centre had drawn participants from ongoing projects, providing them with opportunities to upgrade their skills. One example of that sort of initiative came from Southeast Asia, where FAD had provided (via its four Ph.D.s in adult education, all of whom were placed in regional offices) a course on resource economics to fisheries biologists, followed by one on fisheries biology for resource economists. A happy result was that the two groups were somewhat better equipped to talk to each other and now had some useful insight into the motivations of "the other" on those projects in which they were collaborating.[26]

This suggested old names concealed an evolving Centre. Joe Hulse reflected on this when he told the board that headings could be deceiving, and that while it might appear his division had not changed since the 1970s (witness AFNS's crops, fisheries, animals, forestry, and post-production systems emphasis or its position paper laying out its mandate, which dated from December 1971). That was a far cry from its present reality.[27] The division had changed dramatically, both in administrative apparatus and in areas covered. Budgets for each section had ebbed and flowed, reflecting the decreasing or increasing importance of the various areas in which they had been invested. For example, by the mid-1980s, the division was championing some new approaches like pest or rangeland management and community-based participatory methods. As well, in keeping with the Centre's emphasis, the policy implications of the work were identified at the very beginning of the project development process instead of as an afterthought. Similarly, the division was (slightly) more open to interdivisional co-operation than it had been, although what passed for interdisciplinarity could be construed as rather odd, and will be discussed below. Still, in late 1983 AFNS could point to co-operation with Social Sciences in projects that contained elements relating to production economics and the measurement of technical change; it had not done so before.[28]

That reflected board deliberations that had focused on "the convergence of various disciplines and areas to cope with major problems which are, by their nature, interdisciplinary."[29] For instance, in late 1986, policy issues surrounding multi-disciplinarity were raised, and not for the first time. Despite the intent and a growing commitment to practise what it preached with respect to this concept, the reality sometimes left a bit to be desired. That went back to the Centre's founding practices and remained a difficult, although not intractable, problem to be solved. In a fashion similar to universities that were focused on departmental integrity, there had been "a digging in, a territorial guarding by individual sections or individuals in various areas."[30] As was pointed out, "The problem is one of implementing the concept of cooperation and interdisciplinarity, particularly at the regional level where those who participate in the working out of projects look back over their shoulders to say: What is my principal going to say at headquarters regarding my own particular territory?"

This added up to considerable resistance from Centre staff and management to the concept of substantive interdisciplinary co-operation, despite articulated policy and exclamations of its value. For example, a long-term fisheries project in Sierra Leone proved to be technically successful, but weak in ensuring impact—few of the proposals were adopted by local fishers. That was acknowledged in the AFNS project completion report, but there was no suggestion that social scientists should have been involved or that the Social Sciences division should have worked more closely with AFNS to implement the results.[31] The program completion report implied that fisheries scientists should have been slightly more sensitive to technology dissemination issues, nothing more. What was the Social Sciences' view of co-operation? Contrary to what one might think, given cascading responsibilities, it remained leery of involvement with other divisions:

> We suspect that pressure for collaboration with the Social Sciences Division is building up in other divisions where research typically produces a product— such as a new strain of sorghum, a new vaccine or a new package of practices—which, to have an effect, must be used. Whether and how their product will be used will be determined by social, economic and cultural factors ... the collaborative projects are very time-consuming to develop and sometimes come to an unhappy end ... we are worried that a massive diversion of our resources into this kind of service activity would trivialize the Division.[32]

Quite apart from the difficulties of interdivisional co-operation, it was also true that Social Sciences was experiencing significant stress: "The increase in procedural complexity is becoming more particularly difficult because it tends to inhibit our ability to manage and systematically plan our program of work.... The division had now reached the limit of its capacity to diversify its approach."[33] That statement reflected its involvement with more difficult and demanding institutions in some countries where the institutional base in social sciences was weak. That, when combined with another Social Science characteristic of trying to discover the "young researcher working in difficult circumstances," was a time-consuming, labour-intensive process.[34] It meant divisional staff spending many more hours in identifying suitable researchers and then helping them to write proposals.

But the cultivation process, when it succeeded, was very rewarding. For example, Mahmoud Amr, who is now a renowned Egyptian toxicologist but an unknown scientist working in a marginalized part of the science world twenty-five years ago, remembers his first meeting with IDRC program officer, Gilles Forget. The latter had become interested in Amr's work following a conference held in Dublin, where four of the researcher's papers had been read by others as he could not afford to attend. Forget set out to find him, arranging a meeting in Cairo's Meridien Hotel, where they discussed the work. For Amr, who had never heard of IDRC or of its support for research, "it was the most important meeting of my life"; with Forget's help ("he was my teacher"), Amr wrote the proposal, sent it to Ottawa via the regional office in Cairo, and was awarded a grant of CAN$250,000 for 1989–93, which was renewed with a further injection of CAN$250,000 to 1996. From that time his work has gained local support and the Egyptian government, along with some help from IDRC, established the Toxicology Centre (TC) at the University of Cairo. Since its opening in April 2004, more than ten thousand Egyptians and others who had been poisoned by pesticides have been treated.[35] And while the payoff was incalculable in terms of impact and in the amelioration of lives positively affected by the research undertaken, that sort of intervention took a lot of time and resources that the division did not necessarily have.

Resources were one thing, but internal dysfunction, at least as defined by David Steedman, was another. He complained of difficulties in process and sometimes attitude. As a governor noted following one of Steedman's interventions, "Vous nous parlez des complexités, des règles du Centre, vous nous parlez de choses qui sont plus difficiles de notre point de vue à nous percevoir sans l'expérience du management de chacun des projets." Given that, he had produced a document that had raised some fundamental questions about the operation of the IDRC system. He thought it was time that the Centre undertake a systems analysis of the flow of documentation, how it was done, and its relationship to the approvals process in the hope of streamlining it.

For example, he noted that at the October 1983 board meeting, "there were 26 projects from AFNS that had to go through the board. So at the administrative level within the Centre ... we have similar problems and bottlenecks, and the result is we spend more time talking to ourselves and more time on administration and less time in the field with our recipients." The board might, he thought, consider approving *programs* as opposed to *projects* so that "one could say the Social Sciences Division has permission of the Board to develop over the next three years X number of projects in natural resource management in South East Asia for say $3 million." As well, he would welcome the latitude in terms of project support that such a system provided. The issues raised were very real ones that touched most program officers.[36] His proposal was not then acted upon for a variety of reasons. Not until the mid-1990s and a painful restructuring brought about by a massive reduction in IDRC's parliamentary appropriation did Keith Bezanson introduce program initiatives, the sort of instrument that Steedman had been talking about a decade earlier.

Health Sciences took stock of its position in early 1983, speaking through a new director, E.J. Charlebois, who had come to the Centre from CIDA. It was a planning year and a learning experience for the new director, and she was intent upon investigating "where we have been and where we are now."[37] First, the division would develop regional profiles that would determine "the depth of technical skills, the research institutes, the specific health problems of the region, what IDRC [had] been doing in the region and what it should be doing, and which regions should be ... areas of emphasis." Of some significance, thirteen years after David Hopper had nailed IDRC colours to the door of the rural poor, HS had consciously set out in a new policy direction—its work now specifically included the *urban* poor.

Its two biggest sectors were maternal and child health and tropical and infectious diseases, but Charlebois was also keen to branch out into nutrition studies, particularly as they related to mother and child. Furthermore, she thought it useful to become more involved in field trials of new vaccines (but not any relating to contraception) that were being developed. However, that might be constrained by commitments in other areas; for example, it appeared that the division had underestimated the amount of work that would be coming in the water and sanitation sector, as well as for occupational and environmental health. HS would also continue to fund work done in those areas in which it had always been active—diarrheal and tropical diseases and nutrition.

Finally, the Cooperative Programs Unit had had its budget doubled to CAN$5 million in 1983 over what it had been in 1982. That represented slightly more than .25 percent of Canadian official development assistance, which remained well short of the government's articulated goal of 1 percent. Earth Sciences remained the dominant program supported through CPU, perhaps because of its range of programming—"from red mud to written languages."[38] Given that emphasis, the division changed its name as of January 1988 to Earth and Engineering Sciences. James Mullin had tried to interpret very literally the broad terms of reference given to CPU to support research related to economic or social development. In early 1983, he had under consideration projects relating to marine pollution, engineering and metallurgy, and earth sciences. Still, the division reserved about 66 percent of the funds available to its program for unplanned activities "to allow us to remain as responsive as we can."

There had also been an encouraging development in the operation of his division. During 1982, Earth and Engineering Sciences had spent much time attempting to change the provenance of most of the proposals it received. These had come from Canadian laboratories, written by Canadian researchers who had only sometimes taken the time to search out a Southern partner. Mullin had gone hoarse telling all and sundry that that was not appropriate— the inclusion of developing country researchers was the *sine qua non* of a successful application. However, having spread the word about the existence of CPU to developing country researchers, the division "was now beginning to see a flow of proposals which clearly originate in groups of scientists in the developing world who have decided that, in addition to seeking finance, it would be advantageous to their programs to have [Canadian] partners." And once that happened, CPU would kick its machinery into gear and play matchmaker for the Southern cohort.

As was suggested by Health Sciences, the debate over urban versus rural research was becoming more heated as urban issues competed with the Centre's rural focus. For example, IDRC had been involved in funding these since the early 1970s, even despite its official position. Support had first been undertaken within the Social Sciences division by the rural-urban dynamics program, and after 1977 by the population and the economic and rural development programs. An interesting study in the urban area that had had some impact on target governments, for example, had been one relating to hawkers and vendors. IDRC had financed this research relating to food security and growing conurbations, and hawkers' and vendors' roles in the marketing and food distribution systems of cities. That had come about as a result of certain Southeast Asian governments wanting to rid the streets of those perceived as beggars. Instead, the study had clearly demonstrated their key role in supplying food to urbanites; without them and their activities, city dwellers in developing world countries would go hungry.[39] Following the Centre-funded study, even Imelda Marcos, the wife of the Filipino president and most determined opponent of hawkers and vendors, was convinced of their indispensability in supplying residents' nutritional and caloric needs.

As the Centre set about cultivating research that reflected a broad and varied set of policy concerns and options, it began by expanding and consolidating funding into urban problems in 1982 with the creation of an urban policy program. It was renamed the Regional Development Program in 1988 and the Urban Development Program a year later as it evolved to address changing research priorities within IDRC. Of the roughly ninety-five projects funded by the Centre in that category between 1980 and 1990, many were successful; in a survey undertaken by an external evaluation in 1989, project leaders often listed examples of how IDRC projects with which they were involved had assisted communities to improve their well-being and covered the range of ideas in which the Centre operated, including agriculture, environment, health, and economic livelihood.[40] It would continue to fund work on projects relating to food and food security—"Food Systems under Stress," which began in 1993, and "Cities Feeding People" three years later, among others. The former, the first phase of an intended long-term project that included research in Botswana, Tanzania, Uganda, Zambia, and Zimbabwe, was a series of workshops concerning very local accounts about the nature and causes of local problems related to food security. The approach placed this project, concerned with *community* issues, in clear contrast with those funded by other donors, which tended "to concentrate on the macro-level problems of the economy or of technology."[41]

Still, as the Centre contemplated the growing list of successful *research* projects it had funded, it was apparent that there were often delays in the *utilization* of research results. Jingjai Hanchanlash, the regional director of the Singapore office, had also pondered that: "The problem facing countries in [his] region was not really how to formulate a research agenda or how to relate research work to important development issues but more how to link research with development, how to translate research results into an action plan."[42] That did happen more often than not, but what to do if it did not? A board meeting held in Dakar, Senegal, had come up against this. Following a visit to the Centre national de recherches agronomiques (CNRA), an IDRC-supported organization situated in the small city of Bambey, Sir Geoffrey Wilson voiced his unease about the attitude of its director, who had announced that what happened to the research done at CNRA was no business of his.[43]

Given that situation, what might be an appropriate course of action? The board went around and around on the question with no satisfactory answer. Often researchers in LDCs were the elites in countries of tremendous inequality who had little empathy for their less fortunate comrades. These were people, or so board member Geila Castillo thought, who needed to be "socially re-oriented."[44] And if they, like the director of CNRA, had little empathy, that was in part because there was little interaction between those in the hinterland region and those who lived in gated communities in the cities. Nor was it easy to get those in the latter into the former, largely because of cost: "when we make our research grants, we must make sure that there is money allocated that will take them out to the field … it is an educational process … and [IDRC has not] paid attention to the lower end of the scale in terms of our potential direct or indirect clientele."

Hubert Zandstra, the AFNS director, felt the Bambey case was an example of research being done incorrectly, which necessitated a change in CNRA's research paradigm and not necessarily in IDRC practice. After all, implementation of results was a part of the project design. Still, as Vinyu Vichet-Vadajab, an early recipient of Centre funding, had noted, "researchers [often] consider their task completed when they have written up their findings. There is a serious lack of interest in following up their work by either disseminating their findings to a larger audience or assiduously trying to sell their findings to potential users."[45] As Zandstra had suggested, it remained a constant struggle for Centre program officers; to reorient a fundamental part of a researcher's character would be a slow and painful process that could be helped along by the demonstration effect of research that had been applied. There was a certain art to ensuring impact. There were models, one of which was the International Potato Centre in the Mindoro Valley of the Philippines. It had been funded by the Centre, and its emphasis had been on fieldwork. The project had developed a farmer-back-to-farmer approach so that the problem was defined from that point of view, a solution derived by, then returned to, the farmer. That meant it was a tremendous success, and that was a template to work with.

However, AFNS was not bereft of examples where impact and utilization had taken place and, in a sense, IDRC was getting tied into knots over a situation that, while irritating, was not potentially crippling. It was also a reflection of IDRC attitudes and its penchant for self-analysis; it recognized certain shortcomings and would correct them to its own satisfaction, regardless of the internal disharmony that might cause. Moreover, through its projects the Centre had contributed tremendously to human resource development in the field of agricultural research. That was easily documented by the number of scientists working in the South who had been supported by IDRC during their education, and by the number of research leaders who had grown professionally in close proximity to Centre-funded projects. Similarly, the contribution to institutional development was manifold: IDRC's catalytic role in promoting new initiatives—such as the International Center for Living Aquatic Resources Management, the International Centre for Research in Agroforestry, and the International Network for Improvement of Banana and Plantain—was clear. There was also a regular exchange of staff between the Centre and CGIAR institutions while, by the mid-1990s, several officials in senior Consultative Group positions had been, in times past, funded by IDRC. As well, Centre work in forming networks was an effective mechanism in enhancing agricultural research. Similarly, its acknowledgement that development problems needed to be addressed through more holistic perspectives was a key contribution to the Centre's agricultural development, and was perhaps best seen through its early support of farming systems research.[46]

The new processes also had to do with a changing environment in the South. As Doug Daniels had told the board in October 1983, "we found there was sufficient evidence to propose that the state of the environment in the Third World is now different from what it was when the Centre was conceived, and that we should take a fresh look and make a more formal systematic assessment of this environment in planning long-term Centre strategy."[47] How had the research environment changed? Clearly, consensus around the table, and particularly among those governors from developing countries, was that hostility toward any form of official development assistance had deepened as the mid-1980s approached: "Ten years ago, anyone having anything to do with aid or research was treated as a missionary.... If you brought aid, you were bringing something good. This has now changed."[48]

IDRC was now keen to re-examine the balance it struck between what Daniels called seed money and persistence; it should be tilted toward the latter, or so many thought—the Centre "should stay longer with carefully selected institutions and countries." That selection would be determined by which of these two objectives were more important and its support would be tailored to fit that pattern. For example, in a weak, underdeveloped research environment, staff would anticipate "that the usefulness of the research project as a tool for building research capacity would be enhanced by more coordinated and sustained programs of training, library and equipment support, longer term commitments, all still provided in project phases, all with the express aim of ensuring that an indigenously sustainable and appropriate research capacity is created." This talk about longer terms suggested change as it had not necessarily been part of the Centre's culture; one of the governors, Allison Ayida from Nigeria, remarked that when he had first come on the board in the late 1970s, a project, should it move into a phase III, was very controversial. Now, should there be even a phase IV, "there would be no apologies." He thought that to be a forward-looking development as the long term was necessary, "persistence was a very positive word." That would certainly apply as IDRC undertook what has arguably been one of its most important projects, and that also reflected its focus on SSA, the African Economic Research Consortium.

The African Economic Research Consortium

Funding for projects in Africa had increased, and all divisions had indicated an intent to place more resources there. As was pointed out, the Cooperative Programs Unit and the Fellowships and Awards division had already allocated new staff to the West Africa Regional Office, and Health Sciences had designated Sub-Saharan Africa as its priority area and had redirected a staff position that had been slated for New Delhi to Dakar as the division was planning to increase programming in francophone Africa. Communications was also getting in on the act, increasing its support for African scientific and scholarly publishing. Agriculture, Food, and Nutrition Sciences expected co-operative projects to play a larger role in its programs, and it planned to support fewer projects on the continent in order to make a more significant contribution to strengthening research capacity. Social Sciences was adopting a similar approach, investing most of its funding in Africa.

What were conditions in Sub-Saharan Africa? They had certainly worsened over the course of the previous decade. The scientific community, including those active researchers and institutions that constituted IDRC's clientele, were also affected by the deteriorating circumstances. In order to deal with this, the Centre initiated a broad review to address such questions as: To what extent and in what ways were conditions different from those in other regions? Should IDRC's policies and procedures be altered to be more responsive in the region? The review, undertaken as the decade rolled on, involved an intensive process of information gathering and consultation with staff, management, and the program and policy committee of the board. The thinking that emerged was of a region desperately requiring special consideration. One reflection of that was the increasing percentage of IDRC's grant that went to the region—from 25 percent of its program budget in 1978 to about 35 percent ten years later. As well, almost half of all Centre staff posted outside Canada were in one of the two Sub-Saharan regional offices.

The Centre's mandate was based on the premise that indigenous research capacity gave national development programs access to essential knowledge and technologies. The capacity to create, apply, and manage solutions to development problems and to adapt to emerging problems was necessary if development efforts were to be effective. That was the area in which IDRC wanted to contribute and where its particular mix of talents in terms of its philosophy and style of operation were ideally suited. Its strategy for Sub-Saharan Africa focused on strengthening human and institutional research resources through training and other means of research capacity building. It also worked to promote regional co-operation in applying research results to development problems. That was the sentiment that led to the establishment in June 1988, under IDRC auspices, of one very successful network, the African Economic Research Consortium (AERC), which remained housed in the Centre's Nairobi office for many years. It was later described as "one of the Centre's best known and most successful networks,"[49] and its success was largely the result of a long process of institution-building, dating back "to initial work by IDRC to incubate the Consortium in the late 1980s."[50]

It was an outgrowth of an IDRC-financed network for economic policy research that had operated in Eastern and Southern Africa between 1983 and 1987. The conspicuous success of that program and the strong demand for its services led the Centre to invite other donors to join with it in financing an extended program. Launched in 1987 and led by Jeffrey Fine, a former IDRC program officer, from mid-1988 until early 1994, it was "an extraordinarily successful operation.... It has helped create a network of competent African macro economic researchers, bringing them into contact with each other and with experts from across the world."[51] With an annual budget by the end of 1996 of US$9.5 million and a secured endowment of US$7 million, the Consortium by that time managed over forty research projects annually, involving upwards of 150 African and overseas scholars, as well as a collaborative master's program in economics on behalf of eighteen universities in thirteen African countries. Its bilingual dissemination program "supported the publication of four externally reviewed research monographs per month, several books annually, articles in scholarly journals, international conferences, and a highly acclaimed series of seminars for senior African policy makers."[52]

Being physically located in the Nairobi office allowed the range and quantity of support to be expanded, specialized full-time staff to be hired, donor coordination to be improved, and a formalized structure with a strong advisory committee to be established. Further, one IDRC official agreed with Fine's analysis that it also helped to level the playing field through the training of economics graduates:

This is a great story of research, of new ideas and perspectives emerging as a result of focusing on Southern researchers, of capacity building, of research being put into use. To understand AERC context is important. In the 1980s and 1990s, African countries found themselves in economic crisis, but there was only one source of economic policy advice, namely the Washington Consensus being pedaled by the World Bank and the IMF. I have literally seen Bank-Fund missions of two dozen staff members descend from Washington on an African capital city; each member of the Bank-Fund mission had a Ph.D. or an M.B.A. from a top western university. Sitting on the government side would be maybe half a dozen folks, mostly with B.A. degrees from the local university. The asymmetry of intellectual firepower was striking. AERC was created to equal-ize that balance of intellectual firepower, and to promote a plurality of ideas in economic policy making. AERC succeeded in building those skills, in promot-ing new ideas, in training a new generation of African economists and placing them in influential positions, and of getting their ideas into policy.[53]

AERC remained animated by IDRC values, empowering local researchers, the necessity of research for policy development, and capacity building. Sig-nificantly, the appointment of a Tanzanian research coordinator, Benno Ndulu, was an important step in "Africanizing" the program, as one report called it.[54] As well, IDRC was keen to emphasize a regional approach to defining a common research agenda, along with a team approach to research, with researchers from both academia and government participating in various projects. It also linked support for research with assistance for other related activities like workshops, training, and publications. By the mid-1990s, AERC had become the dominant organization of its kind in Sub-Saharan Africa, being frequently cited favourably in publications of the World Bank. That, admittedly, could be perceived as a mixed blessing in the Africa of the mid-1990s given the Bank's philosophy and practice. It was also seen as a model of cost-effective networking, capacity building, and donor coordination.[55]

The Ten-Week Cure

A policy and management review that began in mid-April 1986—what became known at the Centre as the ten-week management seminar—was held as one response to the ongoing intellectual ferment. It represented the most extensive single examination of the Centre's mandate and function since IDRC had been established in 1970, and was intended to develop a frame-work for its strategic plan, which involved discussion about its mission and objectives. In short, it was to reflect on strategic challenges and had been dictated by the need to assess its overall focus and programs in order to ensure that they reflected the world's changing physical, social, and economic environments. It was agreed that "if people are to benefit from IDRC's work, [it] must endeavour constantly to ensure that the activities it supports reflect in one form or another the essential long-term goals of development ... sustainable growth, equity and participation."[56]

As well, the seminar was an attempt to generate senior management commitment to support more interdisciplinary research, and to more actively foster the utilization of research in practical and policy processes.[57] Head was already mulling over the necessity of approaching these issues in slightly different ways for maximum effectiveness. While systematic and comprehensive evaluations of outputs and outcomes of projects were a complex undertaking that had been increasingly emphasized by the Centre, they had their limitations. Studies of particular projects, while providing insights into and information about one project or a group of them, provided only partial snapshots of the overall outcome of a project or a division's research program. As the notion of utilization became more important at IDRC, so too was it compelled to shift its evaluations focus from procedural issues toward research outcomes like knowledge creation, training, or the development of new products or processes. Head was also concerned about the dissemination processes that made available the outputs of that research, the use of some of those outputs and their outcomes, particularly the longer-term implications of the practical application of research. But that, too, was not as easy as simply providing a good paradigm for policy-makers to use; it was difficult to assess utilization in all its forms. Certainly including government officials in the project design would be helpful. But it was also true that the time frame involved in policy implementation often greatly exceeded the duration of the project. Further, a single project usually represented only one component of the policy development process. Implementation typically required further study and consultation. As well, Lauchlan Munro, IDRC vice-president of Corporate Strategy and Regional Management, has suggested that:

> One of the reasons that it is hard ... to get a handle on [implementation and utilization] is that they didn't seem to think or talk about it a lot. At the same time, we know of lots of cases, and we've documented lots of cases where the results of IDRC projects clearly got used. The famous Waterloo water pump was widely used. The jiko stove, which was developed as a result of an IDRC project, is sold in every market in East Africa. You can't go to a market in East Africa without tripping over a jiko stove. You can multiply those examples. MINISIS was the most widely used library software before the Internet. IDRC clearly was not uninterested in these things—they just didn't talk about it and measure uptake and use.[58]

Lester Pearson, IDRC chair, and Indira Gandhi, prime minister of India, share a moment on the occasion of the Centre's board meeting in New Delhi, March 1972. (IDRC photo)

An early Agriculture, Food and Nutrition Sciences project in the high Andes, Bolivia. (IDRC photo)

Weighing the rice harvest, Thailand. From its early days the Centre was involved in rice research designed to enhance food security. (IDRC photo)

From the early days at IDRC, Southern women were involved in projects. (IDRC photo)

A meeting of the Brandt Commission at IDRC, early 1983. From left: Ivan Head, Willy Brandt, and an unknown researcher. (IDRC photo)

Keith Bezanson observes a textile project in India. (IDRC photo)

Then–UN Secretary-General Kofi Annan and Maureen O'Neil at IDRC headquarters, 9 March 2004. (IDRC photo)

With IDRC funding, the Peruvian microbiologist Palmira Ventosilla has developed a biological method for mosquito control. In this photo, a technician checks for mosquito larvae. (Bruce Muirhead photo)

The M'beubeuss dump outside Dakar, Senegal, and some of the *récupérateurs* who make a living recycling scavenged material. IDRC is funding research on the health and environmental effects of the dump. (Bruce Muirhead photo)

A class of schoolchildren on their lunch break at the information centre in Embalam, Tamil Nadu, India. IDRC has funded work on the effects of ICTs on remote villages in India. (Bruce Muirhead photo)

Urban agriculture, Nairobi, Kenya. The roofs of the world's largest slum, Kabira, are in the background. IDRC is funding research on urban agriculture in various cities around the world. (Bruce Muirhead photo)

Head remained determined to tease out appropriate lessons during the seminar respecting this very contentious subject.

From its beginning it was agreed the Centre must ensure that the activities it supported reflect three essential elements of development—sustainable growth, equity, and participation—and that background informed all discussion. This introspection was inspired by the rather dismal situation in which development organizations were then operating. Budget deficits, public unhappiness in donor countries with money being expended for seemingly little return, and the rapidly widening gap between the Earth's rich and poor all gave cause for concern. In Canada's case, while IDRC's parliamentary appropriation was growing, it was also true that the percentage of gross national product devoted to official development assistance was falling more generally. As well, there was the freeze on civil service hiring, which the Centre respected and which put pressure on programs and officers, and a "dramatically changing context in terms of development problems, research resources and technological potential."[59] The exercise, at least according to Ivan Head, was to prepare the Centre for future effectiveness.

Where did the ten weeks finish up? Most importantly with the idea that research was a means to an end, and not an end in itself. Building research capacity, producing new knowledge, and making linkages were all components in the conduct of scientific enquiry. Indeed, that was the board credo as well: "IDRC's mission is to contribute to development through research and research-supporting activities. The Centre aims to assist in promoting the indigenously determined social and economic advancement of the developing regions of the world, with a particular focus on the problems of poverty."[60] IDRC was an agency that aided development through the medium of research, and was not simply a research-supporting agency. That echoed thoughts in *With Our Own Hands*; the end result lay in "research *for* development."[61]

Further, the Centre's objective must be the creation "of an indigenous competence to utilize science and technology for the benefit of their own societies; to identify and solve problems in a manner respecting individual human dignity."[62] That belief underlay all management seminar discussions. Consensus was also achieved on a number of other issues as IDRC staff were canvassed. Among these was that IDRC's operations were guided by *development* rather than *political* considerations, which set it apart from many donors; it offered untied assistance, recruited internationally, experimented and innovated, and provided small amounts of funding where immediately needed. It was a facility, ironically, beyond the scope of better endowed agencies.[63] As well, it was decided that the Centre would pursue a theme approach as a means of achieving coherence in large part because it was recognized that "the many dimensions of social and economic development are interdependent and overlapping."[64] A series of disconnected sectoral activities could not adequately address development problems in the penultimate decade of the twentieth century. As well, the importance of responsiveness was highlighted—it was "a central tenet of IDRC's philosophy and operating style." It had been the Centre's distinguishing feature and it should continue to be so, subject to the constraint of focusing on certain areas of comparative advantage.

Certainly the ten weeks had been valuable in terms of allowing IDRC to step back and examine itself critically; the result could conceivably be a good launching pad for change. It was also the case that neither the structure nor the method of operations of the Centre changed materially. For example, James Mullin later recalled that it had focused on two concepts, connectedness and utilization—"multi-disciplinarity wasn't one of the things that emerged."[65] Indeed, despite being much talked about by the Centre in all its incarnations—board, management, and staff—multi-disciplinarity remained elusive and, quite frankly, was viewed as less important than the other two. John Hardie thought it was not present in IDRC reality until the mid-1990s. In the 1980s, the divisions continued to pursue their own interests and had established programs specific to particular disciplines with minimal linkages with those of other divisions. As Eva Rathgerber has pointed out, "the attitude within the Centre towards work done by colleagues in other divisions and disciplines was often somewhat negative, ranging from mild criticism to a conspicuous lack of interest."[66] This was not unusual among development organizations set up as IDRC was, or among universities. Indeed, in 2010 disciplinary "purity" remains a jealously guarded practice among the latter. The necessity of paying more than lip service to the idea was to be the conceptual justification of the shift from division-based projects to program initiatives in the mid-1990s, discussed in Chapter 5. As Hardie was to point out later, when the new system was implemented, "It's not fair to say that the divisions were mono-disciplinary, but they were specialists in narrower fields and the conceptual thinking was that to fix any development problem, you need contributions from many branches of knowledge and disciplines. We had to foster interdisciplinarity to the extent possible. So, [we] had hoped that the [program initiative] system would do that."[67]

However, it was certainly not the case that indisciplinarity had been completely ignored with the five thousand projects funded to that time. For example, a very successful project led by the Sri Lankan economist, Hari Gunasingham, based until 1990 in Singapore at the National University and whose work focused on the tea industry in Sri Lanka, was representative of a number of Centre results. With IDRC support, he undertook to investigate the implementation of better tea-drying technology to help those societies dependent on tea as a major source of income and employment. In doing so, he employed, among others, an economist and a sociologist. The former's advice was that tea drying was undertaken by small, inefficient, local co-operatives that needed about US$1,000 worth of computing assistance to enhance their processes, not a prohibitive amount if helped by a donor. The sociologist reported that 85 percent of tea dryers were illiterate males who could not be assisted by their employers using more sophisticated technology because they simply could not use it. That was telling: "It showed the need for social understanding in framing what was originally conceived of as a hard science project. So there began to be much more interest in the interaction of social sciences with the natural sciences, not because of an abstract belief in multi-disciplinarity, but as a necessary means of putting key information into the very basis of the natural sciences development project [IDRC was] going to support." Interdisciplinarity worked, in this case strikingly so, and its inclusion in the mix probably accounted, at least in part, for the tremendous success of the project.[68]

So too, however, did the application, with Centre help, of the technology that Gunasingham had earlier developed, called SYNAPSE. A PC-based commercial process control system that was adapted to optimize the manufacture of tea in Sri Lanka, it allowed the six hundred Sri Lankan tea plantations and four thousand more in India to ensure that drying ovens burned more efficiently, in the process reducing waste and using less fuel. Indeed, as the project completion report noted, it was a "very high-impact project with lessons to be learned for the development of other [small and medium-sized] projects. Should be required reading!"[69] Randy Spence, IDRC's regional director in East Asia, noted that Gunasingham "is a brilliant, shy entrepreneur ... [who brought] together development and technology in a unique way. [His] is the first project of this kind that IDRC has been involved in [and] it has taught us a lot, and to some extent defined a new direction for IDRC in these rapidly changing times."[70]

That "new direction" was recommended in strategy deliberations to identify program initiatives. Development "thrusts" would be identified in order "to provide a coherent approach to the resolution of problems common to a geographic region and/or a particular aspect of development."[71] These thrusts would be well-defined, focused activities carried out within a given time frame, and themes, the paper noted, would be used to define long-term fields of interest for Centre programming. The actual word "thrusts," Head noted, "doesn't necessarily mean anything," but was an attempt to identify, from the regional offices, those areas of activity that seemed to be important to governments and the institutions of the region, at least as interpreted by regional directors. The president explained thrusts as lists of activities—for example, IDRC program officers might feel that a cropping activity was absolutely vital in a region. On the other hand, government might believe that issues like refugees or the creation of jobs were more important. It would be up to these new thrusts to determine what would be done. Themes were long term; in a call to IDRC staff for suggestions, almost thirty possibilities were identified, reflecting the intense interest in the exercise throughout the Centre.

These were eventually reduced to five, which were formally approved by the Centre and the board. They included skills enhancement, physical well-being, economic participation, food security, and technological choice. Themes and thrusts would have an impact on how the Centre comported itself; policy directions would require more integration of divisional activities and the strengthening of coordinating mechanisms.[72]

The ten-week seminar had served a purpose. It had also approved a mission statement and formal objective for IDRC, as well as providing its first ever formal definition of development: "A process for the benefit of people and should be consistent with human dignity, which is best fostered in condition of adequate nutrition, sound health, independence of spirit, pride in indigenous culture and respect for human rights." It had also crafted a strategic statement.[73] Over the next year, management and staff continued to follow up on the broad strategic directions provided in the various self-examinations. At the March 1987 board meeting, Head commented that governors would see "welcome evidence of interdivisional involvement, of coherence, of greater connectedness."[74] The effects of the ten-week management seminar—connectedness and responsiveness, interdivisional collaboration and decentralization, themes and thrusts—all became important elements in the Centre's intellectual operations and planning. Divisions talked seriously about the results and how they could be implemented. The emphasis on responsiveness required a high degree of proximity between program and project decision makers and research partners, and easy and rapid exchange of information between operating staff and potential and recipients of funding.[75] The Centre was now focused upon its renewal, a process that would take it to the end of Head's presidency. That said, themes, thrusts, and sometimes interdisciplinarity never really gathered traction. For those to bite in Centre programming, the divisions would have to go and Head, or so John Hardie believed, "had no intention of doing away with [them]."[76]

Women in Development

One of the more important changes of focus at IDRC had to do with one of the issues mooted as IDRC continued to contemplate its future—women in development (WID). The idea had first been raised in 1970 with the publication of Ester Böserup's *Women's Role in Economic Development*.[77] As had been demonstrated, women's issues were different from men's in the development process; for example, Reem Saad, an Egyptian researcher at the American University in Cairo, noted that gender differences were very strong in such areas as biodiversity and seed selection in rural areas of Egypt in which she had undertaken her work.[78] Moreover, as new technologies were introduced into the agricultural sector, they were usually directed at men rather than women, which, naturally, had further disadvantaged women in the development process.[79] The approach had been informed by the "Report of the Panel of Experts on Science, Technology, and Women" in September 1983. The Panel had addressed itself to strategies and mechanisms for ensuring that the benefits of science and technology in the development process accrued at all levels to females as well as to males. The conclusions reached and recommendations made relating to endogenous research and development and participation of women in education and communication in the fields of science and technology were thought to be of particular relevance to IDRC and its WID program.

In developing a standard of measure, the Panel had stressed reliance on criteria in addition to "economic" issues, which included quality of life issues and policies. The very significant role of publications in the advancement and recognition in science and technology was discussed, and the Panel expressed concern about access to publications for their own work and the coverage given to issues related to women. As well, it had urged national governments, particularly those of developing countries, to build endogenous research and development capabilities by adopting, on a priority basis, a policy of total human resource development that would give women full participation in the research and development process. It was recommended that development projects should include the "users" as primary participants and evaluators of the information collected, thus ensuring their active participation and involvement in projects from the beginning.

Rather late in the game and long after CIDA and other bilateral agencies had first addressed women's development issues, an informal working group composed of staff from the program divisions of IDRC was formed in February 1986 to discuss issues in research related to women. It addressed problems ranging from the difficulties that arose when the concentration was on a particular subgroup as a category of analysis, to the consideration of special strategies for the enhancement of Centre support for WID issues. In view of these problems, the group recommended that Centre management "support more research activities undertaken by grassroots organizations and by NGOs particularly on issues on women in development."[80]

In April 1987, IDRC established Women in Development as a discrete entity, and it was reviewed two years later. As a three-year experimental project, the unit was designed to address the perceived need for more responsible gender-sensitive research. As was pointed out, "Since consideration of gender within development was increasingly being acknowledged as interdisciplinary in scope, bordering on and intersecting different subject areas, the Unit's mandate [was] to operate cooperatively as a Centre-wide facility. As such, the Unit's main objectives [were] to focus on gender issues in development contexts and, where appropriate, to integrate those issues into the Centre's research programs and activities."[81] As well, there was much talk during the internal evaluation and among IDRC staff that the unit would be well advised to broaden the scope to gender and development (GAD) and it became one of the acronyms bounced around the Centre along with women *and* development (WAD) in the late 1980s.[82]

But did WID influence IDRC as much as its supporters hoped? Probably not. Nancy O'Rourke, in her 1989 evaluation, noted that "in order to be truly credible on the front it must [also] meet the classical difficulties of matching words with deeds, and intent with practice."[83] Progress in addressing gender imbalance could only be described as modest, at least until the later 1990s and the appointment of Maureen O'Neil as president. For example, the proportion of female project leaders remained relatively low over time. Indeed, the percentage of female project leaders decreased during the three years from 1991 to 1994 (27 percent) when compared with 1986–90 (20 percent).[84] Further, because female researchers were often in the forefront of research into WID issues, their relative absence suggested that the Centre was falling short of its research commitments in these areas. As Eva Rathgerber has accurately written, "IDRC was slow to adopt WID/GAD approaches." Indeed, a decade later, only 13 percent of project completion reports made any recommendations or gave any evaluative comment with respect to gender, while a mere 33 percent made any mention at all of gender or disaggregated data by sex. While there might have been some awareness of gender equity concerns on a structural level as seen by Centre hiring practices, gender issues were rarely evaluated on the level of individual research projects.[85] Some Centre staff thought it a fad that would pass and, most commonly in IDRC projects, women were grouped with men or they were invisible. That attitude was in stark contrast to more sensitive treatment of women in development elsewhere.

WID was, Rathgerber correctly maintains, "one of the more important methodological breakthroughs in the later 20th century."[86] These researchers working within the WID framework were the first to deconstruct development processes and analyze who benefited from what: "For the first time, customs and traditions which had been taken for granted and which had never been seriously challenged by earlier development researchers, were closely examined and often found to be seriously discriminatory or even detrimental towards women." IDRC was a relative laggard in this case to the point where, in mid-1992, Wendy Pena, the staff association's executive assistant, and Yianna Lambrou, its representative for the Social Sciences division, could write to Keith Bezanson complaining about the lack of women members on a committee put together to develop a generic job description for program officers. "It seems," they wrote, "almost inconceivable that not one female employee would have been of sufficient caliber to join this committee.... Management needs to improve its record on equitable gender representation within the Centre."[87] And while the president could respond to them that it was "a serious oversight" that would not be repeated, the fact that it had happened at all was telling.

More Strategizing

From 1986 to 1988, the Centre made a number of refinements, as has been seen. The clarification of its mission and objectives was accomplished by increased emphasis throughout on coherence among its programs, and on the end results of its activities. As well, there was more than lip service now paid to interdivisional co-operation, and some Centre-wide programs had been created. Further, Health Sciences and Social Sciences had made structural changes in their programs to be more community focused and to support research on an interdisciplinary and interdivisional basis. More funding was also made available to regional offices in order to provide the Centre in its entirety with a better ability to plan. Similarly, revisions to the strategic plan had made the regional perspective more prominent in planning at both the divisional and corporate levels. Intellectual leadership in the Centre was also mobilized in order to allow staff to be at the forefront in their knowledge of development issues.

IDRC had also recommitted itself to addressing Sub-Saharan African issues. The intention was to review the Centre's past activities and its future intentions to determine whether or not it should change its approach or practice for maximum effectiveness. IDRC focused on assessing information on research resources and capabilities, as well as identifying research priorities where it had a comparative advantage. A part of this was in the development of a strategy for South Africa, then in the final throes of its racist apartheid regime, that was presented to the board at its meeting in October 1988, and that will be discussed below. That initiative was to see the flowering of the Centre's involvement with the new multiracial and democratic government of the Republic of South Africa, overseen for its part from its Regional Office for Southern Africa (ROSA) in Johannesburg, set up in 1992.

How would divisional strategies and philosophies alter to reflect these changes? It was now feasible to begin assessing the aggregate picture of strategies in light of the Centre's mission and objectives. Agriculture, Food, and Nutrition Sciences was restructuring in order to better reflect its concerns about the sustainability of agricultural production, resource conservation and rehabilitation, and pesticides and pest management. It was certainly ahead of most other agencies as it would be years before most would begin to consider these issues. In short, the new divisional focus had shifted from an emphasis on increased agricultural production to one where access to food and other basic needs for the individual took priority.[88] In practical terms, this meant increased emphasis was given in the project planning and design to social and economic considerations, to the reduction of poverty, to rural employment and income generation, and to nutrition, all within the renewable natural resource and utilization system.

Concerns that increases in agricultural productivity in the past had some-times been at the expense of the stability and sustainability of the productive resource base prompted the division to pay much more attention to issues of environmental conservation and rehabilitation and natural resource management in general. Similarly, concerns about health and ecological effects associated with the use of toxic agricultural chemicals meant increased emphasis on finding less hazardous pest management methods. Ecological and health concerns were then integrated into AFNS's overall program, and a program officer position was created specifically to promote programming in the environment and sustainable and safe agricultural production systems. In pursuit of this, the program objective for the crop and animal production systems program had been rewritten to underscore its concerns with sustainability, equity, rural employment, misuse of agrochemicals, and strengthening national research capacity. The United Nations Conference on Environment and Development, held in Rio de Janeiro in June 1992, would begin to put global resources, or at least attention, behind this issue, but IDRC remained, as it had been throughout most of its history, in the vanguard of those concerned about the effects humanity had on the global environment.

Health Sciences had also reorganized itself in the latter part of the decade. It had noted, for example, that the division's "activities tend to be discipline-bound and focus on only a few of the target population's symptoms of ill health. Few programs or projects follow a holistic approach and fewer examine causal factors that are not biomedical … [but] behavioural health conditions and those related to social and economic circumstances are of increasing concern in developing countries."[89] Its decision was to promote a more holistic approach to programming in what would eventually become something like the much-vaunted ecohealth program initiative. By 1987, Health Sciences had shifted its focus to, among other things, "develop policies, practices and technologies to improve the physical environment of communities and the physical and social environment of individuals."[90] The programs that emerged dealt with people and their communities, including health and the community, health systems, and health and the environment. The first theme would identify and develop community-based research initiatives. Priority would be given to projects that examined how economic and social conditions and human behaviour affected health, with the emphasis on its improvement.

Also considered was the use of technologies, the transmission of communicable disease, methods to promote participatory research, health education, and strategies to improve the nutrition of women and children. Further, through its "Health and the Community" program, the division would undertake funding for projects focusing on the physical and biological elements in the environment that affected the health of the poor, who were almost too numerous to count. This would result in the establishment of a program of ecohealth, discussed in Chapter 5, which was groundbreaking and innovative, what one staff member has called "one of the greatest ideas to come out of IDRC."[91] This was done to promote the better understanding of health-related environmental factors and the nature of the interplay between communities and their environments. A 1988 document quoted approvingly from an expert in the field, who had noted that "Health is just one element in the total development picture; accordingly, health problems cannot be tackled in isolation from the other elements. In other words, the attack on the problems of health should be mounted as an integral part of a broad frontal attack directed against the multifarious forms of poverty. There can be no hope for a significant and lasting improvement in health in the absence of a simultaneous improvement in all other sectors."[92] That view was widely shared in the division. Health was not the absence of disease, nor could it be achieved by controlling disease. Rather, "Numerous genetic, social, cultural, environmental and economic factors interact to produce both health and illness."

Social Sciences took as its starting point the recommendations coming out of its in-depth divisional review (an administrative innovation implemented during mid-decade) that had been dealt with at the board meeting in Nairobi. It had been very intense and the two governors who had overseen the process, Gerry Helleiner and Jorge Hardoy, had been tough on the division to the point where its director, Anne Whyte, had found it necessary to contest some of the IDDR's findings. Be that as it may, a new program framework had been established that included economic policy, population, education and society, and regional development. Information Sciences had turned its attention to a new strategic plan as well, which would include studies of broad issues such as the utilization of information services and products, the refinement of geographical strategies, and the assessment of newer information technologies. Community-level information services remained a priority, and the division was refining its processes designed to allow it to more effectively respond to local initiatives in disparate parts of the world.

IS also remained focused on improving the management and use of information for development research, decision making, and change. It would continue to support applied information activities, and special attention would be given to development policy-makers and to the intended beneficiaries of the Centre's work—the rural and urban poor. As well, increased attention would be paid during the project development stage to ensure that factors such as potential impact, sustainability, utilization, network linkages, innovativeness, human resource development, and relation to regional office strategies were taken into account. The focus on Africa would be maintained, especially as the division's special strategy for supporting information activities for the continent was entering its second year. This reflected the effort that had begun in 1987 when IDRC had commissioned a series of papers and had organized workshops involving African specialists in order to better plan the design of a regional plan that could respond to their needs. Part of that effort became known as IDRC's "Africa Strategy," reflecting as it did the recommendations in a strategy document, *Sharing Knowledge for Development: IDRC's Information Strategy for Africa*. According to a later external evaluation, this had been "a very effective tool for directing and coordinating its activities and for setting its program priorities ... based on [African's] expressed need."[93] It would also morph into Acacia, a large IDRC-funded information project that would be in place by 1995.

The smaller divisions—Earth and Engineering Sciences (EES), Fellowships and Awards, and Communications—had begun to develop projects of their own. EES had a regular budget, about 8 percent of the Centre's allocation, with which to do so given its change of mandate from the old Cooperative Programs Unit. It set its sights on funding those projects that demonstrated respect for the environment, the increased participation of women, and the utilization of research results. One of the first was "Water in the Environment," designed to fund research on potable water. The emphasis would remain on Africa, and the new division would continue to adhere to the Centre's decentralization policy and would add staff to those regional offices, like Nairobi and Cairo, where it had none. Fellowships and Awards continued to increase its support for institutions and for graduate-level training. Finally, Communications committed itself to increasing support to recipient institutions among LDCs for a more systematic and research-based approach to the dissemination, implementation, and utilization of project results.

All of this activity pointed to IDRC's redefined approach to development research, which included increased interdivisional co-operation, enhanced capacity building, and dissemination of research results and regional perspectives. Divisions had made an effort to coalesce around several development themes, and a number of Centre-wide initiatives on WID, shelter, nutrition, and acquired immune deficiency, had been mooted. All of these focused on particular development problems and were representative of the overall trend in IDRC to pay more attention to regionally focused development problems and the ultimate outcome that its research support pursued. Further, Agriculture, Food, and Nutrition Sciences, Engineering and Environmental Sciences, Health Sciences, and Social Sciences, through the restructuring that had taken place, gave particular attention to the need for adding a broader interdisciplinary focus to their work. Communications, Fellowships and Awards, and Information Sciences put heavy emphasis on the needs and priorities growing out of activities funded by the research program divisions.

As part of this effort, IDRC convened a meeting with a number of other donors and prominent development people whose genesis was a report prepared for the Centre by Princeton's John Lewis, *External Funding of Development-Related Research: A Survey of Some Major Donors*. Among many others, Manmohan Singh, now India's prime minister and sometime finance minister, but then representing the South Commission, attended, as did John Evans, a former president of the University of Toronto and later the founding director of the Population, Health, and Nutrition Department of the World Bank. He was there to give an account of the Commission on Global Health Research. The gathering's purpose was to provide a forum for discussion of strategic issues relating to development research in Southern countries, its

linkages with international and regional research centres and Northern country research, and the role of external support.[94] As well, there was much talk
of the enabling environment, which would lead to provision of adequate
support to development research. This included not only education for
researchers, but also more broadly the whole education process, making
people at all levels of society aware of the importance of the natural and
social sciences and their potential contribution to development.

Following the Lewis study, IDRC had had discussions with the OECD's
Development Assistance Committee about improving the collection of data
on support for research, but that initiative was stillborn as others were not
yet ready to move in that direction. They would in the not-too-distant future.
Still, Klaus Winkel, of the Danish International Development Agency, later
credited the 1988 meeting with focusing attention on the importance of
support for research-capacity strengthening, and the Danish decision to
start a small program in that direction. Tim Dottridge, at the meeting representing IDRC (along with Head), recalls that it "was really to pick up on
the object of the IDRC Act 'to encourage generally the coordination of international development research ... and to foster cooperation in research on
development problems' and to emphasize IDRC's leading role as a funder
of development research and analyst of conditions for research and capac-
ity-strengthening in the South."[95] He also remembers that the president
thought the gathering was a success, not so much for its substantive outcomes, "but mostly in terms of emphasizing the IDRC leadership and convening power role."

The role of the regional offices was also now very important in stimulating collaboration in the field. The proximity of program staff to each other
and to their constituency made shared perspectives and joint action easier.
One of the first examples of this new emphasis on interdisciplinary co-operation was the Asian Fisheries Social Sciences Research Network, which
brought together fish biologists, economists, and other social scientists to
develop fisheries social science research capacity. It was welcomed, as prior
to its establishment there was no mechanism to pull together fishery economists and other social scientists in the region. This was also an important
network as the fisheries sector provided a valuable source of food protein and
was one of the primary sources of livelihood and employment in Asian countries. However, it was also in this sector where extreme poverty persisted, a
situation considered to be a serious social, economic, and political issue.
Clearly, finding solutions to this complex problem would require a multidisciplinary approach. Moving through four phases beginning in 1983, it ended
in 1996 and had been supported by other donors—Ford, the Danish Inter-

national Development Agency, and the Netherlands Ministry of Development and Cooperation—a sure sign of success, which external evaluations confirmed.[96] This Centre creation accomplished important objectives like influencing fisheries policy in Asia, upgrading the degree qualifications of network members, and enhancing knowledge more generally among participants.

Another network, the Joint Investigation of Smallholder Livestock Development, supported by AFNS and Social Sciences, addressed a series of problems that could not be dealt with adequately by only one sector. Pushed by the regional office in Singapore, from 1986 there had been about a dozen new initiatives in the region, bringing together disparate groups. That had been replicated on a Centre-wide basis, with the number and size of interdivisional projects increasing dramatically. Further afield, a project being funded in Paraguay, one of the poorest countries in the Western Hemisphere, was reaping dividends. It evaluated interventions for the prevention of Chagas disease, a particularly debilitating affliction that could result in death, caused by a bug bite or the accidental rubbing of bug feces into the eye after being bitten on the face. Five divisions were collaborating on this one, with specialists involved from several disciplines—materials science and rural architecture, clinical medicine, sociology, and medical entomology.[97] This in itself was no easy task to bring together such different disciplines to address complex issues in rural health and development. As well, a film of the project, the *Chagas Disease Prevention through Improved Housing*, was made, which brought communications, led by the newly appointed David Nostbakken, into the mix. It also had an impact on Paraguayans in terms of reducing the incidence of the disease as communities became more sensitized to the nature of the bug with which they were dealing. IDRC continues to fund research into the disease throughout Latin America.

And what of the regional perspective? This had certainly become more pronounced in the formulation of divisional strategies over the past number of years, with AFNS and Health Sciences very explicit with respect to their intentions to aggregate regional program statements in developing their divisional plans. Regional offices had become key players in the process through annual staff meetings and through their support for a range of activities. As well, management continued to evaluate the results of RO input to divisional strategies. The process whereby information on regional needs, priorities, and research themes was collected and used was evolving, with the regional offices as the focal point and interdivisional collaboration as the central mechanism. All of this was made easier by the introduction of email, a revolutionary new technology that made communication instantaneous. One approach that management had encouraged was that of "thrusts," noted above, which linked together divisional projects addressing different aspects of development problems and regional needs. An example of this new process in action was at the Latin America Regional Office where, in the discussion of a Latin American strategy, development priorities were narrowed down to five well-defined areas amenable to research for which IDRC possessed the competence to support work through an "integrated and intersectoral approach." A working group was established for each thrust and each division supplied program statements on specific development thrusts from its perspective.

IDRC in South Africa

Given the intensity of activity at IDRC during the later 1980s in developing new procedures and expanding programming, additional (and potentially fraught) programs of research should have been the last thing on Head's mind. However, that was not the case and much as had been the case with funding research in the Southern cone of South America, he had taken the prescient step of getting involved in South Africa as the apartheid government wobbled. The Centre had not always been so disposed. For example, at a management committee meeting on 25 May 1984, in response to a question raised, the president had noted that any research funding there "would be counterproductive to IDRC's objectives, credibility and interests.... IDRC policy remains that no IDRC financial support be given to researchers based in South African and Bantustan institutions."[98] Still, the Centre had maintained a strong program of research support for the frontline states that opposed South Africa. That position had changed completely in October 1988, largely as a result of the interest Prime Minister Brian Mulroney had shown in doing what he could to fight the scourge of apartheid, even to the point of alienating two of his closest allies, US President Ronald Reagan and British Prime Minister Margaret Thatcher. While Linda Freeman has suggested that his motives were not altogether altruistic, it remained that Canadian policy toward that country did take a significant turn during the later 1980s, and the Centre responded.[99]

It did so because of institutionalized racism, human rights violations, and widespread political repression. At the same time a new nation was beginning to emerge in South Africa that was erasing artificial racial and ethnic boundaries. By grounding the desirable and the possible on existing reality and emerging trends, research funded by IDRC would play a critical role in the transitional period and in the development of a new society. Indeed, so involved did the Centre become in South African issues that a significant part of the new country's constitution was written in its regional office in Johannesburg, following the ROs establishment in 1992. Centre support alongside others, including the Canadian government, would have a positive impact on South African society through the strengthening of an independent research capability. It would also help to limit an exodus of talent by enabling researchers to remain in the country and by contributing to the continuing development of young group of South African researchers. It could also help to promote the democratization of governance and that could have the important effect of opening the way for a freer and more egalitarian society.

The board, at its October 1988 meeting, directed that IDRC work exclusively with the Democratic Movement and its efforts to undermine apartheid, a policy helped along a number of months later by the release in February 1990 of Nelson Mandela from twenty-seven years of imprisonment. That was, as an IDRC document pointed out, "the greatest political event of the year for this region in particular and Africa in general."[100] As anti-apartheid activist Patrick FitzGerald has suggested, "it marked the beginning of the new South Africa and four incredible years when a state was reshaped, at least in terms of governmental activity, and Black Africans were brought within political discourse."[101] Along with other decisions announced by Pretoria and the anticipated negotiations between the African National Congress (ANC) and the government, powerful new forces for change were spreading across the country. In spite of the South African government's attempts to restrict the Centre's involvement, it did develop a large program supporting the African National Congress and the Democratic Movement in the six years from 1988. During that period, IDRC poured CAN$23 million into projects designed to build policy research capacity and support institutional transformation in key areas that included local government, environment and natural resource management, information sector reform, and science and technology institutional restructuring.[102] The board resolution authorizing IDRC involvement focused on four reasons for involvement: "the Centre would support research projects that have the potential to inform the debate on the process of change and assist it in the development of policies, strategies and programs laying the ground for a future 'non-racial, democratic and unitary society which would be consistent with IDRC's goals of sustainable growth, equity and participation; Centre support would aim at strengthening ANC research capacity; the Centre would support efforts by South African researchers to put in place planning and coordinating mechanisms aimed at identifying research priorities and improving exchanges among researchers and between the research community and the democratic movement; and, the Centre would facilitate contact between South African researchers and their counterparts throughout the world."[103]

Further, while the situation would require that the Centre maintain close relations with the Department of External Affairs and the embassy in Pretoria, it should also endeavour to do what it had done best in times past, which was maintain its independence and ensure as much as possible that IDRC-supported activities were not a part of the Canadian government's diplomatic initiatives.

The program was physically launched through an accidental meeting at the University of Zimbabwe between Marc Van Ameringen, an IDRC program officer and later the regional director of the Regional Office for Southern Africa, and Adzei Bekoe, the Nairobi-based regional director of the East Africa Regional Office. Also involved were several high-ranking members of the ANC: Thabo Mbeki, then the director of the Information Department, Steve Thewete, the former commander of the military, and Zola Skweyiya, the director of the Constitution and Legal department. The Zimbabweans had asked the ANC to participate in the meeting, which then allowed for an important conversation to take place between the IDRC staffers and those ANC members. Most importantly, it afforded Van Ameringen and company with an opportunity to discuss the new Centre policy toward South Africa. As he reported back to Head, "Although the ANC was supportive of the board resolution, they requested that they be consulted on future IDRC initiatives and that the Centre utilize the post-apartheid national research structure that they have created with the assistance of internal organizations to vet proposals."[104]

That was done over the next few years and as Ivan Head was stepping down as president, he could look back on the beginning of a job that would be well done. Between the October 1988 board meeting and February 1991, the Centre had spent about CAN$2 million in research support for ANC and affiliated groups. Manifestly, the situation in South Africa was changing.

> The unbanning of the ANC, the South African Community Party, the Pan-African Congress and other prescribed organizations; the release and return to public politics of Nelson Mandela; the lifting of the State of Emergency; the decision by the De Klerk government to remove from the statute book by the end of the year key pieces of legislation which have provided the legal basis for apartheid; negotiations between the De Klerk government and the ANC on the conditions for the return to South Africa of the estimated 40,000 exiles and the release of political prisoners, and; the agreement between the De Klerk government and the extra-parliamentary opposition to convene a multi-party conference to draft a new constitution.[105]

Clearly, South Africa was entering a period of political transition that was expected to last for two or three years with a new constitution and a democratically elected government. As the political environment in the country had changed, so too should IDRC policy, or so Van Ameringen thought. That, however, would be left to Keith Bezanson as Head handed him the Centre's reins. In 1992, Bezanson had convinced the board that a new office should be established in Johannesburg in view of a change in the political climate in the country. The Regional Office for Southern Africa was set up in that year and eventually had more than fifty staff, making it one of the largest. That act, and the foundation laid down by Head, would secure the Centre's physical position in the country until it closed its Southern Africa office in September 2001. However, IDRC continues to support programming and staff in the country even though it no longer has a physical presence there.

Plaudits for the Centre

It had been a busy few years for the Centre and as it contemplated 1989, it could look back with some satisfaction on the developments that had changed its practices, and well as the intellectual context in which it operated. It also continued to receive accolades from important external sources. For example, Song Jian, the state councillor of the People's Republic of China, made a statement on Chinese television during Ivan Head and Janet Wardlaw's visit to China in August 1988 that IDRC represented "the ideal model of international cooperation."[106] It was unfortunate that Song's utterances were so closely followed by the Chinese government's reaction to the Tiananmen Square protests of April to June 1989. As a result, along with many other agencies that operated in the PRC, IDRC reviewed its activities in the country.[107] However, Head also pointed out to the secretary of state for external affairs, Joe Clark, that "One measure of the reputation of IDRC is its apolitical character. The Centre has never reacted in a political fashion to circumstances in developing countries. Equally, however, it does not ignore the foreign policy realities of the government of Canada. In the instance of China ... IDRC will endeavour to act in Canada's best interest." Head also received, on behalf of the work the Centre had done in China on the forestry file, an honorary degree in November 1990 from the Beijing Forestry University. As well, in October 1989 it had been presented with the first ever "Twenty-First Century Award," given by the prestigious United States Scientific Research Society, Sigma Xi, which recognized the organization that was best preparing the world for the next century."[108] This group said that IDRC's "perceptive, imaginative, and generous modus operandi has profound implications for the stability and well-being of the interdependent world of the 21st century."

Finally, and perhaps most importantly from Ottawa's perspective, the Centre had been identified by the Office of the Auditor General (OAG) as a well-performing organization in the public sector, one of only eight so denominated. As its report noted, it looked at IDRC "from the point of view of its internationally recognized high performance in delivering research assistance to developing nations. IDRC is considered worldwide to be one of the best organizations of its kind. Its high performance is based on a number of elements: people who are competent; committed and value-driven; continuity of leadership; a clear and strong sense of mission and purpose; a strong client focus, autonomy and flexibility at all levels; risk-taking and innovation; freedom from political and central agency interference; tailor-made internal regulations and reporting requirements; and, continual self-scrutiny of strategies and activities."[109] That was real praise from an institution in Ottawa that was known to be harsh in its assessments when harshness was warranted. The Centre, the OAG concluded, had moved "beyond bureaucracy," which meant that it had become "a public enterprise" if the term bureaucracy was construed to mean "red tape and unresponsiveness" and public enterprise to connote "innovation, responsiveness and productivity."

Conclusion

Ivan Head's term ended in mid-March 1991, and he could look back on thirteen quite eventful years. As noted at the beginning of this chapter, in form IDRC resembled what Hopper had built. As John Hardie has noted, however, Head's reforms "were not interventionist in programs, but were interventionist in terms of management structure."[110] As well, certain things had changed, as Head pointed out during his last executive committee meeting: "In October 1990, more than one-third of the projects revealed inter-divisional collaboration; in March 1978, none did. In 1990, a number of projects revealed an IDRC coordinating role for multi-donor initiatives whereas in 1978, none did. Another contrast is found in the strong bias now evident for projects with likely-to-be-utilized results. Finally, the involvement of Canadian institutions as research partners increased from 0 in 1978 to one out of four in 1990."[111]

As Head was suggesting, the Centre was vibrant and healthy with an administrative structure that had been modernized over the previous half-decade by staff and management, and a philosophy and intellectual direction that had been favourably investigated by outsiders several times over during those thirteen years. It had also remained true to its initial calling, as the auditor general had pointed out: "IDRC operates with highly qualified, experienced and dedicated professionals renowned in their fields.... [It] acts as a catalyst, an adviser, a supporter. It monitors but does not manage the research projects its supports."[112] It remained, as William Winegard, a former IDRC board member and then the member of Parliament for Guelph-Wellington, noted "the jewel of Canada's ODA."[113] That extended as well to Winegard's entire committee investigating Canadian official development assistance; even those members who had initially been "very much anti-IDRC [who] thought [it] was the spoiled brat of the whole system" were now among the most perfervid in their support of the institution.

One thing was certain, however; IDRC still had much work to do. As its twentieth birthday came and went, it operated in a completely different environment from that in which it had been created—an increasing world population, crippling debt in many LDCs, holes in the ozone, the old Soviet Union and Eastern Europe plunging into chaos as that empire dissolved, increased narcotics consumption, and the end of the first Gulf War.[114] As was suggested by that list, world happiness remained a distant goal. As 1990 ended, 250,000 children in the South were dying of a preventable disease each month, rural-to-urban migration continued to create ever-larger slums as people sought better lives despite the odds, infectious diseases continued unabated, all of which created unsustainable burdens on the environment. It was an unhappy recitation of much of what was wrong.

Further, the federal government had brought down its budget on 16 February 1991; while the Centre's grant for 1991–92 remained unchanged, the budget did include measures to keep to 3 percent any future salary settlements and a freeze on operational expenditures. As well, the president of the Treasury Board, Gilles Loiselle, had written to Janet Wardlaw, indicating that "the Government expects Crown corporations to help achieve its Plan for Economic Recovery," to which the board agreed.[115] Finally, to add insult to injury, word was received at headquarters that the auditor general had recommended that the Centre, one of the eight Crown corporations then exempt from the *Financial Accountability Act*, be brought in line with the legislation. Corporations subject to it had to file their annual corporate plan and objectives and their proposed annual budget for approval, as well as indicate in their annual report to Parliament the extent to which they were successful in meeting their stated objectives. It was a tsunami of ugly news and developments that IDRC could only hope would pass it by. It would not, but by then, Keith Bezanson would be in control and his Centre would develop a new strategic plan, *Empowerment through Knowledge*. He and his new management staff would have to prevent themselves from being knocked over as not only a tsunami, but an alignment of planets threatened the very viability of IDRC.

Following Head's departure as president, IDRC experienced increasing trouble, the latter not connected with the former; in some ways, it was too small without a real domestic constituency that would fight for its survival. The process of building one had begun while Head was president, but as Ottawa's fiscal situation worsened and the country experienced its largest deficit ever of CAN$42.6 billion, the government looked to cut expenditures wherever it could. While official development assistance received an increase of 5 percent in February 1990, it was to be reduced for the fiscal years 1990–91 and 1991–92, leaving an anticipated shortfall for the Centre of CAN$10 million.[116] Parliament voted CAN$114 million for the Centre in 1988–89, CAN$108.5 million the following year, and CAN$114 million for 1990–91, where it more or less stayed until the draconian cuts in 1995–96. That was a challenge that altered the form and structure of the Centre. This crisis, and many more, intruded into IDRC's rather contented world, causing it to fight just to remain alive as a deteriorating economic situation and a continuing national fiscal crisis caused staff incredible anxiety. That it remained afloat, to end with the metaphor that began with the Head years in Chapter 3, speaks volumes about Keith Bezanson's sense of purpose and unwillingness to lose an incredible organization to the vagaries of politics. Indeed, IDRC owes its continued existence to the new leader and the actions he took to rescue it in the face of government cutbacks.

Notes

1 IDRC–A, Meeting of the Board of Governors, Bangkok, Thailand, 13–16 March 1990, 4.
2 IDRC–A, Meeting of the Board of Governors, B of G Notes (28) 3/83, 3.
3 IDRC–A, Terry Smutylo and Saidou Koala, "Research Networks: Evolution and Evaluation from a Donor's Perspective," Evaluation no. 241, 6 October 1993, 4.
4 Interview with John Hardie, Ottawa, 17 August 2008.
5 IDRC–A, Meeting of the Board of Governors, B of G Notes (30) 3/84, 11.
6 IDRC–A, Meeting of the Board of Governors, B of G Notes (33) 10/85, 113.
7 IDRC–A, "Report of the President to the Board of Governors," 23 October 1985.
8 IDRC–A, Meeting of the Board of Governors, B of G Notes (33) 10/85, 7.
9 IDRC–A, Meeting of the Board of Governors, B of G Notes (28) 3/83, 42.
10 Nasir Islam, "Information Sciences Division: Structure, Processes, and Roles: A Study of PO/RPO Role, Workload, Communication, and Decentralization," September 1987, 46, accessed at https://idl-bnc.idrc.ca/dspace/bitstream/123456789/10968/1/95809.pdf. He goes on to note that: "The central and primary incentive [for travel] is the nature of the work. The majority of the people interviewed indicated that

travel is essential for effective performance. Program staff cannot sit back and wait for projects to be presented to them out of thin air. They have to 'ferret' them out, they have to go beating the bushes. Regional program officers indicate that in many regions of the Third World, face-to-face personal contact is absolutely essential for generating and developing projects. On-site visits are crucial to monitoring and evaluation. Staying abreast with technological and scientific developments in one's field is necessary to improve the scientific quality of IDRC-supported projects. This requires some travel to international conferences in various disciplines. IDRC values its responsiveness to the needs of its clients in the remote areas of developing countries. Travel is essential to promote responsiveness."

11 IDRC–A, Meeting of the Board of Governors, B of G Notes (35) 10/86, 68.

12 IDRC–A, Douglas Daniels, "Issues in Strategic Planning," paper presented at the Canadian Institute for International Peace and Security, 27 February 1989.

13 IDRC–A, Meeting of the Board of Governors, B of G Notes (28) 3/83, 10.

14 IDRC–A, Meeting of the Board of Governors, B of G Notes (37) 10/87, 110. See also *Program and Policy Review IX*, 7. It also emphasized that "the role of the 'top' is not to make all the decisions but to create an organization that will make its own decisions effectively."

15 IDRC–A, Meeting of the Board of Governors, B of G Notes (33) 10/85, 113.

16 IDRC–A, Meeting of the Board of Governors, B of G Notes (33) 10/85, 7.

17 IDRC–A, Meeting of the Board of Governors, B of G Notes (28) 3/83, 16.

18 IDRC–A, Meeting of the Board of Governors, B of G Notes (28) 3/83, 44.

19 *With Our Own Hands: Research for Third World Development: Canada's Contribution through the International Development Research Centre, 1970–1985* (Ottawa: IDRC, 1986), 8–9. Maggie Catley-Carlson had used the occasion of her receipt of the book to thank Head for sending it, even if it did come from a "strange" and "revolutionary" institution. That part of her letter was marked with a "!" However, Rex Nettleford had called it just that—"a revolutionary, if strange, institution." See *With Our Own Hands*, 27. See also IDRC–A, Meeting of the Executive Committee, EC (64) 6/86, 70.

20 Ivan Head, "The African Famine and IDRC" 14 February 1986, accessed at https://idl-bnc.idrc.ca/dspace/handle/123456789/25457.

21 IDRC, "In-Depth Review of the Agriculture, Food, and Nutrition Sciences Division," submitted to the Ad Hoc Committee of the Board, September 1985, xvi, accessed at https://idl-bnc.idrc.ca/dspace/bitstream/123456789/6233/1/68607.pdf.

22 IDRC–A, Meeting of the Board of Governors, B of G Notes (28) 3/83, 68.

23 IDRC–A, Meeting of the Board of Governors, B of G Notes (33) 10/85, 96.

24 *Program and Policy Review IX*, 48–49.

25 "In-Depth Division Review: Fellowships and Awards Division, Program Statement," March 1987, 5, accessed at https://idl-bnc.idrc.ca/dspace/bitstream/123456789/12193/1/96586.pdf.

26 IDRC–A, Meeting of the Board of Governors, B of G Notes (36) 3/87, 86. Another case of group training was in Wusih in the People's Republic of China, in the training of freshwater fisheries personnel from Southeast Asia who were associated with the Network of Aquacultural Centres for Asia. As Gerry Bourrier noted, "We've organized a course in China, we've captured the expertise that exists in China to offer a four-month intensive training course in freshwater fisheries for young biologists. That is the type of group training activity we fund."

27 IDRC, "In-Depth Review of the Agriculture, Food, and Nutrition Sciences Division," 34.

28   IDRC, "In-Depth Review of the Agriculture, Food, and Nutrition Sciences Division," xiv.

29   IDRC–A, Meeting of the Board of Governors, B of G Notes (35) 10/86, 16.

30   IDRC–A, Meeting of the Board of Governors, B of G Notes (35) 10/86, 21.

31   AFNS, as the largest division, often thwarted interdivisional co-operation or defined it in such a way as to make it meaningless. See IDRC–A, Meeting of the Board of Governors, B of G Notes (36) 3/87, 29.

32   Peter Stockdale, *Pearsonian Internationalism in Practice: The International Development Research Centre,* Unpublished Ph.D. diss., McGill University, 1995, 246, as quoted in Eva Rathgeber, "Turning Failure into Success: The Deconstruction of IDRC Development Discourse, 1970–2000," Evaluation #479, September 2001, 30.

33   IDRC–A, Social Sciences Division, *Program of Work and Budget, 1983–86,* 86.

34   IDRC–A, Social Sciences Division, *Program of Work and Budget, 1984–87,* 85.

35   Interview with Dr. Amr Mahmoud, Cairo, 19 February 2007. Mahmoud's Toxicology Centre (TC) is the only one in the Middle East and Africa, and he has made it his life's work to train medical specialists from those areas. It also has agreements with eight universities in the United States, and the flow of information is two-way. The TC has also branched out into investigating the Upper Nile ecosystem in order to improve the health of local peasants. As well, it has been used as a model for others in Latin America and South Asia in terms of "spreading the word on pesticides." Mahmoud hopes that the work with others is synergistic, and that other researchers will add to his results: "take my ideas and put in your ideas and please inform me of your experience."

36   IDRC–A, Meeting of the Board of Governors, B of G Notes (30) 3/84, 23.

37   IDRC–A, Meeting of the Board of Governors, B of G Notes (28) 3/83, 73.

38   IDRC–A, Meeting of the Board of Governors, B of G Notes (28) 3/83, 89.

39   IDRC–A, Sylvia H. Guerrero, "Hawkers and Vendors in Manila and Baguio: Final Country Report," 1974.

40   IDRC–A, D.H. Deby, "Report on the Outputs of IDRC-Supported Research Projects in Urban and Regional Development," Evaluation no. 214, October 1991.

41   IDRC–A, William Found, "Participatory Research and Development: An Assessment of IDRC's Experience and Prospects," Evaluation no. 295, 30 June 1995, 94.

42   IDRC–A, Meeting of the Board of Governors, B of G Notes (35) 10/86, 57.

43   IDRC–A, Assistant Secretary to President, "Project Docket," 18 June 1986 and attached document BG (34 3/86, 27). The memorandum drew attention to a similar situation that had been raised at the March board meeting by Gerry Helleiner. He had "reservations" about the technology policy studies (East Africa) II project, in part because of its "apparent lack of contact with decision-makers. There are comments made about the identification of needs … but there don't seem to be too many governmental people involved." The board agreed with his perspective.

44   IDRC–A, Meeting of the Board of Governors, B of G Notes (30) 3/84, 14.

45   Vinyu Vichit-Vandakan, "The Role of Research in Solving Problems of the Developing Countries: A Third World View," in David Spurgeon (ed.), *Give Us the Tools: Science and Technology for Development* (Ottawa: IDRC, 1979), 180.

46   IDRC–A, W. Coutu and Carlos Sere, "Utilization of Research Results," Evaluation no. 258, December 1993, 4.

47   IDRC–A, Meeting of the Board of Governors, B of G Notes (29) 10/83, 9.

48   IDRC–A, Meeting of the Board of Governors, B of G Notes (29) 10/83, 17.

49   IDRC–A, David Glover, Project Summary, "African Economic Research Consortium, Phase II," File no. 3-P-91-0035, grant approved 21 June 1991.

50 Brent Herbert-Copley, "African Economic Research Consortium (AERC), Phase V," completed as questionnaire, 2 August 2006.

51 IDRC–A, David Henderson and John Loxley, "The African Economic Research Consortium: An Evaluation and Review," 26 July 1996, 10, 75. The evaluation goes on to note that "It has helped restore the institutional base of economic research in Africa and allowed the continent to retain the services of many economists who might otherwise have emigrated. It has created a collaborative MA program which … is showing every sign of meeting the ambitious goals set for it. It has strengthened the capacity and resources of participating universities while, at the same time, giving individual African graduates an opportunity to study in a high quality program with ready access to qualified teachers and to the full range of academic, financial and other support they require…. In short, the AERC has had a very marked and overwhelmingly positive impact on the opportunities for research and post-graduate study facing African economists."

52 Jeffrey Fine, "African Economic Research Consortium," 6, accessed at http://www .macfound.org/atf/cf/%7BB0386CE3-8B29-4162-8098-E466FB856794%7D/NIGERIA CV.PDF.

53 Email, Lauchlan Munro to Bruce Muirhead, 15 February 2009.

54 Glover, Project Summary.

55 Knud Svendsen, "African Economic Research Consortium: Research, Training, and Related Activities from August 1988 to January 1990—An Evaluation," March 1990, 3.

56 IDRC–A, "Health Sciences Division Statement," October 1988, 8.

57 Mullin, as quoted in Tahira Gonsalves and Stephen Baranyi, "Research for Policy Influence: A History of IDRC Intent," January 2003, 12.

58 Interview with Lauchlan Munro, 7 August 2009, Ottawa.

59 IDRC–A, Martha Stone, Paul McConnell, Chris Smart, Richard Wilson, and John Hardie, "Themes Working Group: Final Report," March 1987, 3.

60 IDRC–A, Meeting of the Board of Governors, B of G Notes (34) 3/86, 57.

61 IDRC–A, Meeting of the Executive Committee, EC (64) 6/86, Annex A, 1; emphasis not in original.

62 The discussion of the Ten-Week Management Seminar is found in IDRC–A, Meeting of the Executive Committee, EC (64) 6/86, Annex A.

63 IDRC–A, PPR VII, 21.

64 Stone et al., "Themes Working Group: Final Report," March 1987, 4.

65 Mullin interview.

66 Rathgerber, 30. See also "Health Sciences Division Statement," October 1988, 8. This document notes this as a shortcoming: "The divisions have tended to pursue their own interests, and have established programs specific to particular disciplines with minimal linkages with those of other divisions…. [This responsive mode has] resulted in a very wide scatter of initiatives, with the concomitant risk of being insufficiently 'responsive' to those occasions when the coordinated application of several disciplines could be more effective."

67 Hardie interview. Hubert Zandstra, director of AFNS, had an interesting interpretation of IDRC interdisciplinarity: "I would like to stress that most of our projects are interdisciplinary. They may not cover the social sciences in the sense mentioned … but rarely do we have a single disciplinary project. The difference in reasoning between a forester and a soil scientist is quite considerable, and the gap had to be bridged…. We are very cautious in composing these teams so that they will be

functional and will focus on what is of immediate need in the research.... I would rather see a researcher who is more elastic in his or her discipline and who can move beyond the immediate training and pursue the problem ... to have it solved. That is the kind of scientist we need to support it."

68   IDRC–A, Meeting of the Board of Governors, B of G Notes (36) 3/87, 30. Still, the question had been raised at IDRC with respect to how far program officers could push interdisciplinarity with their Southern partners. If the latter evinced no interest, Joe Hulse once enquired, did the staff member then insist that "You don't know what you're talking about. You've got to bring in all these other things.... How far do we go bashing people on the head and say 'thou shalt not do this'?" It was a problem.

69   IDRC–A, Project Completion Report, Project no. 881022, 27 June 1999.

70   Criselda Yabes, "From Sri Lanka to Singapore," *IDRC Reports*, vol. 22, no. 4, accessed at http://archive.idrc.ca/books/reports/v224/fromto.html.

71   IDRC–A, Meeting of the Board of Governors, B of G Notes (35) 10/86, 71.

72   IDRC–A; for an account of this, see Nasir Islam, "Information Science Division: Processes and Roles," Evaluation no. 136, 27 September 1988, 4.

73   IDRC–A, Meeting of the Board of Governors, "Resolution," March 1986, B of G Notes 34/16, 87.

74   IDRC–A, Meeting of the Board of Governors, B of G Notes (36) 3/87, 7.

75   This paragraph is based on Stephen Rosell, "Renewing IDRC: An Organization for Learning," September 1988, accessed at https://idl-bnc.idrc.ca/dspace/bitstream/123456789/16309/1/99892.pdf.

76   Interview with John Hardie, 12 August 2008, Ottawa.

77   See Ester Böserup, *Women's Role in Economic Development* (London: Earthscan, 1970). The work is "the first investigation ever undertaken into what happens to women in the process of economic and social growth throughout the Third World." According to the foreword in the 1989 edition, "It is [Boserup's] committed and scholarly work that inspired the UN Decade for Women between 1975 and 1985, and that has encouraged aid agencies to question the assumption of gender neutrality in the costs as well as in the benefits of development."

78   Interview with Reem Saad, American University in Cairo, Cairo, Egypt, 20 February 2007. She went on to note that gender did influence such basic tasks as seed selection among poor rural farmers. Women were more interested in seed conservation and collection for storage than men, who tended to focus on the latest high technology hybrids. Gendered spheres of knowledge were certainly divided. For women, there were taste preferences when food products were made from the crop. As women were responsible for preparing meals, they were of the opinion that local varieties were better tasting than the hybrid. Men might have agreed, but that did not mean they were prepared to keep hybrids at bay. As Saad suggested, it was important for men to be associated with the scientific, whereas women, with very little community status and prestige, were not tied to any "hybrid competition."

79   See Eva Rathgerber, "WID, WAD, GAD: Trends in Research and Practice" (Ottawa: IDRC, September 1989), 5. As Rathgerber writes, "Böserup's research was seminal in focusing scholarly attention on the sexual division of labour and the differential impact by gender of development and modernization strategies." See also Eva Rathgerber, "Integrating Gender into Development," *IDRC Reports*, April 1991, accessed at https://idl-bnc.idrc.ca/dspace/bitstream/123456789/24788/1/108936.pdf.

80   Martha Stone, "The Role of Women in the Development of Science and Technology in the Third World: An IDRC Perspective," December 1988, accessed at https://idl-bnc.idrc.ca/dspace/bitstream/123456789/591/1/5092.pdf.

81 Nancy O'Rourke, "An Internal Evaluation of IDRC's Women in Development Unit," October 1989, accessed at https://idl-bnc.idrc.ca/dspace/bitstream/123456789/11695/1/96551.pdf.

82 Rathgerber, "WID, WAD, and GAD," 8 (WAD) and 12 (GAD).

83 O'Rourke, "An Internal Evaluation of IDRC's Women in Development Unit."

84 Stephen Salewicz and Archana Dwivedi, "Project Leader Tracer Study," Evaluation Unit, Corporate Services Branch, March 1996, Section 6, 4/5, accessed at https://irims.idrc.ca/iRIMSTemp/160021D0-9EAA-43AA-910A-4C31E65C6969-6429/rad89D73.PDF.

85 IDRC–A, Annual Corporate Evaluation Report, 1997, 7.

86 Rathgerber, "WID, WAD, and GAD," 38.

87 IDRC–A, MG 92/31, "Report on MG Meeting—April 14–15, 1992," 5 May 1992.

88 For a discussion of this, see IDRC–A, Revised 1989–90 Program of Work and Budget, January 1989, 29–32.

89 IDRC–A, "Health Sciences Division Statement," October 1988, 1.

90 IDRC–A, "Health Sciences Division Statement," 12.

91 Email, anonymous.

92 L. Hendretta, "Health and Development: Review of Policy Options at the Grassroots Level," in W. Lathem (ed.), The Future of Academic Community Medicine in Developing Countries (New York: Praeger, 1979), 59, as quoted in IDRC–A, "Health Sciences Division Statement," 5.

93 IDRC–A, Shahad Akhtar and Martha Melesse, "Africa Information and Development: IDRC's Experience," Evaluation no. 268, April 1994, 17.

94 IDRC–A, "Notes on Meeting of External Support to Developing Country Research," Evaluation no. 158, November 1988, 1. David Hopper attended for the World Bank and Maggie Catley-Carlson for CIDA, while GTZ, Finland's development agency, DANIDA, and SAREC, among others, sent representatives.

95 Email, Tim Dottridge to Bruce Muirhead, 22 July 2009.

96 IDRC–A; see, for example, Parzival Copes, "The Asian Fisheries Social Science Research Network," Evaluation no. 231, 5 June 1992.

97 IDRC–A, See David Black, Chris Schofield, and Luis Yarzabal, "Final Report: Evaluation of the Chagas Disease Prevention Project (Paraguay—IDRC)," 1 October 1992, 1. Chagas disease was transmitted through the feces of blood-sucking triatomine bugs. The most important vector species in Paraguay is one that primarily breeds in the cracks and crevices of poor-quality rural houses, emerging at night to suck the blood of sleeping occupants. Chagas disease cannot be controlled by drugs or vaccines, so the IDRC-supported project was designed to test and compare two specific approaches to preventing insect-borne transmission: (1) by spraying infested houses with modern insecticides, and (2) by using low-cost techniques to improve houses to make them inappropriate for triatomine bugs.

98 IDRC–A, Management Committee Meeting, "Notes on Discussions," MC 84/23, 25 May 1984.

99 See Linda Freeman, The Ambiguous Champion: Canada and South Africa in the Trudeau and Mulroney Years (Toronto: University of Toronto Press, 1997).

100 IDRC–A, "Eastern and Southern African Regional Office: Summary Report for 1990," BG 44/2. See also IDRC Policy toward South Africa, "Decision of the Board of Governors," October 1988, BG 40/30.

101 Interview with Peter FitzGerald, Johannesburg, 12 May 2007.

102 IDRC–A, "Briefing Note: IDRC and South Africa," n.d. (1999).

103 IDRC–A, "IDRC Policy towards South Africa," August 1988, 3.

104　IDRC–A, Marc Van Ameringen to Head, 22 December 1988.
105　IDRC–A, Marc Van Ameringen, "Review of IDRC South Africa Policy," 21 May 1991.
106　IDRC–A, Meeting of the Executive Committee, EC (74) 1/89, Annex A, 4.
107　IDRC–A, Ivan Head to Joe Clark, 19 June 1989. IDRC's proposed course of action was that the board not meet in China for its March 1990 gathering as had been planned; that all current (66 of them in mid-1989) and proposed projects be re-evaluated on a case-by-case basis to ensure that the beneficiaries of IDRC support are scientists and not the Government of China per se…. Should projects be identified that appear to be dedicated primarily to the strengthening of government infrastructure, these would be postponed or cancelled.
108　"IDRC at Twenty: An Anniversary of Development," *IDRC Reports*, October 1990, 27.
109　*1988 Report of the Auditor-General of Canada*, Chapter 4, "Well-Performing Organizations," paragraph 4.3.1.
110　Hardie interview.
111　IDRC–A, Meeting of the Executive Committee, 17–18 January 1991, 9.
112　IDRC–A, "IDRC's Reactions and Response to the 'Report of the Standing Committee on External Affairs and International Trade on Canada's Official Development Assistance, *In Whose Interest?*, Policies and Programs,'" Annex C EC 68/2, 3.
113　IDRC–A, Meeting of the Board of Governors, B of G Notes (36) 3/87, 35.
114　IDRC–A, Ivan Head to Board of Governors, "Towards 2000: A Strategic Framework for IDRC," 18 February 1991, B of G Notes 46/3, i.
115　IDRC–A, Gilles Loiselle to Janet Wardlaw, 1 March 1991, Annex B BG 46/14.
116　IDRC–A, "Revised Two-Year Resource and Operational Plan, 1990–91" (Ottawa: IDRC, June 1990), 7.

Chapter 5

CUTBACKS AND COUNTERMEASURES: KEITH BEZANSON AND IDRC IN RETREAT, 1991–97

The difficulty lies not in new ideas, but in escaping from the old,
which ramify, for those brought up as most of us have been,
into every corner of our minds.
—*John Maynard Keynes, Preface,* The General Theory of
Employment, Interest, and Money, *December 1935*

Rethinking the Centre

"And then there was Keith!" began the roast in April 1997 as Keith Bezanson's tenure as president of IDRC came to an end. Those five words and the exclamation mark at the end encapsulated the sense of almost everything one needed to know about the man who had been appointed on 22 April 1991 to lead IDRC into its new age. He was nothing like the diplomatic, nuanced, subtle, and smooth Ivan Head. However, Bezanson, a blunt and outspoken bulldog who personified the phrase "What you see is what you get," was arguably what IDRC needed at the time. Indeed, as Head, with his skill set and connections, had been a good choice for the Centre in 1978, the new president was equally so in 1991 given the situation that confronted him as he took office and the tsunami of trouble that would cascade over the institution by the mid-1990s. Had Head remained as president, it is likely that IDRC would have been transformed into a departmental corporation, its mandate and practice submerged in Conservative policy that was to affect

207

various Crown corporations and government agencies in 1992. Alternatively, it could have washed up on the shore as detritus following the wave that had smashed other important agencies like the Economic Council of Canada or the International Centre for Ocean Development, a small government organization that had been established in 1985 and was modelled on IDRC.

Bezanson had also had some experience in less prosperous parts of the world, having been Canada's ambassador to Bolivia and Peru between 1985 and 1988. He had begun in the mid-1960s, fresh out of university, as a Canadian University Service Overseas volunteer to teach secondary school in Nigeria. A few years later, he moved over to the University of Ghana as a lecturer, while also consulting with CIDA on a study about technical assistance and capacity building in developing countries. From there, his career was clear, at least to him. He went to work with CIDA, focusing primarily on East Africa, eventually becoming its vice-president of the Americas branch and responsible for all bilateral programming with Latin America and the Caribbean region. When IDRC came calling in 1990, he had moved on to the Inter-American Development Bank (IADB), having been appointed its vice-president of administration. That would come in handy as he began his tenure at the Centre; at the IADB, he had reported to the president on all administrative matters and had supervised field offices and the fifteen hundred people who worked at the Bank, and had prepared, presented, and managed its US$200 million administrative budget.

The new president had his own novel ideas about how the Centre should run, clearly one of the reasons the board search committee had liked his candidacy.[1] It might also have had something to do with Bezanson being the anti-Head; the relationship between the former president and the board had deteriorated by the time he had departed. Head's final three-year term, instead of the normal five, which he had wanted, had been indicative of that. The times they were a changin' and not only for the Centre; as Bezanson was to tell the Study Group later on the Exchange of Development Information during a meeting held in Paris in October 1993, the world was living through "a megacrisis, the dimensions of which we do not fully understand."[2] The idea of global development, which was rooted in the concept that the material condition of all of humanity was subject to ongoing and infinite improvement, which had inspired so much international effort was, in his view, "unraveling and ... is in imminent danger of total collapse. The old nostrums of the past could not be helpful in such a climate." That would animate his attempts to change the Centre. He would, he said, hold weekly meetings with directors and announced that all of them should have weekly meetings with staff in order to get a better sense of the latter's concerns. His goals were clear; the day he crossed the threshold he was determined to change the organization. IDRC was, as he recalled, "the most complacent organization I had ever walked into. The belief was that it was invincible, that it was untouchable, and that we were the greatest. And this talk that went on ... this hubris that was quintessential in the culture of the organization had to be knocked down a notch or two."[3]

One of his biggest conundrums was that the Centre, so highly regarded internationally, was so little known in Canada despite the efforts of the past decade. As Walter McLean, a Cabinet minister in Brian Mulroney's first government and later a member and sometime chair of the House of Commons Standing Committee on External Affairs and International Trade, was to accurately remark, IDRC "was the best kept secret in Canada."[4] No supportive constituency in the country that provided the greatest bulk of its budget could spell bad news; that would be borne out following the 25 February 1992 budget of Conservative Finance Minister Don Mazankowski as IDRC appeared as a prime candidate for a significant change in status. Then, the minister had let it be known that he wanted to be able to tell the good people of Vegreville, Alberta, his riding, that government was taking action on "waste" even if it was only by cutting sundry small and powerless Crown corporations and agencies.[5] Indeed, the smaller, the better as there would be less of an outcry. IDRC fit that description perfectly; when news leaked out that it was on the road to either closure or departmental corporation status, only one letter of protest was sent. Government could easily live with that.

Bezanson highlighted to staff three reasons for change: the first was fiscal as the Centre budget was being held to only 3 percent growth per year. The second was efficiency—IDRC was a hands-on organization to be sure, but one that had also declined in that area; by early 1991, only 60 percent of its funds were being transferred to recipients. That was in keeping with the labour-intensive nature of the work done by program officers, but it was still considerably down from the 80 percent achieved earlier during Head's presidency. The new president had been appalled to learn that of the roughly 130 program officers, one carried a load of one project worth CAN\$65,000 and a few others had two that they were overseeing. As the cost of each officer with benefits was about CAN\$110,000 per year, this was untenable. And while the numbers involved in this sort of thing were tiny—no more than about five in the total program officer complement—they also grated on Bezanson. As he perhaps correctly noted, "If this had hit the *Globe and Mail* or the scandal sheets, it would have been the end of the Centre."[6] At a minimum, he wanted the role of program officers to be explicitly defined, something that had not yet happened in the Centre despite the various exercises that had been undertaken. Governors were to vote on this and decide that by 1 January 1995, the ratio of program to operational costs was to be 70:30.

Third, it was a time for action; much effort had already been spent on meetings and discussions through the consideration of "Towards 2000" and, in words that would have been characteristic of Bezanson, it was now time for "the rubber to hit the road." The president was confident that a new strategic plan would all be wrapped up, at least in its broad strokes, by the end of the October 1991 board meeting. He also had an idea in which direction that road should go; management had achieved consensus on a number of issues. The Centre should, for example, have fewer programs with greater focus; fewer divisions in order to create a more efficient organization; committees should be cut as there were too many with not enough delegated decision-making authority; fewer layers of management were needed despite Head's much-heralded restructuring in the early to mid-1980s, and mechanisms needed to be streamlined. Indeed, the context outlined in Chapter 4, the perseverance of disciplinary silos, had to be changed and interdisciplinarity become more the custom. Areas where consensus had not been achieved included the distribution of human resources among the program divisions and the role, reporting relationship, and functions of regional offices (RO). The last must have come as quite a surprise to many staff given that more than half of them were based abroad, and that they had experienced a huge surge in capacity during the second half of the 1980s. Further, it was important to strategically position the Centre in that it became less an "applied" organization, and more of a "policy" one. Naturally, this would have an impact on its intellectual orientation and would also result in some changes to its structure, like the disappearance of the division that epitomized application—Agriculture, Food, and Nutrition Sciences.[7]

Given all this, some job reductions would be necessary, but those "would be done in the most humane way possible." That must have been of some comfort! It was also the area that threatened to derail Bezanson's train; as his transition team was to note, Centre staff felt a high degree of anxiety over the possibility of unemployment. Rumours abounded of promises made to some and of ad hoc decisions being taken. Many staff were to feel that they were not involved in the transition process and remained distrustful over the manner in which decisions were taken and promulgated. As it turned out, the last part of Bezanson's tenure was precisely like the first; as Caroline Pestieau, first the director general of the Social Sciences division under Bezanson and later vice-president of programs, remarked, "1995 to 1997 was permanent restructuring."[8] It was not a happy time.

The new president was also aware of the nature of the Head exercise that would have led to "Towards 2000" and was not keen on replicating it. While staff reviews, which was how the recent exercise had been done, might have their place, they also had serious disadvantages; "no one [was] willing to fall on his or her sword ... So if you go back to those documents some of the ideas in them were perfectly sound, but they were muted in terms of criticisms of the Centre, which would be people criticizing themselves."[9] Bezanson wanted more of the latter and less of the former in any exercise he carried out. That underlay his intention to introduce a new strategic plan.

But what did the Centre look like as the new president began his makeover? Although slightly different from that which Head had taken over in 1978, it would not have been entirely unrecognizable by those who had left IDRC in that year. It contained seven divisions, four of which had been extant since 1970. It also possessed a confident and comfortable world view (which, as noted above, Bezanson found insufferable), and was engaged with the complexities and challenges of development, grounded in science and technology and, to a lesser extent, in the social sciences. It was also internationally known and respected with its enviable track record of success stories and networks of eminent, as well as not-so-eminent, social and natural scientists. Conversely, it was little known to Canadians, which could prove problematic; it also remained largely absent from Canadian foreign and aid policy milieus, and its board had very limited political leverage with government. He would have agreed with Anne Whyte, his director of Social Sciences, that IDRC needed to be roughed up a bit: "Perhaps we have been too close to Pablum ... nutritional, suitable for babies and old folks, and bland. We have lost our edge, our sharpness of taste that gives the appetite its edge." She suggested, and the new president concurred, that the organization should become more "audacious" as well as empower others: "Let's focus on research institutions and show results in empowering them to do research, build their own linkages, data banks, networks, research capacity à la Bezanson, and let *them* do the research, empower the poor."[10]

It was his intention to shake things up, which he did with a vengeance, but not all the upheaval could be laid at his feet, as will be demonstrated. He wanted to situate the Centre so that it placed increasing emphasis on a "vision of itself as a results-oriented research for development organization."[11] It was also his intention to demand of IDRC that projects and programs be developed with a clearer articulation of objectives and what became known as deliverables, permitting better measurement of their efficiency, effectiveness, and impact. That sort of increased accountability offered opportunities to compare strategies, to document what did work in development, and to continually refine policies and programs to make the most of a shrink-ing real parliamentary appropriation.

Over the summer of 1991 the president began to feel more comfortable in his new office and work on a new strategic plan continued unabated. Meetings of the executive committee were convened in June and September, and the developing strategic plan was discussed. Its main principles reflected Bezanson's beliefs—that there was a need for streamlining Centre opera-tions, for downsizing its workforce, for defining the role of the regional offices, for examining the possibility of strategic partnerships, defining with more precision a niche for the Centre, focusing on its comparative advantages, and moving quickly toward a more results-oriented organization that was con-cerned with its own performance.[12] To accomplish that he offered eight broadly articulated themes that would guide and inform Centre program choices and structure, at least as he conceived them during that first heady summer when the domestic situation had yet to really impose its will on IDRC. These included: (1) the changing global order; (2) the economics of basic human needs; (3) the lag experienced in the South in incorporating sci-ence and technology into their decision making; (4) an appropriate answer to the question of "what works" in terms of international development; (5) the environment; (6) research capacity; (7) evaluation of projects for self-criticism and feedback; and (8) ongoing assessment and a campaign to make Ottawa more aware of the Centre.[13] To that end, he let it be known that IDRC would be downsizing. The Centre was in for a shakeup.

Bezanson also thought that there were a number of areas requiring that his new charge be better placed to address: a changing geopolitical and economic global order; an unequal race in science and technology; the environment, innovation, and empowerment at the grassroots level; and deepening poverty.[14] As well, they should build on partnerships, but in a more focused way than had happened during the Head years. This included part-nerships with key institutions, key country governments, donors and agen-cies, and critical Canadian institutions. That was just as well; in a meeting with officials from the Office of the Secretary of State for External Affairs, Bezanson was told that that was imperative for the Centre's survival: "it was important that the Centre show its relevance to the Canadian popula-tion at large and reach beyond the NGO groups with which it had tradi-tional links. It was vital ... that the Centre build itself a broad constituency within the public so that [he] could count on its support if it ran into budg-etary difficulties down the road.... [Moreover] its image with some policy makers [was poor]. It took time, [the officials] said, to change stereotypes even though they were no longer valid."[15] Bezanson's conception of the new road forward would be a departure for IDRC and would seem to shy away from its mandate as a responsive organization. At a minimum, it would require some explanation as to how it could be both focused and responsive. Whyte suggested that responsiveness in the new Centre "would mean responsive to *problems* rather than to researchers, and that range of problems (or approach to problem-solving) which would now be our hallmark." That new orientation came to pass, marking a fundamental departure from past IDRC practice.

The Change Begins

As the summer wound on, staff were working on the development of the new plan. At a time more usual for vacations, most were reading the tea leaves from the president's cup. The new strategy was eventually decided upon and approved by the board at its October 1991 meeting. The developing strategy and the change in approach and focus reflected a number of issues, including the expectation of reduced resources; the shift of remaining resources, as much as was possible, from administration to programs; the intention to reduce the number of countries and the number of projects being supported; the emphasis on interdisciplinary programs and the importance of Southern institutions in the delivery of IDRC's programming.[16] As well, it anticipated a reduction of 20 percent in Centre staff, a process that began shortly after Bezanson's first board meeting and stretched over months; numbers shrank from 610 employees in 1991 to 486 by the following year.[17] While that was taking place, a new Regional Office for Southern Africa, based in Johannesburg, was mooted to service that area, opening during the summer of 1992.[18]

Bezanson's program included giving effect to proposals for program choices and for a simplified and streamlined structure for the Centre. The new administrative set-up was a marked departure from the one then existing; gone were the four vice-presidents, replaced by directors general of five (not seven) divisions. Its operational strategy included: "improved performance as measured by standard efficiency indicators (e.g., administrative overheads as a percentage of total budget); streamlined administrative procedures; concentrate fewer resources in fewer program areas; focus on a smaller number of institutions over longer periods of time; emphasize the evaluation of what is undertaken; and, ensure that research results are utilized and applied in practical, efficient ways."[19]

This new framework for IDRC was designed to build on the most valuable elements of its experience, while equipping the Centre with sufficient elasticity to respond to changed circumstances and the challenges that lay ahead. One of those, combined with a commitment to become more "entrepreneurial" in order to "diversify the Centre's funding base," led to the establishment within IDRC of a new species of organization, the secretariat. The first to be set up was the Global Micronutrient Initiative (GMI).[20] IDRC was among the very first to experiment with secretariats. Anne Whyte, then the director general of Environment and Natural Resources, thought that "the impetus for offering to host secretariats, or at least a good number of them, was in the hope that they would generate money. It was kind of an accounting thing too, because once you had other donors willing to put their money through IDRC, then you could show on the books that you had more money coming in from other donors."[21] However, it was more than merely finances: "It was [also] building on a much longer history of IDRC working with other like-minded donors in supporting networks, which again were more expensive then IDRC could fund on its own." Similarly, IDRC had often taken a leadership role on the cutting edge of many new areas of research and in the application of innovative delivery mechanisms. Secretariats were one of those program delivery mechanisms and were intended to achieve greater impact on program priorities through the careful targeting of resources and formal collaboration with external partners. They also attempted to establish an international leadership role in a defined area. As well, secretariats represented a movement within the public sector in terms of experimenting with alternative service delivery, which allowed for greater flexibility in the design and delivery of programs. IDRC also eschewed bureaucracy and sometimes rules in its attempts to respond to initiatives; as was pointed out, constraints only discouraged creativity. As was later pointed out, "management rigour should be applied when deciding whether or not to establish a secretariat. It should not be applied to the secretariats themselves. We do not want 'death by policy manual.'"[22]

There was a push under Keith Bezanson to get a number of secretariats, "some of which fitted within the IDRC program and some which were way outside, real oddballs," although all shared certain fundamental characteristics. As the president had emphasized to his staff, revenue diversification was critical, and secretariats would pay for the privilege of being associated with the Centre. Bezanson told Senior Management Committee many times that "only with an increase in resources from outside the government of Canada will the Centre be able to maintain its current work and structure."[23] Historically, IDRC had worked with other donors as a co-funder of project activities; it was now investigating other strategies for collaboration, which included contracting out its services in order to support such ventures.

Included in the first wave were the Secretariat for International Fisheries Research, funded by the World Bank and the United Nations Development Program, along with the Secretariat for the Exchange of Development-Related Information and a Special Unit for Essential National Health Research. These were quickly followed by the Economy and Environment Program for Southeast Asia, the Information Technology Institute, and the African Technology Policy Studies Network (ATPSN), which was designed to improve the quality of technology policy making in Sub-Saharan Africa. It would do this through strengthening the region's institutional capacity for the management of technological development through research, dissemination, training, and linkages to policy-makers and research end users. An external evaluation described it as "an excellent initiative to fill a crucial gap in African development."[24] Bellanet, established in October 1994, and the International Model Forest Network, brought into being a year later, were the last to be established during Bezanson's presidency. These did represent an innovative departure from past ways of managing research and, through them, IDRC hoped to play a leading role in contributing to research on topics of international interest. The Global Micronutrient Initiative, the first, will be used to demonstrate the concept.

Micronutrient deficiencies had become an increasingly important issue, more frequently seen as major impediments to the health, nutritional status, and development of a significant proportion of the world's population. It was estimated in the early 1990s that more than 1 billion people suffered the consequences of vitamin A, iodine, and iron deficiencies. These might include blindness induced by vitamin A deficiency, mental and physical handicaps caused by iodine deficiency, and impaired motor development and behaviour as a result of iron deficiency. Infants, children, and women were especially at risk.[25] A coordinating mechanism for micronutrient work had been discussed at a special meeting of donors, among them, the United Nations Children's Fund, the World Health Organization, the Food and Agriculture Organization, the World Bank, and several bilateral agencies, all of which convened at the Montreal conference on "Ending Hidden Hunger," held in October 1991. Numerous senior government representatives from sixty countries met to launch the global effort to put an end to micronutrient deficiencies. The emerging consensus was that a global micronutrient initiative should be established, and that IDRC and the Task Force for Child Survival and Development, based in Atlanta, be considered as potential candidates for housing it. In December, the Centre, based on its reputation for excellence, was chosen, largely because of the active role it had played in nutrition studies and in the examination of the problems of international nutrition more generally, through coordination of different sectors and interdisciplinary programming. Further, it had broad expertise and experience in nutritional and health sciences, agricultural sciences, social and management sciences, information networking, and communications. The Centre had been actively involved in developing and advising on micronutrient programs in collaboration with a number of other donor agencies. Also, a part of its strategic plan was to develop a micronutrient information network, a version of which IDRC already had operational for its own purposes.

Other, much bigger, agencies, admired the Centre's infrastructure, which would help to support the fledgling GMI. As they knew, a significant part of the latter's objectives were institutional strengthening and the development of local capabilities. In nutrition, it had established partnerships with lead institutions in Benin, Colombia, Kenya, India, Indonesia, and Thailand. The Centre was also well placed to incorporate developing country knowledge into the GMI. Moreover, it shared nutrition information with other international agencies and actively participated in donor meetings. As well, it had provided leadership in bringing together donors in consortia to address specific development issues, like in the establishment of the task force on health research for development. This was assisted by its Swedish equivalent, SAREC, the Ford and Rockefeller foundations, the German Gesellschaft für Technische Zusammenarbeit, and the United Kingdom's Overseas Development Administration.

Finally, and very importantly, over its history IDRC had convened many interagency meetings and was regarded by governments and other aid agencies as a neutral venue conducive to cultivating the broad perspective and input that the GMI required. The secretariat itself would be closely linked to Centre programs, but it would function as a self-supporting unit reporting to an executive board. The first funding agencies were the Canadian International Development Agency, IDRC, the United Nations Development Program, and the World Bank. Others would soon join the effort. The secretariat's first infusion was CAN$3.5 million over two years. By 2001, GMI had become very successful, operating with an almost CAN$40 million budget and a staff of thirty-nine. In early 2000, an external evaluation, the first since its creation in 1992, recommended that IDRC, in co-operation with the other donors, identify a new corporate legal structure for the secretariat; full independent status would take two years to complete. It remains in existence in 2010 and set the template for those that would follow. As Bezanson started the machinery resulting in the establishment of secretariats soon after his arrival, so, too, did he do likewise with a new strategic plan.

Empowerment through Knowledge

Empowerment through Knowledge, a visionary statement of Centre strategy and policy, was primarily written by the president. What was the document all about? First and foremost, it was an attempt "to translate the Centre's mission into a clear program framework that [would] guide and inform the detailed decisions to be made in consultation with [IDRC's] research partners and that will permit an assessment of [its] progress."[26] To accomplish that required a number of things: "a new perspective on development and IDRC's place in it; a sharper program focus; a restructuring of programs to maximize the impact of available resources; greater efficiency in program execution and administration; perseverance in effort; and, flexibility and agility in changing circumstances." Further, the document correctly demanded that the whole notion of "development" be rethought; the underlying conception of the practice as linear was no longer valid. *Empowerment* in its title captured the essence of what development should be. It also reiterated the underlying bedrock of Centre philosophy—that "development" could not and should not be imposed upon a society from outside; it "should mean above all giving people the power, that is, the adequate knowledge and capacity, to decide what is best for them and to act accordingly in fulfilling their own destinies." The so-called knowledge gap had to be closed; only then would people in the South be able to decide and act independently of the North.

Empowerment also contained a plea to members of the international development community, one that IDRC held dear and exemplified the Centre's developing ethic. It was time for development institutions to:

> marshal conceptual, methodological, and technological developments in the theory and practice of social, economic and political change, putting them at the service of development efforts. New concepts of strategy formulation and implementation—for example, multidisciplinary, multi-sectoral approaches; interactive planning; strategic issues management—can contribute to better understanding and management of the problems of the 1990s. Progress in telecommunications, micro-electronics, and modeling tools makes it easier to acquire and exchange information, to experiment with the impact of alternative policies and decisions, and to disseminate ideas and communicate with the public at large. This progress is supported by a growing public awareness of global interdependencies and widespread social mobilization.[27]

That was pure Bezanson, as John Hardie has suggested.[28] Brian Davy, a long-time Centre employee, agrees; much of the early 1990s was spent changing direction and practice, most of which was captured under the rubric of Empowerment through Knowledge (EtK). This EtK mantra was that there was a process of discussion within the Center but it was very activist, driven by Keith, partly because of his perception of this need to change and change urgently or there was no more IDRC. They were seeking outside advice, linking to what other donors are doing. All of these things gave ... a worldview about a new direction. It wasn't just IDRC.[29]

That assertion is exemplified by the quote above from *Empowerment*; the president was interested in the global reconceptualization that was going on in development and how it might assist his charge.[30] He was also keen on changing the basic thrust of the Centre, away from what it had been since its inception (a science and technology organization) to a social sciences one. AFNS had been disbanded, which was a key indicator of the new wind blowing through the organization.[31]

New Divisions and a New Regional Office

Over the next eighteen months of the transition period, programs would be defined and the restructuring would begin. As part of that exercise, two new divisions were created as of April 1992, Environment and Natural Resources (ENR) and Corporate Affairs and Initiatives (CAI). The former was given shape by merging nine former programs—five from Agriculture, Food, and Nutrition Sciences, three from Earth and Engineering Sciences, and one from Social Sciences. The new division would focus on research that capitalized on its multidisciplinary strengths and its ability to put together teams that spanned "earth and environmental sciences, agricultural production, engineering and technological development, linked to social and policy analysis" that could be described as an organizational and programmatic matrix.[32] In order to achieve its mission within the new Centre strategy, ENR proposed a number of innovations in the way it was structured, its method of operation, and in its definition of strategic niches for its programs.

A key innovation lay in how the new program structure would operate and which anticipated the wholesale restructuring the Centre would undergo in 1995–96. That lay in the interaction between programs in the traditional sense in which IDRC had tended to define them, and global program initiative (GPI) teams, which would number less than ten. The GPI teams enabled the division to create a number of small, flexible groups of expertise targeted to the needs of the research or capacity-building task. It also provided more scope for initiative, using the special expertise of staff and sharing the leadership role among more experienced program officers. It was anticipated that each program officer would be a member of several GPIs, and regional program officers would be included. As the project cycle evolved, staff would be drawn in as needed and the time commitment of each team member would be reassessed. That was more in line with a risk-taking and entrepreneurial approach to research development and the need to optimize the allocation of limited resources, or so the new Centre mantra went.

Further, in re-evaluating the Centre's direction, the division would be more responsive to problems rather than proposals. IDRC was now more keen to target the issues on which research would be supported as opposed to responding to projects suggested by Southern researchers. This flew in the face of traditional practice and would surely have raised eyebrows among those Centre employees who had been schooled in the anti-imperialism admonitions of both David Hopper and Ivan Head. However, Bezanson defended it on the basis that each global program initiative would require more investment on the Centre's part in the development phase, in the time over which it would be supported, and in the extent to which IDRC would invest in the utilization components of the project cycle. As was pointed out, "The necessary corollary to [that] is a highly disciplined attitude to the *choice* of what initiatives will be pursued."[33] ENR would invest effort in the selection of its strategic niches given their importance in the ultimate success of the endeavour. It would identify new program initiatives so that the Centre would have what was described as a good portfolio of "'ahead of the game' strategic niches and plain 'good ideas'" that it was exploring.

In some ways, Bezanson was advocating a very significant restructuring of IDRC to allow it, as he would have said, to do its job better. What might some of these be? An incomplete list would have included a number of initiatives, including "moving the Centre's focus from increasing agricultural production in the short to medium term, towards research which took a longer view of achieving productivity levels that could be environmentally sustained; focusing on the upstream (inputs) and downstream (outputs) parts of the production system and letting others concentrate on the production technology components; focusing on those commodities which were being neglected by the research community, that are vital to resource-poor people, and which went beyond subsistence to local and national markets; and, targeting efforts towards the needs of the resource-poor and in threatened ecosystems and marginal lands."

For its part, CAI was organized around four interactive program areas, including research utilization, a research information program that comprised IDRC's library and its public information program; the special initiatives program, which was made up of the training unit, the gender and development unit, the Canadian partnerships program; and the evaluation unit. In the Centre's *Strategy 1991* document, the overarching themes of the effectiveness of research systems and the application of scientific and technological research in the world beyond the research system were raised. This represented a complex and cross-cutting program area for IDRC, whose design and implementation required some care. It devolved upon Corporate Affairs and Initiatives to undertake a study of how a program on the effectiveness of research for development could best be designed to build on the findings and initiatives of other divisions and the regional offices in this field.[34] It was envisaged that this new program would build on the existing Research Utilization Program (RUP), which had been strengthened since Bezanson's arrival in the areas of technology innovations systems and development of institutional capacities.

The RUP's focus was on the practical application of research results and represented a concrete manifestation of that IDRC commitment, much talked about for the past twenty years and now more actively pursued. It involved activities related to knowledge and skill formation, social marketing, diffusion of knowledge, the transfer of technology from the research institutions to the productive sector, those entities that were involved in the development part of research and development, and the development of appropriate two-way linkages and mechanisms that would facilitate that transfer. Key features included a team approach whereby program officers based in the regions worked across those regions and across different disciplines. It was hoped that the RUP would raise the level of interaction between IDRC, its clients, and the private sector in Canada and in developing countries.

There were three subprograms attached to this. The first, applied research and development systems, was to support work that would lead to the commercialization of products and processes and "the dissemination of knowledge to users and beneficiaries through novel and traditional tools and methods of communications."[35] The results of this would, it was anticipated, provide a better understanding of the processes involved in the application of research results and the adoption of research results by users, beneficiaries, communities, and productive enterprises. Institutional capacity for application was the second subprogram and would concentrate on the capabilities of research and research-supporting institutions to engage in activities that would favour the application of research results. It emphasized learning by doing and relevant, specialized training. The third subprogram, innovations systems and policy, was to examine policy issues as they related to the utilization, application, and deployment of research results. "If," CAI's director general suggested, "we are able to determine 'what works,' 'why,' 'how,' 'what does not work,' and 'why' in research utilization, it will be essen-

tial to circumscribe the lessons learned with a view to policy development."
In that connection,

> activities would be oriented toward understanding the broader context in
> which research and development institutions functioned, informing and
> influencing senior policy and advisory bodies, to bring key policy makers
> into the research system at the very definition of the question creating
> favourable conditions for the implementation of policies, to construct link-
> ages between research institutions and the productive sector, linking ele-
> ments within the applied research and development systems, to create a
> dialogue and encourage a mutual exchange of information between actors
> in the research system, the productive sector, and the intended "market," inte-
> grating science and technology elements into broader macro policy frame-
> works beyond economics into such areas as health, education, energy, the
> environment, industrial and sectoral policies, and examining the role of
> international and multilateral institutions in science and technology inno-
> vation policy.

In early 1993, RUP was superseded by the Program on Innovation Systems Management (PRISM), which reflected a dual mandate of support for
research on innovation processes as a coherent field of knowledge and practice, and collaboration with other IDRC programs to strengthen utilization
across all of the Centre's research activities. PRISM was "a programmatic
response to the problem of mobilizing science and technology for purposes
of socioeconomic development by supporting research and action on three
dimensions of the problem: enhancing the effectiveness of science and technology investments; approaching innovation from a *systems* perspective, and;
increasing the capacity of developing countries to manage scientific and
technical change."[36] The program was staffed by a director, three program
officers based in Ottawa, and one each in the regional offices. PRISM was
designed around IDRC's twenty-plus years of experience in the field—much
had already been learned and much of what the program described was
already happening in other sectors. However, as a program dedicated specifically to understanding and promoting the innovation process, it represented
an effort to regularize, institutionalize, and expand those processes, to capture that knowledge through evaluation, to give it a focus, and to incorporate it back into the organizational culture of the Centre. As has been seen,
IDRC had done this regularly since its establishment—what others might
call learning from one's mistakes or from best practices—but much of that
had been more ad hoc than the system contemplated by PRISM. Indeed, the
new program would, over time, *inform* Centre practices.

On a more political level, it was also designed to address the enormous fiscal pressures being brought to bear on public and quasi-public institutions to prove their worth. While the Conservatives were out of office by November 1993, the Liberals, under Prime Minister Jean Chrétien, followed an even more intense deficit-cutting program. Tuned into that network, Bezanson knew full well that taxpayers, through their government, wanted to be able to see and taste the results when it came to justifying the continued existence of those organizations funded with public money. As the president was to correctly tell the board in early 1994, the Centre was operating "in a climate in which the political and public will to sustain cooperation for development was anything but strong."[37] That was an understatement. All Northern countries were facing similar pressures, battered as they were by recession, a jobless economic recovery, and growing uncertainty and fear about the future. IDRC staff were rightly worried about their futures. However, Bezanson preferred to think of this context as an opportunity, one symbolized by the Chinese character for crisis, which involved "the dual components of 'danger' and 'opportunity,' [and] there [had] been opportunities to be seized."

One opportunity he did seize was to firm up Ivan Head's commitments in South Africa, establishing the Regional Office for Southern Africa (ROSA) in 1992. Run by the entrepreneurial Marc Van Ameringen, it turned out to be a huge success in terms of the innovative programming that flowed through its corridors and in its relationship with the new majority government of Nelson Mandela, elected in 1994, which the regional director cultivated so perfervidly. Van Ameringen and his staff were everywhere, drumming up additional resources and pushing it out to willing researchers. Indeed, so involved were ROSA and IDRC in South Africa in the early 1990s that before the country's first democratic elections in April 1994, Mandela noted in a speech that the Centre had played "a crucial role in helping the African National Congress and the Mass Democratic Movement to prepare for negotiations [and] was instrumental in helping us prepare for the new phase of governance and transformation."[38]

And how did it do that? Rashad Cassim remembers his first encounter with the Centre, which is instructive. In the early 1990s, it had set up a trade policy think tank at the University of Capetown, which advised the new government-in-waiting on trade policy matters. As he said, those members were "fighters, not bureaucrats" and would need some help in getting a handle on the intricacies of governance. The role of women in the new South Africa was also under investigation, and Frene Ginwala, later the speaker of the South African House, headed that initiative. In pursuit of a women's charter while in exile, she had asked IDRC for funding, which was provided. Her movement crossed race (some Afrikaner women were involved), religion, and political affiliation, and until the April 1994 elections, her Women's National Coalition was the only representative body in the country. As well, IDRC helped to establish a representative national civil service, largely through funding Al Johnson, the former head of the Canadian Broadcasting Corporation, and allowing him to work out of ROSA. Johnson was instrumental in liaising with South Africans about governance, as well as in working out the details with his interlocutors with respect to a new constitution. As a result, the new state rather closely resembled Canada's federal constitutional structure despite an early ANC predilection for a strong unitary government.[39] Trevor Fowler, until August 2009 the chief operating officer for the South African president's office but in the early 1990s at the University of Witswatersrand, also worked largely on governance issues through IDRC support on a small team, whose leader is now the minister of social development in Jacob Zuma's government.[40]

New President, New Ideas (for Regional Offices)

As had Hopper and Head (twice) before him done, Bezanson set about rethinking the role and place of regional offices in his new domain. Much of the Centre's reorganization and change of focus would be dependent on how regional directors (RDs) reported to headquarters and what their responsibilities might be, so the subject was a matter of some urgency. Accordingly, consultants G.M. Kirby and C. Herzka were hired to come up with recommendations about the roles, composition, and authorities of the ROs. The study was to focus primarily on identifying the role regional offices should play in defining research priorities, developing research initiatives, integrating regional plans with corporate plans, evaluating IDRC-funded research activities, and disseminating the findings of this research. The resulting work, "'A New Day': Recommendations on the Future Form, Responsibilities, and Relationships of IDRC Regional Offices," was published in 1992 in time for the October board meeting.[41] The report also attempted to reconcile a region-centric institution with its centre. As former employee Brenda Lee Wilson remembered, "There was a power struggle between regional directors and directors general; who [had] the power to make programming and staffing decisions, RDs or divisions (programs)? [It brought up front] the regional office question. [The Head] period when regional directors were all nationals from the region [was one thing]. They were big guys, big guns, had a diplomatic representational role, to have IDRC representation in the region. The transition affected the RDs because after [it was implemented], Canadians [who had no local power base] became regional directors. [Also], after the transition, regional program officers became a part of the divisions."[42]

The first consideration of "A New Day" came by mid-year, when the document was submitted to management. Out of that came its discussion by the board, which approved the recommendations. It did alter the nature of the relationship, although not as much as has been claimed. In short, the new regional office responsibility of identifying regional research priorities, deciding how to address those through research programs, and developing projects by which solutions would be found and beneficiaries reached, created a need to redefine the RO role. The Bezanson Centre spoke of a "regional team" forming an integral part of "team IDRC," which would be administered by the regional director, developing its own regional thrusts and implementing processes and procedures that flowed out of the delegation of new responsibilities. In each of these teams, the regional program officer (RPO) had to elaborate with colleagues a common view on regional needs and themes and on the resulting programs and projects. That was a significant change in the RPO's way of working. The change would also see them interacting with the RD in his or her new role as team leader. The regional director became the leader of the team both in program and administrative terms, and would also have a more important representational role in the region, a result of the delegation of power and resources. In short, the regional offices would play an increasingly more important role in strategic planning, networking, project monitoring, project administration, and an increased representational role.

The board was also told that the new role of the RO in the development and management of the Centre's programs required very close linkages with management, and that regional directors had to be involved in the decision-making process. As was suggested, "The monitoring and control of the ROs require[d] more than clear direction, clear delegation of authorities and the specification of the management information to be provided to the ROs."[43] It also required "the integrated oversight of the activities of an office to ensure that its overall operation [was] balanced, productive and consistent with the purpose and priorities of the Centre." Nor would it be one size fits all given the diversity of situation experienced by the ROs: "There should be no reluctance to have very different levels of delegation and reporting demands placed on different offices which reflect not only the quality of the managers within the office, but also the characteristics of the research and administrative environment within which each office operates." Bezanson was adamant that partnerships were to be established between the regions and headquarters in a way that had not happened before. Not only would that allow for the selection of priority themes, which would facilitate the preparation of future programs of work and budget, it would reinforce the decisions to make ROs full partners in support of research for development. The regional offices had apparently come a long way.

The Perils of "Departmental Corporation-ization"

Before the new divisions were established, however, a singular blow hit IDRC. The Conservative budget of 25 February 1992, presented by Finance Minister Don Mazankowski, set the reorganizational cat among IDRC pigeons. Facing a massive deficit and nearing the end of the parliamentary term, Mazankowski was desperate to begin the process of righting a listing ship. Part of that, while not necessarily addressing financial matters, was to remove the Centre from the list of Crown corporations and move it into the departmental corporation category, which would "bring its administrative regime into conformity with that of the rest of the public service." While this was better than what had first been proposed—the closure of IDRC—it was bad. The Centre would then more resemble those agencies over which government had control—the Natural Sciences and Engineering Research Council, the Medical Research Council, the Social Sciences and Humanities Research Council, the National Research Council of Canada, and the Atomic Energy Control Board. It seemed almost punitive; to take an organization with a sterling international reputation that it had developed because of the flexibility and agility conferred upon it by its Crown corporation status and the *IDRC Act* and turn it into a regular federal department was too much. It was also motivated, as Bezanson told the board, "by a single purpose, that being to show Canadians that all aspects of public expenditure is under tight control."[44]

Following the announcement, there was a flurry of meetings between Centre officials and government representatives on working out a process for achieving the change in status, and on the required legislative amendments. The IDRC team was led by Ray Audet, director general of finance and administration, and Robert Auger, the Centre's secretary and general counsel. The government intention was to have discussion wrapped up by mid-April so that the necessary legislative amendments could be ready in early May. As Bezanson told the board in June, the objective of all this activity "was to map out for us the Government's truly formidable policy universe which henceforth could apply to IDRC."[45] It was an alternative reality to the one in which the Centre had operated since its establishment. It seemed not to matter that the auditor general had investigated the institution in 1988 and had noted in his report, "Well Performing Organizations," tabled in Parliament in December of that year, that it was "considered world wide to be one of the best organizations of its kind."[46]

The negotiations represented a few months of tortured, crisis-ridden (at least for the Centre) angst, and the result would have the effect of reducing the Centre's administrative flexibility and would subtract from its attractiveness as a manager of funds on behalf of partners in the donor community. It would also be forced to devote a greater part of its resources to administration than it wanted and, in the process, fundamentally change its nature. Jean-Guy Paquet, a long-serving governor, perhaps put it best, later noting that "Il y avait une période durant les coupures où l'on pensait que le CRDI pourrait disparaître."[47] However, much to the delight of IDRC management and staff, the flurry ended abruptly in May, and an unsettling silence settled over headquarters. Most could not believe their good fortune and wondered when the other shoe would fall. In June 1992, the executive committee agreed that talks with Treasury Board Secretariat should be postponed until such time as a clarification was obtained on whether it remained the policy of government to proceed with its decision given the new role that Prime Minister Brian Mulroney outlined for IDRC at the United Nations Conference on Environment and Development, held in Rio de Janiero during that month. There, he had proclaimed that the Centre would become the implementing agency for the Agenda 21 process. It was all as if nothing had happened.

The Saviour? Agenda 21 and the United Nations Conference on Environment and Development

The United Nations Conference on Environment and Development (UNCED), more commonly known as the Earth Summit, provided life support. While it might be too much to claim that the defibrillator was applied through the careful manipulations of Maurice Strong—once the director general of Canada's External Aid Office, first president of the Canadian International Development Agency and the man who had set the ball rolling along a track that would end with IDRC, and now the secretary general of UNCED—there was also an element of truth in that assertion. We should emphasize that it is not our intention to discuss UNCED itself, but only as it affected IDRC and its future. There is plenty of literature on the United Nations conference and its aftermath.[48] But what was Agenda 21? The first article to the preamble of the document that was adopted by all attendees on 14 June 1992 read:

Humanity stands at a defining moment in history. We are confronted with a perpetuation of disparities between and within nations, a worsening of poverty, hunger, ill health and illiteracy, and the continuing deterioration of the ecosystems on which we depend for our well-being. However, integration of environment and development concerns and greater attention to them will lead to the fulfillment of basic needs, improved living standards for all, better protected and managed ecosystems and a safer, more prosperous future. No nation can achieve this on its own; but together we can—in a global partnership for sustainable development.[49]

For the Centre, it meant salvation. As its *Annual Report, 1992–93* noted, "One of the most remarkable events in IDRC's recent history was the announcement by the Government of Canada at [UNCED] in June 1992 that IDRC would be designated as an implementing agency—in fact, the prime vehicle—for Canada's response to Agenda 21. IDRC was given special responsibility for working with developing countries in achieving the goals of Agenda 21."[50] It was indeed remarkable given what had gone on at the Centre over the past twelve months. Agenda 21 was a six-hundred-plus-page document that had emerged as a consensus from UNCED and which consisted of forty chapters organized across four broad categories: (1) social and economic dimensions; (2) conservation and management of resources; (3) strengthening the role of major groups; and (4) means of implementation.

UNCED was a successor to the landmark 1972 Stockholm Conference on the Human Environment, which had first put environment on the international agenda. The idea of holding a conference on environment and development arose from the World Commission on Environment and Development (or Brundtland Commission, named after Norway's former prime minister, Gro Harlem Brundtland), held in 1986. At that time, the Commission advocated the need for the world to move toward sustainable development, defined as development that met the needs of the present without compromising the ability of future generations to meet their own needs. On 22 December 1989, the United Nations General Assembly passed resolution 44/228 calling for the United Nations Conference on Environment and Development and on the need for the nations of the world to take a balanced and integrated approach to environment and development questions. Agenda 21 was a statement of principles and policy actions for sustainability that identified problems and highlighted solutions and recommendations for action. It was based on the premise that environmentally sustainable development was no longer an option but an imperative.[51] However, it was also not a legally binding document, and its effects were ultimately negligible as heads of state preferred to attend the conference for the photo opportunities it presented than to take substantive action on many of the problems raised. But for the Centre, it was critical.

How did IDRC make that leap? Strong and Mulroney were old acquaintances. When the former had been president of Power Corporation in the earlier 1960s, the latter was a junior lawyer in the firm that handled much of its business. There, the two got to know each other slightly, even though Mulroney was not senior enough to have regular access to Strong. When Mulroney became prime minister, Strong was the chairman of a Crown corporation, the Canada Investment Development Corporation, a position that he had resigned almost as soon as the new government took office in 1984. Later, Mulroney was to make Strong a privy councillor. Clearly, by the time Rio was held, the two had a relationship that went back almost thirty years. Further, it had been Lucien Bouchard, then environment minister in Ottawa, who had put Strong's name forward as a putative secretary general for the conference.

At UNCED, Mulroney, then in the twilight of his years as prime minister, wanted to meet with George Bush and others of the 105 world leaders in attendance, but the Canadian office was far off in the suburbs of a gridlocked city, making any communication very difficult. Strong's office "was obviously the best in the place, right at the centre of things," so he let Mulroney use it.[52] That gave the secretary general a chance "to chat with Mulroney from time to time." He certainly brought up IDRC and its possible role as Canada's Agenda 21–implementing agency and, while Strong takes no credit for the eventual result, it does seem distinctly possible that his intervention helped the Centre's case. Furthermore, Bezanson had earlier consulted with government officials. He told the Standing Committee on External Affairs and International Trade that "as you approached Rio there was a realization that delivery was important and some things had to be put on the fast track if the will, the enthusiasm and the promise of Rio were to work.... So ... we put that on the agenda, that if you want to do something, we can help."[53] Similarly, in the months preceding the conference, he had held meetings with the Environmental Task Force Steering Committee, a group of departmental assistant deputy ministers whose departments had responsibility in the area of the environment and who had been brought together to prepare for UNCED. At one of these meetings he had been asked to convene bilateral donors with a view to developing a database on capacity building, research, and training that related to the environment.[54] As a result, this high-level task force would certainly have known about IDRC's capabilities. Moreover, the Centre had also been funding environmental work in the recent past—Anne Whyte had introduced that theme in the later 1980s—so it seemed a natural fit.

Whatever the reason, the prime minister announced that IDRC's mandate would be strengthened to assume special responsibility as Canada's prime agency for working with developing countries on the implementation of Agenda 21. He also announced that the government of Canada would continue to provide CAN$115 million annually for at least ten years in core support for the organization, and that IDRC would be specifically mandated to contribute to a rapid implementation of the results of the Earth Summit. · It was at least in part because of the new Agenda 21 responsibilities that Flora MacDonald was appointed as chair of the board on 17 June 1992, succeeding Janet Wardlaw, who had served two terms. As the news release from the Office of the Secretary of State for External Affairs pointed out, MacDonald's appointment "followed an announcement at the Earth Summit ... by Prime Minister Brian Mulroney, that the IDRC will be further internationalized and its mandate broadened to emphasize sustainable development issues. The Government wishes to use the IDRC's international network and expertise to facilitate a quick start on the implementation of the UN Conference on Environment and Development's Agenda 21 program of action."[55]

Very quickly IDRC grasped the lifeline the government extended to it. The commitment to Agenda 21 brought in a whole new work order, and staff had to produce "golden bullets—particular initiatives that were going to showcase or address how their work would address the environment."[56] Tim Dottridge, then working in Policy and Planning, remembered that his small group was tasked with coordinating the response. It was important to pick up on, and reflect, the government's desire to have an Agenda 21 organization that would bring "relevance" to new heights. Part of that was the establishment of the Crucible Group, which brought together scientists, media types, policy-makers, and business executives from Northern and Southern countries to discuss contentious issues about the conservation and enhancement of plant genetic resources. Discussion was based on background papers, and the result was a series of recommendations that informed the debate on the subject to the point of leading to changes in some countries' legislation on plant genetic resources and intellectual property rights in several developing states. The project was considered "to be a model knowledge-intensive, multi-stakeholder process that successfully bridged the gap between local concerns and broader policy issues."[57]

Mulroney had also made mention during his speech at Rio about the "internationalization" of IDRC, which was interpreted to mean that the United Nations and the heads of international organizations would be invited to nominate non-Canadian governors to the board. That was a bit of a shock— Mulroney noted in his speech at UNCED that he had invited the Secretary

General, on behalf of the agencies of the United Nations, to propose the 10 non-Canadian board members of the IDRC, further internationalizing it, or so the government believed, and creating a new partnership between Canada and the UN.[58] For an organization that had prided itself on not being a part of the Canadian foreign policy apparatus, the prime minister's promise could alter the very nature of the beast. Ultimately, it never received much traction and it died early on, a victim of a change of government in November 1993, the relative weakness of possible board members suggested by the UN, and the fact that one of the goals of the initiative—to have IDRC funded at least partially by other institutions—did not materialize.

The Centre was quick off the mark in responding to its new status, which emphasized sustainable development, and its programs were described partially in terms of sustainable development rather than disciplines or sectors, although the divisional structure for program delivery remained pretty much as it had been. It could almost be described as a preliminary, halting step toward disciplinary integration without really practising it.[59] How did IDRC proceed? It undertook an extensive examination of its own programs in order to identify those areas that might become priority activities within the context of its follow-up. The process being conducted by each division and regional office caused some staff to grumble that IDRC was becoming little more than an organization that funded environmental research.[60] Centre staff undertook a detailed chapter-by-chapter review of the international agreements and follow-up proposals contained in Agenda 21. That exercise resulted in a document almost as long as that produced during the conference! Following this, staff identified major cross-cutting issues and prepared a first list of possible priority program areas. A separate group, the Agenda 21 Unit, coordinated these activities, acting as a focal point and information centre and as a body that suggested new ideas.

Out of this exercise came a number of projects and one, the Economy and Environment Program for Southeast Asia (EEPSEA), launched in May 1993 to support training and research in environmental and resource economics across the region's ten member countries, was an explicit response to the conference.[61] The choice of region reflected the conference secretary general's observation that the battle for sustainable development would be won or lost in Asia. While that might not be strictly true, it was the case that EEPSEA was a significant success and eventually attracted funding from nine other donors. It was conceived and launched by David Glover, then special assistant to the vice-president of finance at the Centre. As he remembered, his "task was to propose a project that the Centre could launch as a response to Agenda 21."[62] He also recalled Maurice Strong as saying that "he went into the summit believing it was about the environment and came out realizing it was about economics. What he meant was that most of the decisions that came out of the summit were influenced by how much they would cost, what were the benefits, and who would pay and who would benefit. So I proposed that IDRC launch a research program on this topic, which would involve a great deal of capacity building." Its goal was to strengthen local capacity for the economic analysis of environmental problems, allowing researchers to provide advice to policy-makers. The program used a networking approach to provide not only financial support but meetings, resource people, access to literature, publication outlets, and opportunities for comparative research. It eventually morphed into a secretariat and was supported out of the ASRO office by, as one document noted, "the most diverse funding group ... in the number of core donors supporting its work."[63] Further, as an EEPSEA evaluation undertaken in 2000 by the Filipina sociologist, Geila Castillo, and Daniel Bromley noted, it had to be regarded "as a success on practically every dimension of its program."[64] The program had "stimulated more learning and more research in the fields of environment and economics.... Alumni contributed much to local/national meetings and to the use of research results by local authorities. Through their ... participation in environment-related program and policy-making bodies, they have made inputs into the policy formulation and implementation process."

Bezanson also committed his charge to engage in extensive consultations with key institutions and sectors, both within Canada and internationally. In particular, the Centre had always encouraged the participation of developing country organizations in preparing its programs, and would continue to do so with this very important exercise. Further, by September discussions were already under way with key UN agencies, the Earth Council, and with scientific, business, and non-governmental organization partners. Additionally, a small advisory group was brought together to provide input into particular aspects of Centre program development. And when the opportunity presented itself, as it did with the visits to IDRC of Federico Mayor, the director general of UNESCO and, later, Enrique Iglesias, the president of the Inter-American Development Bank, during the summer of 1992, opinions would be canvassed. As well, IDRC established what it called a blue-ribbon advisory group to evaluate programming comprised of Strong, Pierre-Marc Johnson, then the director of research at the Centre for Medicine, Ethics, and Law at McGill University in Montreal;[65] James MacNeil, the secretary general of the Brundtland Commission; and Arthur Campeau, Mulroney's special ambassador to UNCED. The Centre also undertook to collaborate more fully with CIDA and with some Canadian departments, like Forestry Canada, in pursuit of that objective; the three supported the implementation in the South of the model forests program that Mulroney had announced in his speech at the Earth Summit. Internationally, it hooked up with the United Nations Development Program (UNDP) in order to support the sustainable development network, the major UNDP-led follow-up to UNCED. As Terry Smutlyo has said "Rio was a milestone in redefining ourselves as an Agenda 21 agency.... It was a chaotic period in terms of program structure. All sorts of things were happening. There was no coherent central focus to our programming. It was a big milestone for the evaluation function too, because the president said: 'Here is a pile of money. Now let's see the silver [sic] bullet proposals.' Everybody had to be a player in the new world."[66]

In this whirlwind of activity, the Centre was not going to let anyone forget that its role had come from the very top of the Canadian political pyramid. The lifeline was grasped very tightly, even to the point where the threat of being turned into a departmental corporation was no longer as terrifying. A meeting with External Affairs officials in late October 1992 to review a number of issues did not rouse the anxiety that it surely would have without Agenda 21. For Bezanson, that prime ministerial commitment had changed the nature of the debate. At the meeting the president and Robert Auger, the Centre's secretary and general counsel, heard that Barbara McDougall, then the secretary of state for external affairs (and in 2008 appointed the chair of IDRC's board), "attached high importance in abiding by the February budget decision as it concerned IDRC. She did not feel that conversion would prevent the Centre from retaining a pre-eminent position or in following up on Rio."[67] However, McDougall had clearly been overtaken by events. As she now recalls, "it was one of those governmental organizational things that happen all the time. The department throws up an idea and somebody says we need more efficiency or we have to save money or whatever it is."[68] And that was the end of it.

Instead, planning went ahead at the October board meeting about how to proceed with the new mandate of environmentally based themes that were intended to involve all parts of the Centre in a number of programs for sustainable and equitable development, which essentially coincided with the program structure of the divisions and the "responsibility centres" within them.[69] That said, Centre staff were, to some extent, shooting in the dark. As Bezanson said at the first (and only) staff meeting attended by *all* program officers, including those from the regions, "Agenda 21 says everything and says nothing; it sets no priorities; it establishes no specific action plan; it ignores many of the most critical issues." It also demanded a new paradigm for sustainable development without providing the paradigm. However, at the October board meeting a number of papers were presented for consideration that attempted to make some sense of Rio, referring to some aspect of it, and focusing on integrating environment into policy-making. Four themes were taken up: (1) a program of research and training in economics and the environment; (2) national sustainable development plans; (3) strengthening local management for sustainable development; and (4) building capacity in environmental research and policy. Further, the Centre proposed that it fund a program of research concentrating on technology for sustainable and equitable development given its proven track record in supporting research and technology development in several key areas of clean technology like water-quality management, remote sensing, biological agricultural inputs, and industrial waste management.[70] As well, information for sustainable and equitable development was proposed, a program that recognized the role of information as a powerful resource to support development.[71]

Food systems under stress were also tackled. In the South, population growth was generally outstripping food production and, with the former, came environmental degradation, which affected the growing of food. Again, the Centre had had much experience with aspects of the issue. The program would address: areas undergoing desertification, especially in Africa; fragile highland regions in Latin America, Asia, and Africa; and rapidly expanding urban areas, especially in Africa.[72] Out of this general consideration was to come the program initiative "Cities Feeding People" in the last years of the Bezanson presidency. This followed a long IDRC history of research support in two related fields: food security and nutrition among the urban poor and environmental quality, including water and sanitation, in urban areas. In the early 1990s, this had gelled into a program on urban agriculture, while by 1997, it was to become integrated with work on environmental waste and its management.[73] Finally, the Centre adopted the theme that came out of Chapter 8 of Agenda 21, "Integrating Environmental, Social, and Economic Policies." That chapter called for a new approach to policy-making, most notably the integration of environmental concerns into policy.[74] That was quite a post-Rio agenda IDRC had carved out and would absorb much of its attention. It did all this as it pursued earlier commitments, including funding work on spreading desertification. It was a member of the Canadian Interdepartmental Committee on Desertification, and contributed to the drafting of Canada's official position. It also helped to fund many of the projects that came out of it, like the one designed to assist African countries "to participate more effectively in negotiations toward a global Convention on Desertification and Drought, and in finding long-term solutions to deal with problems of land degradation in arid and semi-arid areas."[75]

The first post-Rio national stakeholders' meeting was held on 5 and 6 November 1992. In addition to the Centre, this brought together the principal Canadian actors in the Rio follow-up, including the National Round Table on Environment and Economy, the Canadian Council of Ministers of the Environment, the International Institute for Sustainable Development, and leading environmental non-governmental organizations. That meeting, attended by Conservative Minister of the Environment Jean Charest, was held at IDRC headquarters. Further, the Centre made a presentation later that month to the Standing Committee on the Environment, focusing on its experience and plans with respect to biodiversity. It did likewise with the Liberal Party, following the government's permission to do so. Centre-sponsored round tables had also been established on a regional basis under the leadership of regional offices. In typical IDRC fashion, these involved leading critics from public, private, and non-governmental sectors of society in Africa, Asia, and Latin America. A similar round table was held at headquarters on 18–20 January 1993, bringing together fourteen Southern leaders to provide counsel to the president on the post-Rio challenge. Included among these were Enrique Iglesias, Pierre-Marc Johnson, and Maurice Strong. That was complemented by a one-day session that included a former president of Nigeria and a former prime minister of Sweden, a meeting that had been encouraged by UN Secretary General Boutros Boutros-Ghali. As well, the Centre was invited to provide guidance in the establishment of an Earth Council, designed to be an Amnesty International of the environment, an idea that had come out of Rio. Bezanson participated in its founding meeting in October 1992. Finally, a meeting of selected donors and international scientific bodies was held in Washington, DC, in early 1993 under the auspices of IDRC, the Rockefeller Foundation, and the World Bank, its purpose to examine what steps might be taken to bring about a better integration of science and research organizations with development financing institutions and to explore alternatives in improving coordinated approaches. It had been a hectic several months.

The International Network for Bamboo and Rattan

One of the more important institutions that emerged from the Agenda 21 exercise was the International Network for Bamboo and Rattan (INBAR), and it was appropriate that the Centre was, in a very real sense, its parent, given that it had nurtured bamboo and rattan research for a decade. It was formally established in 1993 by IDRC as a secretariat with co-funding from the International Fund for Agricultural Development (IFAD), following the recommendations of a strategic review commissioned by the Centre. Its creation responded to the principles contained in the Biodiversity and Climate conventions and conformed to the programs of Agenda 21 and the guidelines of the Rio forestry principles. Later, as an international organization in its own right based in Beijing, INBAR was ratified by partners on 6 November 1997. That act consolidated thirteen years of Centre support to research and to an informal network on bamboo and rattan. It had turned out to be significant project; one governor later called it the "flagship" of IDRC—it had everything in it: local focus, women, and the impoverished.[76]

During the early 1980s, IDRC had initiated support for certain scientists engaged in individual bamboo and rattan research programs in several Asian countries. Then based in New Delhi, its work had resulted in the publication of a significant volume of material, albeit oriented toward the technical and biophysical aspects of bamboo and rattan cultivation. Through that decade and into the 1990s, Centre management had left INBAR free to pursue a commodity-based research agenda focused on South Asia and, to a lesser extent, China, "a research direction [which was] increasingly distant from the growing Centre convergence on farming systems and, subsequently, participatory development work."[77] Reflecting an enhanced IDRC commitment to the socio-economic, research was broadened to include those parameters at the behest of Southern partners, a policy that researcher Cai Mantang has called "very innovative."[78] Few development organizations were then funding such research, especially when the subject could be more easily addressed via technical and scientific criteria.

Socio-economic research emerged as a unifying theme for the focus of the research, providing a linkage with development activities and making it more responsive to the constraints and opportunities of small-scale producers, those who were most intimately affected by bamboo and rattan cultivation. As INBAR developed, its mantra came to reflect more of an IDRC bias with its programming focusing more immediately "on enhancing the quality of life of poor and disadvantaged people in developing countries and making a favourable impact on forests and the environment."[79] It also connected governmental and non-governmental organizations and the private sector into a worldwide network. Cai Mantang appreciated the Centre's capacity-building ethos in this area and how it "really gave authority to the [funding] recipient [and] empowered local organizations." Importantly, he brought IDRC ideas with him when he went as a faculty member to the University of Beijing.

IDRC also gave some thought to the role of women in the research it funded, a consideration particularly since the late 1980s and the advent of the Women in Development Program. As phase II of the project funding for INBAR noted, "the role of women and the potential for their economic empowerment through bamboo and rattan was identified ... as a key emphasis for INBAR's future programming."[80] That was important as "specific information on women's role ... [was] almost completely lacking. Since such information [was] essential in designed interventions for development, socioeconomic research and technical assessments will include gender analysis and specific efforts to address identified needs."

INBAR went beyond where most projects stopped, in some ways, even making claims that the research it funded would help to save the planet, or at least parts of its environment. Its programs were to accomplish three objectives: "strengthen the livelihood security of the resource-poor families through the generation of eco-jobs at the village level through a wide range of market-driven manufacture in bamboo and rattan-based products and through the symbiotic social contracts between the corporate sector and families depending for their livelihood on bamboo and rattan-based enterprises; strengthen the ecological security of the planet both by saving forests from denudation for the sake of wood-based products, and by increasing carbon sequestration, taking advantage of bamboo's extremely rapid generation of biomass; and, strengthen sustainable food security through the promotion of bamboo-based agro-forestry systems of solar harvesting and land and water utilization."[81] Bamboo could do all this because it is, in some ways, a miracle grass; it grows up to 30 centimetres each year, takes about three years to mature, propagates by underground rhizomes so there is no need to reseed a harvested plant, absorbs approximately 40 percent more carbon dioxide than trees, is a good soil conditioner, and prevents soil erosion. As well, in countries like India, where groundwater levels have fallen considerably under the impact of the more intensive agricultural production of the green revolution, its roots have been known to draw groundwater closer to the surface. Finally, about 1.2 billion people depend on bamboo for some aspect of their livelihood.

IDRC-funded research has had an impact. For example, the Rattan Project, funded from 1985 to 1991, was awarded the first Science and Technology Award by the People's Republic of China's Ministry of Forestry. "Research on Rattans in China" later won the first-class Science and Technology Award of the State Science and Technology Commission, while Jules Janssen, funded by INBAR, was honoured by the Queen of the Netherlands with the royal decoration of Officer in the Order of Oranje-Nassau for his research on bamboo. Further, a 5,000 hectares rattan plantation was established in China under INBAR auspices, as was a rattan herbarium of over 1,000 species, and rattan was incorporated in 7,000 hectares of rubber plantations in Malaysia. As well, intensive bamboo management technology developed in network research was adopted in 72,000 hectares, resulting in a total income of US$50 million spread among thousands of farmers. Similarly, what would become the beautiful Anji Bamboo Garden—the largest in the world, extending over 20 hectares and including 221 species and the natural setting where the famous Chinese film *Crouching Tiger, Hidden Dragon* was shot—was set up in the early 1990s as a result of INBAR activity. It was visited by about ten thousand researchers, producers, and tourists by mid-decade. Given its increasing importance as a result of IDRC and INBAR-funded research, it was also included for the first time in China's national five-year plan (1995–2000).

Bamboo is also used as a building material, and a number of IDRC-funded projects focused on this aspect. Some of that effort was taken over by INBAR in the later 1990s, but the Centre remained as the primary source of funding. An example of that was a project sponsored by IDRC at the Indian Plywood Industries Research and Training Institute, located in Bangalore, which focused on cost-effective technologies for the production of bamboo mat board to replace plywood in some of the areas like housing, packaging, storage, and transport. During the first phase of the project, "it achieved ... environmental and socio-economic objectives. The direct benefits accrued *viz.*, revival of bamboo mat weaving by women in remote rural and tribal areas, enhanced earning capacity of these people due to increased demand for woven mats, substitution of round wood from natural forests and creation of employment generation, testify to the success of the project and underline the importance of further research."[82] Finally, bamboo was also useful as a foreign policy tool for the PRC; China's Department of Foreign Affairs included bamboo research as an area for assistance to developing countries. In short, it seemed that there was little that bamboo and rattan could not do.

INBAR remains in operation in 2010, no longer nurtured by IDRC. The Centre, having provided funding for various aspects of bamboo and rattan-related research for about twenty years, bowed out in 2004. Its departure also signalled that all was not well. Despite INBAR's earlier success, devolution of the organization and resulting administrative weaknesses created a number of problems that were later cited in a program completion report. However, these do not detract from its innovative approach, which included a focus on the socio-economic and not merely the technical, to a field of research that has the potential to improve the lives of billions who live in the South.

The Continuing Fog of Reorganization: Corporate Program Framework I, 1993–96/97

Bezanson had set in motion a process that was expected to be completed within about eighteen months from the October 1992 board meeting. The resulting corporate policy framework laid out "the broad priorities and areas of activity that will guide programming and allocation decisions.... Its objective is to 'sharpen the Centre's focus,' which is a guiding principle of the Centre's strategy."[83] That certainly sounded reasonable and proactive, but as events transpired, Bezanson's entire presidency was characterized by significant internal upheaval and distress, largely through events outside of his control.

Over the period in question, the president continued to push ahead with single-minded purpose. One item of business that he encouraged, and one that staff might have thought impulsive, but which was so quintessentially Bezanson, was to undertake a collaborative audit of IDRC with the Office of the Auditor General of Canada. Indeed, even AG credulity seeped through the document: "The request for this audit was at the initiative of IDRC. It was under no obligation to seek a value-for-money audit that would be made public. This is the second time IDRC has requested a value-for-money audit. This reflects its interest in improving performance and being accountable." The Centre/AG collaboration was also "innovative": according to officials, the president had "proposed to the AG that the audit be a collaboration that would provide an independent and reliable tool to assess IDRC's performance.... The AG agreed to experiment with this collaborative approach."[84] The results? That the Centre was "exceptionally well-managed [providing] a high level of support for its projects and program officers.... We also found in talking with IDRC grantees that they were generally very satisfied with IDRC's sensitivity, flexibility and speed."[85] The Centre got into the act with its own corporate evaluation, which would be done annually. The first was to take place in mid-1994 and would be focused on reviewing its progress in measuring program performance.[86] As well, the ensuing report would highlight the new evaluation tools and systems that had been introduced for measuring results and development impact. As it noted, "Increasingly, IDRC's challenge for the future is to ensure that development research achieves results." The newly established annual corporate evaluation would help, it was hoped, keep the Centre on that narrow road.

Further, at the end of the year, the Centre funded a project to survey completed projects with a view to "identifying past IDRC research projects whose results have been applied and those whose results have potential for application. A follow-up in-depth impact analysis on selected projects identified in the survey could provide critical information to the Centre as a whole on issues such as research effectiveness, research management, factors affecting the application and use of research results, the measurement and reporting of research output, and public information and dissemination potential of projects."[87] The fact that, as Pierre Beemans wrote in his director general's evaluation, "the transparent design of the Completed Project implied that it will expose both welcome and unwelcome news" meant nothing in pursuit of the objective. The work described in the project summary would allow the Centre "to undergo an objective, tough minded investigation—almost a forensic accounting—of IDRC's past project support." Much as the auditor general had discovered, the Centre was very keen on self-evaluation and self-appraisal in searching for a better way.

As Bezanson looked back on his roughly twenty months as president in late 1992, he could do so with some satisfaction, although the process was by no means complete and staff most likely would not have shared his sense of accomplishment. "It was," as he told the board at the March 1993 meeting with apologies to Charles Dickens, "the best of times, it was the worst of times, it was the age of wisdom, it was the age of foolishness, it was the epoch of belief, it was the epoch of incredulity, it was the season of Light, it was the season of Darkness, it was the spring of Hope, it was the winter of Despair." He itemized those things that governors knew well, beginning with the possible change to a departmental corporation, which had "sapped the energies of much of our staff and had a crippling effect on morale."[88] Further, the year had been spent worrying about the parliamentary appropriation, especially given that in January 1992 there had been much speculation that it was to be slashed. Similarly, the government had mooted the possibility of moving IDRC to a new headquarters in Montreal, which was unsettling for Ottawa-based staff. There had also been the expansion of the Centre's mandate to an Agenda 21 organization, which, while ultimately a benefit, also contained some stressors. As well, the empowerment of regional offices as equals in the planning, programming, and management of IDRC's business was not universally well received, nor was the major restructuring that had taken place and the more inclusive approach to corporate programming. And while the "worst of times" had not happened in that the Centre's status as an independent organization remained intact, the parliamentary grant had not been reduced, and IDRC was receiving increasing recognition as an important instrument in capacity building for sustainable development, it did not lessen the staff's sense of dislocation. John Hardie had suggested to the president that he should emphasize to program staff that all the pain they had gone through, and the failed departmental corporation exercise, had "actually saved our bacon."[89] Still, while Bezanson could be forgiven for quoting Dickens to the board, perhaps the staff would have been more comfortable with "The Second Coming" of William Butler Yeats: "Things fall apart; the centre cannot hold; / Mere anarchy is loosed upon the world."

The president had overseen a process that had articulated a new set of rules and principles for project review. Among these were the demands that each activity be vetted to determine its degree of relevance to Centre policies and program priorities, and that information about project intentions be shared early among relevant staff, assisted by such mechanisms as project identification memoranda, the pipeline database, trip reports, and program review meetings. As Senior Management Committee had pointed out, this was not done "because a 'system' requires it, but because it is part of the way that [the new] IDRC expects its program staff to behave."[90] Further, while certain procedures and components of the system were mandatory across the Centre, officers were given much more latitude in determining the rest. But that also contained potential dangers—program officers would be held responsible.

As well, Bezanson would continue the process of convincing staff to place emphasis on its "vision of itself as a results-oriented research for development organization," as articulated in *Empowerment through Knowledge* and indeed throughout its history. It was necessary to develop projects and programs with a clearer articulation of objectives and deliverables that would permit better measurement of their efficiency, effectiveness, and impact. As Bezanson had said on numerous occasions, such enhanced accountability offered opportunities to compare strategies, to document what worked in development, and to continually refine policies and programs to maximize the impact of a shrinking budget. In such an environment, evaluations would become more important, and the evaluation unit, based in the Corporate Affairs and Initiatives division, would be a more central player in IDRC conceptions of its performance. For example, it would publish a document that would highlight the key lessons learned, which would include summaries of what worked in Centre programming and what did not in terms of strategies for research networks, interdisciplinary research, Canadian partnerships for research, and research capacity building.

The corporate program framework (CPF) laid out the priorities and broad areas of activity that would guide programming and allocation decisions over the three-year period from fiscal year 1993–94. As events were to transpire, however, the president was to ask the board for a one-year extension, to 1997–98, a result of external uncertainties and the sheer volume of change suggested by the document. Its strategy set out the imperatives in the development environment and defined the mission of the Centre while establishing the principles and practices that would guide action over the next several years. The CPF also described the divisional structure and the shift to regional programming. Finally, it laid out a number of ways of achieving greater focus within IDRC; this included fewer program divisions, promotion and experimentation with more integrated approaches that cut across divisions, and fewer levels of management.[91] This would, it was hoped, "sharpen the Centre's focus," a guiding principle of IDRC strategy.[92]

As well, the corporate framework for Centre programming was expressed by three broadly defined strategic dimensions that constituted the primary characteristics of sustainable and equitable development (SED). These encompassed, first, more human development, which meant that IDRC policies would be directed to research on the policies, practices, technologies, systems, and institutions that were required to provide the ingredients for sustainable human development, to develop productive skills, and to enhance the "empowering processes of social participation." The second dimension was better economic management, which pointed to the improved management of economic behaviour and systems in order to promote the more equitable and efficient allocation of resources, in the process empowering those affected to control their own economic well-being in a sustainable way. As Bezanson told the board, "This will involve analysis at three levels, international, national and local, and from three perspectives, policy, technology and institutions."[93] The final strategic dimension focused on the sustainable use of the environment. Its activities were informed by the policies, institutions, and technologies that related to the use, conservation, and management of natural ecosystems so that those affected would benefit, yet the ecosystems would also be left intact for the use of future generations.

The foundation for the strategic dimensions—indeed, the foundation for all programming—was the Centre's commitment to a series of touchstones. These included: "enhancing indigenous research capacity in LDCs; strengthening human resources development; enhancing gender research capacity and gender equity; the importance of information systems and technologies in sharing and using knowledge; ensuring that, where possible, the results of research are used to benefit people; communicating effectively with key publics about the issues and knowledge generated by Centre programs; and, to develop enhanced partnerships with Canadian organizations and institutions." The CPF did not attempt to cover all the key areas that contributed to sustainable and equitable development (SED), to be found in Agenda 21. Instead, senior management had decided that IDRC would exploit its comparative advantage in capacity building, working with developing countries to join together the people, the knowledge, and the organizations to allow them to make decisions based on sound research. The spirit that animated *For Earth's Sake* guided Centre considerations.[94]

Using all of the above as an indicator, the Centre's program framework was developed through consultation from within and without. Over the next three years, IDRC planned to allocate at least 50 percent of its program funds to six core themes on environment and development. Within these were included: (1) integrating environmental, social, and economic policies (22 percent); (2) technology and the environment (20 percent); (3) food systems under stress (19 percent); (4) information and communication for environment and development (15.5 percent); (5) health and the environment (13 percent); and (6) biodiversity (10.5 percent).[95] As well, it planned to allocate an additional 40 percent of its program funds to other initiatives related to SED and 10 percent to new initiatives that might arise during the course of the year, which added up to CAN$84 million.[96]

A further CAN$36.5 million was set aside as operational support. In the new operating matrix, divisions and regional offices were to combine their technical resources in pursuit of larger integrated activities when such an opportunity arose. To reduce operational costs associated with processing numerous small activities, program officers had also been asked to achieve an average project size that was larger than in years past—CAN$250,000 for 1993–94.[97]

Another, largely unwelcome, issue intruded upon IDRC operations given its scarce resources, especially in terms of personnel. External Affairs was keen to get the Centre involved in funding projects in recently democratized Eastern Europe.[98] Western Europeans, and especially Germans, were very interested in pursuing this agenda. What it meant for development budgets directed toward the South was, in 1991, unknown, but IDRC's board felt it could not be beneficial, given the huge demands placed on limited funds for help in bringing those countries that had been under Soviet control up to Western living standards; it was worried about the hemorrhage of donor funding to a relatively wealthy area. Still, when Ottawa evinced an interest in a policy that could have serious implications, one way or another for the Centre, the board was bound to consider it.

And that they did in early March 1993. The discussion was wide-ranging. At the outset, most governors were opposed, arguing that to do so would be beyond IDRC's statutory mandate and that as a matter of policy, it should not detract from its primary concern, funding research for development in the South. That position stated, others were ready to accept that, as a matter of *realpolitik*, the Centre was compelled to take the step contemplated by

External Affairs, but they cautioned against taking any kind of a leadership role in Eastern Europe or the former Soviet Union. As the debate wound down, Bezanson was authorized by the board to continue discussions with External Affairs, bearing in mind the position of the board and on the clear understanding that any activities undertaken by IDRC in Eastern Europe would have to be underwritten by additional funding, which would, of course, avoid the diversion of Centre funding destined for Southern partners. This issue became one that all donors would eventually address, especially those based in Western Europe.

IDRC did provide funding for Ukraine's Dnipro River rehabilitation program, but the support was additional to the Centre's budget, as demanded by the board. Eventually, another CAN$4 million was provided to IDRC, followed by a further CAN$8 million in 1997. That phase ended in 2000. Nor was the experience one of unalloyed happiness. As was noted, "Twenty-five years of partnership with countries from the South did not fully prepare IDRC to meet the specific challenges prevailing in the old Soviet Union, then called the Confederation of Independent States. The Centre had to adapt quickly and tailor its approach to resolving unprecedented problems, most importantly of which was the fact that the old USSR had been a closed society for the better part of seven decades and had therefore missed out on many of the paradigm shifts that had characterized Western evolution in the 20th Century and many of the familiar conditions in which the Centre was comfortable operating were absent or significantly different." That said, its program officers, along with Ukrainians, prevailed and the various research activities funded produced an impressive number of concrete results.[99]

Each division prepared an overview for board consideration of its activities following the presentation of the corporate program framework, showing how their programs fitted into the new direction and structure. For example, Maureen Law's Health Sciences division had organized its activities into two major elements—health, society, and the environment, and health systems—through which it focused explicitly on people and their communities.[100] The Navrongo Health Research Centre, based in Northern Ghana, a very successful IDRC-supported project, fell under this category. With Centre help, it became a leader in African research studies and a forerunner in applying new computer technologies to help make life better for the people of the region; mortality rates were reduced by about 23 percent in a very short time. With funding and advice from IDRC, Navrongo incorporated information technologies into its work—Geographic Information Systems, which made it easier to analyze data and organize research results, and ICTs and access to Healthnet, an IDRC-supported satellite-based communications service.[101] That provided the health centre with linkages to the Internet, email, and other electronic resources, which helped the Ghanaians to access other research findings, share the results of their own, and confer with colleagues around the world. As the health centre's assistant director commented in May 1996, "The Navrongo Demographic Surveillance System and the GIS have become the backbone of major research activities at the Centre," while its director noted that "Without IDRC support ... there was going to be a big problem!"[102] Years later, a new president of IDRC, Maureen O'Neil, paid a courtesy visit to NHRC, long after the Centre's involvement had ended. The entire town of ten thousand turned out to again thank IDRC for helping, moving her to tears.

A like result pertains in China, where, although Centre assistance has long been obscured through the passage of time, its funding helped to fundamentally change government practice in that country. IDRC-supported epidemiological work on the incidence and risk factors for tuberculosis among rural infants, and dengue fever among tropical villagers, and reproductive health work on the high incidence of repeat abortions in Shanghai, started with a strong focus on preventative care and education.[103] This necessitated a Chinese partner looking beyond mere technical supply-side obstacles to develop socio-economic and community-specific needs assessments. The results of this work, "the development of well trained and integrated village-township-county rural infants tuberculosis surveillance, diagnosis and service systems in three counties," was adopted as part of an ongoing national campaign sponsored by Beijing, which coordinated it with the World Health Organization. It became the backbone of similar preventive efforts in about five hundred counties with notable declines in the morbidity of children under five.

Similarly, a program of research undertaken in Tanzania resulted in significant success in terms of reducing the burden of disease. The Tanzania Essential Health Interventions Project (TEHIP) was a joint venture between IDRC and that country's Ministry of Health. Inspired by the World Bank's *World Development Report* of June 1993, such interest was created among international development organizations that the Centre convened a meeting in Ottawa, which was co-sponsored by the World Health Organization, the World Bank, and IDRC. It brought together 150 representatives from developing countries, development organizations, governments, and academia to "examine weaknesses in national and international programs for equity oriented health development in developing countries" and agreed on "practical steps to increase the scope and effectiveness of partnerships and investments for health."[104] As the conference wound to a close, it was decided that IDRC, with (eventually) CAN$16 million of funding from the Canadian International Development Agency, would take responsibility for testing the feasibility of health planning based on local estimates of the burden of disease and cost-effectiveness considerations in the context of decentralization.[105]

Through a long and winding administrative road, TEHIP was eventually established in October 1996 and set out to test the feasibility of an evidence-based approach to health planning in two rural districts in the country, Rufiji and Morogoro. It was tasked to "effectively plan and deliver essential health interventions based on burden of disease and cost-effectiveness, and; to measure, assess and document the overall impact and lessons learned in delivering selected health interventions at the district level."[106] Its impacts would be determined far into Maureen O'Neil's tenure as president, and will be discussed in Chapter 6, so suffice it to note here that it has been construed an important success in the field of applied health research, reducing child mortality by a very significant percentage and greatly exceeding its objectives. For the Centre, it was one more kudo, although it did not conceive of it in that way. Its reputation as a research for development organization was enhanced among the donor community and among Tanzanians as results from TEHIP greatly exceeded expectations.

Anne Whyte and the Environment and Natural Resources division spoke of their commitment to interdisciplinary research and integrated development and how the division had organized its program activities around global program initiatives.[107] These were implemented through teams of program officers working across the division's two programs, Centre-wide program themes included those noted above, such as food systems under stress and technology for SED and ENR global program initiatives. These included water resources management and urban environmental management, and involved program staff in the regional offices and other divisions based at headquarters. It also contained "special initiatives"—Agenda 21, Middle East peace talks (to be discussed below), and others.

Caroline Pestieau, the director general of Social Sciences, laid out her division's plan, which included the theme of integrating environmental, social, and economic policies, and she chaired the task force that brought together representatives of all the divisions and ROs' funding projects in that theme area.[108] As she told the Executive Committee, "The task force approved the theme statement and started the compilation of projects and proposals. Regular meetings and systematic contact with regional office representatives will allow the task force to focus the theme and to monitor the contribution made by the project funded under it." As well, the division "had a particular interest" in the second enunciated theme, technology and environment. Martha Stone's Information Sciences and Systems division had also plugged itself into the CPF,[109] as had Corporate Affairs and Initiatives.[110] The latter's remit lay with special initiatives, the research information program comprising the public information program and the library, the program for innovation systems management, and the evaluation unit. The regional offices also weighed in with their overview statements as they reflected the dominant themes existing at the Centre. It was an entire IDRC chorus, all singing in tune and together.

The months since Bezanson's appointment had been a period of unprecedented change. Some of that had been externally imposed, while other parts had been internally driven. Included in the long list was a new strategy, budget cuts, a downsizing of almost 20 percent, a major restructuring, the introduction of new financial and administrative arrangements, an opening up of planning processes, and the myriad of new responsibilities that had resulted from UNCED. The president told the board that "Taken altogether, it is not hyperbole to state that the extent of our transformation has few parallels in organizations of any type, let alone research organizations."[111] All of this agitation and change had been accompanied by anxiety and worry among Centre staff. Indeed, in some instances, "trauma" would not have been too strong a word to use to describe reactions. However, and while it may have reflected Bezanson's trust that not too much more would be facing IDRC in the future, he also believed that it found itself in an excellent strategic position with a relatively protected financial base that would allow it to give expression to the new strategy and the corporate program framework. While that would prove to be hugely optimistic, whatever happened, he hoped, it would result in a year of consolidation. That, too, was optimistic.

The Expert and Advisory Services Fund (EASF) and Peace in the Middle East?

As IDRC was settling into its new configuration, a challenge emerged, this one reflecting the esteem in which it was held in the Middle East.[112] The process had begun in 1992 with the establishment of the EASF, with funding from CIDA, following an approach to the Centre to manage a mechanism that could support Canada's role as gavel holder of the Refugee Working Group in the Middle East peace process. David Viveash, then at the Department of Foreign Affairs and International Trade (DFAIT) and, later, Canada's representative to the Palestinian Authority, was keen to secure IDRC involvement. He knew the organization well and admired its ability to handle difficult files in inhospitable regions; he also knew that the Centre was "plugged into intellectual networks both in Canada and in the Middle East," which could potentially assist Canada in its work.[113] This was one of the few times in its history that IDRC actively supported the pursuit of Canadian foreign policy objectives. The Centre's initial task was to engage experts to investigate issues raised for both the EASF and for any other of the four working groups on water, the environment, regional economic development, and arms control and regional security. The Expert and Advisory Services Fund became an important instrument for contributing research, dialogue, and networking to the Palestinian refugee issue.

When Israel and the Palestinian state negotiated the Declaration of Principles (also called the Oslo Accords) in August 1993 and signed a framework for the future relations between the two parties on 13 September 1993, the result was the establishment of a Palestinian Interim Self-Government Authority. Momentum was created that promised to change the complexion of the region. IDRC wanted to be there along with the other bilateral and multilateral donors that were poised to move into the region to help secure the fragile peace. This reflected a promise made by Barbara McDougall, the secretary of state for foreign affairs, to "assist the Palestinians to take their future into their hands."[114] As Centre staff knew, the needs of Palestinians living in the West Bank and Gaza (WB/G) were great. Working in the region would not be a new experience for IDRC, only a more rewarding one, or so it was hoped. Since 1985, it had supported a modest number of projects in the WB/G, like funds awarded to Jad Issac's Applied Research Institute of Jerusalem for "Water in the West Bank and Gaza Strip: Current Status and Future Prospects."[115] As well, it had good relations with NGOs and other donors that were active in the territories, while it had also demonstrated that it could act flexibly in a highly volatile and changing environment in a significant capacity-building program for reconstruction.

However, IDRC's mandate in the West Bank and Gaza was envisaged to be much broader than it became; in response to the president's proposition to the board in October 1993, it agreed to the establishment of a Centre presence where the actual arrangements would be submitted to the government for approval. The Middle East Regional Office (MERO), led by Fawzy Kishk, and including a senior program officer from the Middle East office, Eglal Rached, and the regional director from ROSA, Marc Van Ameringen, was charged with developing a strategic and operational framework for IDRC's future involvement in the Occupied Palestinian Territories (OPT) within a regular programming framework. MERO would take into consideration certain special requirements of the OPT, such as strategic planning, governance, science and technology policies, municipal planning, and the rehabilitation of the handicapped, among others. A mission, scheduled to visit on 1–10 March, was to investigate the strategic and operational framework for IDRC's future involvement in the OPT. It would investigate development needs and political/institutional conditions, priorities as seen by the Palestinians, Canadian priorities and policy interests as expressed by CIDA and Foreign Affairs, the Centre's strategic and programming framework, as well as the intentions of other donors. Consideration of this mission ended with Baruch Goldstein's 25 February massacre of twenty-nine Palestinians at the Ibrahimi Mosque.

Still, IDRC continued to consider the situation in the OPT, especially in view of the tragedy. As staff knew, research activities and capacity building in science and technology had been neglected in discussions between Palestinians and donors. This needed to be addressed in order to allow the Territories to tackle their longer-term development needs. The list of problems was long: unemployment had reached 40 percent; public infrastructure and social services were grossly overstretched; and the fragile natural resource base was threatened with irreversible damage. The major preoccupation of many of those involved in the WB/G was the urgent need to stimulate economic development, provide productive employment and income-generating opportunities, address the urgent need for improvements and upgrade public infrastructure like water and electricity supply, solid and waste-water collection and disposal facilities, roads, telephones, and educational and health facilities. Further, there was requirement to build long-term Palestinian research capability; universities like Birzeit located in the West Bank, while not short of students, were short of research funding. As well, the uncertainties of the peace process, despite the recent Oslo Accords, and the atmosphere of political crisis in the OPT worked against any sense of longer term planning. Centre staff involved with the issue hoped that recent events would lead to more political stability, which was a prerequisite for longer term strategic planning. That essential element was not being given adequate consideration by most donors, who were focusing their efforts on infrastructure building and setting up institutions. Reflecting its experience in South Africa, IDRC had an important role to play in this area, and it could be instrumental in assisting in the formulation of longer term research and development plans.[116]

Those were raised in a Centre document, which highlighted the extent of IDRC initiatives in the OPT.[117] Among these were projects involving water or, more accurately, the lack of it. These included land/water/environment, irrigation and water management with the Applied Research Institute of Jerusalem, activities developed through certain working groups like those focused on rainwater catchment. As well, following the change in 1995 to program initiatives, a major project—People, Land, and Water—underwrote support for this very serious issue in the Middle East. Significantly, the Centre also funded a joint Israeli-Palestinian project on the management of a mountain aquifer. This was a particularly important collaborative project that had proceeded even in the teeth of the second Intifada. As the board was told in late 2002 with some understatement, "With the intensification of the Israeli-Palestinian conflict over the last two years, conditions for research in Palestine have become more difficult."[118] Still, researchers on both sides continued to co-operate to the extent it was possible, primarily by email and telephone in order to "avoid any suggestion that they were negotiating with each other." As well, the project's final meetings were held outside the region, but those helped to shore up its findings, and it was to the two teams' credit that, despite a worsening political situation, with IDRC support they continued to research the issues swirling around the two states and their attempts at effectively and equitably managing the shared aquifer that underlay their border.

Work in the Middle East, and particularly in the West Bank, has not been easy. Still, as IDRC programming has evolved, it has helped to reduce the feelings of destitution experienced by people in the region. Among this has been "support for policy-relevant research related to governance and democratization; better management of small and medium enterprises and the promotion of more efficient and equitable allocation of resources; and, better planning and sustainable management of stressed natural resources." As well, on behalf of a number of others, IDRC managed the Scholarship Fund for Palestinian Refugee Women, which supported undergraduate university studies by Palestinian women from refugee camps in Lebanon. This initiative responded to a situation that affected the worst off—women in refugee camps in the Middle East, faced by abject poverty and a lack of opportunity. Finally, the Centre established another program initiative, Peacebuilding and Reconstruction, which has also allocated funds to help support research on Palestinian refugee issues.[119] As this chapter is being written in January 2009, a crisis of enormous proportions is unfolding in Gaza, which makes this funded research even more compelling.

Back to the Future: A New Liberal Government and More Change

On 4 November 1993 the Conservatives were defeated by the resurgent Liberals under Jean Chrétien. This put paid to any thoughts of "relative financial stability." On 22 February 1994, Minister of Finance Paul Martin tabled his first budget, which reduced the international assistance envelope by 2 percent for fiscal year 1994–95. That reflected, the minister said, the country's "very difficult budgetary situation" and the necessity to get its "fiscal house in order."[120] It would be frozen at that level for the following two years. Still, when Minister of Foreign Affairs André Ouellet visited IDRC on 22 March 1995, he told the gathered crowd that "we have tried not to be too harsh on the Centre. We have tried to avoid a slashing budget that would curtail or compromise the good work of the Centre. I had the chance to argue successfully with my colleagues for not too substantial cuts for the Centre."[121]

He might have done that, and the reduction could have been much worse, but for an organization battered and assailed since the early 1990s by various forces, the Martin cuts were too much. For example, program appropriations were only 62 percent of what had been originally envisaged for 1994–95, and it was clear that the Centre would again have to make severe cuts against what it had in the pipeline for 1995–96. Mulroney's much-heralded promised parliamentary appropriation for the Centre of CAN$115 million did not bind the hands of the new government, and the amount for that year was reduced to CAN$111.9 million. During 1995–96 it hit CAN$96.1 million, where it remained during the rest of Bezanson's time as president. As Maureen O'Neil took up the office in April 1997, it was further reduced to CAN$88.1 million, dropping to CAN$86.1 million the next year, where it stayed until 2001–02 fiscal year. John Hardie was to later call these cuts "the water torture effect of the decline in real terms."[122] That meant that Centre possibilities were constrained and the reduced parliamentary appropriation "would necessitate some adjustments."[123] There were few possibilities. The Centre had to maintain its program/administrative cost ratio of 70:30; moreover, Bezanson thought that it would have to demonstrate further efficiencies by moving the ratio closer to 75:25. However, further significant downsizing, he thought, would not be necessary given the efforts IDRC had taken in the area of revenue diversification.

As the fiscal year wound down, the president could not be sanguine about the future, despite all that had happened and the efforts that had been undertaken to construct a more streamlined, cost-effective, and sensitive organization. He correctly told the board that over the recent past, the "climate in which the political and public will to sustain cooperation for development was anything but strong."[124] Canadians, battered by recession, a jobless economic recovery, and growing uncertainty and fear about what lay ahead, gave scant consideration to the even less fortunate in the South. Unemployment, which had climbed to 11 percent, and a federal deficit of CAN$45 *billion* projected for fiscal year 1994–95 were terrifying, and news accounts documenting their effects filled the media. Public opinion polling demonstrated that Northern citizens felt increasingly pessimistic about their lot, and especially that of their children.

Those beliefs were intensified by the international context—conflict in Angola, Cambodia, Somalia, and Bosnia were in the headlines daily, and they continued to drain the lion's share of UN resources and efforts. The much-heralded peace dividend, announced when the Cold War ended in 1991, found itself squeezed between what seemed to be a disintegrating Russia and the global recession. As a result, the 2 percent reduction in IDRC's parliamentary appropriation could be seen as a success, especially given that the Centre remained "relatively little known and poorly understood in [Canada]."[125] It would have to be extremely active at all levels of government and it could now be taken as a given that "our grant can never again be assumed to arrive as naturally as night follow[ed] day."

Bezanson believed that, given all this, over the next ten years many public institutions would cease to exist, and those that did would be very different from what Canadians had known since the end of the Second World War. These new hybrids "will be structured differently, governed differently and funded differently. And they will have three broad elements as defining characteristics—those same elements which governors underscored in IDRC's *Strategy* and in the established objectives for 1994/95: agility/ flexibility/ resourcefulness; perseverance with success (the converse also applies), and continuous strategic planning."[126] The Centre would be one of those that survived if he had anything to do or say about it. Those pressures reminded him, he told the board, of William Shakespeare's famous passage from *Julius Caesar*, IV.iii: "There is a tide in the affairs of men, / Which, taken at the flood, leads on to fortune; / Omitted, all the voyage of their life / Is bound in shallows and in miseries." The former would be the Centre's future, or so he hoped.

What initiatives had IDRC taken to ensure its financial stability, given a declining parliamentary appropriation? As noted above, it had cut Centre staff by about 20 percent. In *Strategy 1991*, it had set a target, met by early 1994, of CAN$1 million in average program appropriations per program officer. IDRC also cultivated other donors. During 1993–94, for example, it entered into CAN$18 million worth of contract research. During the next two fiscal years, it hoped to attract about the same. Associated with contract research was a 10 percent fee to cover the indirect costs of administering funds from other donors, which generated about CAN$500,000. The Centre had also introduced a cost-recovery policy in 1993–94, and during the next fiscal year it hoped to realize CAN$700,000 in research management fees. Finally, IDRC at times administered funds for other organizations, which also helped to increase its bottom line. In 1993–94, it was overseeing fifty-five externally funded projects that contributed CAN$48.5 million to projects into which the Centre put CAN$17.2 million.[127]

The Blue Planet Lottery

The board considered a further initiative, put to it by management and that suggested thinking so far out of the box as to bring into question whether the box had ever existed. The Blue Planet Lottery also demonstrated the desperation that IDRC felt when contemplating its future and, while not strictly speaking a part of its intellectual history, is suggestive of *ideas* that the Centre was willing to contemplate. It was "a high-risk venture" and represented an entirely new attempt to generate financing for world development. As was well known, public funding for ODA was in decline everywhere—indeed, in free fall when measured against past pledges and targets—and the Blue Planet Lottery was a first attempt to establish a constructive alternative and not as whacky as it seemed on first acquaintance.[128]

As described, it was "an international lottery of the skies" that could generate US$500 million to US$1 billion annually to fund sustainable development projects in LDCs. If IDRC kicked in some funding to determine its viability, a fixed percentage of the funds generated by the lottery would be covenanted to the Centre. Revenue would be raised from airline passengers electing to pay an optional US$5 supplement over ticket price to enter the lottery. It was calculated that if only 15 percent of passengers flying annually elected this option, gross revenue raised would amount to about US$1 billion. The Blue Planet Group, a London-based non-profit organization that was undertaking the feasibility study, needed from the Centre CAN$187,500 for its share. It was provided, as was an additional CAN$200,000 at the board meeting in October 1994. Similarly, Ford Foundation contributed US$250,000 and the Rockefeller Brothers Fund kicked in US$75,000.

The whole initiative represented an example of divergent thinking. The project summary for the grant, when discussing it in relation to the Centre's objectives, stated:

> As the ability of central government to raise revenues in support of the wide range of social and economic programs is increasingly strained, priority is given to those programs and services that can only be supported from national revenues while other programs are opened to new funding arrangements most notably by conversion to private sector activities. Foreign aid and development assistance in general and development research in particular are

not readily amendable to transfer to private sector interests. The Blue Planet Lottery of the Skies is a marvelous example of the lateral thinking that offers the opportunity to seek non-government funding for international development activities.[129]

Nor was IDRC alone in contemplating this sort of thing. There had been schemes mooted for UN lotteries; the *Philadelphia Enquirer* had noted in its 25 August 1994 issue that "To those who can't endure a gambling gap while traveling, science, engineering and business management have teamed up to provide relief." All the major airlines had expressed an interest in in-flight gambling.[130] That might not be acceptable to the travelling public (say, blackjack and roulette games being played while one jetted across the Atlantic), but the idea of the Blue Planet Lottery was—that a passenger's airline ticket with its code across the bottom would provide the winning number, as long as the US$5 had been paid. It was an attractive idea.[131]

Bezanson told the board that, given all the adverse activity, this sort of revenue diversification was not only a necessity, it was critical. The Centre had "to broker new and much-expanded financial resources to meet the needs of the new reality." Specifically, "we must hope that Blue Planet succeeds."[132] It was, however, eventually grounded. As Bezanson left the Centre to take up his new position at the Institute of Development Studies in the United Kingdom, the rosy projections offered in the earlier 1990s seemed to be wilting. While the scheme was tried out on a charter airline, Britannia, the amounts projected did not add up to hundreds of millions, but rather "only" hundreds of thousands. The Centre's involvement officially ended in mid-1997. Still, it had been well worth investigating its potential.

More Revenue Diversification

Indeed, anything and everything was worth investigating as IDRC contemplated its viability. In March 1995, a document suggested just that: "La viabilité institutionnelle du CRDI à moyen et long terme est mise en question, d'une part, par la reduction des credits parlementaires et, de l'autre, par l'évolution des perceptions sur la nature des liens entre le governement et les organisms finances à meme les fonds publics."[133] In his October 1994 report to the board, Bezanson had been as specific: "*Research institutes must diversify their sources of funding or they will perish.*"[134] Over the next eighteen to twenty-four months, it was imperative that the Centre do three things, or so management believed. Revenue diversification had to be enhanced and IDRC had to intensify its activities in the South. As well, it had to convince Canadian parliamentarians of the necessity of funding it, and all staff had to adopt a common approach to its survival. The goal, as the document suggested, was "Assurer la sécurité financière dont le CRDI a besoin pour conforter et élargir ses actions malgré la reduction des credits parlementaires." How would it do this? A number of considerations came into play, among these: financing activities and programs with partners other than the government; mobilizing a small group of influential Canadians who knew IDRC and the new government and would apprise the Liberals that it was a worthwhile organization that must be saved; creating partnerships between Centre staff, Southern researchers, and other development organizations that could demonstrate the utility of IDRC's approach; articulating key messages that would mobilize external support; and commercializing those research technologies and advisory services that the Centre had had a role in creating.[135]

All of that implied a shift from a passive to a pro-active mode in pursuing opportunities for outside funding, which generated considerable stresses within the Centre's corporate culture because it challenged long-standing assumptions about the nature and priorities of the organization, how it operated, and its relationship with the private sector. Philosophical discussions about the morality of changing direction in this way clashed head-on with the question of the legitimacy of co-funding arrangements, or contractual relationships with other agencies. And once staff got beyond this sort of discussion, which the pressures of a declining parliamentary appropriation demanded, they moved on to questions like: What kind of co-funding measures? Under what conditions, with whom, using what means, and for how much?

The Creation of the Program Initiative or IDRC as "Postmodern Public Institution"

Still, as turmoil swirled around them ("things were not going well"), Centre staff continued to do their jobs, and the preparation of various strategic documents went ahead.[136] Over the next few years, the pace of change was almost as hectic as it had been during Bezanson's first three years, much to his chagrin. It also had an enormous impact on the Centre's intellectual history, raising such questions as what ideas were worthy of follow-up, how to respond to the government's scorched-earth strategy in its pursuit of addressing the budget deficit, and how to continue its work in the South. Bezanson had spoken of IDRC becoming a postmodern public institution, where it would increasingly resemble a private sector one. Among its characteristics would be "responsiveness to the market and a much-reduced dependency on public financing."[137] Other key features of this new organization were an immediate relevance to national issues and priorities, a dynamic and adaptive management, and the ability to tackle big issues and provide solutions to major problems. That had been IDRC's trademark for the past twenty-five years, but the president was determined to redefine it, at least for parliamentary consumption.

That was made both more difficult and easier at one and the same time as IDRC faced a new fiscal reality in 1995–96; its appropriation was CAN$96.1 million, 14.2 percent less than that received for fiscal 1994–95. However much IDRC staff might complain about what was expected of them, the president took the only discernible course. And even that was not all that clear, covered by underbrush and laced with various traps designed to snare the unsuspecting traveller. Bezanson told the board that "the path we now take and our success on that chosen path will determine not merely what kind of future IDRC will have, but whether IDRC will have a future."[138] While much of what the Centre already had put in place over the previous three years— *Empowerment through Knowledge* and its corporate program framework for 1993–97—would provide guidance in making future choices, it was also evident that staff needed to look for areas of possible adjustment and to review (yet again) different ways of doing things. And (yet again) a further 20 percent reduction in operational expenditures was forecast by 1998–99, which would mean again cutting back on the 470 staff who remained at the Centre. All of this had been forecast by Bezanson very early in 1995. "Never," had he then opined, "have we convened under circumstances [which we now face]."[139]

However, the president also made some unfortunate choices, a major one being his decision to, as John Hardie has said, "dismantle the divisions," perhaps not the act itself, but how it was accomplished.[140] In late June 1995, Bezanson sent the necessary document, "Completing the Transition," to the executive committee.[141] It dictated that the Centre would get rid of its divisions and make redundant three of the directors general—Maureen Law, Martha Stone, and Anne Whyte—and promote Caroline Pestieau to the position of vice-president of programs. Four program divisions were thereby merged into a single Programs Branch, which took effect on 1 August 1995. Of some significance, Health Sciences completely disappeared, unlike the other three programming divisions, which had retained the names of their research fields, such as "economics" and "natural resource management," and "social policy."[142] Still, that did not mean that "health" programming completely disappeared. Indeed, Graham Reid remembered that it was merely disguised: "Basically I joined IDRC Health Sciences Division, arriving in

Ottawa in March 1995. A few weeks later, Health Sciences Division was shut and I questioned why I had been hired out of Uganda since there must have been some pre-warning for such a huge move. It was at this time that I penciled down 'a Trojan horse plan to keep health alive in IDRC but suitably camouflaged within an environmental context.' In partnership with Gilles Forget and Don de Savigny, this plan was eventually accepted and launched as the Ecosystem Health PI."[143] And that was a very innovative, unusual, and successful program initiative.

IDRC had a number of programming choices to make in light of its changed circumstances. While CPF 1993–97 consisted of the six core themes noted above, as well as programs relating to sustainable and equitable development, management was compelled to recognize the need for further focus. Within each one of these themes would be a number of program initiatives that would be large, coherent, integrated program networks.[144] The first of these was by simplifying the corporate program framework (CPF) by integrating the three Sustainable and Equitable Development programs in the area of environment and natural resources into core themes that were no longer treated as separate program areas. Most Centre attention, however, was invested in achieving a greater concentration of programming at the regional level. During 1994, IDRC had undertaken an exercise to identify program priorities in Asia with a view to providing a focus within the broad confines of the corporate framework. The main elements of the Asia program had been approved by the board in October 1994, and comprised seven areas of program focus within the CPF: (1) pan-Asia networking; (2) biodiversity conservation and sustainable use; (3) community-based natural resource management; (4) communities in transition—managing social and economic change; (5) health communities—determinants and responsibilities; (6) adoption of sustainable technologies; and (7) Cambodia human and natural resources.[145]

All programs and activities on the continent had been consolidated into a single Asia program under the Regional Office for Southeast and East Asia (ASRO) regional director. This had provided the base for program concentration in Asia, building large networks of targeted research that would save money as well as, it was hoped, attract it. Indeed, the Asia Development Research Forum (ADRF) was born at this time from discussions between ASRO staff and Bezanson to build on informal networks of senior Asian policy researchers. Anchored in the regional office, ADRF soon developed a prescient policy research agenda focused on economic and financial governance, aging, and environmental and conflict management issues. Key elements of the research were picked up throughout the region. Given the network's existence, it contributed to the Centre's understanding of the region's priorities, program development, partnership building, and linking research and policy.

Still, despite such successes, the war against the Canadian deficit continued unabated and Centre personnel remained convinced that there was every reason to expect a continuation of strong downward pressure on the federal government's budget in general, and in funding for official development assistance in particular. The two principal implications for IDRC were borne out by early 1995; further reductions in operational costs and enhancements would be needed in cost-effectiveness and in the real and perceived value of Centre activities in the areas in which it operated. This program was initially proposed as an experiment with the intention of possibly extending it to other regions once more experience had been gained. However, given the budget pressures to focus resources on a smaller number of program initiatives that could have real effect, and with increased urgency to identify areas that offered the best opportunity for leveraging funds from other sources, the timetable for other regional exercises was brought forward. Work on a set of program priorities to focus activities in Africa and the Middle East was begun even as the Asia document was being presented to the board. Indeed, as has been seen in Chapter 4, the board had decided in 1990 to concentrate programming on Africa and this corporate program framework had reiterated that. Similarly, programs were being worked out for Latin America and the Caribbean, the intention of which was not to examine new program areas, but to examine areas of concentration within the CPF where there was a good prospect both for a developmentally significant set of scientific activities and for the omnipresent necessity of leveraging.

Clearly, the Centre was, as the president told the executive committee, "at a crossroads."[146] It had to devise a strategy that would help in the troubled years ahead. As it had made a unique contribution to development since its creation, it would have to engage in a new type of uniqueness for its future, what Maureen O'Neil was to later call "start[ing] its own experiment."[147] Over the next year, that took place as the Centre took steps toward issue-based programming and away from silos based on disciplinary programs, beginning with a development problem, drew in the relevant disciplines, and linked scientists more effectively in order to learn from each other.[148] Further, policy-makers and civil society were engaged at the outset. That continued a long-term process that had worked for greater effectiveness through enhanced focus and greater multi-disciplinarity, although staff often neglected to comment on its effectiveness in project-completion reports.

However, the priority-setting exercises that IDRC had undertaken through an intensive consultation among the various responsibility centres in Ottawa and the regions had yielded some fruit. The main criteria that staff had been asked to consider when evaluating priorities were development payoff, potential for revenue diversification, and the likely visibility of the "product" and IDRC's contribution. On that basis, the projects proposed for funding in the 1995–96 fiscal year were fitted into clusters, with each cluster representing a separate set of issues where it was judged that the Centre could make a difference. The results of that exercise were fifty-four(!) clusters of program activities allocated to three regional and one global program budget. This solution, described to the board as "interim," left IDRC with a very dispersed program and twelve responsibility centres developing, approving, and monitoring programs. Indeed, given that situation, Bezanson was driven to note that "the Centre's human and financial relationships [were] spread too thinly to provide sound research management and to build partnerships with other funders."[149] The changes in the organization's structure and strategy opened the door to more radical programming changes.

The number of program categories in IDRC was reduced from twenty-seven to five, and all projects were now developed under five sustainable and equitable themes: (1) food systems under stress; (2) integrating environmental, social, and economic policies; (3) technology, environment, and society; (4) biodiversity; and (5) information and communication. It was noted that "As IDRC moves into a more interdisciplinary mode, it is expected that information projects will play a greater role in linking, enriching and demonstrating the potential of all its projects. IDRC will fund projects in health with reference to policy integration and to ecosystem health." However, most Centre funding would now go to program initiatives (PIs) that had been developed with Southern researchers to respond to a particular set of issues. PIs had grown out of the clusters developed earlier, and each was managed by a team of program staff with, usually, three to five core members, and almost all PI teams included both regional and Ottawa-based program staff.

In October 1995, the board had approved the following criteria defining a program initiative:

> definition of a research problematique that is of fundamental importance for development in one or more regions and the establishment of specific goals, objectives, expected results and performance indicators to address the issue(s) over a specific time period (3–5 years); establishment of real, connected networks, i.e., the participating institutions are linked directly with one another (though not necessarily electronically in the short term, as this is difficult in parts of Africa); seeking opportunities to work inter-regionally; cross

disciplinarity; specific identity and the generation of sufficient excitement to attract other donors and agencies to share in the funding; opportunities for Canadian linkages and collaboration; and opportunities to raise IDRC's profile.[150]

All that took some getting used to even though IDRC had been moving intellectually in that direction for some time. As Anne Whyte, the former director general of Environment and Natural Resources, put the new condition, "decision making in the PI teams was extremely difficult because it was kind of a committee approach to things—that has costs and benefits. It's more participatory and therefore it is very much more difficult to get any kind of decision coming out."[151] The shift was also inevitable, or so she thought: "It has partly to do with the fact that the Centre got smaller. If you are bigger you can have these interdisciplinary teams stay within divisions and they are working just fine, but when you reduce your resources and you have to get smaller, then what do you do?" Clearly, the change was "radical and traumatic," yet possessed of "pathbreaking potential." It was also an attempt "to change the grammar of development" in the sense of tackling problems in a more integrated way.

It was also accomplished in about five days—all PIs were determined in less than a week, and then the scramble to secure a position began. The divisions were all blown apart as well, and the structure that had sustained IDRC since its establishment was no more as what would eventually come to be called program areas took their place. It was all very chaotic. John Hardie later wrote that "it can be observed that many institutions have downsized; some have restructured their operations; and a few have tried to reorient their thinking towards a new paradigm. *Very few had done all three at the same time.*"[152] Yet that was what the Centre accomplished—a remarkable institutional innovation that would, over time, contribute to better results. Bezanson put it mildly when, in a memorandum to all staff, he noted that the change that had happened was "perhaps the most radical since [IDRC] was founded 25 years ago."[153] "We are moving into new territory," he told staff, "and will need high levels of tolerance as we try new mechanisms and structures. We will need to accept a degree of ambiguity because it will simply not be possible to lay down all the new 'rules of the game' *a priori* with great precision."

Indeed, the implications of the shift were profound. Hardie noted in a paper prepared after the fact that the complexity of the change was paralleled only by the dislocation it caused. IDRC transformed its own structure based on new ideas about how science was being, and should be, conducted, and its own experiences and circumstances.[154] While some of Hardie's approach smacks of *ex post facto* reasoning, it was also true that the Centre had been concerned about the limitations and inadequacies "of the traditional monodisciplinary approach to science—the 'Western scientific paradigm.'" In an article in the journal *Minerva*, Helga Nowotny, Peter Scott, and Michael Gibbons had described such a shift:

> [*The New Production of Knowledge: The Dynamics of Science and Research in Contemporary Societies'*] broad thesis—that the production of knowledge and the process of research were being radically transformed—struck a chord of recognition among both researchers and policy-makers. Of course, like all theses that gain a certain popularity (and notoriety), this thesis was radically simplified, and collapsed into a single phrase— "Mode 2." The old paradigm of scientific discovery ("Mode 1")—characterized by the hegemony of theoretical or, at any rate, experimental science; by an internally driven taxonomy of disciplines; and by the autonomy of scientists and their host institutions, the universities—was being superseded by a new paradigm of knowledge production ("Mode 2"), which was socially distributed, application-oriented, trans-disciplinary, and subject to multiple accountabilities.[155]

As Hardie noted, the authors pointed to the main contrast with the "traditional" as being "between problem solving, which is carried our following codes of practice relevant to a particular discipline" and "problem solving, which is organized around a particular application." That statement, he thought, "capture[d] the essence of what IDRC is trying to achieve through the program initiative system."

The new system, with its major changes in programming, was put into practice during the 1996–97 fiscal year. "Teams," the board was told, were "transforming a pipeline of often disparate projects into a coherent program and [were] elaborating revenue diversification strategies." This suited Bezanson's agenda, which had, in some ways, grown more hardline over his time at the Centre. That was the case with the freedom that program officers had had since the establishment of the Centre: "Programming ... assigned an exceptional level of discretion and authority to individual program officers and program divisions [that would have to change]."[156] Caroline Pestieau remembered that prior to this change, "a program officer ran with their project for ages and you couldn't move them away from it. There was no sharing of files or partnerships, so there was very little flexibility. When [someone left IDRC], their whole portfolio had to be redistributed. There were also many small projects which were very labour intensive and all more or less disciplinary. The idea behind the program initiatives was, on the one hand, to economize, but it was also supposed to be forward looking and multidisciplinary, there would be more flexibility—you would have a PI team—and you could move people in and out of it."[157] And that flexibility, at least according to Van Ameringen, "was the only way to maintain some dynamism in the organization."[158]

Later, the mechanism for approving program activities was changed. The objective of the new approach was to increase the effectiveness of the PI system by moving the emphasis away from individual projects and more toward the integrated program initiative concept. The proposal had four components: (1) the team prepared a detailed three-year prospectus; (2) its approval would follow an in-depth review; (3) the funding approved for one year would be allocated to the PI, together with delegation of signing authority to the PI team leader; and (4) there would be enhanced monitoring of the program initiative performance and regular reporting.[159] Ray Audet thought the proposal held much potential and was "consistent with our desire to encourage the integrated PI concept, to empower the PI team, to streamline the approval process, to provide Governors with more substantive input into the program planning and to maintain our assurance of accountability." It did do all those things and remains the system at IDRC to this day. This partly administrative, partly ideas-driven change certainly reflected the new direction in which the Centre continued to orient itself.

IDRC's world had been turned upside down by the change of government that had, in turn, sparked language like "blurring" and "lack of clarity." "It was an incredibly stressful and unstable period," as Rohinton Medhora, the current vice-president of programs, remembers: "You didn't know whom you were working for. You were often given responsibilities, such as managing a team, without the authority to do so."[160] Another senior officer called the resulting managerial situation impossible: "team members would dedicate as little as 8 percent of their time to one program initiative. The team leaders that were elected by their teams initially had no managerial authority and were expected to manage the team 'en motivant les gens.'"[161] Further, "program staff selectively voted themselves into PIs at will. Due to the cutbacks, staff tended to vote themselves into three or more PIs, thereby increasing their chances of remaining employed if one PI was dropped. As explained by a former director, it should have been managed otherwise: "People should have been selected, saying: 'Your talents lie best with A, B, C, and not A, B, C, D, E, F, G, H...' Some people signed up for five or six [PIs]."[162] Medhora also pointed out the unreasonable situation that pertained when, over several days, all the PIs were determined. He thought it an object lesson in how not to undertake a transition: "So the end result was chaos. I'm very cognizant of 'letting a thousand flowers bloom' philosophy and innovation and all of that, but that still needs to be managed." Maureen O'Neil agreed with that assessment; while she thought Bezanson's move to program initiatives was inspired, "five days was probably not enough time to accomplish such a fundamental transformation."[163]

Clearly, it fundamentally changed the way IDRC went about its business, intellectually and administratively, and brought into question the issue of how much of its programming was demand-driven, one of the touchstones upon which David Hopper had insisted. When the Centre's lifeblood was programs and divisions, the individual program officer negotiated the project that had to be in the field of his or her competence with a research partner. Still, the initiative almost always lay with the Southern researcher. IDRC's claim had always been that it *responded* to the demands of those it funded. With a program initiative, the *team* became the more important mechanism, and that required coordination of activity and work. The team drew up a research program through a framework paper that several individuals produced. This went through the approvals apparatus and was eventually accepted (or not) by the board. That process provided a much tighter framework within which research partners had to work. The teams would also be mobile, their boundaries permeable. Each one would have a leader, but there was a symbiotic relationship between the leaders and other members on any successful team. In one way it was all more efficient because everyone knew the parameters, but it did change the rules of the game. While it was welcomed by senior management—at least by those who were left—they were under no illusions that the new system would not need to be watched. Bezanson had talked of the "resource immobility" and its detrimental effect on programming that had come with having staff in the same discipline organized in divisions.[164] "However," he told the board, "if we organize according to problems, similar issues of territoriality and inertia will inevitably arise, albeit in a different dimension and in a multilateral setting. Resource mobility is essential for effective, innovative and efficient approaches to problem solving."

Bezanson welcomed that "new" efficiency. Throughout his tenure as president he had often spoken of "controlling chaos" and how, by the mid-1990s, among many private sector corporations, there was "almost no reference to the management tools of the past (e.g., detailed work planning, hierarchical quality-control mechanisms, and Program Planning and Budgeting Systems."[165] He was certainly doing the former now. Still, it was difficult. "The easy years," he wistfully told the board, "are part of what now seems like ancient history. There are no easy years now." He might have talking about himself with that sentence. His term expired on 16 April 1996, and he was not reappointed until eight days later, returning to the Centre on 7 May, but only on a one-year extension following serious government consideration of his presidency.

That blow hurt, especially given all that had gone on during the previous five years. However, it also hurt IDRC. The interpretation that many outsiders made of Bezanson's one-year appointment was that the government was going to wind up the Centre or have it absorbed into CIDA, although this was not true. Bezanson told the board that "sources as diverse as the President of the Association of Universities and Colleges of Canada, members of the Parliamentary Committee to which we make regular reports, developing country partner organizations, and private foundations have all mentioned this interpretation."[166] That had a very bad effect on staff morale, and some were actively seeking alternative employment. It was also detrimental to revenue diversification; staff were being confronted with some organizations' reluctance to even discuss co-funding with IDRC because of the doubts about its future. Given the way the situation was unravelling it was unlikely that targets would be met for that fiscal year, with a negative effect on programming that would spill down the line. However, the government, and in particular Minister of Foreign Affairs Lloyd Axworthy, recanted, later extending an invitation to the president for another full term. By that time, Bezanson had made his arrangements with the Institute for Development Studies and was anticipating his departure.

There was one last ignominy left for the president as Axworthy settled into Foreign Affairs in early 1996—the destruction of IDRC as an entity and its replacement by a "virtual" Centre based at the University of British Columbia and two other Canadian universities. Bezanson was furious and let David Strangway, UBC's president, know exactly how he felt. The dismantling was also encouraged by Ivan Head, then at UBC, an act for which Bezanson never forgave him. Oddly, the idea had come from a speech at IDRC's twenty-fifth birthday party given by Maurice Strong, who had said that the Centre "must be more and more a Centre of ideas, innovative thinking and creative partnerships with other institutions in Canada and throughout the world.... Within Canada, it could become a 'virtual' centre linking with and drawing upon other key centres of excellence and expertise and helping to focus, channel and lever their capacities in cooperative inaction with their counterparts throughout the world."

The UBC *démarche* also led to Bezanson suggesting the establishment of a task force led by Strong and which brought together a small group of "eminent Canadians from academia, business and the non-governmental sector to consider and report on ways and means of preserving and building Canada's intellectual and innovative policy capacities in the field of international development research."[167] That concept was much changed from the one that had initially been put forward as the task force rationale—to find additional funding for IDRC, as well as the North-South Institute and the International Institute for Sustainable Development. Axworthy did not favour the UBC plan, and at a meeting between the minister and the president on 10 July, the former confirmed that it was dead.

The Strong task force also made a contribution to IDRC's intellectual evolution, even though its earlier iteration had focused on increasing funding. Axworthy's response, clear as he wrote the foreword, must have had a soothing effect on the Centre as what the minister included described so much of its mandate:

> [T]his report serves as a wake-up call. It reminds us of the stark reality that Canada in the years ahead will be challenged to maintain its place amongst the world's 15 leading economies, let alone the G7; that our role in the world will depend upon more than our accumulated international reputation; that knowledge-based economies will dominate the 21st century; and that Canada will be obliged to earn its way in that new century, in large part through its intellectual capacity and global leadership. It also tells us that our historical role as international "good neighbour" can no longer be dominated by the donor-recipient exchanges of the past; that our strategic advantage will lie in our potential to become an effective "knowledge broker"; and that our immediate challenge is to build and strengthen the institutional arrangements required for this role.[168]

The key conclusion was that "Canada's place in the world cannot be taken for granted. It will need to earn its position through intellectual and policy leadership and through its strategic advantage as a multidimensional 'knowledge-broker,'" both ideas that played to the Centre's intellectual strengths and its practice for the past twenty-five years. For example, it also noted that "The call for networking has become the mantra of the 1990s"; IDRC had been constructing and facilitating those since its establishment. Furthermore, it believed that in the past, "far too much knowledge for development has been centralized, generalized, and loaded onto a one-way conveyer belt from North to South, without adequate regard to practical problems, local conditions, or its ultimate end-user. The Task Force conceives of a system based on the most up-to-date communications technologies, but which is dynamic and participatory, where the conveyer belt is multi-directional, and where local adaptations can be fed back into the system and disseminated more broadly to other practitioners." That described the ethos at IDRC almost perfectly, and the development of the Unganisha project, described in Chapter 6, was a concrete manifestation of that. It was also far ahead of its time as Robert Valentin and Paul McConnell thought about radical new uses for information and communication technologies (ICTs).

Its effects lingered into the new millennium, and the Centre funded follow-up studies based on its broad principles. For example, a further report, Howard Clark's "Formal Knowledge Networks: A Study of Canadian Experiences," suggested that "more research and understanding was necessary on the nature of knowledge networks and how they promote sustainable development."[169] Furthermore, the report illuminated Canada's competitive advantage in organizing and using formal knowledge networks. The other part of the endeavour was action-oriented, stressing the need for learning by doing. That meant immediate action on forming a knowledge network around a pressing issue, which led to forming the climate change knowledge network in the spirit of the Strong Task Force Report's recommendations. As the project completion report noted, "The consultative project development process enabled under the IDRC grant ... has helped to ensure that the network meets needs identified by the members themselves. The information technology capacity building has been a cost-effective way of improving the ability of developing country organizations to research, communicate and disseminate their work. The climate change network has provided useful, practical lessons for the formation of other knowledge networks intended to promote sustainable development."

However, in terms of broad policy strokes, what was left to Bezanson as he contemplated his future with the organization that he had completely remade? One thing was to continue to address the issue of administrative expenses that had an impact on the intellectual direction of the Centre. It was clear that transaction costs were high and rising in late 1996. New dynamics were required by the move away from smaller projects that were planned and monitored by individual program officers toward much larger, integrated, multidisciplinary activities under the direction of self-directed teams. The learning curve was steep and Centre officers were only just beginning the climb. As was pointed out, one result of that mountain of new education that had to take place was that the consultation and transaction costs between the team leader and different members of the team, between researchers of different disciplines, and between headquarters and regional offices had increased significantly.[170] It was fervently hoped that the promulgation of *Corporate Program Framework (CPF) II* and the selection of specific program initiatives that went along with it would be helpful in terms of dealing with the problem.

Another was to develop the *Corporate Program Framework to the Year 2000*, which also reflected the issues raised above. Adopted by the board in October 1996, it defined IDRC's objectives for the period as: "To foster and support the production and application of research results leading to policies and technologies that enhance the lives of people in the developing regions; and, to mobilize and strengthen the indigenous research capacity in the countries of those regions, particularly capacity for policies and technologies for more healthy and prosperous societies, food security, biodiversity, and access to information."[171] It also offered up six themes that constituted the programming framework under which the Centre would concentrate its resources. They included: (1) food security, (2) equity in natural resource uses, (3) biodiversity conservation, (4) sustainable employment, (5) strategies and policies for healthy societies, and (6) information and communication. Under those themes the Centre funded fifteen program initiatives, the primary programming units, and the driving force of IDRC's programs.[172] It had been a long road with many a winding turn.

Clearly, the program framework that was in place by later 1996 was radically different in form and content to what had prevailed earlier. Underlying that new framework was a complete institutional transformation. Methods of working, reporting relationships, roles and responsibilities, and approaches to accountability and to budget allocation, had all been modified. The amazing thing was that all of it had happened together in the face of a massive external force—a greatly reduced parliamentary appropriation. The sudden impact of that had made charting the way toward the future exceedingly complex, not least because all the components were interdependent. As was pointed out, "Abandoning a divisional program structure based largely on traditional scientific disciplines in favour of one based on development concerns and their corresponding research problematiques is a considerable step into the unknown. It is now imperative for the Centre to design a framework for its programming that will balance the often competing imperatives of focus, innovation and opportunity, and that will establish clear directions for the coming years."[173] That would be left to a Centre without Keith Bezanson even though Axworthy had offered him another term.

Conclusion

Bezanson left for good on 16 April 1997. He could take some solace in the fact that IDRC was still in existence and, while it would take time to manifest itself, could ultimately be pleased that it had been saved from the wrecker's ball largely by the measures he had taken. It seems indisputable to us that he did save it, something for which he has received little credit. While he now claims that he should have implemented change much faster and without so much consultation, it may not have been possible for him to do so in the 1990s given IDRC's corporate ethos. Bezanson might have echoed Gilles Forget's take on the transition: "J'ai appris deux choses: 'Shit happens' et 'There is a silver lining under every cloud.'"[174] The Centre he left in 1997 bore little resemblance to the one at which he had arrived in 1991, a sure sign of the massive upheaval that had taken place. Gone were the divisions, the old fiefdoms from David Hopper's day, replaced by the as-yet largely untested program initiatives. As well, IDRC had become more of an "environmental" organization, one of the intellectual paths it followed to save itself when the government announced that it was Canada's Agenda 21 implementing agency. That gave it an intellectual direction, but that could be followed only if the organization remained financially stable. That led to the other important policy that Bezanson had articulated during his time in office—the search for additional funding as the Centre's parliamentary appropriation nosedived given government obsession with ridding the country of its deficit. Here, he was more successful given that, by 1997, about 20 percent of IDRC's budget was raised from sources other than government. His successor would later comment that he was "imaginative and innovative in making the best of a really bad situation.... If he had not been successful in keeping IDRC off one of the various [Conservative] cut lists, we would not be talking about it now."[175]

Daniel Morales-Gomez, then a program officer, contributed a series of cartoons entitled "Veni, Vidi, Vinci: A Brief Story of Keith at IDRC" to the retirement party, held on 26 February 1997. The "Vinci" was coloured red and a pool of what can only be blood is clearly discernible under it. The first frame is of Bezanson, his right foot placed on three books with the heading *Empowerment through Knowledge*, an unexploded bomb beside him, which had clearly just landed and that had resulted in a crack travelling up the wall of what is IDRC. Later, he is portrayed as consulting his closest advisers—three monkeys, which represent see no evil, speak no evil, and hear no evil. His question is "mirror, mirror on the wall, who's ..." That led to "The staff was energized and inspired," a frame of the president behind a podium, saying, "And finally," while IDRC staff, all asleep and snoring, occupy chairs in front of him. The cartoons went on for about twenty-five pages, each more scathing than the last. That series was probably unfair. He left an IDRC in place for Maureen O'Neil to inherit, which might not have happened had a president with a different skill set than his been in charge. It wore him down, as the final cartoon frame suggests. "Nothing is forever," it says as Bezanson takes his wagon and heads for the Institute of Development Studies at the University of Sussex. To that, he could only have muttered "Thank God."

Notes

1   IDRC–A, Email, Pauline Robert-Bradley to Christopher MacCormac, "All Staff Meeting," 27 May 1991.
2   IDRC–A, KB, "Development: Yesterday, Today, and Tomorrow," Keynote Address to the Study Group on the Exchange of Development Information, Paris, 4 October 1993.
3   Interview with Keith Bezanson, 30 September 2007, Seaforth, England.
4   Interview with Walter McLean, Waterloo, 23 November 2009.
5   Interview, anonymous.
6   Interview with Keith Bezanson by Martin Kreuser, 16 June 2004.
7   Interview with Caroline Pestieau, 12 August 2008, Ottawa.
8   Pestieau interview.
9   Bezanson interview. See also IDRC–A, Pauline Robert Bradley to Management Group, 3 July 1991.
10   IDRC–A, Anne Whyte to KB, "To Continue the Conversation," 12 August 1991.
11   IDRC–A, Evaluation Unit, CAID, "Evaluation Strategy," 1 December 1992.
12   See, for example, IDRC–A, Email, Pauline Bradley-Roberts to Centre, 20 September 1991.
13   IDRC–A, "Report on July 4 [1991] Management Group Meeting."
14   IDRC–A, Anne Whyte to KB, "To Continue the Conversation," 12 August 1991.
15   IDRC–A, BG 49/26, Robert Auger to Governors, 19 October 1992.
16   IDRC–A, FA 49/12, "Regional Office Review; Executive Summary and Status Report," 5 October 1992.
17   IDRC–A, EC 88/10, KB to Members of the Executive Committee, 12 June 1992.
18   IDRC–A, FAC 2001 (01) 11, MON to Finance and Audit Committee, "Review of Regional Presence, 2000–01," 11 January 2001, 2. The board changed ROSA's status in 1993. Originally, "its main purpose was to facilitate Centre collaboration with the democratic forces in South Africa which are preparing the way for majority rule." Further, when the board agreed to change the office to a regional office for Southern (as opposed to South) Africa, "it was pointed out that IDRC will now have four offices in Africa. It was suggested that the realignment of the offices could be considered at some future date." In September 2001, ROSA was closed.
19   Peter Stockdale, "Pearsonian Internationalism in Practice: The International Development Research Centre," McGill University, unpublished Ph.D. dissertation, 1995, 388.
20   IDRC–A, KB to Governors, 19 October 1993. In support of this diversification thrust, IDRC would enter into agreements with such donors as the US Agency for International Development, where it would charge a management fee for overseeing a proj-

ect. See, for example, "IDRC-USAID Collaboration in Capacity Building for Economic Analysis in the WARO Region: The EAGER Initiative," a contract of US$4.068 million, which the Centre managed over a five-year period. EAGER is the acronym for Equity and Growth through Economic Research. Similarly, the UK's Overseas Development Administration, the precursor to the Department for International Development (DFID), used IDRC. As explained by Joanne Alston, the head of central research at DFID, "we have found it very positive to work with [IDRC], on the whole. They have got networks, they have got credibility on the ground, they have got offices on the ground and we don't have that. We have our own offices that deal with bilateral programs and they are like little dotted links between them and our research efforts, but they're run from different business units, so we don't actually have our own staff on the ground dealing with research programs. We think that they have got staff with a very good understanding of how you build up research capacity and a methodology that is very good." Interview with Joanne Alston and Paul Spray, London, 3 October 2007. As Spray suggested, DFID was swayed by "them having the staff and [already established regional offices and] us having the money, to be completely crude about it.... Give them a slug of money."

21 Interview with Anne Whyte by Martin Kreuser, 6 August 2004.
22 IDRC–A, BG 99(01), Meeting of the Board of Governors, 21–22 January 1999, 4.
23 IDRC–A, A.D. Tillett to Regional Directors, "Ottawa Issues: SMC & BOG," 4 November 1994. Naturally, there was some thought given to the effect of resource diversification on IDRC. As Eva Rathgeber wrote, "It is clear that any such partnership will of necessity require compromise in the Centre's programming strategies." Eva Rathgeber, "Turning Failure into Success: The Deconstruction of IDRC Development Discourse, 1970–2000" (Ottawa: IDRC, September 2001), 3.
24 IDRC–A, Daniel Chudnovsky and Lydia Makhubu, "Evaluation of the African Technology Policy Studies Network," Evaluation no. 322, August 1996, 13.
25 IDRC–A, EC 86/9, "Global Micronutrient Initiative," n.d.
26 IDRC, *Empowerment through Knowledge: The Strategy of the International Development Research Centre* (Ottawa: IDRC, 1991), 7. Much of the following text comes from this document.
27 IDRC, *Empowerment*, 14. Still, as Bezanson remarked with respect to interdisciplinarity, that "it should be kept in perspective—theologies are not required." See IDRC–A, "Management Meeting, 1–5 June 1992: Notes of Discussion."
28 Inteview with John Hardie by Martin Kreuser, 29 June 2004, Ottawa.
29 Interview with Brian Davy by Martin Kreuser, 28 June 2004, Ottawa.
30 Brian Davy interview.
31 Interview with Brian Davy, 13 August 2008, Ottawa.
32 IDRC–A, BG 48/5, "Proposed Transition Budget, 1992–93," March 1992, 29.
33 IDRC–A, BG 48/5, "Proposed Transition Budget, 1992–93," March 1992, 30; emphasis not in original.
34 IDRC–A, Director General CAID to Board of Governors, 27 April 1992, 1.
35 IDRC–A, Director General CAID to Board of Governors, 27 April 1992, 3.
36 IDRC–A, EC 90/4, CAI, "Program on Innovation Systems Management (PRISM): A Strategy for Improving Research Effectiveness," 8 January 1993.
37 IDRC–A, HRC 94/2, "IDRC President 1993–94 Performance Report and Proposed Objectives for 1994–95," March 1994.
38 IDRC–A, Naser Faruqui, "Encouraging and Capitalizing on Innovation at IDRC," Evaluation no. 507, November 2001, 10.

39   Interview with Frene Ginwala, 9 May 2007, Johannesburg.
40   Interview with Trevor Fowler, 10 May 2007, Capetown.
41   IDRC–A, 52/31, "Program Delivery: Report to the Board of Governors," March 1994.
42   Interview with Brenda Lee Wilson by Martin Kreuser, 25 June 2004, Ottawa.
43   IDRC–A, FA 49/12, "Regional Office Review: Executive Summary and Status Report," 5 October 1992, 8.
44   IDRC–A, KB to Board of Governors, "IDRC on the Move," 26 June 1992, 3.
45   IDRC–A, EC 88/9, KB to Governors, 12 June 1992.
46   See Canada, House of Commons, Standing Committee on External Affairs and International Trade, 25 March 1992, unedited transcript of hearing. See also Office of the Auditor General, "Well-Performing Organizations" (Ottawa: Queen's Printer, December 1988).
47   Interview with Jean-Guy Paquet by Martin Kreuser, 23 June 2004, Ottawa.
48   See, for example, Gilbert Rist, *The History of Development from Western Origins to Global Faith* (London: Zed Books, 2002), 178–96; Maurice Strong, "Beyond Rio: A New Role for Canada" (Ottawa: External Affairs and International Trade Canada, 1992); Maurice Strong, "After Rio: The Question of International Institutional Reform" (Ottawa: National Roundtable on the Environment and the Economy, 1995); Maurice Strong, David Runnalls, and Roy Culpepper, *Brazil '92: Getting down to Earth* (Ottawa: North-South Institute, 1992); Adam Rogers, *The Earth Summit: A Planetary Reckoning* (Los Angeles: Global View Press, 1993); Caroline Thomas, *Rio: Unravelling the Consequences* (Essex: Frank Cass, 1994); Ranee K.L. Panjabi, *The Earth Summit at Rio: Politics, Economics, and the Environment* (Boston: Northeastern University Press, 1997); Wolfgang Sachs, *Global Ecology: A New Arena of Political Conflict* (London: Zed, 1993).
49   United Nations Development Program, "Agenda 21, Chapter 1, Preamble," accessed at http://www.unep.org/Documents.Multilingual/Default.asp?DocumentID=52&ArticleID=49&l=en.
50   IDRC, *Annual Report, 1992–93* (Ottawa: IDRC, 1993), 2, accessed at http://idrinfo.idrc.ca/archive/corpdocs/003197/1992-93/ar1992-93.pdf.
51   Theodora Carroll-Foster, *A Guide to Agenda 21 Issues, Debates, and Canadian Initiatives* (Ottawa: IDRC, 1993), 4.
52   Interview with Maurice Strong, 6 May 2006, Ottawa.
53   Canada, House of Commons, Standing Committee on External Affairs and International Trade, "Minutes of Proceedings," 23 March 1993, 5813.
54   IDRC–A, Email, Pauline Robert-Bradley to Shelflist, 20 September 1991.
55   IDRC–A, "Flora MacDonald Appointed as Chair of the International Development Research Centre," 17 June 1992.
56   Interview with Tim Dottridge, 13 August 2008.
57   IDRC–A, BG2000 (10) 23, "Sustainable Use of Biodiversity Program Initiative: Request for Board of Governors Approval to Proceed to Phase II," October 2000, 2.
58   IDRC–A, EC 89/4, KB to Executive Committee Members, 21 September 1992. The press communiqué issued on that occasion picked up the idea, but with a slightly different wording: "In order to build up the international network of expertise and contacts necessary for achieving sustainable development, the Canadian Government will invite the Secretary General of the United Nations and other key organizations like the World Bank to propose appointments to the Board of Governors of the IDRC, thereby establishing a new partnership with the United Nations system."
59   IDRC–A, SS-1, John Hardie, "The Program Initiative System in IDRC: Origins and Rationale," 21 May 1998, 3.

60 Dottridge interview.
61 The ten countries are Cambodia, China, Indonesia, Laos, Malaysia, Papua New Guinea, the Philippines, Sri Lanka, Thailand, and Vietnam.
62 Interview with David Glover by Martin Kreuser, 25 June 2004, Ottawa.
63 IDRC–A, BG 2000 (06) 09, Evaluation Unit, "Annual Corporate Evaluation: Report 2000," June 2000, 16.
64 Daniel Bromley and Geila Castillo, *Evaluation of the Economy and Environment Program for Southeast Asia (EEPSEA)*, February 2000, 14.
65 Pierre-Marc Johnson had an interesting pedigree. In 1976, he successfully ran as the Parti Québécois candidate for the district of Anjou. Premier René Lévesque appointed him to the Cabinet in 1977, and he was re-elected in 1981. Johnson served as minister of labour from 1977 to 1980, minister to consumers, co-operatives, and financial institutions from 1980 to 1981, minister of social affairs from 1981 to 1984, and attorney general from 1984 to 1985. He was chosen leader of the party in 1985 following the resignation of Lévesque and, as a result, became premier of Quebec. The PQ was defeated in the December 1985 election and Johnson, until December 1987, served as leader of the Opposition. Of some interest, Maurice Strong encouraged government to appoint him as IDRC president when Head left, which the Mulroney Conservatives rejected. Strong thought Johnson would have made an incredible leader. Interview with Maurice Strong.
66 Interview with Terry Smutylo by Martin Kreuser, 14 June 2004, Ottawa.
67 IDRC–A, BG 49/26, Robert Auger to Governors, 19 October 1992.
68 Interview with Barbara McDougall, Toronto, 2 June 2009.
69 IDRC–A, "Introduction to IDRC's Corporate Program Framework," 1 March 1996.
70 IDRC–A, BG 49/20, "Technology for Sustainable and Equitable Development: Policy Options and Institutional Frameworks," October 1992.
71 IDRC–A, BG 49/21, "Information for Sustainable and Equitable Development," October 1992.
72 IDRC–A, BG 49/25, "Food Systems under Stress," October 1992.
73 IDRC–A, Evaluation no. 425, Anne Whyte and Fiona Mackenzie, "Cities Feeding People: A Review of the CFP Program Initiative of IDRC," 2 July 1999, 4. As the evaluation notes, CFP became "an international champion for the importance of urban agriculture as a development problem to which the major international donors should be paying more attention. CFP could not have done this without drawing on a long track record of IDRC work and leadership in urban agriculture and related fields. Building on past success, CFP has not only positioned itself well with respect to the development problem: it has helped significantly to shape the way the problem is understood and approached by other agencies."
74 See IDRC–A, Julie Hauser to KB, "Outline of Briefing Book," 26 January 1996. INTESEP was defined by the Centre as seeking to develop and promote research to:
 • understand the relationships among environmental, social, and economic imperatives and foster the integration of environmental concerns into social and/or economic policies;
 • develop research methodologies, analytic frameworks, and other tools to enable effective integrated policy development and implementation; and
 • foster the development of communication and decision-making processes between and among researchers, policy-makers, and beneficiaries to enable the formulation of effective integrated policies.
75 IDRC–A, BG 51/22, Anne Whyte to Board, 18 October 1993.

76 IDRC–A, BG 97 (10) and BG 97 (10) 24, "International Network for Bamboo and Rattan Secretariat: Progress Report," October 1997, 13.
77 Stephen McGurk, Project Completion Report, "International Network for Bamboo and Rattan (INBAR) Phase II," 16 April 2002, accessed at https://irims.idrc.ca/iRIMSTemp/8DB9000E-3CC2-49F2-9AC9-F7F0C3EF6796-0BA1/rad5DC18.PDF.
78 Interview with Cai Mantang, 25 November 2006, Beijing. Cai was, in some ways, typical of IDRC-supported researchers. In 1986 the Centre funded his training in Canada, where he attended the University of Toronto for several months, then Laval. It also paid for a fellowship at Oxford, then funded his training in a doctoral program in India. The five program areas that IDRC funded were: (1) production; (2) post-harvest technology and utilization; (3) socio-economics; (4) information, training, and technology transfer; and (5) biodiversity and genetic conservation.
79 IDRC–A, 96-8300-01, Project Summary, "International Network for Bamboo and Rattan (INBAR) Phase II." Grant approved 17 October 1996.
80 IDRC–A, 96-8300-01, "International Network for Bamboo and Rattan (INBAR) Phase II." Grant approved 17 October 1996.
81 IDRC–A, Project Summary, 96-8300-01, "INBAR Phase II," 23 August 1996.
82 IDRC–A, "Evaluation Report of the International Network for Bamboo and Rattan," May 1996, 6.
83 IDRC–A, "IDRC Corporate Program Framework, 1993–1996," March 1993.
84 IDRC–A, EC 93/09, Office of the Auditor General of Canada, "Audit of the International Development Research Centre," December 1994, 3.
85 "Audit of IDRC," 10.5.
86 IDRC–A, BG 53/37, Evaluation Unit, CAID, "Annual Corporate Evaluation Report," October 1994, 1.
87 IDRC–A, "Survey and Assessment of IDRC's Completed Projects," 20 December 1994, 2.
88 IDRC–A, HRC 93/06, KB to Board of Governors, 15 March 1993.
89 IDRC–A, Email, John Hardie to KB, 1 April 1992.
90 IDRC–A, Senior Management Committee, "Principles for Project Review," July 1992.
91 IDRC–A, BG 50/2, Program of Work and Budget, 1993–94, March 1993.
92 IDRC–A, BG 50/1, "Corporate Program Framework," 19 February 1993, 1.
93 IDRC–A, EC 90/5, KB to Executive Committee, 14 January 1993.
94 For Earth's Sake, 1. "The decision to support and fund the Commission on Developing Countries and Global Change originated from a proposal developed in a series of meetings at the International Development Research Centre (IDRC) in Ottawa. The meetings had been convened to consider options for supporting developing countries in the Human Dimensions of Global Change Programme. Both this program and the International Geosphere Biosphere Programme (IGBP) were conceived in recognition of the implications of global warming and other environmental problems, and of the need to study those problems and related responses on a global scale."
95 IDRC–A, BG 50/2, Program of Work and Budget, 1993–94, March 1993, 7.
96 Those programs related to SED were grouped as follows:
    Environment and Natural Resources Systems: Low-input sustainable agriculture, water resources management, green technologies, sustainable cities
    Information Sciences and Systems: Policy research, Capacity building for sustainable and equitable development, software development and applications
    Health Sciences: Threats to health, health policy, and programs
    Social Sciences: Social policy, learning systems for change, macro-economic policy, industrial and agricultural policy, regional integration

Corporate Programs: Evaluation, Canadian partnerships, human resource development, gender and development, innovation systems management, public information, research library

See IDRC–A, BG 50/1, "Corporate Program Framework," 19 February 1993, 10–11.

97 The allocation throughout IDRC was as follows:

Divisions	Allocation ($m)	% Total
Corporate Affairs and Initiatives	$11.9	14.2
Environment and Natural Resources	$11.1	13.2
Information Sciences and Systems	$9.1	10.7
Health Sciences	$7.6	9.0
Social Sciences	$6.7	8.0
ASRO	$5.5	6.5
LARO	$5.4	6.4
WARO	$5.0	6.0
EARO	$5.0	6.0
MERO	$2.9	3.5
SARO	$2.9	3.5
ROSA	$1.4	1.7
Special Program Activities	$8.5	10.1
President's Office	$1.0	1.2
	$84.0	100.0

98 See IDRC–A, BG 49, Doug Daniels, "Presentation to the Board of Governors," 22 October 1992.

99 IDRC–A, Jean-H. Guilmette, "Lessons Learned out of Six Years of Cooperation in Environmental Management Development in Ukraine," 3 November 2000.

100 IDRC–A, Maureen Law to Executive Committee, 5 February 1993.

101 IDRC–A, "Healthnet: Satellite Communications Research for Development," Evaluation Report no. 261, 29 March 1994, 2–3. The satellite had been launched in 1991 and Healthnet's general objectives included: to contribute to the capacity of researchers and professionals in health and health-related fields (focusing on Africa) to effect change through the provision of access to information and communications capabilities; to strengthen the capacity of health-related country institutions to provide more effective support for the research process; and to test, demonstrate, and evaluate the use of packet radio and satellite communication technologies in support of health information flows and networking in order to determine the sustainability and appropriateness of this technology.

102 Terry Smutylo, Sarah Earl, Beth Richardson, "Origins and Achievements of the Navrongo Health Research Centre," May 1998.

103 IDRC–A, Stephen McGurk to Terry Smutylo, "Review of 20 Years of S & T Cooperation with China," 17 April 2000, 3.

104 IDRC–A, "Final Report," Future Partnerships for the Acceleration of Health Development, IDRC, 1993.

105 IDRC–A, Cleopa Msuya, Mohamed Amri, Peter Ilomo, and Mastidia Kahatano, "Essential Health Interventions Project and Tanzania Health Interventions Project: Evaluation Report to IDRC and MOH," Evaluation no. 410, May 1999, 6.

106 IDRC–A, Terry Smutylo, "Feedback to TEHIP: Selected Findings from the Policy Influence Case Study on Tanzania Essential Health Interventions Project," August 2004, 2.

107 IDRC–A, Anne Whyte to Executive Committee, 5 February 1993.

108 IDRC–A, Caroline Pestieau to Executive Committee, 8 February 1993.

109 IDRC–A, Martha Stone to Executive Committee, 22 February 1993.

110 IDRC–A, Report to Executive Committee, 25 February 1993.

111 IDRC–A, HRC 93/5(R) "President's Objectives for 1993–94," n.d.

112 Much of this discussion comes from Bruce Muirhead and Ron Harpelle, "The International Development Research Centre and the Middle East," in Paul Heinbecker and Bessma Momani (eds.), *Canada and the Middle East: In Theory and Practice* (Waterloo: Wilfrid Laurier University Press, 2007), 149–51.

113 Interview with David Viveash, 26 February 2007, Ramallah, West Bank.

114 Barbara MacDougall quote.

115 IDRC–A, BG 51/26, KB to Governors, 18 October 1993. Other projects included: "Environmental and Health Hazards of Energy Sources in the West Bank and Gaza," Recipient: An-Najah University, Nablus; "Environmental Survey of the West Bank," Recipient: Israel/Palestine Centre for Research and Information; and "Pesticide Poisoning," Recipient: Birzeit University. As well, a significant study was undertaken in mid-summer 1993 that focused on the "Joint Israeli-Palestinian Management of the Mountain Aquifer." The aquifer contained the largest source of potable drinking water in the region. As the project completion report noted, "This project has to be seen as much as part of the peace process as a conventional research study. It was funded close to the time of the Peace Accord and advanced in parallel with growing rapport between the two sides. The process, which was enormously successful, was at least as important at the product. Researchers who barely knew one another and, indeed, who were suspicious of one another at the start, were easily collaborating with each other at the end. This is perhaps the best example of a "Third Track" study for water in the peace process (that is academic studies in parallel with the First bilateral and Second multilateral tracks).... The good feelings that have developed among the researchers actively involved in this project cannot be over-emphasized." See IDRC–A, Project Completion Report, David Brooks, "Joint Israeli-Palestinian Management of the Mountain Aquifer," 19 July 1995.

116 IDRC–A, "IDRC Mission to the West Bank and Gaza: A Preliminary Report," 1 March 1994, 3.

117 IDRC–A, BG 53/33, "IDRC Mission to the West Bank and Gaza," September 1994.

118 IDRC–A, BOG 2002 (10) 21, MON to Board, "President's Report to the October 2002 Board Meeting," 11 October 2002, 3. IDRC also oversaw a project that began in 2000, "Sustainable Management of the Dead Sea's Water Resources: A Comparative Analysis with North America," which included Israeli, Jordanian, and Palestinian scientists and planners, assisted by Canadian researchers from the Université de Laval. It was investigating the North American experience in the joint management of shared water resources to promote the sustainable development of the Dead Sea basin. François Farah, a program officer from Lebanon, worked out the general thrust of the program. It was his idea to make the IDRC strength of research management the underlying basis for the Canadian contribution to this potential minefield. In essence, Farah suggested encouraging the parties to share their numbers, data, and definitions, what they thought they knew about refugees, investigating what they could agree on and what needed more research to verify data. As Chris Smart, a former Centre manager, has noted, "One strength of this approach was that if everyone stayed cool and below the media radar, some meetings were able to bring Palestinians, Israelis, Jordanians, Egyptians, and Syrians to the table—though most would have denied it if word got out." Email, Chris Smart to Bruce Muirhead.

119 IDRC–A, BOG 2004 (03) 03, *Program of Work and Budget, 2004–2005*, 58.

120 IDRC–A, Paul Martin to Maurice Strong, 10 January 1994.

121 IDRC–A, Minister's Visit—March 22, 1995, "Statement of the Hon. André Ouellet."

122 IDRC–A, Email, John Hardie to SMC, 30 June 2000.

123 IDRC–A, BG 52/44, KB to Board, 14 March 1994.

124 IDRC–A, BG 52/44, KB to Board, 14 March 1994, 7.

125 IDRC–A, BG 52/46, KB to Directors General, 23 February 1994. However, even given its dismal recognition factor in Canada, it had succeeded in generating some income from outside the country. For example, during the 1993–94 fiscal year, IDRC's budget increased from CAN$115 million to CAN$142 million. The increase derived from the fact that CIDA contributed to two research initiatives; the Micronutrient Initiative (CAN$12 million) and a further CAN$15 million was provided following an IDRC-supported conference in October 1993 on Future Partnerships for the Acceleration of Health Development. Participants at those meetings reviewed the recent World Development Report, which suggested that the delivery of a low-cost, essential package of health support to LDCs could reduce infant mortality and morbidity by more than 30 percent. IDRC, with support from CIDA, the World Health Organization, and the World Bank, agreed to fund a pilot trial of this proposal in East Africa. That would become the Tanzania Essential Health Interventions Project (TEHIP), a hugely successful endeavour.

126 IDRC–A, BG 53/39, KB to Board, 4 October 1994, 6.

127 IDRC–A, BG 52/08, IDRC, *Program of Work and Budget, 1994–95*, 10.

128 Lotteries have been proposed for the financing of numerous things. For example, as Ruben Mendez, *International Public Finance: A New Perspective on Global Relations* (London: Oxford University Press, 1992), 273–74, has pointed out, lotteries were proposed at the United Nations as possible avenues to raising funds for development work.

129 IDRC–A, BG 53/18, KB to Board, 30 August 1994, 2.

130 IDRC–A, BG 53/18, KB to Board, 30 August 1994.

131 IDRC–A, BG 51/25, "Blue Planet: An Airline Lottery for the Globe," Concept Brief, August 1993.

132 IDRC–A, "President's Report to the October Board," October 1994.

133 IDRC–A, BG 54/51, "Assurer Notre Avenir: Un Cadre Stratégique," March 1995.

134 IDRC–A, BG 53/39, KB to Board, 4 October 1994, 4.

135 IDRC–A, Raffaella Zumpano to Governors, "Produits et services de CRDI: un concept de marketing," 16 March 1995.

136 Interview with Caroline Pestieau, 13 August 2008, Ottawa.

137 IDRC–A, BG 54/56, "President's Report to Board of Governors," March 1995, 3.

138 IDRC–A, *Program of Work and Budget, 1995–96*, March 1995, 9.

139 IDRC–A, EC 93/19, KB to Executive Committee, 19 January 1995. Bezanson listed four issues here: (1) Canada's fiscal situation was perilous; (2) the Canadian government was about to take action against that; (3) the actions about to be taken are of a depth and breadth that are unprecedented in Canadian history; and (4) as a result, IDRC's parliamentary grant will be reduced.

140 Interview with John Hardie by Martin Kreuser, 29 June 2004.

141 IDRC–A, Executive Committee Meeting, 22 and 23 June 1995, "Completing the Transition: Strategic Adjustments for IDRC, 1995," 19 June 1995.

142 IDRC–A, PRG-Dec99-B9, Caroline Pestieau, "Note on IDRC's Programming in the Field of Health," 26 November 1999. However, as Pestieau pointed out, the Centre had 140 active projects addressing health issues.

143 Email, Reid to Muirhead, 20 May 2009. Part of the reason as to why health-funded research did not disappear completely from IDRC was as a result of strong pushback from health staff. Caroline Pestieau, who became vice-president of programs following the administrative reorganization, noted in a memorandum to Health Sciences program staff that a meeting she had had with them had given her "a much better understanding than I had before of the strong positions IDRC has established in several research areas and of the possibilities we have to make a difference. But it also confirmed my conviction that we have to make some hard choices as we can't hope to make a difference in all the fields identified.... SMC agrees to consider proposals for two Program Initiatives, one on eco-system Health and one on Public Policy for Health. Senior management is also interested in examining the possibility of establishing a Water Quality Secretariat in the Centre.... I have asked Gilles Forget to assume responsibility for the Water Quality proposal, Don de Savigny for the Eco-system Health one, and Janet Hatcher-Roberts for the Health Policy one." IDRC–A, Pestieau to Health Sciences Program Staff, "Follow-up to August 23 Meeting with Health Sciences Program Staff," 28 August 1995.

144 IDRC–A, "Completing the Transition," 25.

145 IDRC–A, BG 53/31, "The Asia Program: IDRC's Strategy, Program, and Delivery in Asia," October 1994. See also BG 53/34, Resolution, "Asia Program," October 1994.

146 IDRC–A, EC 93/20, "Preparation of Program of Work and Budget for 1995–96: Discussion of Issues by the Executive Committee," January 1995.

147 IDRC–A, "Introduction by Maureen O'Neil, Corporate Strategy and Program Framework, 2000–2005," September 1999.

148 IDRC–A, Program of Work and Budget, 1996–97, March 1996, 29. Many of the following paragraphs come from this document.

149 IDRC–A, KAB to All Staff, "SMC Program Concentration Decisions in August 1995: Process and Criteria," 31 July 1995.

150 IDRC–A, PWB, 1996–97, 30.

151 Interview with Anne Whyte by Martin Kreuser, 6 August 2004.

152 Hardie, "The Program Initiative System in IDRC," 3.

153 IDRC–A, KAB to All Staff, 26 June 1995.

154 Hardie, "The Program Initiative System."

155 Helga Nowotny, Peter Scott, and Michael Gibbons, "'Mode 2' Revisited: The New Production of Knowledge," Minerva, 41, 2003, 180.

156 "Completing the Transition," 1.

157 Pestieau interview. Flexibility also extended to the team leaders, she thought. If there was a deficient senior program officer, he or she could never be demoted. "The idea with PIs and team leaders was that a person would be a team leader for three or four years. However, if the team was reconfigured, or the problem was rethought, then someone else could take the team leadership." It was also a good idea that they became more problem-oriented and multidisciplinary. They could address issues in the field better as issues tended to be multidisciplinary. "It was eighteen months of chaos."

158 IDRC–A, Caroline Pestieau, "Electronic Discussion on Program Management and Regional Presence," 9 February 1998, 3.

159 IDRC–A, FA 97/05, Raymond Audet to Board, 20 September 1996, 3.

160 Interview with Rohinton Medhora by Martin Kreuser, 28 June 2004.

161 Interview with Gilles Forget by Martin Kreuser, 16 June 2004, Ottawa.

162 Interview with John Hardie by Martin Kreuser, 29 June 2004.

163 Interview with MON, 17 October 2008, Ottawa. See also Interview with MON by Martin Kreuser, 30 June 2004, in which she noted that "the final transformation of program branch from a discipline base to PIs was done in a week. I can see why you would have to make the change so quickly because [Bezanson] was under the gun to make cuts and had to act. There is always endless bickering over program lines, not just us but in any organizations. He probably felt that he had to get a new show on the road and had to be able to show the Board and show a Minister that necessary changes had been made, that the Center was going to be fine and that form now on this is how it was going to do business. I'm sure that's what went through his head."

164 IDRC–A, BG 56/29, KB to Board, "Supplementary Note to 'Completing the Transition: Strategic Adjustments for IDRC, 1995,'" 22 June 1995.

165 IDRC–A, HRC 95/04, KB to Board, "My Performance during 1994–95," 17 March 1995.

166 IDRC–A, BG 57/06, KB to Board, "President's Report to the Board," 5 July 1996. However, Bezanson rejects that charge. As he has pointed out, all civil servants at his rank served at the pleasure of the government; it could have gotten rid of him at any time.

167 IDRC–A, Maurice Strong to Janice Stein, 25 March 1996. The other members of the task force were Jack Austin, Tim Brodhead, Margaret Catley-Carlson, John Evans, Yves Fortier, Gerald K. Helleiner, Pierre Marc Johnson, and Janice Gross Stein. They wrote that:

> For the purposes of this report, "knowledge" can be viewed as having three dimensions:
> • the creation of substantive knowledge in the form of both services and products, across a range of development issues;
> • the creation of knowledge-based networks that can multiply, disseminate, and expand knowledge; and
> • the building of the capacity to use, adapt, and build knowledge for sustainable development at the local level, and to build a base upon which effective and appropriate policy can be developed.

168 Maurice Strong et al., *Connecting with the World: Priorities for Canadian Internationalism in the 21st Century*, November 1996, iii.

169 IDRC–A, Project Completion Report, Christopher Smart, "Strong Report Follow-up: Engaging Canadians," March 2000.

170 IDRC–A, "President's Report to the Board."

171 IDRC–A, BG 59/14, *Program of Work and Budget, 1997–98*, March 1997, 35.

172 IDRC–A, "Briefing Note for the Minister of Foreign Affairs, the Honourable Lloyd Axworthy," 28 January 1998. For the fifteen program initiatives, see BG 59/14, *Program of Work and Budget, 1997–98*, 36–42.

173 IDRC–A, Policy and Planning Group, Draft, "Introduction to IDRC's Corporate Program Framework," 1 March 1996.

174 Interview with Gilles Forget, Ottawa, 16 June 2004.

175 Interview with Maureen O'Neil, Ottawa, 17 October 2008.

Chapter 6

MAUREEN O'NEIL AND A NEW MILLENNIUM, 1997–2008: ON THE ROAD AGAIN

> We shall not cease from exploration.
> — *T.S. Eliot, "Little Gidding"*
> *(No. 4 of* Four Quartets*)*

Maureen O'Neil took over a dejected and demoralized International Development Research Centre on 17 April 1997, only two months before a new chair of the board, former Department of Foreign Affairs Deputy Minister Gordon Smith was appointed.[1] As various staff recalled, the word she used most often as she moved around the Centre in those first days was "calm." It figured prominently in everything she said, as did her commitment to create stability in programming following the deep budget cuts of the early to mid-1990s. She later remarked that her "clearest challenge [was] to ensure that an organization that [had] lost so many colleagues over a five-year period [rebuilt] its *joie de vivre* and [felt] a sense of stability so that it could get to work."[2]

Following her inaugural address to staff soon after her arrival, she received a standing ovation from the 325 who remained of the 610 who had wished Keith Bezanson Godspeed as he had taken up the reins of office in 1991. John Hardie, the director of policy and planning, "had never heard it before ... nobody at IDRC had ever applauded a president.... People were just desperate for a period of stability and calm and she provided it."[3] The board took note, and also that she had "arrived in a troubled organization and dealt quickly, effectively, and transparently with difficult situations."[4] That was so characteristic of the new president, a function of her personality, superior management skills, and inclusive demeanour. While she was to benefit during the second half of her presidency from a growing parliamentary appropriation, during her first few years, it was to fall even further from the already-low Bezanson number, making things worse. However, O'Neil played the hand that she had been dealt with skill and finesse, working her cards to the utmost. Her obvious abilities impressed the board, board subcommittees, the president's office, program officers, and staff; watching the game she had entered, they bought into her system. Issues remained, but as Rohinton Medhora, now vice-president of programs, has noted, "at least you [knew] how they would be fixed. We talk a good game ... but from where I sat, I didn't know what that really meant until I saw this whole thing in action."

She came from a background that had been immersed in public policy of one sort or another for decades, some of it centred on domestic issues and some on things international and even developmental. For example, the latter took her to the United Nations. When O'Neil joined Status of Women Canada in 1978, a part of that job was also to represent Canada on the UN's Status of Women Commission, which began in that year and continued until 1986. It was impossible, she recalled, to do that kind of work "without reflecting on women in developing countries. That was a very big part of what the UN Status of Women Commission discussed."[5] The period had covered two world conferences on women, the first in 1975, which had started the United Nations-styled Decade of Women. Then participants worried about disaggregating the impacts in the South on women of different types of public policy ranging from unemployment insurance to development policy to education and property rights to marriage.

The Canadian International Development Agency (CIDA) was funding a number of projects that focused on women's issues and rights, and O'Neil was also sometimes involved with those. She was part of a group that dealt with legal reforms involving women from around the world, as well as how to grapple with the complexities of sorting out what approaches were useful for improving women's rights. When she was appointed deputy minister of citizenship in the Ontario government, her responsibilities included issues that had informed her stay at Status of Women Canada—the settlement of immigrants, human rights, and race relations. Being based in Toronto was also useful for her life's interests as "Toronto being Toronto, the people coming to see me and see my minister were largely from developing countries."

Upon her return to Ottawa in 1986, she took up the position of president of the North-South Institute, an organization that considered the effects of Canadian policies on the South among other things, "whether they were aid, trade, broader foreign policy, development policy—the whole panoply of things." At the same time, she was named to the board of the International Centre for Human Rights and Development, and that, too, was focused on developing countries. She later joined the board of the Institute on Governance, a new creation in the 1990s that connected Canadian public servants with reforms in developing countries, later serving as its interim president. It was here that an executive placement firm found O'Neil and matched her with IDRC, then looking for a president itself as Bezanson had made a commitment to the Institute of Development Studies at the University of Sussex in the United Kingdom.

She had her work cut out for her as the transitional experience that the Centre had gone through over the past half decade went far beyond mere budget-cutting and restructuring. It also involved a fundamentally different approach to programming, program resource allocation and support, with significant effects on the ways in which Centre staff worked together and in how they interacted with partners. Program initiatives were the principal part of IDRC programming now and, along with secretariats and a few corporate projects, were the modalities by which the Centre supported research so their smooth operation was critical for a well-functioning IDRC. But how would Bezanson's creation work and how would it be accepted by staff, especially following the rather chaotic introduction of program initiatives in the last years of his presidency?

As well, a series of issues cropped up, chief among them the increasing importance of impact—that is, influencing policy in those countries in which IDRC funded research. By early in the new millennium, O'Neil's organization would be engaged in a strategic evaluation of the influence of Centre-supported research on public policy, following a path charted by two of her predecessors. As was pointed out, it was necessary "to develop a clearer understanding not only of what we mean by 'policy influence' but what IDRC and Centre-supported research has accomplished thus far. This [would] inform planning at the project level—how to improve the Centre's project support to enhance policy influence opportunities and deepen the Centre's understanding of how ideas enter policy processes; and at the corporate level—what has IDRC done as a corporation and what strategic adjustments does the Centre need to make."[6] The emphasis on policy influence had changed the Centre in another way; during the mid-1990s, there had been a decline in its expertise in the natural sciences and engineering and an increase in that of the social sciences. That reflected the emphasis IDRC was placing on linking researchers to policy-makers to increase the probability of research results being utilized, and on issues of governance.[7]

O'Neil brought this perspective with her when she arrived at the Centre. Medhora recalled that he thought her to be "the social development president ... because of her domestic and international background, [she] successfully brought that to the fore."[8] This was reflected in such initiatives as the so-called Harvard tapes, a gathering held in 2003 that included a number of international luminaries like Nobel laureate Michael Spence and Mohammad Yunnus, who would be so honoured in 2007. IDRC brought them together because "the Information and Communication Technology guys didn't know about poverty and the poverty guys didn't know much about ICTs." Later, an important lecture focusing on the social was given by Amartya Sen on 12 April 2006 entitled "The Violence of Identity," which was, in Medhora's estimation, "the largest voluntarily attended development event in Ottawa that I have seen in the last twenty years. It was supposed to have been held at IDRC, but the demand was so large that we moved it to the auditorium of the National Art Gallery."

Strategy also came into play in other ways. During a wide-ranging board discussion of the president's report in October 1997, issues as diverse as resource expansion in relation to the Centre's mandate and its core parliamentary funding and its implications for IDRC partnerships with Southern researchers was raised. The organization would have to attract sufficient funds to sustain a critical mass of development research on key challenges. Furthermore, and importantly, the Centre would also have to sustain the professional and institutional infrastructure at headquarters and in regional offices in order for it to remain the sort of respected player in development research on the international scene for which it was renowned.[9] All that required money and, at a time when many potential funding partners were experiencing tougher times, the cupboard was relatively bare. That meant a change in the intensity with which certain avenues were explored; co-funding, parallel financing, contract research or research management services, and public–private partnerships were examined more carefully. Indeed, as bilateral donor budgets continued to shrink in the late 1990s, external funding for research was increasingly found in the large integrated projects of international financial institutions and private sector investors.

As well (and of some help at least as far as IDRC's budget problems were concerned), research institutions in the stronger economies of Asia and Latin America, sometimes having been set up by the Centre in times past, were now not so much looking to IDRC as a major source of funding but rather as a partner whose most important contribution might not be financial support but professional advice and links to Canadian and international knowledge networks. The Centre was certainly tied into many of those. O'Neil also brought IDRC closer to the granting councils in Canada, the Social Sciences and Humanities Research Council, the Natural Sciences and Engineering Council, and the Canadian Institutes for Health Research (CIHR) in concrete ways. The classic manifestation of that was the global health research initiative, which is a coalition of CIDA, IDRC, Health Canada, CIHR, and, more recently, the Public Health Agency of Canada (PHAC). This coalition continues to come together for two reasons—to pool money and ideas for projects in pursuit of a common set of rules, and as a forum in which the organization presidents could meet annually.

IDRC's straitened circumstances also meant a change in the way it conceived of its funding relations with Southern partners as well as other donor agencies. As was pointed out, staff would have to "lose some of [their] proprietary attitudes about our projects [they belong to us] and partners ... [and] develop new ways of communicating our messages and disseminating the results of the research we support in order to attract new partners and new resources." That effort would begin with CIDA, traditionally IDRC's major funding partner. In the past, the sorts of co-funding arrangements that the relationship had epitomized had never been considered critical to the Centre's ability to sustain a significant core research program and institutional infrastructure. They had, however, developed into that over the past half-decade and, as IDRC's parliamentary appropriation suffered further, these arrangements became even more critical. They also nicely complemented one another, or so Centre management now thought, as the financial reality of their situation brought them up short. As Pierre Beemans noted in a memorandum to senior management in July 1997:

> IDRC has expertise in key development disciplines and technologies, extensive global networks, credibility and capacity as an international knowledge broker, and an "installed plant capacity" that can be of much greater benefit to Canada and CIDA than they have to date; IDRC projects have produced results that could greatly benefit developing countries, but whose application calls for greater resources than IDRC can afford; on the other hand, IDRC has not been strong in situating its programs within the broader strategic development contexts of the countries in which it operates—nor, for that matter, of Canadian foreign and development policy; CIDA has turned away from its old capital-intensive infrastructure and engineering projects and is explicitly moving towards "knowledge-based programming." These include growing investments in

research-related development activities—often in areas in which IDRC has significant comparative advantages; IDRC's internal scientific and technical expertise can assist CIDA in developing strong and clear operational frameworks for its science and technology-related policies and programming.[10]

As well, the fields of action of both institutions were increasingly converging in the search for better solutions to the long-standing problems of poverty, the environment, sustainable economies, and the like. The new buzzword was synergy. Necessity, as the old saying has it, is the mother of invention and IDRC's ideas about, and approach to, its larger partner demonstrate that. Good relations with CIDA were imperative and it was important that the Centre not market itself as a competitor, even a quiet one, to the Canadian International Development Agency but as a partner that could work with and enhance its activities. While the relationship could be worked out over time, it was absolutely in the Centre's interest to pursue discussions that could lead to a formal arrangement, setting out the priorities and procedures for an ongoing partnership that would reinforce each other's interests and capacities within the context of Canada's broader foreign policy framework. Much of that was accomplished under Maureen O'Neil's presidency. Relations with CIDA were put on a more sound footing and improved, at least at the senior management level; it was also true that the at times hostile relationship was most often replaced by something approaching collegiality.

It was not a monogamous relationship, however, and as the millennium came and went, IDRC was romanced by other suitors wishing to funnel their research funds through the Centre. That spoke to its reputation. And while these funds could never make up for the lost parliamentary appropriation, they went partway there. Moreover, their importance lay as much in what they symbolized as in the dollar amounts negotiated. That was certainly the case with the United Nations Foundation (UNF), established in 1998 to administer Ted Turner's gift of US$1 billion to support global causes. In hopes of initiating discussions that could lead to a major IDRC partnership with UNF in certain program areas, O'Neil met with Tim Wirth, the Foundation's president. He was much taken with the possibility, remarking that "IDRC was the logical conduit for UNF and IDRC's credibility with UNF board members was amazing."[11] A decision was made to explore joint programming in four areas, essential health interventions and eco-systematic approaches to community health, health security, tobacco control, and biodiversity. The first joint venture came in early 2002 when UNF contributed US$750,000 to the Centre to help in funding research on interrelated issues of human health and ecosystems in developing countries. The funds were to assist countries of the South to address the many challenges they faced in the fields of health and the environment. Groups of local specialists were to be trained to find solutions that could be translated into policies for the benefit of people and their environment. The regions targeted included West and North Africa, the Middle East, Central America, and the Caribbean, and a network was to be created enabling them to share experiences. Other partners emerged; Carnegie Corporation of New York, for example, came up with US$737,500 to support the African Technology Policy Studies Network (ATPSN) to pursue its research activities on issues of science and technology policy in Sub-Saharan Africa. From 1998, ATPSN was based in IDRC's regional office in Nairobi. Micro Impacts of Macroeconomic Adjustment Policies (MIMAP) received US$176,700 in parallel funding for the Finance Network from Développement International Desjardins, and so it went. Ford Foundation in Chile and Guatemala, Health Canada for the Research Initiative for Tobacco Control, the Swedish International Development Cooperation Agency and Denmark's International Development Agency, Department for International Development (DFID) from the UK, the Agency for Development Cooperation from Norway, and the Swiss Agency for Development Cooperation all entered into agreements with the Centre to help support certain of its programs.

Each valued the Centre's expertise, connections, and access to Southern researchers, which, for the most part, proved elusive to the bigger organizations. One generic example of this assertion was a contract signed with DFID in 2006 following its realization, through the link with IDRC, that hundreds of African researchers were working on the problem of climate change, many of these with funding from the Centre. As the British development agency was keen to involve itself in the subject, a relationship with IDRC seemed a natural thing. DFID invested CAN$50 million to complement IDRC's CAN$15 million in a five-year effort to strengthen research on how African countries and communities could best deal with the expected effects of climate change through the Climate Change Adaptation in Africa Research and Capacity Development Program. It represented to that time the Centre's largest co-funding partnership. Paul Spray, the former head of DFID's Central Research Office, has noted that, following this agreement with the Centre, the Department for International Development did not have to reinvent the wheel:

> In Britain, there are pretty high-quality researchers on climate change, and the view that we had was that there was very little African research capacity on climate change, but there was lots in Britain. There was a very strong push by British researchers saying that they had very valuable experience in climate change and we would like to share. What you must do is fund us to do the research in Africa, to do the research that would be really useful to Africans. This was from people with the best possible motives. Had it not been

for IDRC, that's probably what we would have done. But actually, what the link with IDRC enabled us to do was to discover that there were really quite a lot of African researchers. In fact there were several hundred [high-quality] research applications for the first round ... far more than I ever dreamt was feasible,... So we actually ended up with a research program that is about funding African researchers on climate change and they can call in outside expertise if they want to. I don't think we'd have done that without the IDRC.[12]

Later, as part of an update to its research funding framework 2005–7 and to provide itself with more precise information with which to inform its decision making in terms of arrangements with international partners, DFID engaged the Overseas Development Institute, one of the United Kingdom's leading development think tanks, to prepare an analysis of sixty-three putative partners, including such notables as AusAID, CIDA, Deutsch Gesellschaft für Technische Zusammennarbeit, the Norwegian Agency for Development Cooperation, and USAID. Under the heading of qualitative indicators, the report noted:

> Turning now to considerations of quality ... highly reputed donors were also characterised [sic] as those effective in fostering innovation as well as research-based policy dialogue and research uptake within development practice.... What is striking from the key informant interviews, however, was the wide range of assessment of quality research donors among bilaterals. The only bilateral to stand out consistently in term of positive evaluations (including among both northern and southern key informants) was the Canadian International Development Research Centre.... The reputation was based predominantly on their role in supporting innovation, capacity building/mentoring and a focus on research-policy linkages.[13]

That was high praise indeed.

Those sentiments, however, were in a not-too-distant future; for the present, many of the issues confronting Bezanson had not gone away. Some had intensified as the Centre's parliamentary appropriation continued its downward spiral. Using 1992–93 as the base year, in *real* terms it hit CAN$75.6 million during 2000–1, the same amount in real terms it had received from government in 1975–76. That was astonishing. Nor could management contemplate an increase in the years ahead, even though the Liberal government was well into the process that would set the country's books in order. During her first term in office, the average actual amount of the parliamentary appropriation was CAN$87.7 million; in *real* terms, using the same base year, it was CAN$78.88 million. O'Neil had characterized this to the board in late 2000 as "the precipitous decline in ODA and IDRC's grant from 1991–92 (when it was CAN$123 million) to CAN$88 million now." Staff had come up with efforts to change that trend, but success had proved elusive as federal efforts were focused on deficit reduction. For example, Chantal Schryer, the chief of public affairs, had prepared a note for presentation to Deputy Minister of Finance Kevin Lynch about "a) the (important) research topic, b) the (excellent) result IDRC had already achieved, c) then what the Centre would do with further resources. The idea is to evoke the response 'Oh wow, we will get a lot of bang for our buck by giving the money to IDRC; they could really take the ball and run with it. They'll make Canada look good because they are working on important stuff and can do a good job, no problem.' *En gros*, that's the thinking anyway."[14] It did little to convince Lynch then, although he later became a strong proponent of the work the Centre does.[15] Clearly, IDRC had become a lean and efficient instrument for supporting multidisciplinary research, but it was also constrained. It was somewhat miraculous that, with savings on the operational side, the Centre was able to *increase* the program appropriations budget. Still, to make decisions about research funding, to maintain seven regional offices, and to keep the administrative apparatus in shape was increasingly difficult in such an environment. That is where we begin.

The Program Initiative System at Work

The introduction in July 1995 of the program initiative (PI) system had involved much trial, error, compromise, and debate, and had very much altered the intellectual constructs that had guided the Centre since its founding. Indeed, it represented a foundational change in the *way* it went about its business and in the *thinking* about how it did so, although not so much in the output of that business, funding research for development. It is also very significant as the new way of doing business represented a shift in the nature of the *ideas* that animated the Centre's program development. PIs were also cut to fit the new IDRC cloth—their number was capped at twelve, and there were three program areas (PAs) under which all PIs fell, which included environment and natural resource management (ENRM), information and communications technologies for development (ICT4D), and Social and Economic Equity (SEE). IDRC conceptualized program areas at several levels: concrete outputs of research programs, the reach of programs with respect to key partners, and the longer-term outcomes that could reasonably be attributed to the work the Centre funded.[16] Each of these mirrored a particular strength of the organization—for example, with ENRM, the

Centre, a leader in support of research on the management of natural resources in all regions in which it operated, assisted researchers on focusing projects on community-based alternatives to traditional top-down natural resource management in rural areas, as well as on studies of national and regional policies that expanded the space for local management.[17] In China, for example, partly as a result of work funded that focused on the activities of village farmers, provincial governments changed legislation and practice to reflect this community-based, bottom-up process that helped 220 million agriculturalists be able to better gain a livelihood. SEE supported work in areas like governance in Sub-Saharan Africa (SSA), peace-building and reconstruction in Southern Africa, Central America, and the Middle East, as well as the Tanzanian Essential Health Inventions Program and Ecosystem Approaches to Human Health. The last was an innovative and pioneering approach to development research that focused on improving human health through better ecosystem management. It supported research on three sets of stressors that had implications for human and ecosystem health: mining, urbanization, and intensive agriculture. In the case of ICT4D, the Centre supported far-reaching and very successful programs of funding designed to help recipients participate in the twenty-first-century communication revolution, like Acacia.

As well, O'Neil took steps to remedy the deficiency in middle management caused by the 1995 Bezanson reorganization, which had placed too great a responsibility on the vice-president of programs. In 2000, she brought in "Director[s] of Program Areas (DPAs).... That was in terms of making the transition work, and I think it's now working a hell of a lot better than when it started," or so John Hardie believed.[18] Another team leader remarked that "I think that with DPAs in place ... we have [a] better sense of where new ideas come from, how they percolate, how they develop; in other words, how an exploration becomes a program."[19] Following the development of *Corporate Strategy and Program Framework III* (2000–5) and the promulgation of a new decision-making matrix, this also worked well. The matrix managers, the six regional directors, the DPAs, and the vice-president of program and partnership, as well as the director of policy and planning, oversaw the whole thing. The matrix structure permitted the relatively smooth development of such cross-program and cross-regional issues as information and communication technologies and poverty, or biotechnology and development. Following 2000, every program issue was treated within the context of the matrix, recognizing its regional and thematic dimension.

The program areas also served a useful purpose. One of the problems that Bezanson and O'Neil had encountered was program officers' reluctance to give up on "their" program initiative—the feeling was that if it disappeared, so too would their jobs. There had been enough layoffs over the previous number of years to confirm that, or so staff thought. Program areas suggested otherwise, as O'Neil later noted. The PI system that had developed in the months following its introduction in 1995 was unworkable given the straitjacket into which it put Centre programming as program officers scrambled for a clawhold on as many program initiatives as they could to ensure their own viability. While it would evolve, there was not then real capacity to deploy program staff within areas related to their specific program initiative(s). "Program areas," O'Neil remembered, "changed that. Now, for example, people are working in the Social and Economic Equity area. Whether all the PIs have the same title in the next cycle matters less. You've got a group of people with skills relevant to managing research on social and economic equity. No matter how you redefine individual PIs, you've got a team that usually can be deployed and redeployed within a program area. It's more logical in terms of human resource management."[20] It also helped to convince staff that their *position*, as opposed to a specific job, was safe, which, in turn, allowed them to more completely buy into the new way of doing things.

PIs were based on three guiding principles: (1) there was but one Centre; (2) they had a presence in developing regions; and (3) they were the primary programming units and driving force of Centre programs.[21] Approval, leadership, implementation, and monitoring of program initiatives were key program activities. The first point mentioned above—that there was but one Centre—reflected the notion that the old divisional structure had ultimately damaged IDRC by slicing its efforts into a number of pieces that only rarely interacted with one another in a substantive way and made it, some believed, less than the sum of its parts. Program branch would oversee all program activity as a whole in order to ensure that it did not end up "with 15 different programs, to ensure consistent quality control, to learn from evaluations and to provide forward, strategic thinking on IDRC's place in the research-for-development universe."

Generally, IDRC staff saw the change to PIs from discrete projects as a good thing. Remaining responsive to Southern demands was also challenging as PIs were much larger in scope than the old projects and were supposed to conform more closely to Centre themes as laid down by the board, permitting less flexibility in program adjustments. Indeed, this became a conversation among regional directors and senior management committee as it went almost to the core of IDRC's practice and history. A significant part of the discussion revolved around what was meant by "flexibility." For example, if an opportunity arose to become involved in a project outside the parameters spelled out in a prospectus, should it happen? No, or so Caroline Pestieau thought. Even if the activity was fully funded by another donor, it was "likely to involve future commitments of a moral, legal or financial nature."[22] The opportunity cost of time not spent on planned activities also had to be calculated into the mix. That would be worse for the Centre and its program initiatives if an opportunity required a diversion of resources from planned activities and entailed staff modifying their plans. If that happened often enough, then program officers would be justified in claiming that "distractions" prevented them from carrying out their prospectuses.

Further, as PIs were implemented beginning in the second half of 1995, program officers indicated some confusion about directives: Were they to focus on research excellence or capacity building (which, at times, were not complementary), press for early appropriations from headquarters for certain PIs, or wait for potential additional donors to sign on with IDRC? However, following the October 1998 comprehensive assessment of program initiative performance, a number of positive results were noted that would be linked to PIs, like Acacia. They led to projects that had more relevance, as well as possessing a more finely tuned problem and policy focus so that researchers were better linked to policy-makers and other users of research, a point that had been an issue for IDRC for the past twenty years. PIs also served, it seemed from early experience, to promote a greater gender and environmental sensitivity, as well as encouraging networking and program synergies, all very important considerations in the Centre's evolving nature.

For example, reflecting the O'Neil influence, gender was very important for the successful realization of the objectives of Micro Impacts of Macroeconomic and Adjustment Policies (MIMAP), a program initiative that aimed to provide decision makers with alternatives that minimized the adverse impacts of economic policies on the poor and the vulnerable. It played a key role in developing tools and approaches for the multidimensional analysis of poverty; that included a heavy concentration on gender considerations as women were affected in disproportionately high numbers by changes in economic paradigms. Randy Spence, the regional director in the Singapore office, noted in his trip report to the fourth annual meeting of MIMAP in September 2000 that gender issues had been an animated topic of discussion, and had included "gender modeling work, and emerging real breakthroughs in addressing gender inequity and issues in the analytical and modeling work." As well, it had resulted in progress in the Gender Network on gender indicators in poverty monitoring systems.[23]

MIMAP brought together specialists on poverty monitoring both physically (through the annual meeting) and virtually (through email communi-

cation). As a result of IDRC assistance, there were also opportunities for collaboration with the World Bank's Economic Development Institute and its "Initiative on Poverty." In terms of resource expansion, the PI was also a
success—bilateral and multilateral donors were becoming more active in
funding parts of the network. As an example, Spence pointed to "the surge
in activity of the Asian Development Bank in poverty reduction in Asia" that
directly followed on MIMAP work. Other donors' interest could then lead to
an exit strategy for IDRC from certain parts of the programming, given its
reduced resources; "national projects [would] become funded by others,
leaving IDRC to pursue the leading edges at the all-network level."

The experimental and novel nature of the program initiative structure
had led the Centre to assess it intensively, with much of that evaluation done
through external appraisals. Those investigations confirmed what staff increasingly believed—program initiatives were conceptually strong, had coherence
and rigour, and used innovative approaches. The new structure and philosophy also allowed PI teams to be involved in continuous evaluations of their
area and to build the results of those evaluations into program redesign in
a way that had not necessarily been the case with the old structure. These
happened in two ways. Responses from recipients were systematically collected
yearly on a range of indicators such as building capacity, external impacts,
and replication and extension of lessons learned to other situations. Recipients were also trained in methods of participatory monitoring and evaluation
of their own projects. The results of these external evaluations suggested
that IDRC continued to be seen as a leader in research conceptualization
and problem identification.[24] By the end of the twentieth century, most of the
teething problems associated with the introduction of PIs had been overcome and IDRC had refined its niche in terms of programming.

A Strengthened Priority: Programming in Sub-Saharan Africa

An increasingly important part of that was Sub-Saharan Africa (SSA), which
remained a Centre focus under O'Neil as it had been with Ivan Head and, to
a lesser extent, Keith Bezanson. It was also true that as budget cuts had dec-
imated IDRC, those regional offices (ROs) that serviced Sub-Saharan Africa—
Dakar, Johannesburg, and Nairobi—had also been cut. Given that, could
they continue to make a meaningful contribution to program development?
For example, eleven of the fourteen program initiatives were active in Africa
and IDRC now had only *ten* program staff resident on the *entire* continent
(which included the Middle East Regional Office based in Cairo), a far cry
from the 54 percent of all program officers resident in regional offices in

those four offices in the early 1990s; clearly something would have to give.[25] At the same time, downsizing had increased the level of insecurity and over-work among program staff that had translated into PI team members' pre-occupation with reaching co-funding targets or attaining objectives as laid out in the prospectus. Moreover, regional tailoring of program initiatives had not been an explicit priority, which complicated some activities in Africa through the dispersal of responsibility to other regions. To deal with these sorts of issues with a reduced workforce, senior management had contem-plated instituting a system of regional poles of expertise on the continent. If that were to happen then, say, the East Africa Regional Office (EARO) would become the leadership pole for environment, technology, and economics; the Regional Office for Southern Africa (ROSA) would support democratic process, governance, and Acacia, while the West Africa Regional Office (WARO) would focus on social policy, learning, and Acacia.

Whatever transpired, the Centre would have to support mechanisms designed to ensure that the regional office presence was effective and main-tain the unity and quality of the overall program without weakening the PI team's ability to attain the objectives set out in the prospectus. However, given the budgetary circumstances then prevailing, that was a tall order. As events had unfolded, it was the four regional offices in Africa that were examined as the Centre's financial problems tightened further. The issue became one of ensuring appropriate support for program initiatives in Africa, which translated into an increase in financial support to those researchers and certain institutions. By 2000, about 38 percent of program spending took place there as compared with a total of 38 percent for Asia and Latin Amer-ica combined, a significant amount indeed that would need some oversight.

But that might be difficult, at least according to some regional directors (RDs) who felt largely ignored by head office, the result of the almost decade-long restructuring that had left them with skeletal offices. Reflecting the upheaval that had been so common during the Bezanson era, the regional director of EARO wrote: "One of our problems as an institution is that we have rushed to try new ways of doing things, often before we thought through all the implications. Inevitably ... it seems that ROs have suffered. For example, ROs and especially the RDs were really the forgotten actors in the ideas con-tained in the 1995 *Report on Scientific Excellence*, which led to major pro-grammatic restructuring [into PIs]."[26] Given the opportunity to change in what they perceived to be a positive direction, the four based in Africa, as well as their colleagues in Montevideo, New Delhi, and Singapore, grabbed it. Generally, they believed that strong and vibrant PIs could take shape only if regional offices were better integrated into the evolving Centre. That would require headquarters to have a change in attitude as during the turmoil of the mid- to late 1990s IDRC might not have had, some regional directors believed, "a shared set of concrete values, a vision of what we as [the Centre] want to achieve in strategic terms."[27] However, that was not the spirit that animated O'Neil's IDRC, a sense that took hold as her approach took root.

As O'Neil set her mind to sorting out that side of the relationship, it was complicated by the fact that ROs were essential at IDRC. The board had said so, and regional offices were one of the things that set the organization apart from many other development agencies. Further, IDRC's reputation for relevance, detailed knowledge of its environment, and overall credibility were in part derived from its network of regional offices. The benefits to the Centre from such a presence had been expounded often enough with presidents past and were largely repeated in mid-1997; they were to provide visibility, regional intelligence, and a mechanism through which to build partnerships.[28] If that was the ideal, the reality fell short, at least as far as suggesting that regional directors were "leaders 'in ensuring that the Centre maintains a strategic sense of programming priorities."[29]

Senior management set out to clear up some of those ambiguities and to better integrate the regional office system into the new program initiative matrix. The introduction of the program initiatives in 1995 *had* changed the relationship of regional directors to programming from direct to indirect, while at the same time increasing the importance of other roles. As a result of the strategic and program planning that had gone on since the changeover to PIs, and the introduction of the resulting *Corporate Program Framework to the Year 2000* in April 1997 (which had coincided with O'Neil's accession to the presidency), the responsibilities of regional director had been changed. The order of priority for regional directors as applied to Sub-Saharan Africa were as program manager, entrepreneur, networker, strategist, and diplomat.[30] Similarly, the shift away from discipline/sector-based programming to interdisciplinary program initiatives had important implications for the role of the regional program officer (RPO) after 1995. The purpose of a program initiative was to seek out and support the deployment of the optimum interdisciplinary mix to address a development-related research problematique. It was also expected that the RPO would supply the specific regional intelligence—the local knowledge of institutions, social and political circumstances, and prevailing conditions—that was essential for the successful operation of the program initiative. All of these currents required some serious consideration.

Most importantly, in 1997 it was decided that all four offices located in Africa "*must*" be kept open. The president had confessed her uncertainty about this to the standing committee on Foreign Affairs and International Trade during her first visit to testify in November 1997: "There had been a lot of to-ing and fro-ing on what we were going to do with regional offices. Could we afford to keep them? Could we not? ... It was our advice to the board that we keep the regional offices. Our credibility rests on our ability to stay in close touch with what is going on in the regions."[31] One way of doing that was through a strategy that focused on the strengthening of human and institutional research resources though training and the promotion of regional collaboration and co-operation in the application of research results to development problems.

The most significant problem in Sub-Saharan Africa was a research community starved of resources that was below the critical mass required for effective operation. The idea conceived at headquarters and given birth in the field was that program initiatives would encourage viable networks that were focused on particular knowledge gaps and that would create sturdy and dynamic offspring, which would mature into grown-up research communities. That was, however, a labour-intensive process that would require an adequate field presence. Participating institutions would have to be connected with one another and with other relevant knowledge communities, not always an easy task. However, Centre ingenuity came into play through a path-breaking project named Unganisha and the lessons learned from it.

Unganisha

What was "Unganisha," apart from being a Swahili word for connectivity, which also conveyed a sense of unity? Approved by the board at its October 1996 meeting and implemented by the Bezanson Centre as of 1 March 1997, it "was innovative and important,... a 'campaign' to help IDRC partners in the developing world with access to email so they could communicate more effectively."[32] An external evaluation undertaken in mid-1999 pointed out that it was designed "to extend the Centre's connectivity to its projects and facilitate collaboration between projects, between IDRC program initiatives and program officers, and between different groups within the Centre."[33] Unganisha was to jumpstart the connectivity of existing IDRC research partners across all the program areas, a recognition that easier access to information and the ability to disseminate it inexpensively had the potential to dramatically improve the effectiveness and efficiency of researchers, as well as enhance communication with IDRC staff. That, in turn, was a reflection of the decreasing cost of ICT technology by the later 1990s, and its increasing sophistication from email to video conferencing to the growth of ICTs themselves. The technology was, in short, breaking down the barriers of geography, a very important factor as "Distances between haves and have-nots do not cease to widen."[34]

Tim Dottridge remembers that "The person recruited to set things up was Steve Song and for a couple of years he traveled the world, probably with screwdriver in hand, but also with technical advice and funding for our research partners. He later became head of ICT4D for Africa. Unganisha was a recognition that there was a new way (or an additional way) of IDRC connecting with its partner researchers and institutions, and strengthening their capacity. Part of the idea came from Robert Valantin, who was to become the head of what became ICT4D—the real ICT push started with Acacia in 1995–96, and was directly inspired and pushed by Keith Bezanson, and Robert was the one chosen by Keith to get work moving."[35] Further, the Pan Asia Networking (PAN) program initiative, covering Asia and eventually Latin America and established in 1996, was also in the mix.[36] All of this meshed nicely with activity at headquarters; Valantin and Paul McConnell, the organization's Advisory Committee on Information Management cochairs, had written that "As a leading international development research organization tracking hundreds of projects, with an active global presence, multiple partners, and a commitment to knowledge sharing, it is inevitable that the use of information technologies is playing an increasingly significant role in the Centre's business."[37]

Unganisha was funded as a project by IDRC to extend the Centre's connectivity to its projects and facilitate collaboration among those, between IDRC program initiatives and program officers, and among different groups within the Centre.[38] It made important contributions to both IDRC and the recipients of Centre funds. For the latter, support was provided in the form of subsidies for Internet connections, technical advice, training, and assistance from help desks. With respect to the last, as anyone who has wrestled with the complexities of ICTs knows, access to a help desk is very welcome. Within the Centre, Unganisha played a pioneering role in the introduction of new methods and tools of communication such as the development of the intranet, the testing and introduction of IPass roaming services designed to allow Internet and mobile phone access anywhere in the world, the facilitation of listservs, and the use of computer conferences. According to questionnaires circulated, staff appreciated that it experimented with such things as smaller computers for use in the field and video conferencing for communication among PI members. As well, the training provided by the experts was very useful in large part because it could "open people's eyes" to what was in fact possible with the new communication technologies.

Examples of how Unganisha had made IDRC more productive included such things as the local Internet service provider's training for project staff, paying trainers and per diems of project staff for Africa-wide network personnel and testing and using ITrain materials for Internet training sessions. In one case, the training demonstrated how to organize connectivity within a network and with others outside the main group. Assistance in this case included both local help to facilitate connection, as well as the provision of links to help desks that were being established. The guidance supplied by Unganisha allowed groups of researchers to become involved in network communication, increased the use of the Internet for networking, led to the creation of project websites, and improved email communication with IDRC and other network members. Indeed, it seemed there was little it could not do. It made one wonder how it had all been achieved in the past, before technology had so changed communication.

Unganisha also benefited by being a project and located within Programs Branch, which was not merely fortuitous—staff had thought about this beforehand. As a result, it enjoyed the flexibility and funds necessary for both experimentation and innovation, being able to purchase its own server and look into problems related to external access to email, work on the development of web-to-email services, experiment with video conferences, test the appropriateness of IDRC staff's use of small computers for field use, and purchase and test new software to determine if it might be useful to IDRC or its recipients. In this sort of introspective endeavour, the Centre was definitely ahead of the curve. As well, staff combined technical expertise in Internet technologies with development experience, and were applauded by those on the receiving end of information for having listened to people's needs and suggested appropriate solutions; they did not simply push a specific technology or software solution. Very quickly, Centre staff came to call upon Unganisha for technical advice on Internet technologies and the use of these technologies to promote improved communication and more collaborative working arrangements. Further, it pushed some innovation within the Centre, becoming "a focal point to reflect on issues and problems and an important part of the ferment of thinking in IDRC about ICTs and their use."[39] The computer geeks who ran the program also recognized the importance of thinking about the use of ICTs for development, and it was out of this that the program initiative, information, and communication technologies for development (ICT4D) emerged.

That evolution certainly helped IDRC programming in Sub-Saharan Africa overcome crucial barriers. As the dawn of the information age in the region was breaking, the Centre was already there, using widely accessible computers and email, a part of what became an international effort to empower Sub-Saharan Africa with the ability to apply information and communication technologies to its own social and economic development. It facilitated things like learning for change, fostering lifelong learning opportunities. It also made more possible research in areas like ecosystem health, which encompassed "the complex interplay among the environmental and the socio-economic, cultural and political conditions of any group of people."[40] All of this was incredible, given IDRC's small size and its struggle to incorporate debilitating budget cuts in the late 1990s and early 2000s. Clearly, it had made the best of the hand that it had been dealt, developing Unganisha and then ICT4D against all odds. It also set the Centre on a path that it still treads in 2010, of making ICTs accessible to those who have the least access to them.

And so it went as IDRC found its way forward in Sub-Saharan Africa; sustainable employment in SSA emphasized small, medium, and micro-enterprises, and innovation and technology, which also investigated the role of women in small business. Trade, employment, and competitiveness had a large portfolio of projects in the region, helping to support two secretariats, Trade and Industry Policy in South Africa and the Secretariat for Institutional Support for Economic Research in Africa. As well, funding continued to flow to the African Economic Research Consortium, while Micro Impacts of Macroeconomic and Adjustment Policies, which had started in Asia, now pushed out into SSA. The themes of food security, as well as equity in natural resource management, were also active in Sub-Saharan Africa in areas like urban agriculture, while People, Land, and Water was designed to help communities enhance the equitable, sustainable, and productive use of land and water resources to improve the quality of life of impoverished farmers.

All of these PIs in that region and elsewhere meant a labour-intensive commitment. As was pointed out, the Centre recognized that its particular conditions—weaker institutions and research capacity relative to Asia and Latin America—demanded program officers on the ground. Nor did they only act as research funding managers. Instead, they concentrated on working on a peer basis with researchers in partner institutions in fulfilling a number of roles: "encouraging greater recourse to multi-disciplinarity and helping researchers circumvent obstacles to it; helping researchers to link up with policymakers and ensuring that the latter were involved early on in the research process; promoting collaboration in integrated and participatory approaches; strengthening attention to the gender dimension in research; promoting the dissemination and utilization of research; and nurturing networks of researchers and encouraging development of peer review groups in the region."[41]

Indeed, this *human* element of IDRC-supported research was arguably as important to researchers as was the actual financial contribution. That was borne out by the Tracer Study of past project leaders supported by the Centre, which emphasized the centrality of this nurturing and facilitating role, especially for activity in a large and diverse region like Sub-Saharan Africa. Undertaken in early 1996, it "was the first aggregate assessment, from the perspective of the project leaders, of the impact of [IDRC] support."[42] It set out to obtain a historical overview and demographic profile of project leaders. As well, it would assess the capacity-building effect of IDRC-supported research projects on project leaders, document the effectiveness of IDRC support and the level to which the Centre had met part of its corporate objectives, and generate lessons learned for Centre-wide policy-making, project development and design, and training. The praise from project leaders was rather fulsome—a great majority of the 317 alumni surveyed reported that "the support provided by IDRC staff—and the networking opportunities resulting from their involvement with the Centre—have helped them professionally."[43] Survey respondents ranked networking opportunities as IDRC's most important contribution to their careers. As one project leader noted, "Through networking, I improved my department's image internationally.... Every time I convened a meeting with foreign colleagues, it was easier because I was known to them because of my work with IDRC." Another key finding was the high level of enthusiasm for IDRC's approach to program delivery: "IDRC reviews project designs very thoroughly, but once they are funded, project leaders are encouraged to learn by doing," the study's co-author Stephen Salewicz explained. "It's not like at some agencies, where Northern consultants are sent to oversee or to participate in the project."

Further, many project leaders indicated that IDRC had opened up new approaches to research: "Before the IDRC-supported project, I was working on my own," said one. "During the project I got to work with geographers, doctors, epidemiologists, and I understood the complementarity of various disciplines. The work was easier and more comprehensive. An interdisciplinary research approach is now included in all my projects."[44] Indeed, what became very clear from the study was that the principal reason for approaching the Centre "was not for funding support but for the non-pecuniary benefits that this relationship brought, such as assistance with research and publications and opportunities presented for networking." Clearly, despite the grumblings of some regional directors (who also quickly came to support it), buy-in across IDRC, both among program staff and researchers for its new way of doing business and the changes that were being implemented, was high.

The Acacia Initiative

Acacia represented a significant challenge for IDRC; some claimed an overly ambitious one. In October 1996, the board had approved initial support for this initiative and had set aside CAN$1 million for the preparatory phase. For fiscal year 1997–98, CAN$8 million was appropriated, a large sum given the Centre's straitened circumstances. Moreover, the Centre figured on requiring CAN$125 million over a five-year period to achieve a critical momentum. While this was massive in IDRC terms, it was miniscule in terms of Africa's needs and it would be necessary to ensure that the Centre's investment had a catalytic effect on governments and other donors. For IDRC, the ambitious goal was to raise five times that sum from other funding partners in the private and public sectors. Ultimately, the Centre held individual discussions with about ten partners, and Bellanet established a consultative process with other agencies.[45] The initiative came partially out of the proceedings of the Information Society and Development Conference, held in South Africa in May 1996. As a participant, the United Nations Economic Commission for Africa presented a document, "Africa's Information Society Initiative: An Action Framework to Build Africa's Information and Communication Infrastructure," which offered the conclusions of a high-level working group on ICTs in Africa that IDRC had supported under the project "African Networking Initiative."

An international effort led by the Centre, it was a major initiative dealing with Communities and the Information Society in Africa in order to empower Sub-Saharan African communities with the ability to apply new information and communication technologies to their own social and economic development. IDRC had laid out its concerns about the dangers of ICT marginalization in Africa, which had been flagged by leading African researchers during the mid-1990s. Ultimately, Acacia became one the of the most "African-owned" of ICTs for development on the continent, receiving strong backing from participants, as well as from those governments involved in the four-country ministerial-level Maputo Declaration—Mozambique, Senegal, South Africa, and Uganda. It was also fortuitous that it had the support of the then Minister of Foreign Affairs Lloyd Axworthy. One of his priorities was the development of a global information strategy and Africa, he thought, was the perfect place to begin.

And what were those "new" ICTs? They were technologies that allowed for the collection, storage, processing, packaging, and communication of information that provided access to knowledge that controlled physical processes and which were, in the late 1990s, transforming societies and economies.[46] As well, access to such technology implied access to channels and modes of communication that were not bound by language, culture, or distance and that could, or so program officers at the Centre hypothesized, nurture "new forms of social organization and productive economic activity [and] become transformational factors as important as the technology itself." Finally, why Sub-Saharan Africa? Pierre Beemans perhaps reflected the rationale in an address he gave in Halifax:

> Africa ... [was] becoming even more marginalized in the 1990s than it had been in the previous development decades. If you will pardon some sweeping generalizations, Africa doesn't have much to offer in the new globalized financial and trading economy, it is no longer of any critical geopolitical importance, it is increasingly wracked by nasty little wars and genocides, its education and health systems are a shambles at all levels, and on and on. Is Africa going to slip farther and farther behind, except for the happy few that live in favoured urban economic enclaves, or is there some way that African communities can be enabled to harness their capacities more effectively and to leapfrog some of the obstacles and stages before them?[47]

At IDRC, the application of new information and communication technologies to the problems besetting the Sub-Saharan part of that continent would mean access to the information and knowledge it needed, while the proposed network would support those efforts across countries, which would have a cumulative effect. For people at the Centre, it was important that SSA not be marginalized from the information revolution of the twenty-first century as it had been from the Industrial Revolution of the twentieth and to that end, policy and capacity building remained the first priority in Africa. Clearly, knowledge was quickly becoming a most important commodity on the global market, and new ICTs were the key to linking knowledge to development as IDRC had been doing since the earliest days of the old Information Sciences division of the 1970s. As a result, IDRC launched its largest single venture— African Community Access to the Communications and Information Age, which spelled out the acronym ACACIA; it was also the name given to a tree common on the continent.

Approximately 15 percent of the Centre's entire program budget was invested in it, and about 40 percent of what IDRC spent in total in Africa. It would support research activities undertaken by African institutions to discover which policies were conducive to Acacia's objectives. IDRC would also work with people to develop content that could be shared across the continent and to test various forms of African communities' access to ICTs, as well as to investigate various forms of social organization to generate and use the knowledge. As a reflection of that, the Centre also initiated the Evaluation and Learning System for Acacia (ELSA). At its launch, ELSA was seen as the most innovative aspect of Acacia through which successful ICT for development lessons would be learned, extracted, and mainstreamed. It was also conceived as the powerhouse through which Acacia I was "to achieve the goal of demonstrating the benefits of information and communication technologies for solving development problems in disadvantaged sub-Saharan African communities." ELSA was later adopted as one of the principal planks of the Global Knowledge Partnership's Action Plan at its second international conference in Kuala Lampur, held in March 2000, a sure sign of IDRC impact.[48]

Barriers to access to ICTs in Sub-Saharan Africa would have to be tackled head on. A basic communications infrastructure was lacking in large swaths of the continent, and there was little indication that the investments needed for an increase in connectivity would be forthcoming. Indeed, quite the contrary. Those institutions—normally the repositories of the knowledge society like universities, schools, and research centres—had been seriously eroded over past decades, victims of what had euphemistically been called adjustment, but were usually the result of civil war, increasing poverty, and World Bank structural adjustment programs. In a world where access to knowledge and technology defined the new fault lines, Sub-Saharan Africa was virtually certain to fall deeper into poverty unless some way could be found to circumvent those barriers.

The guiding hypothesis that informed Acacia focused on the power of technology and associated social innovations that might allow poor countries to leapfrog stages of development. As its concept paper noted, "In the face of accelerating innovation and the increasingly evident link between prosperity and knowledge, we must accept the challenge inherent in the hypothesis that ICTs can serve as catalysts to viable African communities, locally grounded, globally connected, and capable of addressing their own development problems in equitable and sustainable ways." That reflected the sentiments expressed in an IDRC paper, "A New International Framework for Information, Communications Technologies, and Development: A Canadian Initiative." Its first line read "the extraordinary development of ICTs presents the international community with a unique opportunity to apply new innovations to address problems of poverty and underdevelopment."[49] Target sectors would include education, health, employment and income opportunities, natural resources management, and governance. With hard work and a bit of luck, it would build connections and innovative delivery mechanisms that would illustrate a new Canadian development partnership model and would help to answer the pressing question of the transformative and developmental potential of information and communications technologies at the community level. The Centre had the advantage of being able to work successfully with intermediary and non-elite groups in various African countries, as it had been doing this for decades, which would help to smooth the way. That would be important as Acacia would support the needs of communities, of women, and of indigenous non-governmental organizations. And that was not the norm on the continent. Investing approximately CAN$22 million over four years, Acacia targeted Mozambique, Senegal, South Africa, and Uganda with outcomes resulting from, as the Phase I evaluation noted, three sources: "its national programming approach, project type/programming and its evaluation and learning system for Acacia studies.[50]

As well, program officers quickly absorbed such things as "government policy is key," "gender equity is very hard to achieve," and "the management of community ICT projects is complex." These would be addressed in the phase II program design. It was also true that although large numbers of people were using ICTs, larger numbers were not, being left out of the information age because of gender, age, illiteracy, poverty, and location, which reinforced and aggravated disparities. The project would be ongoing and the traditional IDRC participatory research approach was relevant, albeit very time-consuming. It remained that Acacia's primary objective was to empower the poor by providing them with information, thereby improving their daily lives.[51] There was also a danger to be avoided—that it could become too policy-oriented or taken over by some Sub-Saharan Africa governments. It should, the board believed, only address policy issues to help resolve problems at the *community* level. Perhaps that was what a Bloc Québécois Member of Parliament, Maud Desbien, had in mind when questioning Maureen O'Neil during an appearance before the House of Commons Committee on Foreign Affairs and International Trade. The MP was concerned that IDRC might help repressive regimes by providing them with ICTs. O'Neil was able to assuage her concerns about Centre behaviour to Desbien's satsifaction.[52]

The MP's concern would have been eased had she been more aware of IDRC philosophy and practice. ICT4D's Annual Learning Forum, called eALF, which included staff from the regions and Ottawa, and which was focused on policy influence, claimed that policy was not "a 'head without a body.'" The relationships and interactions between those who make policy changes (the head) and those who were affected by these changes (the body) were always considered.[53] Put another way by participants, "The antidote for a snake [was] a safari of ants. The metaphor describes well the role of citizens in bringing about change when governments [comprised of national elites, perhaps divorced from the reality of their citizenry] tended to act as they usually did, with little understanding of the effects of their policies on the communities they govern." It was IDRC practice and policy "to invest in the body so that it [did] not become a safari of ants."

And surely Desbien would have been comforted by the reaction of some of the people positively affected by the new technologies: "Mobile phones [were] everywhere [by the early 2000s], a part of the reality of African development. Ten years ago it would have been impossible to imagine ICTs being used in schools, in medicine, and in trade. And [in 2001], phase III of Acacia [was] trying to create a research network, [for Africans] to do research in ICT4D."[54] Indeed, 2003 was the first year in which there were more mobile subscribers than land lines in the world; by 2005, about 80 percent of all telephones on the African continent were mobiles, holding tremendous potential for innovative approaches to health care delivery from continuing medical information to demographic surveillance to patient monitoring. They were "changing the livelihoods of women in Africa, as well as changing the relationships between the sexes. ICTs were having an impact on economic growth and they had a hand in improving services with government, its accountability and transparency, as well as enhancing communication between administrations and their constituencies.[55] And that meshed nicely with another IDRC program area—social and economic equity—and one of its broad trends that focused on the changing role of the state as governments recognized the inadequacy of their past responses to governance and human security concerns. The list of positive effects went on. The clear message was that people were better off as a result of the more widespread use of the technology. The Centre in this case was a "catalytic organization, keeping things moving, an organization which inspired confidence and credibility."[56]

And so it has continued. The latest prospectus for Acacia covers the years from 2006 to 2011 and it still espouses a "people first" approach—access to ICTs, proper content, and a steady power supply. Indeed, to the desperate situation in Africa that had inspired Acacia could be added a new one: "Rural Africa, where more than 60 percent of Africans live, seems very remote from the world of high technology; it is a world often with no access to electricity, let alone access to communications. Nearly half the African population lives on less than a dollar a day and on average, life expectancy on the continent is falling; Africa is home to two-thirds of the estimated 38 million people suffering from HIV/AIDS."[57] In this context, one is driven to ask "What is the relevance of ICTs to development for those Africans whose priority is clean drinking water, basic health, shelter, safety, and adequate sources of food? Are ICTs not a comparative luxury in this context? Shouldn't development funds be directed toward more basic needs?" The prospectus provided the response: "The answer is not *either/or* but rather *both/and*.

Appropriately applied, ICTs have the power to accelerate individual, social, and economic development in Africa. A key message is that ICTs are transformative at a variety of levels." However, it would also take time—loads of it. It did evolve into information technologies "and people persisted and it became satellites, RADARSAT, Canadian technology applied to developing countries ... and Acacia was a natural evolution. You had the staff who were able to look at potential and who knew their stuff. Acacia is a good example of the organization having partly a role of stimulating an idea, but also being able to identify the characters and having the staff onboard already to get involved. If you had asked people at the beginning [whether IDRC should get involved], they probably would have said it was too much of a gamble. But the Centre has not shied away from funding that sort of thing."[58] Disseminating findings to remote areas that spoke to telecentres, school networking, and the community-based use of ICTs would be difficult, although it was completed by late 2004. As well, IDRC was intent upon extending the reach of Acacia, which it did, to Angola, Benin, Ghana, and Kenya. In short, the millions of dollars with which the Centre had supported the program initiative had paid off handsomely in better lives for those Africans positively affected by its development, although the task remains unfinished.

Information and Communication Technologies for Development

To some extent, ICT4D emerged from Acacia, then had Acacia folded into it. IDRC established the program area in 2000, and it quickly achieved an international acclaim that reflected the Centre's expertise and reputation in this area. It was the case that its involvement in ICTs for development was about investing in moving targets to bring more efficient and lower cost technologies within the reach of beneficiaries.[59] When IDRC first entered this area of programming, it was one of the very few so involved. As the old saying has it, imitation is the sincerest form of flattery and, if true, ICT4D was a much flattered program; as other agencies took note and international policy incorporated this sort of programming, the Centre was, as ICT4D's team leader, Richard Fuchs, noted, "often at 'top of mind' when new initiatives [were] considered." As others began to pay more attention to ICTs, they also tended to consider IDRC to be a thematic and sectoral leader in this area, which eventually resulted in partnerships and resource expansion. By 2004, about 40 percent of the Centre's resource expansion came from ICT4D initiatives.

ICTs were also something that O'Neil had thought long and hard about in the years before she moved to IDRC. As she sat for her interview before the board's hiring committee, she contemplated some policy elements that had informed her past. In the mid-1970s, for example, she had worked in the Department of Communications, which was supervising Canada's communications technology satellite and experimenting with what the social uses of the Communication Technology Satellite would be—telemedicine and bringing diverse communities together. It occurred to her as she was being interviewed "that what the Centre was doing on ICTs for development had a very familiar ring, and the ring was right back to 1973 when Canada was trying out those ideas at a much less advanced stage of technology, trying out ideas about how video could be used for social change. In the '70s, I sat on the NFB's Challenge for Change Committee that was experimenting with the use of video in communities so that people could tell their stories, tell truth to power and back it up with pictures."[60]

As a result of its experience, IDRC was involved from the beginning of the attempt by the world's most powerful governments, meeting together as the G-8, to bridge the digital divide. The Digital Opportunity Taskforce (DotForce) was launched at the Kyushu-Okinawa summit, held in July 2000. DotForce would "examine concrete steps to bridge the international digital divide, and prepare a report for the next G8 Summit to be held in Genoa, Italy in 2001."[61] Each participant in the meeting named several members to represent its interests, and O'Neil was selected as one of three from Canada. The other two were the influential Peter Harder, deputy minister of Industry Canada, and Charles Sirois, chairman and CEO of Telesystem. It was a natural, therefore, that when, at the Summit of the Americas held in April 2001 in Quebec City, Prime Minister Jean Chrétien had proclaimed the establishment of the Institute of Connectivity in the Americas (ICA) in an attempt to narrow the digital divide (or, put positively, to create digital bridges) between North and South, O'Neil and IDRC would be called upon to fill a gap by "facilitating the coordination, collaboration, and sharing of ICT expertise across countries, serving as an active agent to enable strategic partnerships and financing, and providing leadership and support."[62] By 2004, the Centre would be engaged in different areas designed to forward that agenda; e-Link Americas (admittedly a failure), an independent non-profit company created by the Centre's Institute for Connectivity in the Americas to provide low-cost ICT solutions to research and educational institutions and non-governmental organizations in the region, @Campus Mexico (one of the reasons why Mexican President Vicente Fox visited the Centre in October 2004),[63] and the launch of the Latin America and Caribbean Network Internet Centre. Provided with CAN$20 million by the federal government, it was housed in IDRC, both at headquarters and in the Montevideo office, an indication, again, of the Centre's reputation.

The same was true when Canada hosted the G-8 summit in June 2002 in Kananaskis, Alberta, which came out with the Canada Fund for Africa, a CAN$500 million initiative that was, in part, a response to the New Economic Partnership for Africa's Development (NEPAD),[64] launched in July 2001 by a number of African countries and for which CIDA oversaw the Canadian contribution. Included here was the Centre for Connectivity in Africa (CCA), supported by the Canada Fund to the tune of CAN$15 million per year, located at the Centre and managed by it and the United Nations Economic Commission for Africa. CCA operated in parallel with the Centre's Acacia initiative; indeed, IDRC approved programming support for CCA through Acacia. Again, IDRC was a logical choice to oversee this program: With its years of experience in working on these issues in the developing world, and being involved at several levels of the G-8 Digital Opportunities Task Force, O'Neil could note in a press release that "IDRC was one of the first development agencies that embraced ICTs as key for development and poverty alleviation. We have brought that history to our work with the DOT Force." It also brought to bear its penchant for innovation and application; in the Connectivity Africa initiative, it would help to construct a network developed from the ground up that was based on local demand from African partners. It would also encourage African institutions to develop and fund projects in areas such as innovation in the use of ICTs, as well as help to connect national strategies with regional infrastructure priorities in order to help build connectivity throughout the continent, and encourage research and development in African ICTs.

As a pioneer in the integration of ICTs and social and economic development in the South, the Centre knew the file. Furthermore, through its regional offices, it could tap into discussions in the region on NEPAD, and more accurately reflect the views of African governments and civil society. It would focus on four areas: (1) fostering policy, regulatory, and network readiness; (2) improving connectivity, increasing access, and lowering cost; (3) building human capacity; and (4) encouraging participation in global e-commerce networks.[65] In pursuit of those objectives, IDRC helped to launch the Research ICT Africa (RIA!) network in 2003. Emerging out of the Acacia initiative, it was designed to help African researchers and institutions develop a rigorous and relevant ICT research base that could guide decision makers in their efforts to development and implement effective ICT4D policies.[66] By 2006, RIA! had incorporated francophone members in addition to Cameroon, which had been included from the beginning. Benin, Burkino Faso, Côte d'Ivoire, Rwanda, and Senegal had joined. The Centre also provided CAN$2.5 million toward NEPAD programming. Two other African areas that were highlighted for support were "promoting dialogue within Africa between civil society, researchers and policymakers on the basis of the findings from research [and] supporting the creation of a research and policy institution in East Africa to provide policymakers in the region … with the findings from field-based research on people's health needs and the most effective and efficient response to providing services to meet these needs."[67]

Through all the work, IDRC staff remained, at least according to Richard Fuchs, "cheerleaders for people in the regions who were trying to find ways to benefit from the information economy."[68] They remained as willing listeners, advisers, evaluators, and colleagues of those whose work their organization funded. The Centre also used this area as an entrée through which to support Canadian foreign policy objectives. It participated in the World Summit on the Information Society held in December 2003 in Geneva, which provided an important venue "to showcase IDRC's expertise in the use of ICTs for Development program area within the Canadian delegation [to Geneva]."[69] Indeed, Sergio Marchi, the head of the Canadian mission to the UN in Geneva, referred to the Centre's work in ICTs during his official address to the summit.

Perhaps a payoff for all this involvement, quite apart from the work done in the developing South, was the recognition bestowed upon IDRC by Microsoft, no slouch itself when it came to innovation and thinking outside the box. The latter had approached the former to become its partner, a sure reflection of the Centre's reputation in the field. In mid-2004, IDRC was named as the principal host to a new Telecentre Support Network–Worldwide (TSN–W), which involved both global and regional support to telecentre practitioners involved in ICT4D. Microsoft would invest US$9 million over five years in the project. However, while Microsoft would be a partner, it would not be the dominant one. The president pointed out that "The TSN–W, and its regional offshoots, will be hosted at IDRC as a corporate project within the ICT for Development program area. Very similar to the Institute for Connectivity in the Americas, the TSN–W … will fall squarely within the governance and management of IDRC."[70] And while there were risks to a public corporation tie-up with a very dynamic private sector Microsoft, the fact that the Centre was managing and governing the initiative would be enough to prevent, if such were necessary, any untoward influence by the company. As well, the business plan for the service had been developed in close consultation with the director of ICT4D. Perhaps as a result of that, the agreement with Microsoft did not tie Telecentre.org to the use of Microsoft products, and the initiative has used Microsoft, as well as non-Microsoft, software, including open-source software. This was an important recognition of Centre programming, as well as being a part of the furrow that it continued to plough; partnerships had been important to IDRC over time and would continue to be so.

Planning for the Future: Corporate Strategy and Program Framework III, 2000–5

However, that was in the future and for the present, with its *Corporate Strategy and Program Framework II* expiring in late 1999, IDRC began the process of constructing a successor. But what was this creature? It was the reference point for all decisions made at the Centre and how it was governed.[71] Its development exercise allowed staff to "stop doing their regular work and spend a couple of days reflecting on the future. It means that there is a kind of joint thinking." It focused on issues like "complete capacity building," which suggested to IDRC research partners a clear direction when building support for communications and policy outreach activities from the beginning of every project. It also reflected the changed circumstances in which the Centre found itself. With reduced financial and human resources at its disposal, ambitions also had to be constrained. Qualitative elements had to reflect the quantitative context—without the financial wherewithal, new ideas about an appropriate management structure and its ensuing procedures had to be set in place. Further, the external environment required some consideration; while other donor agencies had considerable goodwill toward IDRC, there was also, as O'Neil pointed out to the board, "some puzzlement and uncertainty about the evolving nature of the Centre."[72]

While that reflected IDRC's declining financial situation, it also spoke to what the president had called "an over-zealous approach to 'revenue generation'"; the Centre seemed to be straying too far from its roots. However, some of that damaged image had been repaired by changing the policy to one of "resource expansion" for developing country partners through partnerships with other funding agencies. Further, a Centre with much less money meant saying "no" more often, which had irritated some potential partners and funding recipients. O'Neil believed, however, "that we must recognize that as we search for the most effective ways to use the resources both from our parliamentary grant and from co-funders, we do need to think carefully about how we communicate the changes to our partners and to the broader community." It also meant that a new strategy was needed that could help IDRC more effectively focus the resources it did have.

That was the *CSPF*'s prime directive. Included were the challenges posed by the paradox of globalization and fragmentation, contrasting greater homogeneity with renewed affirmation of local identity, the huge backlog of unsatisfied need and of continuing desperate poverty, the problems of environmental degradation, and the importance of paying attention to governance issues. The global order seemed to be increasingly fractured along economic and social as well as ethnic and religious lines. That sentiment was put more starkly through reference to average GNP per capita—in the twenty-five richest nations (US$25,000), it was fifty-three times that of the fifty poorest countries (US$480).[73] IDRC staff believed that economic and social progress depended on the way in which decisions were made and on the effectiveness with which societal policies were implemented. Another key factor included in the mix were the revolutionary developments in information and communication technologies and the opportunities, but also dangers that they posed for the South. As we have seen, IDRC had been involved in this area since its establishment with the old Information Sciences division. It was against that backdrop that the CSPF was considered, combined with where it was felt the organization could make a difference with its (scant) resources. Interestingly, it was also the first time that CIDA, the Department of Foreign Affairs and International Trade, and the Privy Council Office participated in the development of a Centre strategic plan, being formally consulted on its programming directions.

IDRC's mission remained empowerment through knowledge, a concept that had emerged in the first year of Bezanson's presidency, which meant helping to maximize the creation, adaptation, and ownership of the knowledge that the people of poor countries judged to be of greatest relevance to their own prosperity, security, and equity—in short, a continuing emphasis on the notion that men and women must control their own social and economic destinies. It also retained those principles, sustainable and equitable development, that had come out of the UN Conference on Environment and Development in 1992; those would undergird all of its programming.[74] Indeed, they remained a cornerstone of the Centre's belief—"that equitable and sustainable human activity depended on men and women's control of their own social and economic progress, on equitable access to knowledge of all kinds, and on an indigenous capacity to generate and apply knowledge."[75] Knowledge, they knew, was the key to progress. Flexibility had been built into programming in order to permit IDRC to respond to emerging issues. The three broad corporate program areas mentioned above (eventually headed by a director of program area) were: (1) social and economic equity, (2) environment and natural resource management, and (3) information and communication technologies for development.[76]

John Hardie also suggested that O'Neil take some time to consider the implications of certain measures in order to ensure "that we begin by moving forward and not back."[77] Some of these might include reference to IDRC and its mission to "concentrate on building research capacity defined in terms of human resources ... not being all things to all people, but certainly retaining adaptability, e.g., by relying quite heavily on the creative judgment of good program staff and their on-the-spot discretion." As well, the Centre should maintain a willingness to take risks and experiment and to "promote evaluation as a planning, learning, and management tool, building capacity for evaluation, and assessing the impact of the work that we support." The *CSPF* also threw into the mix that IDRC should "make greater efforts to ensure that there is indeed an impact by closing as many loops as possible."

As well, thinking about the new *CSPF* meant that the Centre was reinvigorated in its efforts to explore the evolution of knowledge-producing institutions, and in examining the institutional and policy frameworks that facilitated the application of scientific knowledge to development problems. The evaluation unit, established in the early Head years as part of the Office of Planning and Evaluation and as a separate entity in 1992, had done this internally. The Program on Innovation Systems Management (PRISM), set up by Bezanson in the early 1990s, had accomplished this on the programmatic side. And while the intensity of the work carried out by Evaluations and through PRISM had diminished by the mid-1990s because of budgetary pressures and the question of "whither [wither?] the Centre," IDRC had maintained a role through its support of such activities as the African Technology Policy Studies Network and as a result of reviews of national science and technology policies in South Africa, China, Vietnam, and Chile.[78] Further, a range of other activities touched on the concern for the conditions under which knowledge could be applied to development problems, including work on indigenous knowledge, the worry about traditional ecological knowledge with trade-related intellectual property rights, and work done on small, medium, and micro-enterprise innovation and technology to promote innovation by smaller firms.

Much of the methodology employed in what could almost be termed first-generation research on research had undergone a change that was reflected by the late 1990s at IDRC. Most importantly, what was called the linear conception of the innovation process in which research flowed from laboratory to users needed to be abandoned "in favour of a more complex model, emphasizing the multiple flows of information and knowledge between users and producers, and the importance of practical experience as a complement to formal scientific knowledge." Furthermore, it was pointed out that the innovation process was conceptualized in "systems" terms—the creation and application of knowledge resulted from the interaction of a wide range of institutions in both the public and private spheres. In recognition of these shifts, the new *CSPF* advanced the term "knowledge systems" to describe this field of research. Its central focus would remain, to quote the *CSPF*, "a concern with effective ways to conduct research and to apply knowledge for beneficial change."

Indeed, an exploratory program, Research on Knowledge Systems (RoKS), flowed out of the *CSPF* designed "to explore, from a developing country standpoint, the evolving process of knowledge production and use, and the policy and institutional frameworks which govern this process."[79] It cut across all areas of IDRC work and was, in some senses, a return to some of the issues the Centre had dealt with in the 1970s and 1980s under science and technology policy, although RoKS would take a broader approach by investigating knowledge systems. Knowledge was increasingly recognized as a critical factor in social and economic development, and a key influence on organizational performance. Along with gender, the *CSPF 2000–2005* identified RoKS as one of two cross-cutting dimensions of the Centre's work. As Caroline Pestieau noted, "It hearkened back to the 1970 *IDRC Act*, which empowered the Centre 'to initiate, encourage, support and conduct research ... into the means for applying and adapting scientific, technical and other knowledge" to the problems of the developing regions of the world.[80] It was also a field in which senior management felt the Centre could make a unique contribution, both by ensuring that developing countries had a voice in debates over the issue, and also by broadening the debate from a focus on institutional management strategies toward a concern with the interplay among actors and institutions in a wider knowledge system.[81]

During the ramping-up phase, RoKS program officers hoped to accomplish a number of objectives, including promoting analysis and debate at various levels on key issues in the evolution and functioning of knowledge systems, and re-establishing IDRC's reputation as a leading player in this area, and in particular as a channel for independent Southern perspectives. They also wanted to identify longer-term activities and partners with whom the Centre could work to pursue those initiatives. By early 2000 it was easy to assert the importance of knowledge as a critical factor in economic and social development and as a key influence on organizational performance. It was, IDRC staff member Brent Herbert-Copley remarked, "leaving its mark on development discourse and practice ... because it was based on a core set of insights about the nature of knowledge production and application, which [were] themselves the product of accumulated research and practical experience over the past half-century."[82]

CSPF 2000–2005 also referred to knowledge intensity and the fact that IDRC could not "achieve its goals of strengthening research capacity, and of fostering research that will benefit people's lives through funding alone. Two resource flows [were] required: money and people."[83] That, too, had been the Centre's forte and mantra since its establishment. Further, the *CSPF* dictated that the Centre retain the capacity to adapt and experiment in order to remain as relevant and effective as possible. It called for "innovations in the way that science is conducted and managed" and for program officers to "choose from a wide range of options to ensure that the support we provide is optimally tailored to the needs of ... different regions."

The final document met with board approval; governors liked its regional dimension, the focus on indigenous capacity, the use of local knowledge, and the explicit intent to help Southern countries carry out negotiations with international organizations like the World Trade Organization. They also liked the concentration on such issues as genetically modified organisms, governance in Africa, capacity building and e-commerce, and especially the development of privacy and other legislation. As well, it emphasized links to policy, a topic that one governor labelled "a most vexatious subject." This was called "closing the loop," which focused on the third element in the IDRC trinity and nicely complemented the first two; to build capacity to analyze key development issues, to produce technically sound research, and to make IDRC-funded research policy relevant. By the 1990s, this had become much more prominent and IDRC was demanding to see results for its money, while by 2001, the issue of utilization received concerted attention with the development of numerous "closing the loop" activities.[84] Later, the trinity was provided with more substance:

> [It would be] directly relevant to local problems and sensitive to changing local conditions and opportunities, IDRC supported research serves to modify behavior in the public interest by enhancing knowledge, understanding and awareness among researchers, policy-makers, users and communities. Possessing the flexibility to adapt in order to seize opportunities that were not foreseen at the outset, IDRC research projects will influence the way in which research is undertaken, encouraging experimentation and innovative approaches leading to the more effective use of research to enhance the well-being of people in developing countries.[85]

Overall, the *CSPF* provided clear direction that the knowledge- and people-intensive approach for which IDRC had become renowned should be maintained. As it pointed out, "IDRC houses a core competence in a wide range of expertise and experience.... The Centre will maintain its field presence and its in-house expertise."[86] The document also insisted that IDRC retain the capacity to adapt and experiment in order to remain as relevant as possible. It called for "innovations in the way that science is conducted and managed ... [and that the Centre will] choose from a wide range of options to ensure that the support [it] provides is optimally tailored to the needs of the ... different regions." And regional presence was important; a program matrix formed its core and it was adopted to achieve "a more judicious balance between the substance of research on broad program areas, and tailoring what IDRC supports to the specific priorities of each region."[87]

Programming took place within a matrix that balanced broad program areas and issues along one axis, and regional priorities and opportunities along the other. Discovering a proper equilibrium depended on an evolving set of relationships among Centre managers. Indeed, following a meeting of senior managers the consensus was that "the success of the matrix structure depends on sophisticated interpersonal skills, clarity of expectations and responsibilities, feedback mechanisms for staff development, and exquisite communication."[88] Happily, that reflected IDRC capabilities. The *CSPF* also pulled together the program initiatives into a coherent whole and provided, at least according to some critics, "new vitality, greater flexibility and exciting new opportunities."[89] As programming diversity remained the key to the Centre's capacity to respond to rapidly changing conditions, its emphasis on PIs remained relevant as the best way to achieve this. It was the creativity and scientific competence of its program staff that allowed IDRC to stand out in the international development arena. The *CSPF* provided a strategic direction for the Centre, as well as reinforcing some age-old truths. It also allowed O'Neil to press researchers and others in the South for their views of the development of the Centre. Interested in their perspective, she discussed priority issues with researchers, politicians, and public servants on all her trips abroad as IDRC president, some of which appeared in the final document.

Gender as an Issue

O'Neil had been proactive on the gender front, which was reflected in IDRC's more intense consideration of it. For example, the Centre had hosted the first annual meeting of the new international alliance, "Women in Informal Employment: Globalizing and Organizing," in April 1999, which brought together members from grassroots women's organizations, research and statistical institutions, and international development agencies. The opportunity was seized to share IDRC's new approach to gender, much to the delight of the participants. Indeed, a part of O'Neil's performance evaluation was based on the steady progress in the integration of gender in Centre-supported research. As she pointed out, PI teams had undertaken a great deal of work during 1999 in preparing appropriate subject and regional tool kits to assist Southern country research partners in improving the quality of their gender research. *CSPF 2000–2005* spoke to that issue: "Over the last few years, we have been concerned about ensuring that researchers consider the differential impact on men and women of the issues they are studying. But this is insufficient. There are issues that explicitly relate to women gaining greater control over their lives.... We then have to ask whether our programs directly address any of these issues. At a general level, yes, you can fit women into anything. But it's not the same thing as asking if research can contribute to the essential steps to improve women's lives."[90]

As a reflection of the new dynamic that animated the Centre, a newly renamed Gender Unit was established in 2000 and supported with CAN$600,000 (increased to CAN$1.1 million in 2002 and CAN$2.4 million by 2005). In one of its first papers, the Unit suggested that work be refocused on research and that it set up a program of "cutting edge, gender-focused research."[91] It was also mandated to produce a positive "lessons learned" document highlighting the gender-related findings of the Centre's PIs as well as to enhance the Centre's profile in international debates regarding gender and development through the implementation of an expanded program of research. That reflected an increasing concern with the role of women more generally at IDRC. The old days of the "two-for-one" special, when program officers were overwhelmingly men and their wives stayed home to raise children and keep the home fires burning while they travelled the world, were over. As O'Neil remarked with some emphasis, when she arrived at IDRC, there was no maternity leave and the Centre "was way behind other federal agencies. I don't understand how that happened; nobody paid any attention to it." David Brooks, the acting head of the Gender Unit in the early 2000s, agreed that the Centre had lagged behind, going back to Ivan Head's tenure as president: it had experienced "a political roller coaster, ... mainly as a result of 'the view from the top.'"[92] In other words, the presidents had set the tone.

While mainstreaming[93] of gender issues had happened, O'Neil was surprised at how little programming actually focused on women's inequality, a far cry from the central vision of a Centre-supported researcher, who had noted that "[h]uman development, if not engendered, is fatally endangered."[94] IDRC "was not funding work on that, and how to overcome those barriers to women having greater personal freedom, like property rights in marriage, like land title. There was no women's rights agenda for research. It had gotten mired in the gender question." Following O'Neil's arrival, the Centre pushed on with an intent to increase awareness. As was noted in 2000, "Over the last few years, the Centre's main effort has been in 'mainstreaming' considerations of gender equity, ensuring that they were addressed appropriately in all the research it funds. This effort continues. We also now intend to have a specific program of research support to advance international debate of gender issues. The starting point will be disciplinary expertise in one of the three main program areas, to which gender analysis and its practical application can be directed. The research program will be carried out in collaboration with the most closely related program initiatives."[95] However, it could be difficult in some cultures to press women's issues too strongly. While PI team leaders were expected to provide intellectual leadership in terms of focusing on areas they wanted to investigate, they also had to know "when enough is enough and they can't push too much more within the context of the culture and behaviors within a country. Being sensitive to how far you can 'push' on gender issues in some projects, but not losing the focus completely."[96]

Still, it would be some time before gender became a totally accepted facet of program development. As an early 2004 evaluation of ENRM pointed out, with respect to gender, "The teams are now sensitized but they have still not fully assimilated the concept."[97] Jean Lebel, the author of the management response to the external evaluations of ENRM, noted that "The shortcomings ... are attributed to multitude factors, the most frequently cited of which are: the variability of our staff's capacities, the difficulty of translating the concept in the field, specific regional circumstances, the lack of experience among researchers, the lack of follow-up and monitoring, and resistance to a concept 'imposed' by IDRC." Clearly, given some resistance in the field to incorporating gender issues into program initiatives, the Centre would have to establish some sort of mechanism to integrate them more effectively. Over the next several years it did so, pursuing gender-based research in a more focused way, a development that is seen in the example of a five-year project called Swayamsiddha.

Coordinated by the Bharatiya Agro Industries Development Research Foundation (BAIF), an organization set up on the IDRC model in 1979 and initially funded by CIDA and IDRC, the project focused on women's health and empowerment and was implemented by nine partner institutions in six Indian states. BAIF had been "mentored" by the Centre and, as a result, Narayan Hegde, the organization's president in 2006, could say that as a result, it was able "to visualize how important women were to development.... For development, a patient–doctor relationship is needed and the latter needs to listen and prescribe very precise medicine."[98] That was what IDRC did in the case of gender. As a result, he believes, the project "exceeded expectations." Its final report noted that its "purpose was to improve rural female health, and empower them to address their own needs, by initiating gender responsive collective actions and institutionalizing processes. To this end, a multifaceted process was implemented to increase women's knowledge, build their confidence, and enhance their ability to apply their newly acquired knowledge, both individually and in groups.... Practical needs identified collectively by women at the beginning of the project shaped the activities that they ... worked to address."[99]

The project emphasized the role of the collective in empowerment, and reached 5,202 women through 616 community-based organizations (CBOs) in its investigation of health outcomes. For example, one indicator related to women's knowledge of their bodies, causes of illness, reproductive health, and preventative health. As an IDRC evaluation pointed out, "in March 2002, only 38 percent of women CBO members were deemed to have fair health knowledge and skills [about these issues]. At the end of the project, 73 percent of women were assessed as having good skills and knowledge, reflecting a substantial increase in primary and reproductive and preventative health knowledge and practice."[100] It was as if women were finally getting to the kitchen with mainstreaming of gender issues at IDRC: O'Neil had pointed out that "I used that analogy that you really wanted to renovate your kitchen, but first you approach it through the bedroom then the living room and you hope that that will do it, but you never really get to the kitchen. And the women's rights questions are really focused on the kitchen, sometimes literally, so we created a new program [that came into being on 1 April 2006], Women's Rights and Citizenship."[101]

The new program was cutting edge and was the result of a long debate over what IDRC should call it. O'Neil was quite insistent that it was about the rights of women and girls, a reflection of her formative years, shaped by a deep knowledge of human rights and the human rights machinery. She was also more than a little distrustful of some of the gender social science, finding it excessively dense, jargon-filled, and impenetrable in its language. Further, she found it often not very useful to the people who wanted to make a difference in promoting the rights of women and girls. As a result, she had a very detailed view of what the new program should be, challenging the then-team leader "to put yourself in the place of the head of women's rights in the social affairs ministry in some developing country. What information, what research do you need to further your case in that highly male-dominated environment where you are the head of women's rights in a second-tier ministry in the social affairs realm in [that] developing country? Well down the totem pole. What do you need to move women's rights up the agenda?" As Lauchlan Munro, now vice-president of corporate strategy and regional management, pointed out, "She challenged the team leader to think in those terms because the initial discussions around the prospectus had a lot of post-modernist and gender studies jargon to which Maureen was allergic."[102]

Goodbye to ROSA

As has been seen, much had been accomplished at the Centre since O'Neil's arrival. However, the range of IDRC involvement in various areas of the globe was proving financially difficult given the Centre's straitened circumstances. For that reason, the Regional Office for Southern Africa, was targeted for closure. That had everything to do with IDRC's parliamentary appropriation; savings had to be found as the new millennium dawned if the Centre was to survive.[103] The Operational Review Working Group was tasked with coming up with recommendations designed to reduce the Centre's operational costs in order to protect a minimum level of program funding directed to its Southern partners in light of operational constraints. In October 2000, the program committee met to discuss IDRC's program of work and to examine priority areas given its current level of resources. That included a discussion of the regional presence strategy to determine the feasibility, from a programmatic point of view, of rationalizing the costs of IDRC's regional presence. At the time of the last review in 1997 total program appropriations in IDRC had been CAN$64 million and the four offices in Africa had cost CAN$4.5 million; by 2000, the numbers were CAN$44 million and CAN$6 million, respectively. Four regional offices in Africa were now (at least) one too many given costs, and the resulting recommendation was to close the Regional Office for Southern Africa, even though the Centre's parliamentary appropriation was to rise by almost CAN$6 million for fiscal year 2001–2, the first increase in eight years. No other regional office would be similarly affected, although Montevideo was to be downsized through attrition. It was expected that CAN$1.6 million in savings would result.

However, as O'Neil told the board in March 2001, cost was not the only factor, especially as the Nairobi office was more expensive than ROSA. Rather, "the choice lies at the intersection of cost, program and broader regional considerations." Nairobi would be kept open to maintain the programming IDRC intended to support in the region—"there would be more to lose by closing Nairobi and operating only out of Johannesburg."[104] Furthermore,

IDRC has had a presence in Nairobi since 1975 and EARO has become a highly visible and recognized partner in the research environment of many countries of Eastern and Southern Africa. Since the 1960s, Nairobi has been the regional centre for Eastern and Southern Africa, acting as a hub for many regional activities, e.g., UNEP, UNICEF, IUCN, CGIAR, and a number of major donors (Ford, Rockefeller). Despite the evident problems of insecurity and political instability in Kenya ... it must be remembered that since the 1970s, Ethiopia, Uganda, Tanzania, Somalia, Rwanda have all been involved in wars, while Kenya has avoided open conflict. The considerable concentration of international and regional institutions creates its own pressure for a reasonable level of services and coping mechanisms. Also, the relatively stronger research infrastructure in South Africa means that there are better prospects for devolving responsibility for some program activities than there would be in Nairobi.

Moreover, O'Neil believed that the time when IDRC needed an office in Johannesburg had passed; ROSA "had been a brilliant idea in the pre-Mandela, pre-democratic government days and IDRC, heavily funded by CIDA, had run fascinating programs ... when the focus was on improving the capacity of the African National Congress to become the governing party."[105] That had led to commissions on macro-economic policy, on urban affairs, on environment, and a lot of work on women's issues. There was also a companion program run by Al Johnson, many times a deputy minister in Ottawa and a former head of the CBC, on public service reform. That, too, was done under the IDRC umbrella; indeed, a section of the new South African constitution was written in the Centre's Johannesburg office.[106] As O'Neil later explained, the activities that ROSA undertook were focused and highly specific. As well, all programming in the region could be supervised from either Nairobi or Ottawa, and the Centre would continue to base a program officer in Johannesburg to represent its interests and research would continue to be funded. TIPS and SchoolNet South Africa, two major initiatives that operated out of the Johannesburg office, would be established as separate entities, while the program officer for Acacia would be placed in a South African university.[107] South Africa also had very strong institutions already in place; East Africa was another question entirely and the need was to have an office in Nairobi. Politics had also moved on in South Africa: "It was very important to have these neutral spaces in the years before majority rule. In the beginning, IDRC was a real meeting place. In fact, half the people in Mandela's first Cabinet had been on the end of an IDRC policy research project grant," O'Neil remembered. She also believed that that sort of access would decline over years as the government became established and capacity increased—"the romance and dynamism would have paled."

That was probably true, and it was equally as probable that the regional director, Marc Van Ameringen, was vehemently opposed to the pending closure, as was ROSA staff. Of some significance, Nelson Mandela, now a private citizen, also wrote to Prime Minister Chrétien opposing the closure, as did the prime minister of Mozambique, Pascol Manuel Mocumbi. The latter expressed his "very strong feeling … that we stand to gain a lot if IDRC establishes a stronger point of presence [in Johannesburg]."[108] In October 1995, while still president of the Republic of South Africa, Mandela had noted that "South Africans have benefited greatly from the IDRC's assistance."[109] He went on to point out that in the difficult years before 1994 and the return to majority rule, the Centre had played "a critical role in helping the ANC and the Mass Democratic Movement to prepare for negotiations." Similarly, IDRC "was instrumental in helping us to prepare for the new phase of governance and transformation." His *démarche* to Chrétien in September 2001 as a private citizen reflected his intense concern over the pending office closure. This was remarkable, prompting board chair Gordon Smith to remark that "The South Africans are certainly pulling out all the stops."[110] None of the lobbying carried the day, however, and on 30 September 2001 the last person out of ROSA turned off the lights for good. It was a sad occasion and the decision still elicits quite strong reactions in 2010.

Nor did the closure of the office mean the end of all IDRC programming. While it might be reduced in scope and volume, it did continue. An example of that is seen with the very successful Trade and Industrial Policy Secretariat (TIPS), created in 1996 to serve as a research and knowledge clearing house for South Africa's Department of Trade and Industry (DTI). By 2001 it was a very successful initiative, addressing as it did the new context for trade and industrial policy formulation in South Africa "by building capacity within and outside the government, establishing linkages between the available expertise in this sector within the state, private sector and research community, and by addressing the serious skills shortage in trade and industrial policy."[111] It was also funded by USAID and Germany's Geshellschaft für Technische Zusammenarbeit. Trade policy was a cornerstone for achieving equitable economic growth and development, and many leading South African economists, in the years immediately following the establishment of majority rule, saw poor export performance as the major factor prohibiting the entire economy from growing at a faster rate. Through assistance to DTI, the project strengthened its policy analysis capacity while constructing linkages between the department and outside policy researchers. As well, it established a forum to allow the department, the research community, the private sector, and other parts of civil society to determine priorities for research on trade and industrial policy, and expand the pool of researchers through strengthening training and research capacity in trade and industrial policy. In short, TIPS assisted the department in harnessing all relevant trade and industrial policy research for DTI, in the process influencing trade, industry, and technology policy in government by nurturing, as Rashad Cassim, now the deputy director general of Economic Statistics of Statistics South Africa but in the late 1990s the head of TIPS, recalled, high-quality, policy-relevant research and creating the capacity to absorb the findings. The program initiative document had said just that: "TIPS strength and relevance lies in: (1) its input into policy formulation through the recruitment of experts to assist the South African government; (2) its efforts to move the frontiers of the debate in these subjects forward, and; (3) its assistance in improving the quality of policy-relevant research and the absorptive capacity of the government."[112]

As Cassim remembers, "IDRC provided a training ground. Being head of this unit, you got into contact with experts and you got resources to go to conferences."[113] Most importantly, IDRC, while never the biggest donor, did get major results for the funding invested in part because it was "core funding and the others gave more project funding. The bigger money basically meant nothing if you couldn't get core funding." IDRC funding was also a benefit because "you were linked to a network which had members in Vietnam and Latin America—it provided capacity and exposure to develop policy in a way that would help the country." Further, the Centre was a knowledge broker, whereas its larger cousins were donor agencies; that was a key difference. Finally, IDRC was not linked to the foreign policy considerations of Canada, a fact that Cassim recalled fondly.

That work continues. TIPS, devolved from IDRC with the closure of the ROSA office in September 2001, did not experience any difficulties and continued to produce high-quality work for the South African government and the region. That was confirmed by the seventh annual TIPS conference, held in 2002. As was pointed out, "Almost three hundred academics, policy makers and experts in the trade field gathered for three days to hear papers and discuss *Global Integration, Sustainable Development and the Southern African Economy*."[114] The conversation, Connie Freeman, the regional director based in Nairobi, noted, was lively and candid between policy-makers and scholars. As well, "The discussion on South-South trade collaboration and its difficulties was pioneering." Importantly, among the three hundred present, "IDRC was universally recognized and applauded as the founder of TIPS and as a continued force in its success."

Regional Offices and Their Place in IDRC

The agitation around ROSA's closure led to further consideration of the role of regional offices, as had happened at least once during each presidential era. They had come to be regarded as more than "administrative outgrowths of headquarters [and] ... many now saw them as a part of the Centre's "particular personality as an institution."[115] Under O'Neil's guidance, small regional activity funds were created, which allowed regional directors "to respond strategically and rapidly to particular requests from local partners and stakeholders." However, intellectually, what role did they play in IDRC's world? Clearly, they were an integral part of the Centre; in *CSPF 2000–2005* "regional presence was reaffirmed as a distinguishing feature ... and essential for the successful implementation of the program laid out in the Corporate Strategic and Program Framework." The remark by a governor in 2001, "There is still no substitute for being there," certainly resonated in IDRC hallways.[116]

Centralizing all project administration in Ottawa was explicitly rejected even though significant savings could most likely be achieved via such a policy. Indeed, management knew that regional presence added value to knowledge intensive activities, as the Overseas Development Institute analysis for DFID, quoted above, had suggested. An example of that was the establishment of the Asia Development Research Forum, which had come out of the Singapore office trying to catalyze a "made in Asia" forum of researchers that would focus local research on problems of regional significance. A paper written by Randy Spence, the Regional Office for Southeast and East Asia (ASRO) director, on the Asian financial crisis of 1997 was the single most popular item on the pan-Asia networking site. Preparing it had involved digesting and synthesizing more than one hundred other papers and reports, and it has set the example for Asian members of the forum who, by 2000, were taking the lead in such activities and presenting their own high-quality research findings.[117] Similarly, South Africa's Consultative National Environmental Policy Process had been a regional office initiative launched in 1994 in connection with the South African Mass Democratic Movement. It had been aimed at identifying key natural environmental policy priorities. The resulting report had been endorsed by the South African president, Nelson Mandela, while the then Minister of Environmental Affairs and Tourism Dawie de Villiers had asked IDRC to assist the government in managing a national policy formulation process. In like fashion, the East African Regional Office was critical in establishing a workshop for senior managers from five research organizations in East Africa to share their evaluation experiences with fifteen others, and to offer their expertise on how to use evaluation to build capacity. These are only several of hundreds of such ventures that had come out of IDRC's network of regional offices. Clearly, regional presence did add value to knowledge-intensive activities. It also added credibility, convening power, and technical and administrative capability. As *CSPF III* had noted, "IDRC's field presence provides an extra edge to its special knowledge and awareness of Southern research and development conditions."

It was one thing to assert this, but quite another to prove it. This was done in part through the context of managing the program matrix that formed the core of the *CSPF 2000–2005*. The matrix had been adopted to achieve a better balance between the substance of research on broad program areas, and tailoring what IDRC supported to the specific priorities of each region. As was pointed out, "The [2002] approach [was] expressed in a complete and inter-related set of job descriptions for the managers most directly involved in making the matrix work: the Directors of Program Areas, the Regional Directors, the Program Initiative Team Leaders, Program Officers based in Ottawa, and Regional Program Officers. The main responsibilities of the Regional Directors—and by extension the main role of the regional offices— is to ensure the effective delivery of the Centre's program in the region, including *inter alia* identifying new research areas and needs, fostering partnerships and resource expansion, and promoting the dissemination and use of the results arising from IDRC-supported research for policy change."[118] A paper, "Update on IDRC's Strategic Approach to Regional Presence," was prepared for consideration at the June 2002 executive committee meeting and underlined the necessary complementarity between the thematic and regional dimensions of the program matrix. This made it difficult to talk only of a regional presence (or that of headquarters) as management and program responsibilities were shared among staff, wherever they might be; there were very few things for which either staff in Ottawa or in the regional offices had sole responsibility.

IDRC continues to place value on the regional presence, despite its cost. Management uses regional intelligence to, for example, inform future program development and to learn from experiments that are being undertaken in the regions in terms of assessing their wider use. The establishment of networks also remains centred, to some extent, on regional offices and drawing in regional partners. Regional offices also draw other development agencies to IDRC because of the expertise that has been developed over decades. As Joanne Alston, DFID's head of central research, has noted, her organization finds the Centre's regional offices much to its liking as the two develop joint programming; ROs have "been a big factor in why we think it's worthwhile engaging with [IDRC]."[119]

The Centre Moves Ahead: More Dollars, More Commitments

IDRC's fortunes improved in terms of its parliamentary appropriation by 2003–4, when it reached almost CAN$108 million. The following year it was to hit CAN$116.5 million. These were substantial increases and the Centre was keen to take advantage of the enhanced capability they provided. Reaffirmation of IDRC's mission took place at the board of governors meeting in late 2003, an occasion where the usual hand-wringing and anxiety about the parliamentary appropriation was noticeably absent. Capacity building remained the primary focus among the three program areas—Environment and Natural Resources Management (ENRM), Social and Economic Equity (SEE), and Information and Communication Technologies for Development (ICT4D). Capacity building also took an enormous amount of time if done properly; IDRC remained committed to flexibility and perseverance in environments where, at times, success was not obvious and might even be counted as the absence of outright failure. Capacity building was easier to achieve, however, given the rising parliamentary appropriation. The way forward, at least for IDRC, was to continue its tendency "to blend perseverance on issues with a curiosity and an openness to new opportunities … this openness to new opportunities and new ways of doing things was as important as perseverance."[120] The management matrix, developed for the *CSPF 2000–2005*, had allowed directors more time to look "above and beyond program boundaries [and it had] facilitated the development of opportunities for more collaboration."

IDRC had also championed the use of methods for bringing scientific disciplines, civil society representatives, politicians, and communities together in the joint development and pursuit of research activities. This represented a major breakthrough in fields of research that had been traditionally dominated by, as one account had it, "reductionist and narrowly uni-disciplinary approaches."[121] Further, various program areas had placed stress upon participatory approaches in order to "encourage the community to take ownership for understanding the problems, for developing and participating in the research process, and for using its outcomes to ensure the sustainability of activities and their impacts." It had also made some progress in terms of sensitizing decision makers to innovative fields of research, or making sure that their views were included in the program design to move from a situation where researchers were "pushing" the research agenda to one where the policy-makers' demands were "pulling" it, making the idea of "closing the loop" a foregone conclusion.

All of that was reflected in an ERNM program initiative, Ecosystem Approaches to Human Health, commonly called Ecohealth. Begun in the later 1990s by Gilles Forget, its premise lay in the notion that human health was linked to the environment in which people lived and improvements in both could be, and often must be, simultaneously achieved. It was also established as the Bezanson Centre had ended health programming, at least in theory. As Forget recalls, "La transition a débuté quand le nouveau Président a décidé de changer des structures qu'il n'arrivait pas à contrôler tels qu'elles existaient. À ce moment là on m'avait approché et on m'avait dit ... le Président m'a dit : 'Écoute Gilles la santé on n'en veut plus au Centre et on va seulement garder une chose et ça c'est 'santé et environ-nement' et c'est toi qui devrais s'occuper de ça."[122] That reflected IDRC's Agenda 21 commitments.

It was also driven as much by the foresight of Centre staff as it was by a clearly expressed need from Southern partners. Ecohealth had found fer-tile ground for growth in the innovative thinking that animated IDRC's work during the last days of the Bezanson presidency despite the horrendous fis-cal situation and accompanying administrative upheaval. Its program deliv-ery reflected the Centre's mission of empowerment through knowledge by strengthening and mobilizing the local research capacity of developing coun-tries. The 2004 PI further identified "humans as a part of their own ecosys-tem and [posited] that successful interventions must take into account the symbiosis that exist[ed] across elements of the ecosystem."[123] The unifying hypothesis that underlay its attractiveness was key:

> Principle I[124] of the Rio Declaration summarizes well what we must do to achieve sustainable development. It cannot be achieved if there is debilitat-ing illness and poverty, and health cannot be maintained without healthy envi-ronments and life support systems. And yet, we currently face all of these development challenges: high poverty and inequity, a global burden of dis-ease of which 25 percent is estimated to be due to poor quality of the envi-ronment, poorly managed natural resources and new, emerging, and re-emerging infectious diseases. This suggests an urgent need to understand the linkages between health, environment, and development and the nature of the trade-offs in the choices made by the poor. It suggests the need to identify interventions that are multi-sectoral, involving not just the health and/or environmental sectors. It requires a recognition that health is both an outcome and a resource for sustainable development, and an understand-ing of the role of health and well-being in poverty reduction strategies. It calls for integrated thinking, innovative approaches, inclusive processes, partner-ships and empowered communities.[125]

As the proposed prospectus went on to note, it had also carved out a unique niche: "the Ecohealth PI focuses on the interacting social and ecolog-ical contexts that influence health and human well-being. It is engaged more with issues of health rather than with those of disease, on prevention rather than just cure. It moves beyond health to concerns of sustainable development and continued well-being." It had identified three ecosystems in which it would carry out its research support, including agriculture, the urban environment, and mining, all fraught with difficulties, disease, and calamity in the South. The rationale for selecting those areas was clear; they were places where human and environmental health were simultaneously being degraded in a way that particularly disadvantaged the poor and the weak, which could inhibit any rational approach to development.

Ecohealth was well recognized among researchers and development organizations working in health and the environment, was identified with IDRC, and was viewed as creative and effective.[126] The concept of broad problem definition that encapsulated both health and environment, and a research approach that included local communities, was particularly well suited to the needs of developing country populations who faced multiple adverse effects from environmental and health risks, but who also had to be involved in finding credible solutions. The idea built capacity among developing country researchers to engage in research of direct relevance to their communities. As was noted, "the innovativeness of the Ecohealth approach [lay] in its focus on understanding the social and ecological context of human lives, and on efforts to achieve improved health that engage the multiplicity of actors, processes, and agencies implicated in these complex linkages."

During the early 2000s, about three hundred developing country researchers had been involved in research projects, more than one hundred had applied for research funding, and at least eighty had been involved in a training experience. Those experiences had allowed transdisciplinary[127] researchers to develop collaborative teams, as well as to form relationships with other researchers in other parts of the world. As the 2004 evaluation noted, "long term impact [was] expected from the local, regional and international networks of researchers created through these activities and likely to be sustained through new efforts to develop a Community of Practice [in Echohealth]." In addition, almost forty Southern research institutions had benefited from their researchers' involvement in these projects, benefits that had included such things as greater diversity of intellectual activity, inclusion in relevant networks, greater cohesion among their faculty, and improved relationships with nearby communities. They also reflected more tangible assistance like small amounts of infrastructure and overhead support and access to improved funding streams.[128] As well, certain international organizations like the World Health Organization, the UN Environment Program, and the Pan American Health Organization had incorporated some of its findings

into their own work, as had various Canadian federal government departments with similar interests.

This was impact spelled with capital letters.[129] And Centre staff had
become increasingly focused on impact, pushed by Jean Lebel, the program
area director. As he had noted in a report to the board, the major breakthroughs that had followed Ecohealth "will have to be supported by hard
evidence that these 'innovations' are leading to better access, better utilization and better quality of the environment and of resource management and
that, thanks to those improvements, we will be able to improve the welfare
of the populations concerned."[130] That would mean more reference to, for
example, yield increases of 1.5 tonnes per hectare in rice paddies adjacent
to a community-based reforestation management project in Cambodia, or
the nation-wide scaling up of waste-water treatment technology in urban
and peri-urban areas of Jordan, or the decline in the incidence of malaria in
Mexico through ecohealth approaches that had supplanted the use of the
harmful chemical DDT.

Work has continued on the program initiative to the present time (2010).
Indeed, throughout the first decade of the twenty-first century, it has grown.
For example, following the Ecohealth Forum held in Montreal in May 2003,
new directions were contemplated. As well, Ecohealth continued to pursue
its support of the System-Wide Initiative on Malaria and Agriculture (SIMA)
of the Consultative Group on International Agricultural Research, a multinational network that had been initiated in 2002 with the Centre's support ·
and coordinated by the International Water Management Institute. IDRC support helped SIMA to fund two new projects on malaria and agriculture in
East and Southern Africa to complement the three already being funded. In
addition, the PI continued to support the development of a global Community of Practice on Ecohealth, which had been strongly represented at the
Forum and which was already supported through collaboration with one of
the federal granting agencies, the Canadian Institutes of Health Research.
As an element of that, and recognizing the importance of supporting young
researchers to increase the reach of Ecohealth and ensure its sustainability,
the Ecohealth Awards were re-established. The field has also developed into
an academic discipline, supports its own academic journal, *Ecohealth*, has
hosted successful international meetings, and overseen the continuing establishment of global networks of Ecohealth practice and the adoption of the Ecohealth perspective by other agencies and funders. However, this brief recitation
of a few Ecohealth projects represents a small portion of the total; by the
end of July 2004, there were thirty-two ongoing activities being funded, at
least in part, by IDRC.[131]

The Tanzania Essential Health Interventions Project (TEHIP), introduced in Chapter 5, had a similar catalytic effect on research and process in the South, as well as demonstrating how, if carefully applied, small amounts of funding and an innovative paradigm could yield big benefit. By 2004, Centre support for the initiative was winding down following years of assistance, yet it was also true that IDRC programming and the New Partnership for African Development had meshed nicely with TEHIP, which had proved to be enormously successful and suggestive of a way forward. Indeed, the *Globe and Mail*'s Africa reporter, Stephanie Nolan, had been entranced by its capabilities and simplicity and perhaps most noticeably by its cost. As she wrote, "How's this for bang for your buck? At a time when problems of poverty and underdevelopment often appear grimly intractable, a Canadian-funded research project in Tanzania has proved that it is possible to cut child deaths by almost half with just a tiny injection of cash—in this case, less than $2 (US) a person each year."[132] The influential *Economist* had also commented on the tremendous success of the initiative: "The results of all this were stunning.... The proportion of children dying before their fifth birthdays dropped by 14 percent from 140 per 1,000 to 120."[133] An IDRC evaluation had noted that "Through its impacts on capacity building and its influence on policies, [TEHIP] and its team have had a remarkable influence on development in the country."[134] The program had clearly demonstrated that decentralization of government service delivery could result in better targeting of health expenditures, but only if local communities and decision makers had accurate and convincing information on local needs and sufficient resources. And that was what it had provided, with IDRC help, through developing a series of decision-making tools that allowed district-level health officials to better understand the burden of disease facing their district, and the way in which existing financial and human resources were deployed. The result was a better match between health care needs and expenditures, and a notable improvement in health status in the Rufiji and Morogoro districts where TEHIP was active. The Centre was planning to assist in the creation of a new institution to promote evidence-based planning of health interventions in Eastern and Southern Africa and Nigeria as part of TEHIP's legacy.

The good news just kept coming—a Special Examination of the Centre undertaken by the Auditor General's Office at the behest of IDRC in 2002 had gone very well, and the Centre was well pleased with the report.[135] For the 2004–5 fiscal year, its parliamentary appropriation rose to CAN$113.5 million, which, when combined with other Treasury Board votes to cover part of the compensation costs, totalled CAN$116.1 million. The year following it was CAN$128.2 million, while by 2006–7 it had reached the heady level of CAN$135.3 million. In the final year of O'Neil's tenure as president, it was CAN$145.2 million. That was made possible by the Liberal government's promise in its February 2003 budget to double the amount spent on international assistance by 2010, and the adherence of the Conservatives, following their election in January 2006, to that same commitment. Indeed, the Centre was specifically identified in that budget document as receiving "an eight percent increase in their [sic] budget in the next two fiscal years ... [in] recognition of its world-class reputation for supporting research aimed at funding innovative solutions to challenges facing developing countries."[136] This was the only time that IDRC had received a mention and must surely presage a better world for the organization, or so it was hoped. Moreover, a recent World Bank study had shown that the Centre remained one of the very few organizations to take its lead from foreign researchers and was "perhaps unique in putting development research grant-making at the core of its mandate."[137] That had some traction in Ottawa among the Liberal government. It was also the result of proselytizing work done by Centre staff; as the president pointed out and which had been made clear to senior officials in Ottawa, "IDRC is the only organization to work at the intersection of two of the new government's key priorities: its innovation agenda and its development agenda."[138]

Whatever the reason, it was welcomed, and senior management believed that much good would come from it: "tremendous opportunities—and possibly turbulence—present themselves with the expected buoyancy in Canada's ODA budget, the new regime [John Manley as finance minister] that has recently taken over the reins in Ottawa, and developments at the global level, politically and financially." That made planning for the next CSPF a little easier—continuity with the old would be maintained where appropriate, but some flexibility could also be built into the new strategic plan. And while, in real terms, IDRC's parliamentary appropriation remained about 30 percent below its 1988–89 peak year, it was also moving in the correct direction, according to staff. Still, given that sobering number, Rohinton Medhora, vice-president of programs, could note that in late 2004, "IDRC is not the organization it was 15 years ago and choices [have been made] on the types of issues we address."[139] Still, those choices had not detracted from the Centre's reputation among its peers where its brand remained dynamic and innovative.

CS + PF 2005–2010

That was the climate in which the new corporate strategy and program framework plan was considered—quite different from that of five years previous when *CSPF 2000–2005* had been developed. Medhora cited what he called IDRC's core business—addressing the knowledge and research capability gap—as well as the five themes that were to be addressed in the new CS + PF:

- Extreme poverty and hunger; the links between food security and sound environmental management; trade and agriculture; the use of ICTs to improve environmental management and rural incomes, and GMOs— are they a continuation of the problem or part of the solution to the problem of poverty and hunger?
- Education as a key component of development. Throughout the program structure, there is support for education, e.g., through the introduction of ICTs in classrooms, through support for SchoolNets, and through modest institutional support.
- Health and the effective delivery of health services through decentralization; the links between health and the environment, the links between health and the global governance debate and the potential for biotechnology to make a difference for health in developing countries
- Environmental sustainability and issues focusing on water, climate change, and marginal lands
- Global governance and issues relating to how the world organizes itself to deal with new challenges[140]

Further, a new program area would be developed to complement the three that had existed for some time: Innovation, Policy, and Science. It was conceived as a response to the federal government's innovation and development agendas and brought related themes under one umbrella.

In a sense, this exercise helped to close the loop on the process that had begun more than twenty years before in Ivan Head's Centre, when he had become very concerned about what was a dearth of data on the measurable "impact" of IDRC programming. That was not to say impact did not happen—it was just very difficult to measure in those relatively unsophisticated days. Impact could certainly be confirmed by external sources and O'Neil could point to several excellent examples, including Alternative Approaches to Natural Resource Management in Latin America and the Caribbean-supported project to develop agro-industries and markets for arracacha, an ancient Inca root crop, in Cajamarca, Peru. TEHIP was an overwhelming success, a fact captured in *Fixing Health Systems*, which attracted extensive and very positive coverage from a number of sources, including the *British Medical Journal*, the *World Report on Knowledge for Better Health*, various UN Millennium task forces, the *Globe and Mail*, and many others.

Arracacha was chosen as the most successful project in Latin America at a workshop held in Chambéry, France, on "Strategies for Improving Liveli-hoods through Income-Generating Activities in Mountain Regions." Simi-larly, the results of the EcoPlata joint research initiative[141] had been presented at a session of the Coastal Zone Canada 2004 conference, held in June in St. John's. It was recognized for its achievements in science and technology and management of the coastal area for encouraging the commitment and participation of communities. The United Nations Educational, Scientific, and Cultural Organization had called EcoPlata one of the most successful initiatives in improving expertise and technical abilities in the area in which it conducted research.

Much remained the same, which was comforting, especially following the extensive consultation that had taken place over the past several years as *CS +PF 2005–10* had been maturing as a plan. As was pointed out, "The fact that there weren't a vast number of changes [from *CSPF 2000–2005*] reflects the reality that the Centre is in its own way constantly in a process of adjustment. It doesn't stand still. We had it about right."[142] External inter-locutors agreed with that, especially given its emphasis on flexibility and responsiveness and the ability to host large resilient programs. Most funda-mentally, IDRC continued to pursue what some called "two seemingly con-tradictory objectives—'investing ahead of the curve' while remaining a 'listening organization.'"[143] As Rohinton Medora told the board, those qual-ities, as well as the Centre's intent to focus on capacity building, research, and analysis, would be promoted in the new strategy. As well, its guiding prin-ciples remained sustainable and equitable development, sensitivity to gen-der, an emphasis on multidisciplinary research, and a focus on Southern researchers. Similarly, networks and partnerships remained at the centre of IDRC practice; it was anticipated that their formation would accelerate dur-ing *CS + PF 2005–2010*. However, they were also now explicitly counted on to achieve capacity building and influence policy. The three program areas also remained as they had been, albeit with variations in theme and project and one name change. On 1 April 2005, SEE became SEP, which translated into Social and Economic Policy. It was necessary, or so the director of the PA, Brent Herbert-Copley believed, "in order to more clearly signal the focus of work on issues of public policy." As one respondent to the post-CS + PF exercise noted, "the reality is that we are always adjusting around the edges, but the nuance is extremely important. The nuance has been significant pro-gram change."

Part of that change lay in the development of a new program area—Innovation, Policy, and Science—in March 2005. That reflected a renewed recognition of the importance of science, technology, and innovation (STI) for development, something that the Centre had moved away from over the past decade. It was also the result of "the fruits of the revolution in [ICTs] which are now being seen in almost all developing countries, buttressed by the potential for advances in bio- and nano-technologies to also impact humanity."[144] And IDRC had had much experience with the former. Certainly it had been a leader in the area with its groundbreaking 1970s project, Science and Technology Policy Instruments. The new program area also emerged from a task force report that had been commissioned in early 2003 to explore the issues involved in the rapidly growing area of biotechnology and development. It had reported to the board in March 2004 and IPS had been the ultimate result, reflecting "an increased demand for applied research that [could] inform and contribute to enhanced innovative capabilities, as well as strong policy and institutional foundations for developing country innovation systems."[145] The range of issues that demanded attention included a host of things not even conceived of a few years earlier, like new transformative technologies including genomics, genetic engineering, and nanotechnology. IDRC was also keen to support research on the economic, environmental, ethical, legal, and social issues regarding their development and use, as well as to enhance research on questions of governance, public understanding, access, and benefits associated with new transformative technologies in and for the South. IPS goals were "to more effectively position the Centre in the emerging STI agenda in Canada and internationally by supporting STI programs and policies in developing countries and by strengthening linkages between the relevant institutions in developing countries and Canada.[146] That also meant increasing engagement with Canada's granting councils— the Natural Sciences and Engineering Research Council, the Social Sciences and Humanities Research Council, and the Canadian Institutes of Health Research. The result is a series of international research chairs, funded 50/50 by IDRC and its granting council partners.

As well, it would fund research in science and technology innovation policies that were directed toward poverty alleviation, increasing equity in science and technology policy discussions in low- and middle-income countries. The new program area soon proved its worth; IPS became instrumental in supporting science and technology within the framework of the New Economic Partnership for Africa's Development. In September 2005, at the second science and technology ministerial conference held in Dakar, ministers attending had adopted an ambitious new consolidated action plan on science and technology for Africa; IPS was instrumental in supporting the core secretariat for NEPAD's science and technology effort, as well as key research

activities carried out by the secretariat, for which the Centre had been singled out by the chair of the minister's conference for its support of science
and technology.[147]

The other program areas remained largely unchanged following consideration in *CS + PF 2005–2010*.[148] Environment and Natural Resource
Management remained focused on helping countries find feasible and sustainable approaches to enhance water and food security, human health and
natural resources management, building their foundations on democratic
participation, good governance, and social equity. An important component
of the program was to strengthen the linkages between research, policy, and
its implementation in order to ensure that its findings were translated into
policy. Social and Economic Policy focused on "public policies that can lead
to poverty reduction and enhanced social equity," which it hoped to achieve
policy change in three ways: (1) by strengthening long-term capacities to
carry out, manage, and disseminate research; (2) by supporting policy-relevant research and analysis on issues of immediate policy concern; and (3) by
assisting researchers and civil society organizations in the facilitation of public accountability by informing debates on key policy issues. Meanwhile,
ICT4D continued the work described earlier in this chapter.

As IDRC buckles down to the challenge of creating another corporate
strategy and program framework for 2010–15, surely much that is in its
predecessor will also find expression in the new document. Since the late
1990s, there is a valuable consistency in Centre strategic plans, which has
proven to be very useful for Southern researchers and their societies. The fundamental thrust of programming will remain the same, even though some
revision around the edges will undoubtedly happen. IDRC has long been
known (and not only by its recipients and staff) as the jewel in the crown of
Canadian development assistance. Certainly that has been the opinion of a
number of national leaders like Mexico's Vicente Fox, Nelson Mandela of
South Africa, and Manmohan Singh, prime minister of India.

A board retreat, held in early 2009 and led by a new president, David
Malone, was devoted at least in part to this developing exercise—that is, to
arrive at broad directions for the Centre's future. It was also an opportunity
"to reflect upon how IDRC carries out its mandate, and envision the Centre's
future role ... [that would] guide program development over the coming
years."[149] Following regional consultations, a number of possible points to be
discussed by the board were suggested, including: "an appropriate balance
between program themes (knowing the research substance) and regional
sensitivity (knowing the context where IDRC works); the balance among the
types of support IDRC can offer; an appropriate balance between support to

individuals ... and strengthening organizations; the value added by IDRC interventions beyond financial support (e.g., framing the problem, guiding research design, connecting with peers, providing missing opportunities for critical inquiry); and the appropriate balance between supporting research and brokering knowledge."

Conclusion

Clearly, Maureen O'Neil's eleven years as president of IDRC worked out very well. Following the cataclysm of the six Bezanson years, caused by events well beyond his control, the Centre was anxious for some stability in programming and in personality. She had also been bequeathed a new programming system by her predecessor, which worked out very well over time, albeit with some further refinements. Jean-Guy Paquet, a governor for a total of sixteen years until 2004, noted in that year that, "Aujourd'hui c'est un autre CRDI comparativement à celui que j'ai connu il y a dix ans. La culture pour moi c'est la façon de faire, d'interagir ensemble, de communiquer à l'interne, de partager, de travailler sur des projets communs, de viser le succès du CRDI. C'est beaucoup plus intégré, les gens travaillent plus dans la même direction. Ils sont plus motivés malgré les difficultés qui ont été vécues lors des coupures budgétaires. Les projets sont mieux ciblés, mieux évalués, on comprend mieux, on sait où l'on va à travers le plan stratégique. Pour un organisme comme le CRDI, qui est une société d'état, je pense que c'est un exercice qui a été très positif."[150] It was also a reflection of her personality and intelligence that she got along as well as she did for as long as she did. O'Neil was consultative, inclusive, and empathetic in her approach to issues; her staff responded in kind. As a result, the Centre was reinvigorated and repositioned to embark on a journey under her leadership.

She was also a citizen of the world and knew it better than most. While the same claim could be made for the Centre, O'Neil was active in pushing its boundaries. They were both aware of an increasingly interdependent world in which Canadian research for development assistance also served the best interests of Canada. Those areas where IDRC put its money—disease, environmental degradation, and underdevelopment—clearly transcended boundaries. As she told the annual meeting of faculty at Ryerson University: "The transmission of diseases across borders is reduced when health issues are addressed in countries worldwide. Addressing development challenges contributes to sustainable development and increased stability, and, therefore, has peace and security implications at regional and global levels. Canada's continued support of Southern science research has won for our country a great deal of respect and goodwill in international arenas."[151] All of that was true, and the IDRC way of doing it had also been validated over time—that a country can develop only when its citizens have acquired the capacity to address their own development problems.

IDRC has continued to walk the path, the one less travelled, that it first took forty years ago. That might be best summed up by Rohinton Medhora: The organization was "not necessarily about delivering the keynote address, we are about building the platform so that other people can deliver their own keynote addresses."[152] This is a theme of which the Centre is rightly proud and one that researchers find difficult to absorb, even four decades later. Alternatively, it has been framed in terms of a "Kodak moment" where IDRC is not present; the project that was funded, often long before other agencies were interested, has become a global or a continental or a regional success and the Centre, sometimes sustaining the research for ten years, has vacated the field as it encouraged others to take it up. As prime ministers, presidents, or other VIPs gather on podiums for the official ribbon-cutting, IDRC program officers are conspicuous by their absence, even though the work would not have been accomplished without the long, nurturing care provided by the Centre. And it wants it this way, shunning the limelight as it moves on to other projects and areas.

O'Neil, in her own way, personified this. Loved and respected by the people who worked for her, she could also be very firm when occasion demanded, clearly demonstrated by the closure of the Regional Office for Southern Africa. She was no micro-manager, but maintained an organization in which ideas and research impact were the most important things. Importantly, O'Neil also had traction in official Ottawa and was universally admired for her savvy and intelligence, factors of considerable weight. As Medhora remembers, "She knew how to situate things for IDRC."[153] She continued the IDRC tradition of being ahead of the curve in conceiving of its program areas and projects, as well as being a listening organization. Sometimes the former came from the latter, a very unusual development in world of international assistance, but it was quintessentially IDRC. Under her presidency, IDRC came to quickly reflect twenty-first-century issues, like the effects of new communication technologies on development or those of bio- and nano-technologies. As had been the case since its inception, O'Neil's IDRC framed its programming as a reflection of the intelligence, competence, and capability to be found in the South.

In a sense, IDRC practices of the past thirty-seven years were weighed by government in 2007. In that year's federal budget, it was announced that there would be a strategic review of all government spending. Agencies,

Crown corporations, and departments would assess all of their program-ming, rank it all according to priority (and government priorities) by using such indicators as performance—that is, what had worked and what had not. IDRC saw this as a wonderful opportunity to tell its story to ministers, given that Treasury Board Secretariat had asked for the review. The idea was that every four years every agency would go through such a review and make adjustments accordingly. It was a relatively simple exercise for IDRC as it had been doing something similar for as long as anyone could remem-ber; at the Centre it was called "three arrows—up, stay the same or move down."[154] As Lauchlan Munro has pointed out, "We have a thorough discus-sion every October at the program and operational meeting ... that looks at all the programs, what their capacity is, how well they are performing, what teams can absorb more money next year, what teams are going through tran-sition for whatever reason, ... what programs are of more interest politically. We take into consideration all these variables—who is performing well, who has absorptive capacity, what's hot and what's not—and that forms the basis for our submission to the [IDRC] board in the form of program of work and budget. At the same time, the other parts of IDRC outside of programs go through a similar process and rethink. How they are organized, what their priorities are, how they are doing, what they should be changing."[155] The first group to go through included the Centre, as well as the Department of For-eign Affairs and International Trade, CIDA, and the rest of the international assistance envelope—the bits that are managed by Finance and other depart-ments. The other group that went through was the heritage portfolio—Her-itage Canada, the museums, Parks Canada, and Statistics Canada. The two represented about 15 percent of total government program spending. As a result of long practice, the Centre submission was superior; it had not dis-covered excellence or good management recently—it went back twenty-five years to its first evaluation in 1982. That being the case, "Every now and again we get a phone call from Treasury Board Secretariat saying that there is another group going through strategic review and can we send them over to you to be briefed on how to do it."

Perhaps the last word should go to the Office of the Auditor General (OAG) for Canada, a harsh critic of those government departments its audi-tors find wanting, but a supporter of those found to be performing well. The latter has been the case with IDRC from its inception. Yet another special examination report undertaken (again) at the behest of the Centre by the OAG in 2008 spoke to a very well-run, productive, and dedicated organization—no small praise:

Developing countries have a vast need for research. While many organizations provide development assistance, IDRC is among a smaller number supporting local development research. Given the rapidly changing global environment and IDRC's limited resources, its choices are critical: it must continually assess why, where, and how to intervene to have the greatest impact.[156]

What did the audit find? That the Centre had "no significant deficiencies in systems and practices," high praise in auditspeak. Moreover, "IDRC's systems and practices in several areas *have contributed to its success*."[157] It had "sound systems and practices" to manage its funding, its core function as the special report pointed out. It also "uses an appropriate process to select and approve the research projects it funds, and it monitors projects to ensure that they are completed to a suitable standard of quality. The financial aspects of projects are adequately controlled.... In a number of cases, it has been active in linking project recipients with other potential partners and donors to ensure that projects are sustainable after its own role has ended." It also dealt with its employees fairly and valued their work. As a result, "its reputation as a learning organization continues to attract and retain highly qualified staff who have developed effective processes for sharing knowledge and for capturing and disseminating research results." The report was a paean to IDRC's practices and personality. It was also richly deserved.

Notes

1 Smith wanted the chair of IDRC. During a plane trip home from a G-7 summit, which he had attended with Prime Minister Chrétien, the latter, upon learning of Smith's desire to retire from the public service, asked him what position he would like to undertake in retirement. Smith answered, without a moment's hesitation, "chair of IDRC." Interview with Gordon Smith, May 2006, Victoria.
2 Canada, House of Commons, Standing Committee on Foreign Affairs and International Trade, "Evidence," 4 November 1997, 10.
3 Interview with John Hardie, 12 August 2008, Ottawa.
4 IDRC–A, "Annex to Master Minutes," Meeting of the Board of Governors, 30–31 March 2000.
5 Interview with Maureen O'Neil, 17 October 2008, Ottawa.
6 Abra Adamo, "Strategic Evaluation of Policy Influence: What Evaluation Reports Tell Us about Public Policy Influence by IDRC-Supported Research," 30 April 2002, 1.
7 IDRC–A, Programs Branch, "Key Elements of Program Management and Delivery," 15 December 1997, 13. For a very interesting account of this, see Fred Carden, *Knowledge to Policy: Making the Most of Development Research* (Ottawa: IDRC and Sage Publications, 2009). Lauchlan Munro, vice-president of corporate strategy and regional management, saw it slightly differently: "Social sciences versus natural sciences? Maureen's training is in social sciences, yes. Before she got to IDRC she spent 30 years

as a policy worker in the Canadian government and the provincial government and in NGOs. Her bias would be 'great to have a new idea, great to have new technology, but there has to be policy space for this to be accepted, picked up and used.' ... The idea had become quite impregnated in IDRC staff.... Everyone in IDRC was inculcated with the idea that whatever we do, it has to have some impact and that means influencing the policy and/or the practice of the public authorities. If that means that IDRC took a more social science slant, well, yes ... but I don't see it as a natural science versus social science thing. I see it as a research into use question and the 'into use' always involves the social sciences regardless whether the research comes from the social or natural sciences or the applied sciences like engineering." Interview with Lauchlan Munro, 7 August 2009, Ottawa.

8   Interview with Rohinton Medhora, 6 August 2009, Ottawa.

9   IDRC–A, BG 98(01)28, Pierre Beemans, "Resource Expansion, Partnership, and IDRC," 12 December 1997.

10 IDRC–A, BG 98(01)29, "Resource Expansion: Operational Policy Issues," 24 July 1997, 9–10.

11 IDRC–A, BOG 2000 (10) 32, MON to Board, 29 September 2000, 4.

12 Interview with Joanne Alston, head of Central Research, and Paul Spray, deputy director, Caribbean and Overseas Territories Department, Department for International Development, 3 October 2007, London, England. See also BOG 2006 (06) 38, Rohinton Medhora to Board, "Approval to Negotiate a Partnership with DFID on ICT4D Research Activities in Africa and Asia," 19 June 2006. Following the successful joint effort announced in May, the UK organization entered into another arrangement with IDRC for £5 million (about CAN$10.2 million) in support of ICT4D's applied research activities in Africa and Asia. The funds would be disbursed over a five-year period, with 70 percent going to Acacia and the remainder going to PAN Asia. IDRC's links with DFID went back to 2000 and the G-8 DOT-Force. In its strategic plan from 2005, DFID also noted that "Too much aid in the past was badly used, often because it was driven by the priorities and preferences of donors rather than of poor people and poor countries." The association with IDRC helped to address that.

13 Nicola Jones and John Young, "Setting the Scene: Situating DFID's Research Funding Policy and Practice in an International Comparative Perspective," Overseas Development Institute, 30 June 2007, 4–5.

14 IDRC–A, Email, Chantal Schryer to Caroline Pestieau, 1 September 2000.

15 Interview with Barbara McDougall, 6 June 2009, Toronto.

16 IDRC–A, BOG 2004 (03) 16, Brent Herbert-Copley, "PI External Reviews: Synthesis Report, Social and Economic Equity Program Area," March 2004, 3.

17 IDRC–A, BOG 2000 (03) 05, *Program of Work and Budget, 2000–2001*, 46.

18 Interview with John Hardie, 29 June 2004, Ottawa.

19 Interview with Rohinton Medhora by Martin Kreuser, 28 June 2004, Ottawa. See also interview with MON by Martin Kreuser, 30 June 2004, Ottawa. As O'Neil noted, "Although directors of program areas were finally approved in 2000, the thinking on it started earlier then around the time of the consultation in Cairo that was the lead-up to the 2000–2005 CSPF. I was meeting with PI team leaders at that time and explained that we needed to reintroduce middle management. Too much had been taken out. It was very fashionable at the time to get rid of middle management. But middle management is where the learning takes place and in our case also where the allocation of people takes place. Also, you need to have the negotiation of the

borders of the programs, you need somebody there. In other words, Rohinton or the vice-president needs a management team and you didn't really have one."

20 Interview with MON, 30 June 2004.

21 IDRC–A, Caroline Pestieau to SMC/The President, 3 December 1997. See also *Corporate Program Framework II*, 15.

22 IDRC–A, Caroline Pestieau, "Electronic Discussion on Program Management and Regional Presence, Continued," 9 February 1998.

23 IDRC–A, Trip Report 7-2000, Palawan, Philippines, Randy Spence, "Fourth MIMAP Network Meeting," 31 August–10 September 2000.

24 IDRC–A, BG 99 (10) 21, Caroline Pestieau to Board, 17 September 1999, 8.

25 In late 1995, there were twenty regional program officers as compared with more than fifty a few years earlier, a drop of about 60 percent.

26 IDRC–A, Eva Rathgerber to Tim Dottridge, "Comments on Preliminary Paper on Regional Presence," 14 February 1997.

27 IDRC–A, Email, Carlos Serré to Caroline Pestieau, 12 November 1997.

28 IDRC–A, FA 97(10)09, O'Neil to Board, "IDRC Regional Presence in Africa and the Middle East," 26 September 1997.

29 Rathgerber to Dottridge.

30 IDRC–A, John Hardie, "Discussion Notes: Options for More Cost Effective Program Delivery and for Reducing the Costs of IDRC's Presence in Africa," 7 June 1997.

31 Canada, House of Commons, Standing Committee on Foreign Affairs and International Trade, "Evidence," 4 November 1997, 10.

32 Email, Richard Fuchs, regional director, East Asia. In today's world where email accounts and access to the worldwide web are taken for granted, it is important to remember that, while perhaps not in its infancy by 1996, emailing was restricted to certain groups, like those connected with universities or government service. Muirhead's first email was sent in March 1992.

33 Michael Graham, "Unganisha: An Assessment of Results and Effectiveness" (Ottawa: IDRC, June 1999), 5.

34 IDRC–A, Carlos Afonso, "A Report on PAN-Supported Internet Service Providers," Evaluation no. 397, February 1999, 6.

35 Email, Tim Dottridge, Ottawa, 18 March 2009.

36 IDRC–A, BG 2000 910) 18, Pestieau to Board, 19 September 2000 and attached PAN Networking Prospectus. Phase I had been approved at the October 1997 board meeting and was tasked with "support[ing] research on programs and activities that promote equitable access and democratic use of ICTs, and it takes advantage of opportunities for development in the new information economy in order to: understand the positive and negative impacts of ICTs on people, culture, economy and society; strengthen ICT uses that result in positive outcomes for sustainable development; promote policy environments conducive to socially responsible uses of ICTs, and; develop and experiment with innovative applications using leading-edge ICTs for development." As well, ICT impact on gender was a key part of the PI.

37 IDRC–A, Robert Valantin and Paul McConnell, "Information Technology at IDRC," 10 September 1997. The ACIM also played a significant role at IDRC, focusing on the dissemination and application of the Information and Communications Management Strategy; assessing the effectiveness of the strategy; situating it as a key component in IDRC's overall strategic approach to information, communication, and knowledge; and keeping senior management informed about trends and opportunities with respect to information and communications technologies and how they relate to IDRC.

38 Michael Graham, "Unganisha: An Assessment of Results and Effectiveness," June 1999, accessed at https://irims.idrc.ca/iRIMSTemp/34DE0791-57D6-46F8-AA5D-6 F6293D5CFD4-356E/rad3DD5C.PDF.
39 Graham, "Unganisha," 6.
40 IDRC–A, BG 97(10)22, For Discussion by IDRC Management and the Board of Governors, "IDRC Regional Presence in Sub-Saharan Africa," October 1997, 6.
41 BG 97 (10)22, 8–9.
42 Stephen Salewicz and Archana Dwivedi, "Project Leader Tracer Study," March 1996.
43 Salewicz and Dwivedi, "Project Leader," 5.
44 Curt Labond, "Project Leader Tracer Study Reviews IDRC's Performance," *IDRC Reports*, 1996.
    Project Leader Tracer Study: Key Findings
    • Project leaders were asked to rate the impact that IDRC project support had on eleven skills. Of the skills reported to have been "greatly improved," "project management," "leadership," and "communication" skills were rated the highest by the greatest number of project leaders (72 percent, 65 percent, and 54 percent, respectively).
    • For certain skill types, younger, less experienced researchers significantly improved their skills relative to their older, more experienced colleagues.
    • The percentage of project leaders who reported very extensive collaboration with IDRC program staff declined from a high of 76 percent in the 1970s to 55 percent in 1991–94.
    • One-third of project leaders reported that collaboration and contact with program staff had greatly supported their career advancement.
    • Sixty percent of respondents reported that IDRC's most important influence on their careers had been in linking them to networks of other researchers and organizations. In so doing, project support gave them the opportunity to contact the best researchers in their relevant fields, to develop links with policymakers, and to enhance their profile and reputation within the national and international research community.
    • Project leaders were asked to rate the influence that IDRC had had on the adoption of new research approaches. They reported that IDRC had the greatest "positive influence" in promoting the "utilization of research results" (84 percent) and the "need for multi-disciplinarity" (78 percent). IDRC had the least influence on "gender considerations" in research (35 percent).
45 The individual discussions were held with World Bank, Rockefeller, Carnegie, UNDP, UNESCO, ITU, FAO, Ford, and ECA. The Bellanet consultations involved all of the above, as well as MacArthur, SIDA, DGIS, CIDA, USAID, Soros, UN-DPCSD, CTA, GTZ, SDC, ORSTOM, UNITAR, UNCTAD, ODA, UNEP, COMSEC, WHO, and Danida.
46 IDRC–A, "Communities and the Information Society in Africa: A Canadian Initiative for the Millennium," 4 July 1996.
47 IDRC–A, Pierre Beemans, "SID-Ottawa Luncheon Seminar, 18 May 1999. Some of the debate had been informed by Robert Kaplan's article, "The Coming Anarchy," which had been circulated at the Centre following its publication in the February 1994 issue of *The Atlantic Monthly*. Robert Kaplan, "The Coming Anarchy," *The Atlantic Monthly*, February 1994, vol. 273, issue 2, 44–63. The article begins with an almost ineffable sadness: "The Minister's eyes were like egg yolks, an after effect of some of the many illnesses, malaria especially, endemic in his country. There was also an irrefutable sadness in his eyes. He spoke in a slow and creaking voice, the voice of

hope about to expire. Flame trees, coconut palms, and a ballpoint-blue Atlantic composed the background. None of it seemed beautiful, though. 'In forty-five years I
have never seen things so bad. We did not manage ourselves well after the British
departed. But what we have now is something worse—the revenge of the poor, of the
social failures, of the people least able to bring up children in a modern society.'
Then he referred to the recent coup in the West African country Sierra Leone. 'The
boys who took power in Sierra Leone come from houses like this.' The Minister
jabbed his finger at a corrugated metal shack teeming with children. 'In three months
these boys confiscated all the official Mercedes, Volvos, and BMWs and willfully
wrecked them on the road.' The Minister mentioned one of the coup's leaders,
Solomon Anthony Joseph Musa, who shot the people who had paid for his schooling, 'in order to erase the humiliation and mitigate the power his middle-class sponsors held over him.'"

48 As its website claims, Global Knowledge Partnership (GKP) was founded in 1997
and is the world's first multi-stakeholder network promoting innovation and advancement in Knowledge and Information and Communication Technologies (ICT) for
Development. GKP brings together public and private sectors and civil society organizations with the goal of sharing knowledge and building partnerships in knowledge
and ICT for development. Its activities and programs foster the innovative application of knowledge and technology to address and solve development issues in four
strategic themes: (1) access to knowledge, (2) education, (3) poverty reduction, and
(4) resource mobilization. GKP members influence policy at a global level.

49 IDRC–A, "A New International Framework for Information, Communications Technologies, and Development: A Canadian Initiative," 25 July 1997.

50 IDRC, rad43608.doc, "An IDRC Program Initiative for Africa: Prospectus 2001–2005,"
October 2001, 14.

51 Interview with Embalam, Tamil Nadu, December 2006. While not a part of Acacia,
the example epitomized by this village in Southern India in terms of ICTs and the betterment of life is indicative of computer power's potential. The authors visited the
village with its knowledge centre funded by IDRC. To a tumultuous welcome, villagers
recounted how access to ICTs had changed their lives in such simple ways as allowing them to access certain government forms online to apply for pensions and other
government assistance programs without having to spend the five rupees (CAN$0.25)
to travel to the nearest large city, Pondicherry, to apply. Some villagers cried as they
recounted their stories. They could also check such things as the price of rice or
chickens online and avoid being cheated by unscrupulous dealers from the city. IDRC
had also funded the development of a series of icons for the keyboard that were
readily understood by illiterate villagers. The centres had originally been called
"Communication Centres," but following the revelation of their power to change
lives, the villagers insisted that they be called "Knowledge Centres."

52 Canada, House of Commons, Standing Committee on Foreign Affairs and International
Trade, "Evidence," 4 November 1997, 17.

53 IDRC–A, BOG 2006 (06) 29, "Annual Corporate Evaluation Report 2006," n.d.

54 Interview with Alioune Camara, Dakar, 18 May 2007.

55 IDRC–A, BOG 2005 (10) 41, "Acacia Prospectus Development—Status Report, October 2005," 21 October 2005. Nobel laureate, Muhammad Yunnus, offered a similar interpretation in 2003. In the first Harvard tapes exercise, "he held up a cell
phone and said 'this is the best tool, if you want to bring a poor Bangladeshi woman
out of poverty.' It was quite a dramatic gesture. Now, five or six years later, it is

quite obvious that he was correct. The spread of cellphones in the developing world has been enormous. They are used not only for telephonic communications but for web-based communications, for texting, for sharing information about market prices between urban markets and rural producers, about meteorological information, about storms for fisherman. All those sorts of applications to say nothing of the encouragement it has given to small businesses. You can now put up a sign that says 'plumber' with a cellphone number. Now it's obvious that Yunnus was right when he made that gesture at Harvard, but it was revelatory at the time. It was obviously a far-sighted observation." Interview with Lauchlan Munro, 7 August 2009, Ottawa.

56 IDRC–A, Meeting of the Board of Governors, 31 March–1 April 2005, 4. The characterization of IDRC in this way had occurred in India, but it applies equally here.

57 IDRC, radF6C82.doc, "Acacia Prospectus, 2006–2011," 17 February 2006.

58 Interview with Paul McConnell, Ottawa, 22 December 2008.

59 For an account of the run-up to the ICT4D PI, see Robert Valentin, "ICTs and Development: A Proposed Strategy for IDRC's Corporate Program Framework III," 29 January 1999.

60 Interview with MON, 17 October 2008.

61 Ministry of Foreign Affairs of Japan, "First Meeting of Digital Opportunities Taskforce," 30 November 2000, accessed at http://www.mofa.go.jp/POLICY/economy/it/df0011.html.

62 Peter Boehm, "Contribution of Canada as Host of the Third Summit of the Americas," *Achievements of the Summits of the Americas: Institutional Contributions* (Washington, DC: Organization of American States, 2003), 5.

63 Fox remarked that "We must thank Canadian and Mexican institutions that have collaborated in developing this @Campus initiative which is invaluable for [a] more efficient and lower-cost government—to contribute to competitiveness in Mexico, and to participate in equal terms with our partners, Canada and United States, in NAFTA," accessed at http://www.idrc.ca/en/ev-85868-201-1-DO_TOPIC.html. The government of Mexico had introduced a law to establish and support a professional and nonpartisan public service. Approved in April 2003, it stipulated that promotions and hiring were to be based on merit rather than on political influence or connections. The law also required the government to evaluate and offer training to public servants, who must undergo certification at least once every five years in order to retain their jobs. @Campus Mexico was designed to create a training and evaluation framework for the government as it moved to implement the new law.

64 The objectives of NEPAD, to which IDRC subscribed fully, were:
   • to eradicate poverty
   • to place African countries, both individually and collectively, on a path of sustainable growth and development
   • to halt the marginalization of Africa in the globalization process and enhance its full and beneficial integration into the global economy
   • to accelerate the empowerment of women

65 IDRC–A, "IDRC's Program Initiatives, Secretariats, and Corporate Projects," 16 October 2002,15.

66 IDRC – A, "President's Report to the Board of Governors," n.d.

67 IDRC–A, BOG 2002 (06) 03, Meeting of the Executive Committee of the Board of Governors, 26–27 June 2002, "Resolution—Support for NEPAD Initiatives."

68 IDRC–A, BOG 2003 (10), Meeting of the Board of Governors, 15 October 2003, 6.

69 IDRC–A, BOG 2004 (06) 26, "Meeting Communications Objectives: A Communications Retrospective for 2003–2004 and Look Forward to 2004–05 and Beyond to Supporting CSPF 2005–2010," 30 May 2004, 6.
70 IDRC–A, BOG 2004 (06) 19, MON to the Board, 27 May 2004.
71 IDRC–A, BOG 2006 (06) 07, Munro to Board, "Review of the Planning Process for the CS + PF 2005–10," 24 May 2006, 4. Much of the discussion of the CS + PF comes from this document, written by the director of policy and planning, Lauchlan Munro.
72 IDRC–A, BG 99 (03) 14, MON to Board, 12 February 1999, 4.
73 IDRC–A, IDRC, BG 99 (10) 13, "Corporate Strategy and Program Framework, 2000–2005," 15 September 1999, iii.
74 IDRC–A, BG 99 (03) 19, "Corporate Strategy and Program Framework, 2000–2005," Discussion Draft, March 1999.
75 IDRC–A, BG 99 (10) 13, "Introduction by Maureen O'Neil, Corporate Strategy and Program Framework, 2000–2005," 15 September 1999.
76 SEE would encompass governance, peace-building and reconstruction, innovations in managing public goods, managing economic globalization, and supporting economic livelihoods. ENRM would oversee food and water security, ecosystem management for human health and development, and equity in access to biodiversity. ICT4D would support research in universal access and benefits and the information economy.
77 IDRC–A, Hardie to O'Neil, n.d. He framed his note to the president by noting that "there are those who, for whatever reason (acute deafness, amnesia, too busy to read basic documents—or simple disagreement) feel that they are not sure of what your view of the future shape of the Centre is."
78 IDRC–A, PRG-Dec99-B11, Much of this discussion comes from Brent Herbert-Copley, "'Research on Knowledge Systems': Options for IDRC Programming Background Document for the Program Committee Meeting, December 1999."
79 IDRC–A, Brent Herbert-Copley, "Concept Note: An Annual 'RoKS' Research Competition," 19 January 2001.
80 IDRC–A, BOG 2001 (06) 14, Caroline Pestieau to Board, "Research on Knowledge Systems: Program Strategy," 28 May 2001.
81 IDRC–A, BOG 2001 (03) 19, MON to Board, "President's Report to the March Board," 16 February 2001, 5. RoKS was rooted in (1) extensive consultation with policymakers and research partners working on science, technology policy, and indigenous knowledge issues as they are understood in the development dialogue; (2) IDRC's experience in this field through past and current programming; and (3) IDRC's programming and staff expertise in this area.
82 IDRC–A, BOG 2005 (03) 24, MON "Annual Evaluation Exercise: Statement of Achievements for the Year 2004–05, 3 March 2005.
83 IDRC–A, BG 2000 (03) 08, Discussion Paper, "Strategic Approach, Cost Structure, and Benchmarks," February 2000, ii.
84 Eva Rathgeber, "Turning Failure into Success: The Deconstruction of IDRC Development Discourse, 1970–2000" (Ottawa: IDRC, September 2001), 61.
85 IDRC–A, Corporate Assessment Framework, John Hardie, Federico Burone, and Roger Finan, "Research Results for Policy and Technology Influence."
86 IDRC–A, CSPF para 47.
87 IDRC–A, BOG 2002 (06) 25, MON to Board, "Update on IDRC's Strategic Approach to Regional Presence," 11 June 2002, 3.
88 IDRC–A, Notes from IDRC Meetings, 12–14 December 2000, "Meeting with Senior Staff, Caroline Pestieau, David Brooks, Chris Smart, and Celine Gratton," 8.

89   IDRC–A, Gilles Forget to Caroline Pestieau, MON, M. Van Ameringen, R. Medhora, S. McGurk, and J. Hardie, "Summer Thinking," 25 September 2000.

90   *Corporate Strategy and Program Framework 2000–2005*, 12.

91   IDRC–A, BOG 2001 (03) 09, *Program of Work and Budget, 2001–2002*, March 2001, 60.

92   IDRC–A, PRG-Dec99-B7-R, David Brooks, "Note on Gender," 23 November 1999.

93   Interview with MON, 17 October 2008. O'Neil was never convinced about the merits of mainstreaming: "The notion is that you have a tiny central function and you are trying to get everybody to understand … so, for example, the Ecohealth program would really have to understand what the impact on men and women was of the work they are doing and they would have to think about that when they are dealing with researchers and also convincing their researchers that this is an issue that is important and that they need to understand it in order to frame their research questions. The objective is to get all of the programs to ask themselves those questions [but the practice should permeate the research].… What I felt was missing [in IDRC work] was any focus on actual women's equality. We weren't funding work on that and how to overcome those barriers to women having greater personal freedom, dealing with all the issues Canadian women had to deal with.… There was no women's rights agenda for research. It had gotten mired in the gender question."

94   IDRC–A, MON, "Reflections on the Human Development Report in South Asia: The Gender Question," 5 December 2000. Here, O'Neil approvingly quotes from Khadija Haq and the Mahbub ul Haq Centre for Human Development report, *The Gender Question*, which was the fourth in the series of Human Development in South Asia Reports.

95   IDRC–A, rad BE91B, "References to Gender in CSPF 3," *CSPF III: Cross-cutting Dimensions, (i) Research on Gender*, CSPF III, para 89, 29.

96   IDRC–A, Notes from IDRC Meetings, 12–14 December 2000, "Meeting with Senior Staff, Caroline Pestieau, David Brooks, Chris Smart, and Celine Gratton," 4.

97   IDRC–A, BOG 2004 (03) 35, Jean Lebel, "External Evaluation of Program Initiatives under the 'Environment and Natural Resource Management' Program Area," 17 February 2004, 4.

98   Interview with Dr. Narayan Hedge, 18 December 2006, New Delhi.

99   IDRC–A, irims.idrc.ca/iRIMSTemp/334A213A-B2F5-4090-B2BD-ADE90D0A0C27-38A7/rad1FFAD.pdf "Swayamsiddha: Women's Health and Empowerment, 23 June 2000 to 23 December 2005," vol. I, Final Report, June 2006, ii.

100   IDRC–A, BOG 2006 (06) 29, "Annual Corporate Evaluation 2006," n.d., 14–15.

101   MON, 17 October 2008.

102   Interview with Lauchlan Munro, 7 August 2009, Ottawa.

103   IDRC–A, BOG 2000 (10) 32, MON to Board, 29 September 2000, 3.

104   IDRC–A, FAC 2001 (01) 11, MON to Finance and Audit Committee, "Review of IDRC Regional Presence, 2000–01," 11 January 2001.

105   Interview with MON, 17 October 2008, Ottawa.

106   Interview with Marc Van Ameringen, 6 October 2008, Geneva.

107   While neither TIPS nor Acacia were a problem in terms of the closure of ROSA, SchoolNet was. By 2000, the project was in deficit, there were personnel concerns, it lay outside of IDRC's program area, and, perhaps most importantly, it was no longer of interest to the minister of education in South Africa.

108   IDRC–A, Prime Minister Pascol Manuel Mocumbi to Prime Minister Jean Chrétien, 15 March 2001.

109 IDRC–A, Nelson Mandela to IDRC, 18 October 1995.
110 IDRC–A, Email, Gordon Smith to John Hardie, 3 October 2001.
111 IDRC–A, File Number 95-8907, Marc Van Ameringen, "Trade and Industrial Policy in South Africa," 22 February 1995.
112 IDRC–A, BOG 2001 (03) 09, *Program of Work and Budget, 2001–2002*, March 2001, 50.
113 Interview with Rashad Cassim, Johannesburg, 12 May 2007.
114 IDRC–A, Constance J. Freeman, ESARO RD, "TIPS and South Africa, Trip Report," 8–13 September 2002.
115 IDRC–A, BOG 2000 (03) 05, *Program of Work and Budget, 2000–2001*, 63.
116 IDRC–A, BOG 2002 (06) 25, "Update on IDRC's Strategic Approach to Regional Presence," June 2002, 4.
117 IDRC–A, BG 2000 (03) 08, Discussion Paper, "Strategic Approach, Cost Structure, and Benchmarks in IDRC," February 2000, 6.
118 "Update on IDRC's Strategic Approach," 3.
119 Interview with Alston and Spray.
120 IDRC–A, BOG 2003 (10), Meeting of the Board of Governors, 15 October 2003, 7.
121 IDRC–A, BOG 2004 (03) 35, Jean Lebel, "External Evaluation of Program Initiatives under the 'Environment and Natural Resource Management' Program Area," 17 February 2004, 4.
122 Interview with Gilles Forget by Martin Kreuzer, 16 June 2004, Ottawa.
123 IDRC–A, BOG 2004 (03) 27, Rachel Nugent and Roberto Briceño-Léon, "PI External Reviews: Summary of Report Ecosystem Approaches to Human Health," March 2004, 1.
124 Principle I asserted that "Human beings are at the centre of concerns for sustainable development. They are entitled to a healthy and productive life in harmony with nature."
125 IDRC–A, BOG 2004 (11) 03, "Prospectus for the Ecosystem Approaches to Human Health Program Initiative for 2005–2010, 2 November 2004.
126 See, for example, Jacobo Finkelman, Nancy MacPherson, Ellen Silbergeld, and Jakob Zinsstag, "External Review of the IDRC Ecohealth Program Initiative: Final Report," November 2008. "The Review Team recognizes that IDRC, from its inception, has established and maintained a unique position in the landscape of funders and actors in development research by increasing the knowledge base relevant to anticipating, diagnosing, and solving problems in developing countries. The Review Team found that the Ecohealth Program Initiative since its inception has enriched IDRC through the development of the ecohealth concept and its emphasis on the holism of environment and health, the importance of community-based participatory research, the need to respond to locally identified problems, the commitment to influence on policy and behavior, and attention to gender and social aspects.... The Review Team found much good work taking place and concludes overall that the Ecohealth Program Initiative continues to be a well-founded and important program for IDRC and for the ecohealth and development community at large and deserving of continued support."
127 IDRC–A, rad41ADB, "Backgrounder, Ecohealth and Risk Analysis," n.d. As the document notes, "Transdisciplinarity refers to the integrated form of carrying out research by teams of scientists from various complementary disciplines in dialogue with local knowledge systems and experts. It characterizes a collaborative working process that allows going beyond the limits of individual expertises in order to generate new

logical frameworks, new methods, new intuitions and insights born from the synergy that ensues from the collaboration."

128 IDRC–A, "External Review of Ecosystem Approaches to Human Health PI," n.d.

129 IDRC–A, radDEB66, Jean Lebel, "Ecosystem Approaches to Human Health Program Initiative: Proposed Prospectus 2005–2010," iv. For example, those agencies and institutions in Canada that followed up on Ecohealth's path-breaking work included the Université de Québec à Montréal, University of Guelph, University of Toronto, University of British Columbia, University of Alberta, University of Winnipeg, CIDA, Environment Canada, Health Canada, the Department of Foreign Affairs and International Trade, CIHR, PATH Canada, Association of Universities and Colleges of Canada, and Biodôme Montreal. International organizations and foundations were equally as wide-ranging: the World Health Organization, the Danish National Institute of Public Health, the Pan-American Health Organization, TDR for Research on Diseases of Poverty, a Special Programme for Research and Training in Tropical Diseases, Ford Foundation, United Nations Foundation, The Energy and Resources Institute, American University of Beirut, National Institutes of Health, and the National Zoonoses and Food Hygiene Research Centre.

130 IDRC–A, BOG 2004 (03) 35, Jean Lebel, "Summary Report: External Evaluation of Program Initiatives under the 'Environment and Natural Resource Management' Program Area," 17 February 2004.

131 radDEB66, Lebel, 23.

132 Stephanie Nolan, "Canadian Project Halves Tanzania's Child Deaths," Globe and Mail, 24 January 2005, A-1.

133 The Economist, 17 August 2002, vol. 364, issue 8286, 14.

134 IDRC–A, MON to Finance and Audit Committee, "TEHIP Audit Report," 2 February 2004.

135 Auditor General for Canada, "International Development Research Centre: Special Examination Report," 19 July 2002. In the dry language of professional auditors, Richard Flageole, the assistant auditor general for Canada, noted in the report that "with respect to the criteria established for the examination, there is reasonable assurance that there are no significant deficiencies in the systems and practices we examined" (3).

136 Canada, Department of Finance, Budget 2003—Budget Plan, Chapter 6—"Canada in the World," February 2003, accessed at http://www.fin.gc.ca/budget03/bp/bpc6-eng.asp.

137 IDRC–A, BOG 2004 (11) 11, "Corporate Strategy 2005–2010: Proposal Submitted to the Board of Governors," 2 November 2004, 13.

138 IDRC–A, BOG 2005 (03) 24, MON "Annual Evaluation Exercise: Statement of Achievements for the Year 2004–05, 3 March 2005.

139 IDRC–A, Meeting of the Board of Governors, 2–3 November 2004, 10.

140 Meeting of the Board, 11.

141 EcoPlata is improving the management and conservation of the 300 kilometre-wide Rio de la Plata, South America's largest estuary. Ten years of collaborative research by Uruguayan and Canadian researchers on the Rio de la Plata estuary may lead to decisions to preserve the estuary and conserve its valuable resources. The results to date—a wealth of data on many aspects of the river system and coast—have led to the creation of a multi-stakeholder commission to address the region's problems. In the process, a valuable collaborative network has emerged.

142 "Review of the Planning Process," 7.

143 IDRC–A, BOG 2004 (11) 11, "Program Framework 2005–2010: Proposal Submitted to the Board of Governors," 2 November 2004, 1.
144 IDRC–A, BOG 2005 (03) 06, Medhora to Board, "Strengthening and Situating S & T Programming in the Centre," 21 February 2005, 1.
145 IDRC–A, BOG 2006 (06) 02, Richard Isnor to Board, "Prospectus for Innovation, Technology, and Society," 19 May 2006, 1. A March 2005 report to the board noted that the Centre has been very active in biotechnology and emerging technologies exploration and programming. Consultations had been undertaken in every region, along with gender, intellectual property rights, and other consultations in Ottawa and the South. Programs and projects were initiated in areas of agricultural and health biotechnology, ABS and IPR management, global and national biotech and nanotech governance/policy/regulation, and some new technology areas. See IDRC–A, BOG 2005 (03) 05, Medhora to Board, "Biotechnology and Emerging Technologies Task Force: Progress Report," 21 February 2005, 3.
146 IDRC–A, Meeting of the Board of Governors, 31 March–1 April, n.d., 22.
147 IDRC–A, President's Report to the Board of Governors for the period 1 June–30 September 2005, 19 October 2005, 5–6.
148 For the Environment and Natural Resource Management prospectus, see BOG 2005 (10) 09, for Social and Economic Policy prospectus, see BOG (10) 06, and for the ICT4D prospectus, see BOG 2005 (10) 07.
149 IDRC–A, "Board Retreat: Speaking Point for David Malone," n.d.
150 Interview with Jean-Guy Paquet by Martin Kreuser, 23 June 2004, Ottawa.
151 IDRC–A, MON, "Stop the World! I Want to Get on: Reconnecting the Canadian University with the World," 18 May 2000.
152 IDRC–A, Meeting of the Board of Governors, 2–3 November 2004, n.d., 11.
153 Interview with Rohinton Medhora, 6 August 2009, Ottawa.
154 Interview with Bruce Currie-Alder, 9 August 2009, Ottawa. As Currie-Alder pointed out, most critics believed that once a government (or IDRC) program was set up, it existed forever. "The idea that there was a senior management team that constantly considered issues like 'What do we cut? What do we move forward?' [was unusual]. Something like 15 percent of our programming ends each year, so at the end of a five-year period, what we are funding could be quite different from what we did at the beginning."
155 Interview with Lauchlan Munro, 7 August 2007, Ottawa.
156 Office of the Auditor General for Canada, "International Development Reseach Centre: Special Examination Report," 27 March 2008, 1.
157 "Special Report," 2; emphasis not in original.

Chapter 7

CONCLUSION

What a concept! Take a well-disposed Canadian Parliament intent upon "doing good" in the world; a visionary federal official, Maurice Strong, who had a distinct idea about the sort of organization he knew was needed; the engagement of a number of like-minded officials to implement the plan laid out by the visionary federal official; two prime ministers, Lester Pearson and Pierre Elliott Trudeau, who also liked what they saw, followed up with David Hopper as the first president, an iconoclast who was as different in attitude and demeanour as one could be in the broader federal public service, and all the ingredients for a successful launch of the International Development Research Centre were present. Then, to ensure its ongoing viability, select as presidents to follow Hopper individuals who were uniquely qualified to lead the organization into the different contexts encountered along the way. The skill set of each somehow, fortuitously, seemed to reflect the age in which they served: Hopper, the scientific technocrat, to get it started and set the initial standard that would characterize IDRC from that point; Ivan Head, the international lawyer and a politically well-connected Ottawa insider, to solidify his predecessor's initial moves; Keith Bezanson, the gruff, no-nonsense former civil servant and Ottawa official to undertake the brutal cuts that were necessary to save the Centre during the worst fiscal crisis in Canada since the Great Depression of the 1930s; and Maureen O'Neil, the very bright, calming yet forceful personality with the large Ottawa rolodex who successfully pressed government on appropriate occasions to restore that funding to IDRC

taken away in the years since 1990. Indeed, as a match to challenge presented, each was an inspired choice.

This volume has traced the ebb and flow of IDRC evolution over the
past forty years. It was established at probably the one time in postwar Canadian history during which it could have been—five years earlier and the
unprecedented wealth and concomitant government activism was not yet
apparent; five years later and the economic situation was so dire as to prevent even the consideration of such an initiative. It was indeed a creature
of its time, dedicated to research for development, a very odd concept for
other countries and their aid agencies to grasp in the late 1960s. IDRC's
focus put the onus on the developing country researcher and institution to
develop and articulate projects, eschewing in the process anything that
smacked of research imperialism. It reflected the Centre's uniqueness, as
did its history and structure—creation by one national government, governance by an international board, independence from the usual aid strings
and requirements, and multinational staffing. It also followed that the role
of the first president would be crucial in determining the eventual shape
that the words in the *IDRC Act* would take over time; he (and it would be a
he given the times) would lay the blueprint that all in his footsteps would
follow. Happily for the Centre and the millions of Southern residents whose
lives have been enriched by the work IDRC has funded, the Hopper years were
very successful ones as the organization got off on a sound footing.
Researchers were supported and projects were funded that in many cases
were groundbreaking and innovative.

Hopper's implementation strategy for IDRC was designed to satisfy two
goals: the establishment of the Centre in a manner that would preserve its
unique character relative to its Act, and the buildup of credibility and respect
among LDCs and within the international development community. Nasir
Islam put it well in an evaluation of Information Sciences he wrote a quarter-century ago: "IDRC is a rather unique organization fulfilling an equally
unique mandate. Its hybrid structure defies normal principles of organization
design or theory."[1] As well, it began to address a glaring lacuna in Canada—
that of a dearth of Canadian area and development studies programs and associations, development conferences and journals and their ability to conduct
research and communication activities. This thrust would intensify over time.
This support "has allowed Canadian-based scholars to create networks outside of US-dominated anglophone North American academic associations
for discussion of development and area studies issues, and [has assisted]
them in bringing scholars and agents from developing countries to Canada
to participate in those discussions."[2]

The four divisions set up by Hopper—(1) Agriculture, Food, and Nutrition Sciences; (2) Health Sciences; (3) Information Sciences; and (4) Social Sciences—and the programming that they funded remained at the heart of IDRC for the next two decades, even as a few more were added to reflect the demands of a changing world. Science and technology, and their application in research for development, were most important in the Centre's early incarnation, changing over time to reflect an approach that provided more balance between the social sciences and their natural science counterparts. The early days were also "passionate and hot." Program officers had an immense amount of freedom to go out and investigate what could be done in co-operation with Southern researchers. While there was accountability to both the board and senior management, they were also very much on their own, guided only in passing by themes or programs determined at headquarters in Ottawa. Roving program officers also contributed to the betterment of IDRC, as well as to its developing reputation. If they saw something innovative and interesting in one place, they would tell of it in another or offer funding to help prospective researchers turn an idea into a reality. These ideas reflected the first Centre mantra, which provided a rough matrix that incorporated its philosophy: "a strong orientation to assisting research that has a practical or an applied significance for the economic and social advancement of developing nations."[3]

That direction was continued as Head took over in 1978. Indeed, IDRC remained, by and large, unchanged during his tenure as, apart from certain administrative changes, the first president would have recognized the essential structure of IDRC when the second retired in 1991. The ideas that animated behaviour at the Centre also remained, more or less, similar. For example, Head's Centre would continue to focus on the welfare of peoples living in the rural areas of developing countries; the 1980 Brandt Commission report, *North-South: A Program for Survival*, had observed that "mass poverty remains overwhelmingly a rural affliction, and it is rural poverty that seems so harshly intractable ... the poor in India, Bangladesh, Indonesia and nearly all of Africa are still, to the extent of 70 percent or more of the total population, in rural villages."[4] That reflected the IDRC rationale well and argued for the continuing investment in increasing food production, research that would lead to the provision of adequate health care, water supply and sanitation facilities, education, renewable resources, and the list went on. Further, IDRC would continue to cultivate research networks. By the mid-1980s, the Centre was supporting more than three hundred, which took an enormous amount of time, energy, and resources. It also emphasized practical action research and remained reluctant to support research activities unless there was some sort of payoff in terms of application. Indeed, this became a greater priority for both board members and senior management over the 1980s, and its consideration would take much more time.

But that did not mean that certain things did not change within IDRC. Perhaps of singular importance for its long-term survival, it became much more conscious of Canadian roots. Head's intent to spread the IDRC message to both citizens and parliamentarians was key to the Centre's continuing effective operation. This outreach included the involvement of Canadian institutions as research partners, which increased from none in 1978 to one out of four by 1990. The Cooperative Programs Unit was an essential and flexible add-on to that effect in support of its overall objectives. As well, IDRC opened up vistas to include the People's Republic of China, just emerging from the ravages of the Cultural Revolution. That was very significant and was testimony to the Centre's global reputation—the Chinese sought it out and signed an MOU while most other development organizations were still scrambling around, attempting to determine what the death of Mao meant for them.

IDRC's mandate, corporate values, and global orientation had led to the emergence of a flexible organization in which operating divisions functioned with a certain degree of autonomy. Furthermore, as it had evolved from awkward child to more accomplished youth, the emphasis on interdivisional collaboration was more in evidence, as was an increase in IDRC's coordinating role for multi-donor initiatives. The Centre was vibrant and healthy with an administrative structure that had been modernized over the previous half-decade by staff and management, and a philosophy and intellectual direction that had been evaluated several times over during those thirteen years. It had also remained true to its initial calling as the auditor general had pointed out in his 1982 "Comprehensive Audit Report": "IDRC operates with highly qualified, experienced and dedicated professional staff, many of whom are internationally renowned in their fields. Most project recipients we interviewed considered the IDRC approach superior to that of other international aid agencies." As well, the Centre acted as "a catalyst, an adviser [and] a supporter."[5]

As Head stepped down, there was a significant cloud on the horizon—a sharp spike in the price of oil caused by the first Gulf War, which began in August 1990 and precipitated an economic slowdown in the global economy that had hit Canada very hard. It would be five years before the country could claim to be out of a very bad situation. It was also the time when Keith Bezanson took over. And while the Centre's parliamentary appropriation in actual dollars continued to rise until 1993–94, in real terms it fell. However, by 1995–96, in both ways IDRC was receiving less funding from government, and that, of course, caused the turmoil that wracked the organization for years and which had a profound effect on its programming and intellectual history. It also led to some interesting innovations, like the development of program initiatives to replace the old projects funded through the various divisions.

Indeed, the Centre Bezanson left in 1997 had been fundamentally transformed. Gone were the divisions, the old fiefdoms from David Hopper's day, replaced by the then largely untested program initiatives. As well, IDRC had become more of an "environmental" organization, one of the programming paths it followed to save itself when the government announced that it was Canada's Agenda 21 implementing agency. That gave it direction and life, but that could only be followed if the organization remained financially stable. That led to the other prong of Bezanson's period in office—the search for additional funding as the Centre's parliamentary appropriation fell as part of government's deficit reduction efforts. On that, he was more successful; by 1997, about 20 percent of IDRC's budget was raised from sources other than Ottawa.

Maureen O'Neil's Centre carried on that tradition, as well as entrenching practices to ensure that it maintained its recognized strength as a responsive organization. As was generally conceded, she had her work cut out for her as she assumed office as the transitional experience that the Centre had gone through over the past half decade went far beyond mere budget-cutting and restructuring. It also involved a completely different approach to programming, program resource allocation, and support, with significant effects on the ways in which Centre staff worked together, and in how they interacted with partners. Program initiatives were the principal part of IDRC programming now and, along with secretariats and a few corporate projects, were the modalities by which the Centre supported research so their smooth operation was critical for a functioning IDRC. But how would Bezanson's creations work and how would they be accepted by staff? As well, gender, and its inclusion in programming, became a much more important issue in the IDRC of the twenty-first century. Indeed, upon her arrival, O'Neil had been surprised by senior management's lack of interest in the subject.

As well, a series of issues cropped up, chief among them the increasing importance of influencing recipient policy through Centre programming and research funding. By early in the new millennium, O'Neil's organization would be engaged in a strategic evaluation of the influence of Centre-supported research on public policy, following a path charted by two of her predecessors. The emphasis on policy influence had changed the Centre in another way; during the mid-1990s, there had been a relative decline in its expertise in the natural sciences and engineering and an increase in that of the social sciences. That reflected the emphasis IDRC was placing on linking researchers to policy-makers to increase the probability of research results being utilized, and on issues of governance.[6] This had been targeted by Centre programs for years and was given more urgent focus by O'Neil's Centre. It was certainly ahead of the curve in this area, developing programs on governance long before most development agencies believed it to be important. That was reflected in programming like Acacia, where "closing the loop" was made a critical part of the project design. Further, other mechanisms, such as evaluations, were implemented to ensure the Centre remained a vibrant and dynamic institution. Such an emphasis also made the Centre qualitatively better. As well, it sharpened its focus through its rediscovery of research on knowledge systems. Importantly, the overall objective of the program, launched in the early 2000s, was to explore "from a developing country standpoint, the ways in which knowledge is produced, communicated and applied to development problems, and the policy and institutional framework which govern this process."

During the ramping-up phase, program officers hoped to accomplish a number of objectives like promoting analysis and debate at the local, national and international levels on key issues in the evolution and functioning of knowledge systems, re-establishing IDRC's reputation as a leading player in this area, and in particular as a channel for independent Southern perspectives, and identifying longer-term activities, and partners with whom the Centre could work to pursue those initiatives. An important area to consider, it was easy to assert the importance of knowledge as a critical factor in economic and social development and as a key influence on governance and organizational performance. The results of the work permeated program design and, indeed, much of the other work of the Centre.

For example, regional presence was important; a program matrix formed the core around which IDRC organized itself in order to achieve "a more judicious balance between the substance of research on broad program areas, and tailoring what IDRC supports to the specific priorities of each region."[7] As was pointed out, programming took place within a matrix that balanced broad program areas and issues along one axis, and regional priorities and opportunities along the other. Discovering a proper equilibrium depended on an evolving set of relationships among Centre managers. Indeed, a consensus developed that "the success of the matrix structure depends on sophisticated interpersonal skills, clarity of expectations and responsibilities, feedback mechanisms for staff development, and exquisite communication," all of which IDRC strove to achieve.[8] By the early 2000s, program initiatives had also been fitted into a coherent whole and provided, at least according to some critics, "new vitality, greater flexibility and exciting new opportunities."[9] As programming diversity remained the key to the Centre's capacity to respond to rapidly changing conditions, its emphasis on program initiatives remained relevant as the best way to achieve this. PIs allowed a more holistic consideration of the problem being addressed incorporating into the team scientists, social scientists, development specialists, and others as needed. It was the creativity and scientific competence of its program staff that allowed IDRC to stand out in the international development arena. The context in which the Centre operated had been modernized following O'Neil's accession to the presidency. She also remained very interested in soliciting informed Southerners for their views of the Centre and its future development, discussing priority issues with researchers, politicians, and public servants on all of her official trips as IDRC continually evaluated its work.

And what of its future? Can it remain a creative, innovative, ahead-of-the-curve, listening organization funded by the government in Ottawa with some leavening of other money thrown in? Indeed, is there a role for the Centre in 2010? Arguably, the need for IDRC is greater now than at almost any time in its history. The plethora of challenges the world confronts—from climate change, to alterations in forms of global governance, to future directions of national innovation and science policy reviews—confound the development process. How does one include gender in a project that investigates agriculture in Yemen? What about the continuing role of information and communication technologies in development in less advantaged parts of the world? How will desertification affect certain parts of the world and deforestation others? There are thousands of questions like these that the Centre has the expertise to investigate if it has the resources. It is indeed the case, perhaps more so than ever in 2010, that the words in a book written in 1981 ring true: "It is hard to argue that donor countries 'know best' in relation to political issues and it is even more difficult to argue that they are in a position to judge issues in which economic considerations are deeply entangled with social forces and political motivations."[10]

One of the Centre's strengths is its reputation as a listening organization, more intent upon *responding* to Southern concerns than imposing its interpretation. Clearly, as the world changes IDRC's research for development mandate allows those most affected to interrogate their own situations through questions that they devise, a policy that goes back to the genius of the IDRC Act and Hopper's conception of what this kind of organization should do. IDRC had led by example over the past forty years, and a number of critics and organizations are now coming around to its perspective, even if they have not heard of the Centre. In *"The White Man's Burden": Why the West's Efforts to Aid the Rest Have Done So Much Ill and So Little Good*, William Easterly, an unremitting and influential critic of development as it is now conceived, writes about this problem using words strikingly reminiscent of IDRC practices:

> The core problem … is that few Western aid programs ever seek feedback from their consumers, the world's poor. Aid bureaucrats seldom feel account-able to anyone other than their rich-country principals…. On the basis of this analysis, [his] advice to Western donors is that they should stop thinking of themselves as Planners and begin thinking of themselves instead as "Searchers." They should investigate what is in demand in impoverished countries, adapt to local conditions, and stress accountability.[11]

The idea seems so simple and obvious that one is left wondering why it has not gotten greater traction in development organizations' strategic plans.

Hopper's words, which ended Chapter 1, remain relevant as the Centre stares into the future:

> By [2010] … the heavy, awkward footprints of astronauts will have marked many planets, and the shape and pace of our life on earth will have changed beyond belief. But by that time also, about 5 ½ billion people will live in what we now call the world's "developing" countries. Will their lives have changed too? We hope so. We hope that through a higher standard of living and eco-nomic integration with the "developed" world, they may have the freedom to enrich all of the earth's peoples by the quality of their lives and cultures. And we hope that the International Development Research Centre of Canada might contribute to that.[12]

While it has done much to make the lives of those who inhabit the South-ern reaches of the planet better, more remains to be done. The world would have been a much worse place without the Centre and its activities over the past forty years and the more than twelve thousand projects it has funded. It remains as vital as ever now. Its flexibility and willingness to experiment with new forms of management and listen to the researchers it funds is leg-endary among development practitioners. As has been shown throughout this book, IDRC has been the envy of many of those organizations who have sought to copy its practices and team up when the correct situation pre-sented itself. The assertions made here will no doubt come as a surprise to most Canadians, but they would not be so to many of those who are trying to make the developing world just that. Perhaps we should end with the words of the prime minister who began the process, Lester Pearson: "In today's world, concern with improvement of the human condition is no longer divisible. If the rich countries try to make it so, if they concentrate on poverty and backwardness at home and ignore it abroad, they will merely diminish and demean the principles by which they claim to live."[13]

Notes

1 IDRC–A, Nasir Islam, "Information Science Division: Structure, Processes, and Roles," Evaluation no. 136, 27 September 1985, 1.
2 Anonymous reviewer.
3 IDRC–A, David Hopper, "Research Policy: Eleven Issues," IDRC-014e.
4 Willy Brandt, *North-South: A Program of Survival: Report of the Independent Commission on International Development Issues* (Cambridge: MIT Press, 1980), 50.
5 Office of the Auditor General, "Comprehensive Audit Report to the Board of Governors of the International Development Research Centre," August 1982, accessed at http://www.idrc.ca/uploads/user-S/11558266111Comprehensive_Audit_(1982).pdf. See also IDRC–A, "IDRC's Reactions and Response to the 'Report of the Standing Committee on External Affairs and International Trade on Canada's Official Development Assistance, *In Whose Interest?*, Policies and Programs,'" Annex C EC 68/2, 3.
6 IDRC–A, Programs Branch, "Key Elements of Program Management and Delivery," 15 December 1997, 13.
7 IDRC–A, BOG 2002 (06) 25, MON to Board, "Update on IDRC's Strategic Approach to Regional Presence," 11 June 2002, 3.
8 IDRC–A, Notes from IDRC Meetings, 12–14 December 2000, "Meeting with Senior Staff, Caroline Pestieau, David Brooks, Chris Smart, and Celine Gratton," 8.
9 IDRC–A, Gilles Forget to Caroline Pestieau, MON, M. Van Ameringen, R. Medhora, S. McGurk, and J. Hardie, "Summer Thinking," 25 September 2000.
10 Just Faaland (ed.), *Aid and Influence: The Case of Bangladesh* (London: Macmillan, 1981), 3.
11 Review article, Joshua Kurlantzick, "Planners & Seekers: William Easterly, '*The White Man's Burden': Why the West's Efforts to Aid the Rest Have Done So Much Ill and So Little Good*," *Commentary Magazine*, June 2006, accessed at www.nyu.edu/fas/institute/dri/Easterly/File/commentary_plannersandseekers.pdf.
12 IDRC–A, "Comments," 7 July 1970.
13 Lester Pearson, *The Crisis of Development* (New York: Praeger, 1970), 35.

APPENDIX

Relationship of IDRC Parliamentary Appropriation to ODA, 1970–2008 ($ millions)

Fiscal Year	ODA	Actual Parliamentary Appropriation	% ODA	Parl App (real terms)	CPI
1970–71	346.12	1.4	0.4	5.97	24.2
1971–72	396.66	2.5	0.6	9.94	24.9
1972–73	514.19	8.0	1.6	30.65	26.1
1973–74	596.06	14.0	2.3	49.82	28.1
1974–75	749.10	19.0	2.5	61.09	31.1
1975–76	909.67	27.0	3.0	78.26	34.5
1976–77	971.69	29.7	3.1	80.05	37.1
1977–78	1,049.35	34.5	3.3	86.25	40.0
1978–79	1,139.95	36.9	3.2	84.63	43.6
1979–80	1,285.76	36.9	2.9	77.52	47.6
1980–81	1,311.57	42.0	3.2	80.15	52.4
1981–82	1,491.16	47.2	3.2	80.14	58.9
1982–83	1,676.55	59.2	3.5	90.66	65.3
1983–84	1,797.08	67.4	3.8	97.54	69.1
1984–85	2,104.56	81.0	3.8	112.34	72.1
1985–86	2,247.61	86.0	3.8	114.67	75.0
1986–87	2,551.77	100.0	3.9	128.04	78.1
1987–88	2,624.06	108.1	4.1	132.64	81.5
1988–89	2,946.60	114.2	3.9	134.67	84.8
1989–90	2,849.87	108.5	3.8	121.91	89.0
1990–91	3,035.34	114.1	3.8	122.29	93.3
1991–92	3,182.46	114.8	3.6	116.55	98.5
1992–93	2,972.70	114.1	3.8	114.10	100.0
1993–94	3,075.27	115.0	3.7	112.97	101.8
1994–95	3,092.46	111.9	3.6	109.71	102.0
1995–96	2,683.55	96.1	3.6	92.40	104.0
1996–97	1,676.44	96.1	5.7	90.75	105.9
1997–98	2,524.56	88.1	3.5	81.88	107.6
1998–99	2,591.14	86.1	3.3	79.28	108.6
1999–2000	2,749.26	86.1	3.1	77.92	110.5
2000–01	2,586.97	86.1	3.3	75.86	113.5
2001–02	2,900.71	92.5	3.2	79.47	116.4
2002–03	3,302.80	92.5	2.8	77.73	119.0
2003–04	2,719.77	107.7	4.0	88.06	122.3
2004–05	4,144.68	116.5	2.8	93.50	124.6
2005–06	3,491.53	128.2	3.7	100.71	127.3
2006–07	3,582.72	135.3	3.8	104.16	129.9
2007–08	3,880.32	145.2	3.7	111.44	130.3

INDEX

Swiss Agency for Development Coopera-
tion, 285
SYNAPSE, 183
System-Wide Initiative on Malaria and
Agriculture (SIMA), 326

Talwar, G.P., 86
Tanzania, 66, 83, 174, 244, 245, 318
Tanzania Essential Health Interventions
Project (TEHIP), 244, 245, 288, 327
Task Force for Child Survival and Devel-
opment, 215
team leader(s), 224, 261, 262, 265,
276n157, 315
technology, as IDRC concern, 133–34;
with development, 183–84
Technonet, 123; funding for, 73
Technonet Asia, 72
Telecentre Support Network–Worldwide
(TSN–W), 307
ten-week seminar, 179–84
Thailand, 57, 88, 141, 153, 167
Thammasat University, 57
Thant, U, 9, 25
Thatcher, Margaret, 136, 137, 194
Thérien, Jean-Phillipe, 5
Thewete, Steve, 196
Thorson, D.S., 39
thromboembolism, 86
thrusts, 82, 183–84, 193, 194, 224
Tiananmen Square, 197
Tillett, Tony (A.D.), 76, 149, 150
Tono, Henrique, 69
Toxicology Centre (TC), 171
Tracer Study, 298, 339n44
Trade and Industrial Policy Secretariat
(TIPS), 318, 319, 320
Trade and Industry Policy in South Africa,
297
"travel or perish," 165
Treasury Board Secretariat (TBS), 52, 60,
70, 95–98, 115, 116, 117, 131, 162,
226, 335
triticale, 82–83
Trudeau, Pierre, 34–35, 38, 40, 41, 51,
96, 107, 108, 112, 136, 153, 347
Truman, Harry, 3
Tunisia, 9
Turner, Ted, 284

Uganda, 75, 76, 118, 174, 299, 302, 318
Ukraine, 162, 243

UN, 3, 69; Development Decades, 8, 9,
10, 139; international development
and, 5; World Bank and, 5
UN advisory committee on the applica-
tion of science and technology to
development, 34
UN Children's Fund, 215
UN Commission on International Devel-
opment, 25
UN Conference on Environment and
Development (UNCED), 188, 226–34
UN Conference on New and Renewable
Sources of Energy, 114
UN Conference on Science and Technol-
ogy for Development (UNCSTD), 24,
93, 94, 114, 133–40
UN Conference on Trade and Develop-
ment (UNCTAD), 10–11, 52, 110
UN Development Programme (UNDP),
76, 88, 124, 232
UN Economic Commission for Africa,
109, 299, 306
UN Environment Programme (UNEP),
76, 325
UNESCO, 88, 145, 147
UN Foundation (UNF), 284–85
Unganisha project, 265, 294–98; funding
for, 295
UN General Assembly, 9, 52
Ungphakorn, Puey, 57, 58, 87
UNICEF, 85
Unitarian Service Committee (USC), 6
United Kingdom, 3, 9; Department for
International Development, 285, 286;
Ministry of Overseas Development, 9,
119; Overseas Development Institute,
286
United Nations Educational, Scientific,
and Cultural Organization, 330
United States Agency for International
Development (USAID), 64, 95, 109,
124
Universal Declaration for the Eradication
of Hunger and Malnutrition, 84
universities, Canadian, 6, 30, 32, 77, 82,
97, 115, 263; funding and, 113. *See
also specific universities*
University of Alberta, 107, 115
University of Beijing, 235
University of British Columbia, 115, 145,
263
University of Cairo, 171